20TH CENTURY® TYPEWRITING

SIXTH EDITION

By

D. D. LESSENBERRY

Director, Courses in Business Education
University of Pittsburgh

and

T. JAMES CRAWFORD

School of Business, Indiana University

Complete Course

Published by

SOUTH-WESTERN PUBLISHING COMPANY

Cincinnati 27   Chicago 5   San Francisco 3   Dallas 2   New Rochelle, N. Y.

T40—H1456

Printed in U. S. A.

INDEX

PREFACE

The building of a usable skill in typewriting is the primary aim of a course in typewriting. Rightly understood, though, skill is not merely the ability to type at so many words a minute, but the ability to type materials that have a use value at an appropriate rate and with acceptable accuracy. This is the concept of skill building that is emphasized in this sixth edition of 20TH CENTURY TYPEWRITING. The student is thus challenged to learn as a whole being and not as a one-sided specialist.

A few of the new features of this edition are listed below to indicate the variety of practice procedures and materials included in the textbook:

Levels of Practice. Three levels of practice in building typing skill are identified to make the practice meaningful and the outcomes certain.

The exploration level of practice (the high-speed level) is used when the purpose is to push into a new area of speed.

The skill-building level of practice (the intermediate level) is used when the purpose is to build sustained typing power. This level of practice calls for a rate that is 5 to 10 words slower than the exploration level of typing.

The control level of practice calls for a drop back of 10 to 15 words below the exploration (or forced speed) level of typing. Work at a suitable rate and with a high degree of accuracy is produced for use purposes.

Direct Dictation. Material is provided to achieve two purposes: (1) To lead the student from typing one letter at a time to typing on the higher order of word-recognition response; and (2) to test the mastery of related learnings.

Calling the Guide. This procedure is not new to this edition, but its use has been extended to make it more effective as a skill-building device. The call of the guide tells the student that he is typing too fast, not fast enough, or at approximately his selected goal rate. It is used with sentences for guiding the typing without spurts or pauses. It is used with paragraphs to do three things: (1) To maintain a steady and consistent rate to achieve a selected goal; (2) to type with the line endings of the paragraph called to control the rate of typing; and (3) to type with each succeeding line of the paragraph a few strokes longer, thus calling for the gradual increase in typing speed.

Production Typing. As provided in this textbook, production typing is more than split-second timing of spurt speeds on short problems. It is based (1) on production comparison so that each student will know when he achieves an appropriate production speed in relation to his straight-copy speed; (2) on the organization of problems in a sequence of (a) learning the nature of the problem, (b) skill building in typing the problem, and (c) measurement of production in typing the problem; and (3) on large problem units for building sustained production power.

Some of the features of former editions that will be found in this edition are (1) the daily lesson plan; (2) the timing of each part of the lesson; (3) the use of paragraphs of specific syllable intensity; (4) the use of problems that force the student to think in terms of the meaning of the material typed; (5) emphasis at stated intervals on composing at the typewriter; and (6) a variety of practice materials. The actual business letters, tabulated reports (some in script and some in problem form), invoices, telegrams, legal documents, manuscripts, and many miscellaneous office forms provide a rich experience in arrangement and in typing through which students will learn to type with understanding, appropriate speed, and acceptable accuracy.

Appreciation is expressed to the many teachers, students, and office workers who have given criticisms, materials, and suggestions for this sixth edition of 20TH CENTURY TYPEWRITING. All these have given generously of their time, their work, and their ideas to the end that a better textbook may be available for the better teaching of typewriting.

D. D. LESSENBERRY

T. J. CRAWFORD

OPERATIVE PARTS OF THE TYPEWRITER

A part that is common to two or more different typewriters is given the same number in the illustrations on the following pages. Parts that are shown on one typewriter and not on others are indicated by letters of the alphabet. The names of the parts are not the same on all typewriters even though the function of the parts may be the same. The names of the machine parts used in this textbook are those that are commonly used in the teaching of typewriting.

Name	Machine Part Number
Aligning Scale	34
Backspace Key	30
Card and Envelope Holders	12
Carriage-Release Lever, Left	4
Carriage-Release Lever, Right	18
Cylinder (or Platen)	14
Cylinder Knob, Left	2
Cylinder Knob, Right	19
Cylinder Latch	17
Cylinder Scale	20
Line Finder (or Ratchet Release)	6
Line-Space Regulator	5
Line-Space and Carriage-Return Lever	1
Margin Release Key	25
Margin Stop, Left	7
Margin Stop, Right	15
Paper Bail and Scale	11
Paper-Bail Rolls	13

Name	Machine Part Number
Paper Guide	8
Paper Guide Scale	9
Paper-Release Lever	16
Paper Table or Rest	10
Ribbon Carrier	21
Ribbon Control and Stencil Lock	22
Ribbon Reverse	32
Shift Key, Left	28
Shift Key, Right	26
Shift Lock	29
Space Bar	27
Tabulator Bar or Key	24
Tab Clear Key	31
Tab Set Key	23
Touch Regulator	35
Variable Line Spacer	3
Writing Position Indicator	33

THE ROYAL TYPEWRITER

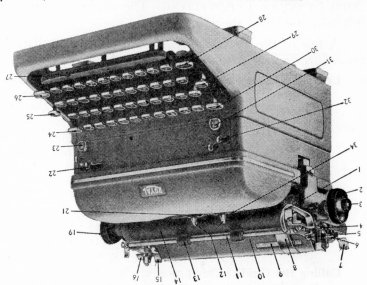

SETTING THE MARGIN STOPS

To set the left margin stop: Pull the left margin lever (No. 7) toward you; move the carriage to the point where you wish the margin to begin; then push the lever back to its original position.

To set the right margin stop: Pull the right margin lever (No. 15) toward you; move the carriage to the point where you wish the lines to end; then push the lever back to its original position.

ADJUSTING THE PAPER GUIDE

Set the paper guide (No. 8) so that the indicator at the left points to 0 on the paper guide scale (No. 9).

ADJUSTING THE RIBBON CONTROL AND STENCIL LOCK

When the ribbon control indicator (No. 22) is in the "blue" position, the type will strike on the upper portion of the ribbon. When the ribbon control indicator is in the "red" position, the type will strike on the lower half of the ribbon. When a two-color red and black ribbon is used, this "red" position of the ribbon control indicator will cause the typing to be in red. When the ribbon control indicator is in the "white" position, the ribbon is thrown off entirely and there will be no readable typescript.

from the imprint of the keys. This "white" position is used when it is desired to type in the stencil position.

DETERMINING THE CENTERING POINT

When the left edge of a standard-size sheet of paper is at 0, the centering point is 51 for elite-type machines or 42 for pica-type machines. For ease in centering, 50 can be used as the centering point for elite-type machines.

CENTERING TITLES AND HEADINGS

Move the carriage so that the paper is centered. Backspace once for every two letters or spaces as you spell the copy to be centered.

THE UNDERWOOD TYPEWRITER

SPECIAL PARTS: Front Scale (A)
Left Margin-Release Latch (B)

SETTING THE MARGIN STOPS

The margin stops (Nos. 7 and 15) are on a rod at the front of the typewriter with the front or margin scale (A). The stop at the right (No. 15) is used to control the left margin; the stop at the left (No. 7) is used to control the right margin. To set the margin stops, move the stops to the desired position on the front scale (A).

ADJUSTING THE PAPER GUIDE

For Underwood typewriters on which the paper guide scale (No. 9) begins at the left at 0, set the paper guide at that point. On other Underwood typewriters, set the paper guide at 10 on the paper guide scale. Then the left edge of the paper will be at 0 on the front scale (A).

ADJUSTING THE RIBBON CONTROL AND STENCIL LOCK

When the ribbon control indicator (No. 22) is set in the "blue" position, the type will strike on the upper half of the ribbon. When it is set in the "red" position, the type will strike on the lower half of the ribbon. When a two-color red and black ribbon is used, this latter position of the ribbon indicator will cause the typing to be in red.

When the ribbon control indicator is set in the "white" position, the ribbon is thrown off entirely and there will be no readable typescript from the imprint of the keys. This "white" position is used when it is desired to type in the stencil position.

DETERMINING THE CENTERING POINT

When the paper guide is adjusted in the manner explained under Adjusting the Paper Guide, the centering point is 51 for elite-type machines or 42 for pica-type machines. For ease in centering, 50 may be used as the centering point for elite-type machines.

CENTERING TITLES AND HEADINGS

Move the carriage so that the writing position indicator (No. 33) is at the centering point. Backspace once for every two letters or spaces as you spell the copy to be centered. Begin typing at the point at which the backspacing ends.

The foregoing method may be used with all Underwood typewriters. But with Underwood typewriters on which the scale on the paper table does not begin at 0, the following method is often used: Insert the paper so that the reading on the scale on the paper table is the same on the left and right edges of the paper. Move the carriage until the writing position indicator is at 0 on the white front scale. Strike the space bar once for each character and space in the heading to be centered. Note the figure on the green scale at which the writing position indicator stops; then move the carriage so that the indicator is at the corresponding number on the white scale. Begin to type at this point.

THE SMITH-CORONA TYPEWRITER

SPECIAL PARTS: Page Gage (A)
Total Tabulator Clear Key (B)

SETTING THE MARGIN STOPS

To set the stop for the left margin: Lift the automatic margin lever (Nos. 7 and 15) and hold it in the "L Set" position; then move the carriage so that the writing position indicator is at the desired point on the scale. Return the lever to the "Lock" position. To set the stop for the right margin: Depress the automatic margin lever (Nos. 7 and 15) and hold it in the "R Set" position; then move the carriage so that the writing position indicator is at the desired point on the scale. Return the lever to the "Lock" position.

ADJUSTING THE PAPER GUIDE

Set the paper guide (No. 8) so that the pointer is at 0 on the paper guide scale (No. 9). The left edge of the paper when inserted will then be at 0 on the paper-bail scale (No. 11).

ADJUSTING THE RIBBON CONTROL AND STENCIL LOCK

The letters R M B S are above the ribbon control knob (No. 22) and indicate the different settings of the ribbon control. When the pointer is at R, you will type on the lower (the red) portion of the ribbon; at M, the middle portion of the ribbon; at B, the upper (black) portion of the ribbon; and at S, the stencil position. When a two-color red and black ribbon is used, the "red" position of the ribbon control knob will cause the typing to be in red. When the lever is at S, the ribbon is not used and there will not be a readable typescript from the imprint of the keys.

CLEARING TABULATOR STOPS

Before setting tabulator stops, clear all previous settings to eliminate false stops. To do this, depress the total tabulator clear key (B). It is not necessary to move the carriage back and forth to clear all stops. To clear an individual stop, tabulate to the position at which the stop is set and press the tab clear key (No. 31).

DETERMINING THE CENTERING POINT

When the left edge of a standard-size sheet of paper is at 0, the centering point is 51 for elite-type machines or 42 for pica-type machines. For ease in centering, 50 can be used as the centering point for elite-type machines.

CENTERING TITLES AND HEADINGS

Move the carriage so that the paper is centered. Backspace once for every two letters or spaces as you spell the copy to be centered. The point at which the backspacing ends is the point at which the typewriting will begin.

THE REMINGTON TYPEWRITER

SETTING THE MARGIN STOPS

To set the left margin stop: With the left hand, move the carriage to the right as far as it will go. Depress the keyboard margin control key (KMC) and hold it down with the right hand. Use the left hand to move the carriage to the place where the margin is wanted. Release the KMC key.

To set the right margin stop: With the left hand, move the carriage to the left as far as it will go. Depress the KMC and hold it down as you move the carriage to the place where the right margin is wanted. Release the KMC key.

SPECIAL PART: Key Release (A)

ADJUSTING THE PAPER GUIDE

On the new model of the Remington typewriter, 0 is in the center of the scale on the paper table. The scale runs 50 for pica- or 60 for elite-type machines to the left and right. If you are using standard-size paper, slide the paper guide (No. 8) so that the point on its left edge is at the black arrow.

ADJUSTING THE RIBBON CONTROL AND STENCIL LOCK

When the ribbon control indicator (No. 22) is in the "black" position, the type will strike on the upper portion of the ribbon. When the ribbon control indicator is in the "red" position, the type will strike on the lower portion of the ribbon. When a two-color red and black

ribbon is used, this latter position of the ribbon indicator will cause the typing to be in red.

When the ribbon control indicator is in the "white" position, the ribbon is thrown off entirely and there will be no readable typescript from the imprint of the keys. This "white" position is used when it is desired to type in the stencil position.

When a single color ribbon is used, the ribbon control indicator may be set in a fourth position— the center position—to permit typing in the center of the ribbon.

DETERMINING THE CENTERING POINT

If the paper guide is adjusted so that the left edge of the paper is at 0 on the cylinder scale, the centering point is 42 for a pica-type or 51 for an elite-type machine. For ease in centering, 50 may be used as the centering point for elite-type machines.

When the Remington typewriter is used, the paper may be centered from the paper-bail scale. If the paper is inserted so that the reading on the scale is the same at each margin, the paper will be centered.

CENTERING TITLES AND HEADINGS

Position the carriage so that the paper is centered. Backspace once for every two letters or spaces as you spell the copy to be typed. The point at which the backspacing ends will be the point at which the typewriting will begin.

ELECTRIC TYPEWRITERS

In addition to the electric typewriter illustrated on page IX, the Remington, Royal, and Underwood companies also manufacture electric typewriters. All of these typewriters are similar in having the operative parts of the machine controlled electrically. The location of the parts will not be the same on the different typewriters, of course; but each part is

adequately identified and familiarity with one electric typewriter will enable the operator to adapt to the use of another electric typewriter without difficulty. It will be helpful if the operator will get the instruction booklet from the company manufacturing the particular electric typewriter to be used.

		STROKES
To: *Carl J. Dilworth*	**Date:** *Current*	33
From: *Frank E. Lamont*	**File:** *RB-6105*	57
Subject: *Reporting Machine Repairs*		83

	STROKES
Effective March 1, all office machines	122
in need of repair will be reported on appropriate	171
forms especially prepared for that pur-	209
pose. It is believed that greater efficiency	255
in maintaining our equipment can be	291
realized if some standardized procedure is	334
followed in reporting the machine out of	375
order. To that end, therefore, we are soliciti-	421
ing your support in inaugurating this new	463
and considerably different routine.	498

PROBLEM 12—BUSINESS LETTER

Directions. Prepare this letter in modified block style with open punctuation and no indentions for paragraphs. Address an appropriate envelope.

	STROKES
Current date Mr. David K. Millar Sales Manager National Fabrics, Inc.	74
637 Highgate Street Buffalo 9, New York Dear Mr. Millar	130
(P) We have just compiled a list of Conventions and Home Shows to be	195
held in the Midwest this spring. Each of the meetings listed will necessi-	269
tate special planning for appropriate exhibits. You should begin now to	342
assemble advertising materials for these conventions; and you should	411
take steps to see that your entire sales organization is notified and ready	487
for these exhibitions. (P) The following list shows the name of each con-	556
vention or meeting, its location, and the inclusive scheduled dates:	626

			STROKES
Spring Home Show	Peoria, Illinois	March 10-15	672
State Realtors Show	Elkhart, Indiana	March 17-21	721
Homebuilders Show	Madison, Wisconsin	April 19-24	770
Civic Planners Show	Gary, Indiana	April 27-30	816
Better Homes Show	Toledo, Ohio	May 3-10	856
Modern Homes Show	Joliet, Illinois	May 12-15	901
Builders Supplies Show	Racine, Wisconsin	May 17-22	952

	STROKES
(P) Inasmuch as exhibit space will be assigned six weeks prior to each	1019
meeting, it is important that you write immediately to the director of	1090
each show indicating whether or not you plan to participate in the ex-	1159
hibits. With your letter, too, you should include a check in payment of	1232
the required registration fees. (P) It is our sincere hope that you will	1302
have both an interesting and profitable convention season. Very truly	1373
yours ADVERTISING ASSOCIATES, INC. Robert R. Rankin Execu-	1430
tive Director crb	**1447**

IBM TYPEWRITER

SPECIAL PARTS: Electric Switch Indicator (A)
Multiple Copy Control (B)

two-color red and black ribbon, the adjustment of the ribbon control indicator in the lower position will cause the typing to be in red. For the best action of the ribbon mechanism, set the indicator in the upper or center position except when it is necessary to type in red or in the stencil position.

CLEARING TABULATOR STOPS

Before setting the tabulator stops, clear all previous settings to eliminate false stops. To do this, move the carriage to the extreme right of the line and, while holding down the tab clear key (No. 31), touch the carriage return key (No. 1). To clear a single tabulator stop, use the tabulator key (No. 24) to move the carriage to the tabulator stop to be cleared; then press down the tab clear key (No. 31).

OPERATING THE TABULATOR KEY

On the electric typewriters, it is not necessary to hold the tabulator key down until the carriage stops its movement.

DETERMINING THE CENTERING POINT

When the left edge of a standard-size sheet of paper is at 0, the centering point is 51 for elite-type machines or 42 for pica-type machines. For ease in centering, 50 can be used as the centering point for elite-type machines.

CENTERING TITLES AND HEADINGS

Move the carriage so that the paper is centered. Backspace once for every two letters or spaces as you spell the copy to be centered. The point at which the backspacing ends is the point at which the typewriting will begin.

MULTIPLE COPY CONTROL

The multiple copy control lever (B) is graduated from 0 to 5. For ordinary correspondence with an original and two copies, the control should be set at 0. Generally, the lever should be advanced one position for every three extra copies, although the weight of the paper will affect the setting.

SETTING THE MARGIN STOPS

To set the left margin stop: Return the carriage to the beginning of the line. Depress the keyboard margin set key (Nos. 7 and 15) and, while holding it down, move the carriage to the point at which the new line is to begin; then release the set key.

To set the right margin stop: Move the carriage to the end of the line. Depress the keyboard margin set key (Nos. 7 and 15) and, while holding it down, move the carriage to the point at which the new line is to end; then release the set key.

ADJUSTING THE PAPER GUIDE

Set the paper guide (No. 8) at 0 on the left of the paper guide scale (No. 9). The left edge of the paper when inserted will then be at 0 on the paper bail scale.

ADJUSTING THE RIBBON CONTROL AND STENCIL LOCK

The ribbon control indicator (No. 22) can be set for three different printing positions: upper, center, and lower. It can also be set for stencil position by pressing the control key all the way down. When the ribbon control indicator is set for stencil writing, the ribbon is not used and there will be no readable typescript from the imprint of the keys. With a

PROBLEM 9—INVOICE

Directions. Prepare this invoice for the Harrington Company in a form similar to that shown in Illustration 56, page 222.

in Illustration 56, page 222.

Sold to **Hart & Adler Book Store Kirkwood at Indiana Bloomington, Indiana** Date Current No. 7246 Terms 2/10, n/30 Shipped Via **National Truck Lines**

Quantity	Description	Price	Amount	STROKES
				57
				110
				131
				165
				199
6 ea.	#786 Metal Desk Lamps	2.25	13.50	241
5 ea.	11 1/2 x 11 1/2 x 16 File Cabinets	49.50	247.50	296
2 doz.	#432 Imperial Desk Blotters	6.75	13.50	345
10 ea.	14 1/2 x 34 in. Typewriter Tables	9.95	99.50	399
6 ea.	#603 Executive-Type Desk Sets	3.25	19.50	449
3 doz.	3/4 in. Large Sign Type Sets	52.68	158.04	499
3 ea.	#9132 Electric Desk Clocks	8.75	26.25	546
				553
			577.79	559

PROBLEM 10—TABULATED REPORT

Directions. Arrange this report on a full sheet of paper.

Employed Persons by Major Occupation Groups

Group	Northeast	North Central	South	West	STROKES
					17
					44
					186
					226
					297
Professional and technical	1,519,000	1,451,000	1,228,000	746,000	364
Farmers and farm managers	308,000	1,692,000	2,090,000	363,000	430
Managers and officials	1,420,000	1,412,000	1,404,000	774,000	493
Clerical and kindred workers	2,156,000	2,116,000	1,596,000	908,000	562
Sales workers	999,000	1,180,000	1,020,000	541,000	616
Craftsmen and foremen	2,321,000	2,356,000	1,922,000	1,034,000	678
Operatives and kindred	3,632,000	3,386,000	2,970,000	1,066,000	741
Private household	367,000	336,000	612,000	142,000	799
Service workers	1,150,000	1,271,000	1,083,000	641,000	855
Farm laborers	241,000	712,000	1,256,000	294,000	909
Laborers, except farm and mine	869,000	934,000	1,089,000	456,000	979
					1049

PROBLEM 11—INTEROFFICE MEMORANDUM

Directions. Prepare the message at the top of page 340 on an appropriate form of **the** T. D. Benson Company. Address an envelope and mark it LOCAL MAIL.

CONTENTS

PART 1—FOUNDATIONS OF SKILL BUILDING

PART 2—PERSONAL AND OFFICE TYPING PROBLEMS

PROBLEM 6—BUSINESS LETTER

Directions. Type this letter in modified block style with indented paragraphs and mixed punctuation. Address an appropriate envelope and mark it AIR MAIL.

STROKES

Current date Mr. Paul S. Conley 36
1206 North Bennett Street Louis- 77
ville 7, Kentucky Dear Mr. Conley 111
Subject: Investigation of Delinquent 149
Accounts (P) Summaries of pay- 175
ments for the fiscal period just closed 215
reveal that 34 clients in your district 245
are delinquent. These 34 customers 281
have erratic records punctuated by 316
late payments, cancellations, pro- 349
tests, and special requests for exten- 386
sion of their credit periods. In all 424
cases, there have been repeated and 460
unsuccessful attempts at follow-up 495
from the Home Office—the accounts 530
are still unpaid. (P) Within the next 565
six weeks, therefore, I should like 601
to have you investigate, personally, 638
each of the clients in your district 675
to determine his fitness for further 712
credit and service from our organi- 746
zation. Upon completion of your 779
investigations, a report stating the 816
approximate financial status, esti- 850
mated indebtedness, and anticipated 886
income for each client should be filed 925

with me. When all reports have 957
been submitted, I shall summarize 991
their contents and forward a report 1027
to the Home Office for final disposi- 1062
tion. (P) Inasmuch as the clients in 1096
question have a long record of in- 1129
stability, it is important that you be 1168
very thorough in your investigation 1204
of their status. If, after personal 1241
contact with each client, you feel 1276
that some should no longer be car- 1309
ried on our books as active accounts, 1346
indicate in the space provided for 1381
special comments on the enclosed 1414
report form your recommendations 1447
for deciding their future status with 1485
our company. (P) It may be that 1514
there are clients other than the ones 1552
listed whose records indicate that 1587
they should also be included in this 1624
credit checkup. If there are ones of 1662
that type, please send a detailed re- 1698
port of their accounts to me at once. 1737
Very sincerely yours Credit Man- 1768
ager crb 1776

PROBLEM 7—BUSINESS LETTER

Directions. Type two additional copies, without carbons, of the letter typed in Problem 6. Send the letters to: **Mr. Ralph J. Shepard** 419 North Lang Avenue Dayton 7, Ohio; and **Mr. Joseph R. Sniderman** 1402 Homewood Avenue Portland 6, Maine. Change the number of clients in each letter to read as follows: Shepard, 23; Sniderman, 15. Address envelopes for both letters.

PROBLEM 8—TELEGRAM

Directions. Send this message as a night letter. Charge to the sender.

STROKES

Metropolitan Wholesalers, Inc., 1856 Asheboro Street, Roanoke, Virginia 72
Shipment 1000 ladies dresses style X-B9867 loaded N & W freight 136
yards Saturday, June 19. Cars to be shifted at siding Roanoke 200
Wednesday, June 23. Dealers in Roanoke area should contact 260
R. W. Wilson, Chief Freight Dispatcher, for shipments consigned 324
to each dealer. Notify this office immediately upon receipt of 388
car shipment at Roanoke. 414
Dartmouth Weaving Mills, Inc. 443

PART 3—OFFICE TYPING PROBLEMS

PART 4—WORK EXPERIENCE

CARE OF THE TYPEWRITER

The typewriter must be kept clean. This is the responsibility of each typist. Dust the machine each day. Remove surface dust with a soft rag. A long-handled brush will enable you to remove dust and dirt from the carriage trough and other places not readily accessible with a rag.

Cleaning the Type. Wipe the type dry with a cloth. Use a prepared fluid in a small quantity. Do not let the fluid run down into the typewriter because it destroys all oil that it touches. If a prepared fluid is not obtainable, brush the type vigorously with a stiff brush dipped in benzene.

Care of the Cylinder. Clean the cylinder (or platen) with alcohol, or rub it lightly and evenly with very fine emery.

Oiling the Typewriter. Like all other machines, typewriters should be oiled at certain intervals. Use just enough oil to lubricate the part. The carriage rod should be oiled. Move the carriage to the extreme end; place a drop of oil on the rod; move the carriage back and forth; then wipe off the excess oil.

ARTICLE III

Officers—Terms and Duties

Section 1. The officers of the Society shall be President, First Vice President, Second Vice President, Secretary, and Treasurer, who shall hold office for the Current Year and until their successors are elected. (P) Section 2. The President shall preside at the meetings of the Society and be chairman of the Board of Directors; with the Secretary, or in his absence the Treasurer, he shall sign all written contracts and obligations, except checks. (P) Section 3. The First Vice President, or in his absence the Second Vice President, shall have all the powers and perform the du-ties of the President in the latter's absence. (P) Section 4. The Secretary shall keep the minutes of the Society and the Board of Directors, conduct all correspondence, send out all notices, and have custody of the seal. With the President, he shall sign all written contracts and obligations, except checks. (P) Section 5. The Treasurer shall collect and receive the moneys due and owing to the Society, have custody of its funds, keep regular and correct accounts, and pay all bills upon being duly certified as to their correctness. He shall render monthly reports to the Board of Directors, and shall give bond in such amount and with such surety as the Board may direct.

(Stroke counts: 39, 71, 106, 139, 175, 209, 245, 276, 311, 345, 378, 411, 448, 482, 513, 551, 585, 618, 656, 687, 722, 758, 795, 832, 868, 903, 936, 973, 1006, 1043, 1077, 1114, 1155, 1190, 1224, 1258, 1294)

PROBLEM 3—MAILING LIST

Directions. Type this mailing list on a full sheet of paper with one carbon copy.

MAILING LIST

Name	Address	City	Strokes
Andrews, Paul C.	5510 Jackson Street	Worcester 8, Massachusetts	66
Bauman, Walter J.	4627 Seaton Avenue	Kalamazoo 6, Michigan	135
Campbell, James W.	7398 Stanton Avenue	Stockton 11, California	198
Dawson, William B.	1504 Fordham Drive	Duluth 12, Minnesota	257
Fairley, Robert I.	2963 Academy Place	Denver 10, Colorado	315
Hanley, Melvin T.	8056 Laketon Road	Jackson 9, Mississippi	374
Kistler, Phillip C.	1392 Beverly Place	Portland 10, Oregon	433
Lockhart, George E.	4856 Vermont Avenue	St. Joseph 5, Missouri	495
Melwood, John H.	3012 Wallace Street	Mobile 12, Alabama	551
Peterson, Ernest H.	9853 Merriman Avenue	Wilmington 9, Delaware	615
Reardon, Paul O.	7046 Smithfield Drive	Columbia 5, South Carolina	681
Sinclair, Ralph N.	3162 Ellsworth Avenue	Paterson 17, New Jersey	746
Taylor, Charles M.	5890 Blanton Boulevard	Houston 9, Texas	805
Vaughan, Arthur L.	4613 Duffield Road	Bridgeport 5, Connecticut	869
Wright, Frank C.	2805 Clermont Avenue	New Orleans 10, Louisiana	932

PROBLEM 4—FILL-IN AND ENVELOPE ADDRESSING

Directions. Use the mailing list typed in Problem 3 to complete the letters mimeographed in Problem 1. Fill in the appropriate inside address and supply the salutation. Place a copy of the enclosure duplicated in Problem 2 with each finished letter; then address an appropriate envelope for each. (To the strokes given with the list add 35 strokes for each date line and salutation.)

PROBLEM 5—INDEX CARDS

Directions. Prepare an index card for each person on the mailing list given in Problem 3. At the bottom of each card type the following notation in all capitals: COPIES OF ARTICLE III MAILED MARCH 15.

FOUNDATIONS OF SKILL BUILDING

INSTRUCTIONAL BLOCK 1
BASIC TECHNIQUES FOR TYPEWRITING

SECTION 1. Initiating Keyboard Control

LESSON I

Place this book on the desk at the right of your typewriter. Have the top of the book turned from the machine for easy reading. Use a bookholder or place something under the top of the book for a good reading position.

Locate on the illustration of your typewriter, pages v to ix, the paper bail (No. 11)*,

* The numbers are those assigned to machine parts on page v.

the paper guide (No. 8), the paper table (No. 10), the right cylinder knob (No. 19), and the cylinder (No. 14).

Locate on your typewriter each of the five machine parts named above. Touch each part as you think of its name. You will learn the use of each part as you insert the paper.

INSERTING THE PAPER

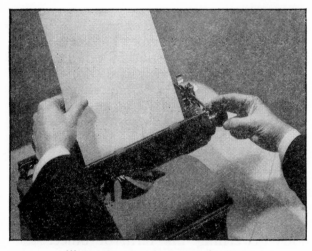

Illustration 1 — Inserting the Paper

Pull the paper bail from the cylinder. Pick up a sheet of paper with the left hand; drop the paper back of the cylinder and against the paper guide, letting it rest lightly against the paper table; then twirl the right cylinder knob with a quick movement of the first two fingers and the thumb of the right hand. Adjust the paper bail to hold the paper firmly against the cylinder.

Margins. Before you begin to type, you may need to set the margin stops for a 50-space line. Your teacher will tell you whether to set the margin stops now or defer this activity until Lesson 2. Instructions for setting the margin stops are given on pages v to ix.

FINGER POSITION

Typing position for your fingers is on the second row from the foot of the keyboard. Look at the keys. When the fingers are not making a reach-stroke, they are curved and held in typing position with the fingers of the left hand covering the keys *a s d f* and those of the right hand covering the keys *j k l ;*.

Look at Illustration 2. Note the curving of the fingers and the placement of the tip of a finger over the center of a key. Place the fingers of your left hand curved lightly on their home keys, the *a s d f* keys. Place the fingers of your right hand lightly on their home keys, the *j k l ;* keys.

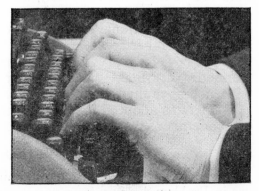

Illustration 2 — Finger Position

INSTRUCTIONAL BLOCK 24

PRODUCTION MEASUREMENT

SECTION 54. Production Unit

LESSONS 296 TO 300

General Directions. In each lesson, you are to type for 30 minutes on the problems designated. Correct all errors as you type; uncorrected errors will be penalized. At the end of the fifth lesson, compute your stroking rate per minute. You will receive credit for each stroke typed. If you finish typing all problems before the end of the fifth lesson, go back to the beginning and retype as many problems as possible in the time remaining. Follow the specific directions given for each job. Prepare one carbon copy for each problem.

DAILY OUTLINE FOR LESSONS 296 TO 300

Conditioning Practice ....5 minutes   Production Typing ....30 minutes
Assembling Materials ....5 minutes

CONDITIONING PRACTICE 296 TO 300
5 minutes

Directions. In each lesson, type each line twice. Double-space after the second typing of the line. Retype the lines as often as time permits.

STROKES

Lewis requests six dozen July chicks for August or September delivery.	70
A builder left 95 bricks, 73 doors, 82 sashes, and 10 Venetian blinds.	70
The lady in charge of this work did not believe it was very well done.	70

PRODUCTION TYPING 296 TO 300

PROBLEM I—LETTER TO BE STENCILED

Directions. Prepare a stencil for this letter. Run 20 copies and retain them for use in Problem 4.

STROKES

Current date **(P)** During the past 33
three years, local chapters of the 68
National Business Society have been 104
discussing the need for revisions in 141
the national by-laws. One item un- 175
der constant criticism has been Ar- 209
ticle III dealing with the terms and 246
duties of officers. As a result, dele- 284
gates to the National Council meet- 318
ing in November were instructed to 353
vote on revisions previously recom- 387
mended. **(P)** I am enclosing here- 415
with hectographed copies of Article 451
III as it was adopted in the meeting 488
of November 25. This article now 522

STROKES

sets forth in clear, concise terms 557
the duties and responsibilities of 592
each officer, together with regula- 626
tions governing his term of office. 663
For clarification, the article has been 703
divided into five specific sections. 741
(P) Will you see that all of the en- 772
closed copies are distributed to the 809
officers of your local chapter. I 844
shall appreciate your help in get- 877
ting this new information into their 914
hands as soon as possible. Very 947
cordially yours Executive secretary 983
ALBarnes/crb Enclosures 1006

PROBLEM 2—HECTOGRAPH REPORT

Directions. Prepare a hectograph master for this article. Run 20 copies and retain them for use in Problem 4.

STROKING THE HOME KEYS AND RETURNING THE CARRIAGE

Directions. Strike the keys covered by the fingers of your left hand, beginning with the left forefinger (named the *f finger*). fdsa Type the keys covered by the fingers of the right hand, beginning with the right forefinger (the *j finger*). jkl; Hit one key at a time and release it quickly before lightly and rapidly hitting the next key.

Type a short line of the letters fdsajkl;

When you type to the end of the line (or if you hear the bell ring), move the left hand, palm down. and with the fingers bracing one another, to the carriage-return lever and throw the carriage.

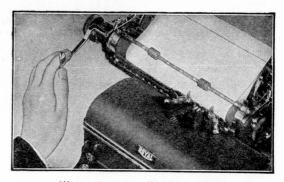

Illustration 3 — Carriage Throw

CONTROLLING THE SPACE BAR

Type another line of the letters, but space between the groups of letters as shown below. The space between the groups of letters is made by hitting the space bar (the long black bar at the bottom of the keyboard) *with the right thumb*. Raise the thumb quickly after striking the bar.

fdsa jkl; fdsa jkl; fdsa jkl;

REACH-STROKE PRACTICE I—*u, e, g*

u is controlled by the right forefinger (*j finger*)
e is controlled by the second finger of the left hand (*d finger*)
g is controlled by the left forefinger (*f finger*)

1. The reach to *u*. Move the *j finger* forward without moving the other fingers from their home keys. Study Illustration 4. Watch your finger as you type juj several times.

2. The reach to *e*. The *e* key is above the *d* key and is controlled by the *d* finger. As you move the *d finger* to *e*, lift the *f* finger slightly and keep it curved. Watch your *d finger* as you type ded several times.

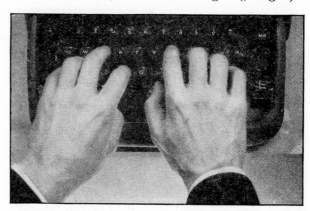

Illustration 4 — Reaches to u and e

3. The reach to *g*. Move the left forefinger (the *f finger*) to the right to the center of the *g* key without moving the other fingers from their typing position. Study Illustration 5. Watch your *f finger* as you type fgf several times.

You have watched your finger make the reach-stroke. This is right for this initial learning; but when you type lines made up of different words or letters, you must keep your eyes on the copy as you type so that you can type with continuity.

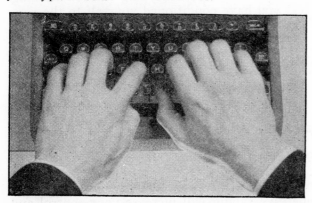

Illustration 5 — Reach to g

all caps →

Proficiency Standards for Beginning Stenographers — 50

(Suggested by NOMA). — 71

Year	*Typewriting	Shorthand	Transcription	
				113
1950	45 wpm.	80 wpm.	30 wpm.	142
1953	55 "	100 "	35 "	166
1960	60 "	120 "	45 "	190

* *Typing of straight-copy material for 10-minute period* — 245

with no more than 5 errors. — 272

SKILL MAINTENANCE 290 — *10 minutes*

Directions. Use each sentence for 1-minute writings. Determine your nwpm.

	STROKES	WORDS
Unsuccessful efforts may be caused by failure to use right techniques.	70	14
Excel in your work. Be exact in all you do. Expect much of yourself.	70	14
Your duty to your country, today and forever, can be done only by you.	70	14

INSTRUCTIONAL BLOCK 23

RECONSTRUCTION OF TYPING POWER

SECTION 52. Speed Emphasis

LESSONS 291 AND 292

Use the materials for Lessons 226 and 227, pages 97-99, to bring your basic skills for typing to as high a degree of control as possible. Use the lessons as directed, typing the conditioning practice at the beginning of the period until you feel you have conditioned yourself to the control of yourself and the control of the typewriter.

Make this repetitive typing of Lessons 226 and 227 effective in building an improved stroking skill. Emphasize ease and continuity of stroking. This meaningful repetitive practice will pay rich dividends in better typing skill.

SECTION 53. Typing for Control

LESSONS 293 TO 295

Use the materials of Lessons 228 to 230, pages 100-102, for three periods of typing on the control level. Type each lesson as directed. This repetitive typing will increase your control and build the feeling of certainty that will make for better production typing.

Directions. Type each line two or three times.

juj uj uj ded ed ed uj ed uj ed due due uj ed due

fgf gf gf uj gf uj gf jug jug uj gf uj gf jug jug

jug jug due due jug due jug due jug due jug due jug

due due dug dug jug due jug due dug dug jug due dug

Hold your eyes on the copy as you throw the carriage.

Direct Dictation. Close the book or cover this page, and type from your teacher's dictation.

u u g g jug jug u g jug e e due due due jug due dug

REMOVING THE PAPER AND CENTERING THE CARRIAGE

Hold the paper-release lever (No. 16) down and remove the paper with the hand not controlling the lever. Return the lever to the original position.

To center the carriage, depress the right carriage-release lever (No. 18) and move the carriage so that it is approximately centered. Begin the habits of good housekeeping with this first lesson. Pick up all paper—do not crumple it. If you are instructed to cover the typewriter at the end of each period, see that the cover is placed over the machine properly. Clear the desk of waste paper and push the chair under the desk as you leave.

LESSON 2
5 minutes

Beginning with this lesson, a time schedule is introduced to tell you the approximate number of minutes an average student will need to learn what is taught in each section. Learning rates differ, of course; so if it seems best for you to shorten or to increase the time assigned to a particular lesson or a portion of a lesson, do so with the approval of your teacher.

Typing Readiness. Place this textbook to the right of the typewriter. Have the front of the frame of your typewriter approximately even with the edge of the desk. Place your chair so that you are seated 8 to 10 inches from the base of the typewriter and slightly to the right of the center of the keyboard. Place the paper to the left of and turned endwise to the typewriter.

Pica- and Elite-Type Machines. Pica type has 10 spaces to a horizontal inch; elite type has 12 spaces. Note the difference in the type:

Pica type: 10 spaces to an inch.

Elite type: 12 spaces to an inch.

Compare this type with the type of the machine you are using. Know whether your typewriter has pica or elite type.

Adjusting the Paper Guide. The paper guide is used to guide the left edge of the paper as it is twirled into the typewriter. You will find instructions for setting the paper guide on pages v to ix. Read the instructions for the machine you are operating. Check the placement of the paper guide each day.

Setting the Margin Stops. If you did not study the directions for setting the margin stops in the preceding lesson, turn to pages v to ix and read the directions for setting the margins on the typewriter you are using.

For this lesson set the stop for the left margin at 17 if you are using a typewriter with pica type or at 25 if you are using a typewriter with elite type. Move the stop for the right margin to the end of the scale. Because you will type the copy line for line as it is given in the book, you will not need to set the stop for the right margin to get the line length desired.

JOB I—TYPING A DISCUSSION BULLETIN

Directions. Type the bulletin in two 3-inch columns with a half inch between the columns and left and right margins of 1 inch each. Center the heading QUESTIONS over the left column and ANSWERS over the right column. Draw a line one space below the last line of each question and extend the line across the blank column so the space for the answer will equal the space for the question. Use a 2-space paragraph indention.

Prepare a work copy. The first two questions are given in pica type to show one work copy. Diagonals have been inserted in the short lines to indicate the blank spaces that must be inserted as you type the line. After you have prepared the work copy, retype it with a uniform right margin. To do this, you may need to insert extra spaces or squeeze a word to absorb a space.

QUESTIONS

```
   1.  How can we better corre-
late the work of our salesmen/
with our advertising and sales
promotion programs in order to
increase sales?
```

```
   2.  It is probable that trav-
eling expenses will increase or
decrease during the next six//
months.  What will cause any//
changes that do occur, and how
extensive will these changes//
be?
```

3. Is there a demand for any new products that we should add to our present line? If so, what are these products and how extensive is the demand for them?

4. In what ways may our window and counter displays be improved so that they will be more attractive (a) to merchants who handle our goods and (b) to the ultimate consumer?

5. How many more calls is it possible for a salesman to make when he travels by automobile than when he travels by train? by bus?

6. Does traveling by automobile increase or decrease selling expenses? Does it increase or decrease the average cost of making each call? Does it increase or decrease the average cost of selling a dollar's worth of merchandise?

SKILL MAINTENANCE 289

Directions. Use the sentences for 1-minute writings if time permits.

	STROKES	WORDS
Quick responses to a quiz question quite frequently require quick wit.	70	14
That time I took dictation and transcribed my notes on the typewriter.	70	14

LESSON 290

CONDITIONING PRACTICE 290   *5 minutes*

	STROKES
Hal expects the squad will make the jump if the breeze is very strong.	70
Paul is 26 years 9 months and 7 days old; Dick, 30 years and 8 months.	70
The more skill you have, the more you can feel equal to the first job.	70

PROBLEM TYPING 290   *25 minutes*

JOB I—TABULATED REPORT

Directions. Your employer has asked you to type a copy of the report at the top of page 335.

Directions. Type each line two or three times or until you feel your fingers have recalled the reaches taught. Type with ease. Do not hurry, but keep the carriage moving steadily.

juj uj uj ded ed ed uj ed uj ed due due uj ed due

fgf gf gf uj gf uj jug dug jug due due gf dug dug

jug dug jug dug jug dug due due dug jug jug due

fdsaf jkl;j fdsaf jkl;j fdsaf jkl;j fdsaf jkl;j

Hold your eyes on the copy as you throw the carriage.

REACH-STROKE PRACTICE 2—*r, h, .* (Period)   *20 minutes*

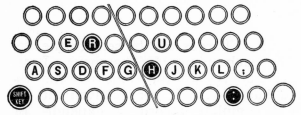

r is controlled by the *f finger*

h is controlled by the *j finger*

. is controlled by the *l finger*

1. Illustration 6 shows the reach to *r*, made with the *f finger,* and the reach to *h*, made with the *j finger.*

Move the *f finger* to the center of the *r* key without moving the other fingers of the hand.

Move the *j finger* to the left to the center of the *h* key without moving the other fingers from their typing position.

Watch your fingers as you type rf hj several times.

Illustration 6 — Reaches to r and h

Illustration 7 — Reach to . (period)

2. Illustration 7 shows the reach to *.* (period), made with the *l finger.* The *.* is beneath and slightly to the right of the *l* key. As you touch *.l* lightly, hold the little finger in typing position, lift the other fingers of the right hand slightly, and strike the *.* without changing the hand alignment with the keyboard. Watch your finger as you type l.l a few times.

Directions. Type each line two or three times. Hit each key lightly and swiftly. Release the key quickly. *Hold your hands and arms quiet; let your fingers do the work.*

rf rf uj rf uj rf uj fur fur fur rf uj fur fur fur

hj hj ed he he fur he jug hug fur jug he he fur he

Hold your eyes on the copy as you type.

fd jk fds jkl fdsa jkl; he he she she led she led

Space once after a semicolon.
he led; he led a lad; he led a lad; she has a fur;

---

* Each part of a lesson is given the number of the lesson even though that part may not have been used in the earlier lessons.

JOB 2—MULTIPLE COPIES

Directions. Type seven copies of the letter, using bond paper of medium weight. An office typist has told you of two speedup procedures that you will use in completing this typing job:

1. When it is difficult to get the cylinder to "take" a number of sheets of paper, use a "feeder" or guide sheet. First, insert a sheet of paper and twirl it in until it is only about 4 inches from the bottom of the page; then place the seven sheets of paper to be inserted back of the cylinder and in front of the feeder or guide sheet; and roll the paper pack in just far enough for the machine to grip and hold the paper. (NOTE: You can also place the assembled sheets of paper under the flap of an envelope or under the creased edge of a folded piece of paper and get the same result.)

2. Place the carbon sheets between the sheets of paper with the carbonized surface toward you. As the carbon sheets do not extend to the top edge of the paper, it will be easy to remove all of the sheets at one time by pulling them out as you hold the left top edge of the sheets of paper.

	STROKES
Mr. Appleton	13
Mr. Chester	25
Mr. Greene	36
Mr. Norton	47
Mr. O'Donovan	61
Mr. Parkinson	75
Mr. Sanders	87

Gentlemen A card enabling you to 120 sign for charges of meals, hotel 153 rooms, etc., in more than 131 restau- 189 rants and hotels in 32 different cities 229 is available from the EXECU- 256 TIVES' DINNER CLUB if you 282 wish it. Charges will be sent to the 320 office each month for payment. I 354 have had a card for some months 386 and have found it very convenient 420 as a complete record of expendi- 451 tures. (P) The enclosed pamphlet 481 lists the hotels and restaurants that 519 honor the EXECUTIVES' DIN- 544 NER CLUB card. Check the names 576 of the hotels in your territory to see 615 if a card will be of service to you. 653 Sincerely yours R. F. Thornton, 685 President Enclosure 704

SKILL MAINTENANCE 288   *10 minutes*

Directions. Use each sentence for 1-minute writings. Determine your nwpm.

	STROKES	WORDS
Can their cook concoct delicacies which excel this crab-meat cocktail?	70	14
Our opponents ought to know the official reason for our other actions.	70	14
Perhaps Phillip has permission to postpone his appearance until April.	70	14

LESSON 289

CONDITIONING PRACTICE 289   *5 minutes*

	STROKES
The music was very good, but an excess of jazz makes Paul quite weary.	70
In 1870, only 3,008 people lived in Waco, Texas; then in 1950, 84,300.	70
It pays to do as well as you can as often as you can. Good work pays.	70

TIMED WRITING 289   *8 minutes*

Directions. Use the timed writing on pages 296 and 297 for a 5-minute writing. *Type on the control level.* Determine your nwpm; or correct each error as you type, if this is approved by your teacher.

DIRECT DICTATION

5 minutes

Directions. Close your book or cover this page, and type from your teacher's dictation.

u u j uj g g gf gf jug jug e e due due dug jug due

r r rf fur fur jug fur h h hj he he he fed he fed

SHIFTING FOR CAPITALS

5 minutes

To type a capital controlled by a finger of the right hand, as *H,* for example, depress the left shift key (No. 28) with the *a finger.* Hold the shift key down until the key for the capital has been *struck and released;* then release the shift key and return the controlling finger to its typing position without delay. Stretch the little finger into position to depress the shift key without moving the elbow or changing the arm position. Study Illustration 8; then watch your left hand to see that it does not move out of position as you type Hal.

Illustration 8 — Reach to Left Shift Key

Directions. Type each line two or three times. Space twice after a period at the end of a sentence.

He led. He led Hal. He led Hal far. Hal led a lad.

Hal has a fur. He had a jug. Hal had a large jug.

LESSON 3

5 minutes

Typing Readiness. Have your work materials arranged properly. Be prompt in getting ready to type. Check the placement of the book, paper, chair, paper guide; and see that the front of the frame of the typewriter is even with the edge of the desk.

Adjusting the Paper Bail. If your typewriter has a paper bail (No. 11), adjust it for paper insertion by lifting the bail or by pulling it forward.

INSERTING THE PAPER

In the two preceding lessons, you inserted paper before you began to type, of course; but in this lesson you will study the details of correct paper insertion so that you can follow this uniform plan each time you insert paper into the typewriter.

Directions. 1. Place a sheet of paper on the desk at the left of, and turned endwise to, the typewriter; then grasp the paper with the left hand, placing the left thumb under the paper and the fingers on top.

2. Drop the paper behind the cylinder (No. 14) and against the paper guide (No. 8); *at the same time* bring the right hand to the right cylinder knob (No. 19). Place the thumb under the knob and the first and second fingers on top.

3. Twirl the right cylinder knob with a quick movement of the fingers. Hold the forearm and elbow steady.

4. Adjust the paper bail (No. 11) to hold the paper firmly against the cylinder.

considered in good relationship to 1821   pany for a term of three years. 2542
expected sales for this year. (P) 1852   Other directors whose terms did not 2578
For the first three months of this 1887   expire are Walter C. Thorpe, James 2613
year, sales were 5.2% above those for 1925   S. Moore, Walter C. Thorpe, Jr., 2646
the same period last year, despite 1960   Edgar L. Pyton, E. F. McClure, and 2681
the difference in the Easter Season. 1998   N. Griggs Thomas. (P) Officers of 2712
Easter business will be reflected in 2035   the company listed in the Annual 2745
the second quarter of the year. (P) 2068   Report were re-elected by the Board 2781
Mr. Thorpe concluded his remarks 2101   of Directors following the Share- 2813
by stating that merchandise stocks 2136   holders' Meeting. (P) A quarterly 2844
are being controlled closely in order 2174   dividend of $37\frac{1}{2}\cent$ per share was de- 2877
to take advantage of any change in 2209   clared payable on June 2 to share- 2910
the price or quality of goods. He 2244   holders of record May 15. (P) Your 2942
emphasized the importance of the 2277   directors and officers are pleased to 2980
cooperation and interest of share- 2310   furnish you with this information 3014
holders, employees, customers, and 2345   concerning the Annual Meeting of 3047
suppliers to the continued progress 2381   Shareholders and welcome all sug- 3079
of the company. (P) Paul L. Ho- 2408   gestions toward improving the op- 3111
bart, Harold E. Cook, and J. Clar- 2441   eration of your company. 3137
ence Shaffer were re-elected by 2473
shareholders as directors of the com- 2509

     By order of the Board of Directors. 3174
     W. S. Thurmond, Secretary 3199

SKILL MAINTENANCE 287   *10 minutes*

Directions. Use each sentence for three or four 1-minute writings. Determine your nwpm.

	STROKES	WORDS
Work failure does not seem to be caused by lack of ability to do work.	70	14
A smile costs you nothing, but it can pay rich dividends in many ways.	70	14

LESSON 288

CONDITIONING PRACTICE 288   *5 minutes*

	STROKES
My move next July will be required for lack of right size store space.	70
Poor personal traits cause the failure of 65 to 85 per cent of workers.	70
To give a helping hand to another in need should give you lasting joy.	70

PROBLEM TYPING 288   *25 minutes*

JOB I—TYPING LABELS

An easy and exact way to insert labels into the typewriter is to use the back-feeding method. To do this: 1. Insert a sheet of paper so that the top edge is a half inch above the ribbon. 2. Place the label back of the top edge of the paper and against the cylinder. 3. Roll the cylinder back (toward you) until the label is in position for typing the first line.

Directions. Address a label to each person included in the mailing list of Production Typing 245, page 295. If labels are not available, use slips of paper about 5 inches by 3 inches.

Machine Adjustments. Set the stop for the left margin at 17 for a pica-type machine or at 25 for an elite-type machine; move the stop for the right margin to the end of the scale. (Directions for setting the margin stops are given on pages v to ix.)

(Directions for setting the margin stops are given on pages v to ix.)

RECALL PRACTICE 3
7 minutes

Directions. Type each line two or three times or until you feel that your fingers have recalled the reach-strokes taught in preceding lessons.

rf hj rf hj ed uj ed uj rf hj ed uj gf hj gf hj uj

Throw the carriage quickly.

Start to type without pausing.

fur jug fur jug rug fur jug rug fur jug rug fur fur

Space twice after a period at the end of a sentence.

he he she she he she he she led led she led she led

Hal led. Hal led a lad far. He had a large jug.

SETTING THE LINE-SPACE REGULATOR

You can adjust the typewriter to type material with single, double, or triple spacing. To do this, set the line-space regulator (No. 5) for the desired spacing. The line-space regulator is located near the left cylinder knob on most typewriters. When the carriage is returned, the paper automatically moves forward the number of spaces for which the regulator has been set.

Directions. Set the line-space regulator for single spacing.

REACH-STROKE PRACTICE 3—*i, t*
20 minutes

i is controlled by the *k finger*

t is controlled by the *f finger*

Illustration 9 — Reaches to i and t

1. Illustration 9 shows the reach to *i*, made with the *k finger*, and the reach to *t*, made with the *f finger*. These reach-strokes are made with low, short, forward reaches and with a sharp blow to the center of the key, followed by a quick pulling of the finger toward the palm. As you touch *ik* lightly, lift the *j finger* slightly to give freedom of movement to the controlling *k finger*. Watch your fingers as you type ik a few times.

2. The reach to *t* is made with the *f finger*. As you touch *tf* lightly, straighten the *f finger* and hit the center of the *t* key without moving the hand forward. Watch your fingers as you type tf several times.

Directions. Use each sentence for 1-minute writings.

                          STROKES   WORDS

	STROKES	WORDS
Mr. King's collection has 58 prints, 392 books, and 417 piano records.	70	14
There is so much to be done in this world, we must not waste any time.	70	14

LESSON 287

CONDITIONING PRACTICE 287   *5 minutes*

	STROKES
Webb & Fox have justly criticized the report I am making on the query.	70
Earnings per share in 1949 were $4.46; in 1950, $4.68; in 1951, $4.46.	70
It is well to recall that the sword that cuts a foe has a second edge.	70

PROBLEM TYPING 287   *25 minutes*

JOB 1—TITLE PAGE

Directions. Center the material vertically and horizontally.

               STROKES

	STROKES
STERLING STORES COMPANY	24
Annual Meeting	39
of	42
Shareholders	55
April 8, 195—	69
Newark, New Jersey	87

JOB 2—REPORT TO SHAREHOLDERS

Directions. Type the report in acceptable report form.

           STROKES

	STROKES
May 1, 195—	12
To Common Shareholders of	38
Sterling Stores Company:	64
(P) The Annual Meeting of Share-	91
holders was held at the General	123
Offices in Newark, New Jersey, on	147
April 8. Signed proxies for 1,875,749	186
shares were returned by 4,188 share-	222
holders. These proxies accounted	256
for 88% of the total outstanding com-	292
mon stock. (P) Mr. W. C. Thorpe,	322
Chairman of the Board of Directors,	358
served as chairman of the meeting.	394
In his discussion of operating results	433
for the past year and the company's	469
progress in the coming year, he made	506
the following comments: (P) Sales	537
of $168,897,669 were 12.2% more than	574
in the preceding year. Sterling, not	612

	STROKES
including the Moore subsidiary, pro-	647
duced average sales of $740,851 per	683
store to total $165,209,845 for the	719
year. (P) Earnings of $18,216,129,	751
before federal taxes and non-recur-	785
ring income, were $1,038,003 better	821
than in the preceding year. This	855
increase, together with the non-re-	889
curring income of $1,382,122 from a	925
refund of excess profits tax for the	962
period 1940-1945, was more than off-	997
set by the $10,437,000 increase in	1032
federal taxes. Net earnings after	1067
taxes and non-recurring income were	1103
$7,779,129 compared with $9,416,126	1139
for the past year. (P) The changed	1171
relationship between taxes per share	1208
and earnings per share of common	1241
stock during the past three years is	1278
a striking illustration of the effects	1317
of government spending upon the	1349
corporation and the individual share-	1385
holder:	1394

	1949	1950	1951	
				1409
Earnings per share	$4.46	$4.68	$4.46	1446
Taxes per share	3.47	4.68	6.04	1479

	STROKES
(P) Dividends on common stock	1505
last year were $2.37½ per share com-	1540
pared with $2.25 the preceding year.	1578
The dividends included 50 cents paid	1615
in October as a result of the tax re-	1651
fund. (P) Total working capital in-	1682
creased $5,860,801. Investment in	1717
merchandise was $23,800,644 at the	1752
end of December. This amount was	1786

Directions. Type each line three times. Double-space after the third typing of each line.

```
ik ik tf tf ik tf ik tf if if it it if it if it if

it is; it is his; if it is his; if it is his light;

Hal has a light.  Hal has just the right light.

Jake had a fight.  Hal asked if he had a fair fight.

I like this lake.  I like this life at this lake.
```

Space once after a semicolon.

Space twice after a period at the end of a sentence.

DIRECT DICTATION 3
5 minutes

Directions. As your teacher dictates these words to you, try to think each word (instead of the letters) and type it as you think it or, if you are permitted to do so, as you say the word quietly.

```
if if if it if it if it if it is if it is fit

he he he the the the if it is the if it is the
```

SHIFTING FOR CAPITALS
5 minutes

To type a capital controlled by a finger of the left hand, as *A*, depress the right shift key with the *; finger*. Hold the shift key down until the key for the capital has been struck and released; then release the shift key and return the controlling finger to its typing position without delay. Use the "hinge" motion of the wrist to stretch the finger to the shift key. Type each of the following lines once.

```
A; A; Alf Alfred has a light.  A;

Alfred is here.  Alfred is here.
```

Illustration 10 — Reach to Right Shift Key

LESSON 4
5 minutes

Typing Readiness. Do things in the same right way day after day, and you will establish a pattern of procedure that will add to the ease and the certainty with which you work. Vary this pattern but little and then only as you learn how to improve the way you work.

1. Clear the desk of unneeded books and papers. Place your work materials on the desk so that you can use them with an economy of movement—the paper at the left and the textbook at the right of the typewriter.

2. Uncover your typewriter. Fold the cover and place it out of your way, but not on the floor. The folded cover can be placed under the top of the textbook to give it needed elevation for a better reading position.

SECTION 51. A Day in an Office

LESSON 286

CONDITIONING PRACTICE 286

5 minutes

STROKES

The squad was lucky in moving the jeeps before the next strong breeze.   70

In 1870, just 1,307 persons lived in Albuquerque; and in 1950, 97,012.   70

Many workers lose positions because they lack good personal qualities.   70

PROBLEM TYPING 286

25 minutes

JOB 1—STATISTICAL TYPING

Directions. Your employer has asked you to type the following copy in acceptable form.

	STROKES	WORDS
STOCK FACTOGRAPH	32	6
for	36	7
UNITED OIL AND GASOLINE REFINERY COMPANY	77	15

	STROKES	WORDS
Incorporated in Texas in 1896, the company was a constituent of the	145	29
old Standard Oil trust which was dissolved in 1911. Office: 539 South	218	44
Main Street, Houston 9, Texas. Owns an extensive pipe line system. Last	292	58
year, had 7,824 producing oil wells on 243,698 acres of "operated" leases,	367	73
producing 28.1 million barrels. Working capital on December 31 $42.1	439	87
million. Dividend payments made in 1912-32, 1934-38, and 1940 to date.	508	102

JOB 2—LETTER TO A SENATOR

In the letter of this job, the reference initials are typed *after* the enclosure notations. There is no reason for this—except that the dictator wants it typed that way. Do so.

Directions. Type the letter in single-spaced, indented form with close punctuation and 5-space paragraph indentions. Illustration 74 shows a correct way to type the address of a letter to a senator. Make a carbon copy for the files. On the file copy, type the identifying items for the enclosures. Illustration 75 shows the form for the closing lines.

Honorable Joseph Lester,
  United States Senate,
    Washington, D. C.

My dear Senator Lester:

Illustration 74 — Form for Address for Letter Directed to a Senator

STROKES

Honorable Joseph M. Lester, United   52
States Senate, Washington, D. C.   85
My dear Senator Lester: Mr. Snow-   118

STROKES

den has asked me to acknowledge   150
your transmittal of April 28, sub-   183
mitting a letter you had received   217
from C. G. Abbott, president of the   253
Abbott-Mills Electric Company, of   287
Oklahoma City. (P) We are return-   316
ing Mr. Abbott's letter to you to-   349
gether with a copy of the letter we   385
have written to him. Please feel   419
free to call upon us if we can be of   455
any further help to you. Sincerely   491
yours, C. M. Rollins Secretary to   525
W. S. Snowden *(68)* Enclosures 2   552
C. G. Abbott letter cc letter to   585
C. G. Abbott   597

C. M. Rollins
Secretary to W. S. Snowden

Enclosures 2
  C. G. Abbott letter
  cc letter to C. G. Abbott

CMR:NLE

Illustration 75 — Form Showing Closing Lines for Office Copies

3. Dust the typewriter if a cloth is available. Remember to wipe the surface of the desk under the typewriter if the machine is not fastened to the desk. Brush the type with a forward and backward motion. (Do not brush the type with a sidewise motion.)

4. Make a daily machine checkup:

a. Check the placement of the paper guide.

b. Adjust the paper-bail rolls (No. 13) so that the paper will be divided approximately in thirds. Place the paper bail to hold the paper firmly against the cylinder.

RECALL PRACTICE 4 *7 minutes*

Directions. Set the stop for the left margin at 17 for a pica-type machine or at 25 for an elite-type machine; move the stop for the right margin to the end of the scale. Use single spacing. Type each line three times in single-spaced form. Double-space after the third typing of the line

```
ik tf if ik tf it if it if it is if it is this

ed hj he rf hj fur jug hug he the he had the fur

it fit it; if it is it; if it hit; if it is fit;
```

Space twice after a period at the end of a sentence.

```
This is it.  This is right.  This is the right drill.
```

REACH-STROKE PRACTICE 4—o, c, n *20 minutes*

o is controlled by the *l finger*

c is controlled by the *d finger*

n is controlled by the *j finger*

1. Illustration 11 shows the reach to *o*, made with the *l finger*. As you touch *ol* lightly, raise the *j* and *k* fingers slightly to give the controlling finger freedom to make the reach to *o*. Hold the *; finger* in its typing position and keep the *j* and *k* fingers curved near their typing position. Type the word **old** a few times.

Illustration 11 — Reach to o

2. Illustration 12 shows the reach to *c*, made with the *d finger*. As you touch *cd* lightly, lift the *f finger* slightly to give freedom to the controlling finger. Hold the *a finger* in its typing position, but let the other fingers of the left hand move slightly with the *d finger*. Hold the hand in its normal typing position without moving the elbow out. Type the word **cold** a few times.

Illustration 12 — Reach to c

Directions. Use Timed Writing 280, page 322, for a 5-minute writing. *Type on the control level.* Determine your nwpm. Contrast the results of this writing with the nwpm of Lesson 280.

LESSON 285

CONDITIONING PRACTICE 285 — *5 minutes*

	STROKES
We request the big executives to speak a dozen times from May to July.	70
After living at 2658 since June 1937, we now live at 4061 Park Avenue.	70
It is well to think less of the starting pay than of where you can go.	70

TIMED WRITING 285 — *8 minutes*

Directions. Type Timed Writing 230, page 277, for 5 minutes *on the control level.* Determine your nwpm; or correct each error as you type, if this is approved by your teacher.

PROBLEM TYPING 285 — *25 minutes*

PROBLEM 1—ARTICLES OF INCORPORATION

Directions. Type one copy of the articles of incorporation. Use the current date. Provide a backing sheet, type an endorsement similar to the endorsement for the last will and testament shown in Illustration 68, page 316, and bind the pages together.

ARTICLES OF INCORPORATION
OF
McCLELLAND BUILDING COMPANY

The undersigned, all of whom are citizens of the United States, desiring to form a corporation, for profit, under the General Corporation Act of Ohio, do hereby certify:

FIRST: The name of said corporation shall be the McClelland Building Company.

SECOND: The place in Ohio where its principal office is to be located is Akron, Summit County.

THIRD: Said corporation is formed for the purpose of constructing and maintaining buildings to be used for hotels, and to acquire by purchase or lease and to hold, use, mortgage, and lease all such real estate and personal property as may be necessary for such purpose, and the doing of all things incident thereto.

FOURTH: The maximum number of shares which the corporation is authorized to have outstanding is One Thousand (1,000), all of which shall be with a par value of One Hundred Dollars ($100) each.

FIFTH: The amount of capital with which the corporation will begin business is Fifty Thousand Dollars ($50,000).

IN WITNESS WHEREOF, we have hereunto subscribed our names, this _____ day of _____, 195__.

_____
_____
_____

State of Ohio }
County of Summit } ss.

Personally appeared before me, the undersigned, a Notary Public in and for said county, this _____ day of _____, 195__, the above named Harold E. McClelland, Victor M. McClelland, and Ralph C. Nichols, who each severally acknowledged the signing of the foregoing articles of incorporation to be his free act and deed, for the uses and purposes mentioned.

Witness my hand and official seal on the day and year last aforesaid.

_____
Notary Public

SKILL MAINTENANCE 285

Directions. Use the sentence for 1-minute writings as time permits.

	STROKES	WORDS
The 1870 population of Los Angeles was 5,728; in 1950, 1,957,692.	65	13

3. Illustration 13 shows the reach to *n*, made with the *j finger*. As you touch *nj* lightly, make the reach without twisting the elbow or hand and without moving the other fingers from the keys. Type the word **can** a few times.

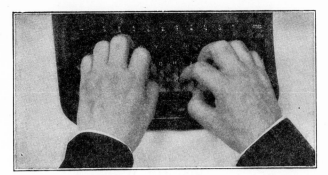

Illustration 13 — Reach to n

Directions. Type each line three times in single-spaced form. Double-space after the third typing of the line.

Technique Emphasis. After striking *o*, pull the finger quickly toward the palm of your hand and to typing position. After typing *c* or *n*, pull the finger quickly upward and to typing position.

```
ol ol old fold told fold told fold gold sold fold

cd cd cad cad old cold cold deck deck cold deck

nj nj an and and can can and old cold cold cold

I can go.  He can go for his son in an hour or so.

Dan did not go.  He and I can sing the old songs.
```

DIRECT DICTATION 4   *10 minutes*

Directions. As your teacher dictates this material to you, think each word and type it as you think; or, if you are permitted to do so, say the word quietly and type it.

```
he he if if he the the it it if it it fit if it fit

an an and and and or or for for for and for and for

He can go.  He can go for an hour or so.  He is in.
```

LESSON 5   *5 minutes*

Typing Readiness. A good typist must know the typewriter to be used and must check the machine before beginning to type. Make this daily machine checkup a part of your planned program for learning to type.

1. Check the placement of the paper guide, the paper-bail rolls, and the paper bail.
2. Set the stop for the left margin at 17 for a pica-type or at 25 for an elite-type machine; move the stop for the right margin to the end of the scale.
3. Set the line-space regulator for single spacing.
4. Set the ribbon control for typing on the upper part of the ribbon. (See Adjusting the Ribbon Control and Stencil Lock in the discussion of the typewriter you are using, pages v to IX.)

IN THE COURT OF COMMON PLEAS OF LAWRENCE COUNTY, PENNSYLVANIA

McNEELEY JEWELRY COMPANY,
a corporation,
New Wilmington,
Pennsylvania,

Plaintiff

vs.

FRED H. MORGAN,
Pulaski, Pennsylvania,

Defendant

No. 7202

July Term, 195-

AFFIDAVIT OF DEFENSE

Now comes Fred H. Morgan, the defendant in the above-mentioned case, and says that he has a just and equitable defense to plaintiff's claim, the nature and character of which are as follows:

The defendant admits that on or about August 1, 195__, he executed and delivered to the plaintiff his 90-day promissory note and a conditional sales contract substantially in the form and tenor given in plaintiff's statement of complaint, but he says that said note and said conditional sales contract were executed under the following circumstances, to-wit:

The defendant, at the time the said note and conditional sales contract were delivered to the plaintiff, purchased from the plaintiff a Truemark 17 jewel movement wrist watch set in a platinum case containing 8 baguette diamonds, 8 round diamonds full cut, and 12 round diamonds single cut, which watch plaintiff agreed and guaranteed to deliver to defendant at his place of business at 10 Vine Street, Pulaski, Pennsylvania, one week after date of purchase.

The defendant, relying on the guarantee of plaintiff to deliver to him a watch conforming to the exact foregoing description, signed a conditional sales contract containing the foregoing description and gave his note as part payment of the purchase price, to-wit: One Hundred Dollars ($100) paid in cash at time of purchase, and his 90-day promissory note for the balance of Four Hundred Fifty Dollars ($450), said balance to be paid in three (3) monthly installments according to the terms stipulated in the conditional sales contract.

The defendant says that plaintiff, according to agreement, delivered to him exactly one week after date of purchase a watch purporting to be of the foregoing description, but that upon thorough examination of the watch which plaintiff delivered, defendant found that the representation of plaintiff in regard to said watch was false and fraudulent. The examination of the watch which plaintiff delivered to defendant disclosed that said watch contained only a 14 jewel movement instead of a 17 jewel movement, as guaranteed, and that the platinum case contained only 4 baguette diamonds instead of 8 baguette diamonds, the number guaranteed to be in said case.

The defendant further says that he has repeatedly offered to return said watch to plaintiff if plaintiff would refund defendant's down payment of One Hundred Dollars ($100), but plaintiff has wholly failed and refused to make such refund; and further plaintiff has at no time offered to exchange said watch now in defendant's possession for a watch conforming to the foregoing description.

_____
Defendant

STATE OF PENNSYLVANIA ⎱
COUNTY OF LAWRENCE   ⎰ ss.

Sworn to and subscribed before me this _____ day of _____, 195__.

_____
Notary Public

My commission expires
(Use date one year hence.)

THROWING THE CARRIAGE

Improve your skill in throwing the carriage. Move the left hand, palm down and turned slightly sidewise with the fingers bracing one another, to the carriage-return lever (No. 1). Place the first finger against the lever (not around it) between the first and second joints; then push the lever until the slack is taken up, and throw the carriage with a quick wrist motion. Let the hand drop to typing position without following the carriage to the end of the line.

Illustration 14 — Throwing the Carriage

RECALL PRACTICE 5   *7 minutes*

Directions. Type each line three times in single-spaced form. Double-space after the third typing of the line.

```
u uj e ed o ol c cd t tf i ik g gf n nj r rf h hj

I can go.  I can go to the fight in an hour or so.

Don can sing.  Sue thinks he can sing those songs.

He can learn.  He can learn to do this just right.
```

TYPING POSTURE   *2 minutes*

When you are typing, sit in an alert manner and let the body lean slightly forward from the hips, the back away from the chair (unless you have an adjustable chair). When you remove your hands from the typewriter, take the at-rest, or relaxed, posture with your back resting against the chair.

Height of Desk. There should be approximately 6 to 8 inches of space between the top of the knee and the frame of the typewriter. This will usually place the arms at the approximate slope of the keyboard, a 30-degree angle that is best for good stroking of the keys.

Placement of the Chair. Place the chair so that the front of your body will be 8 to 10 inches from the base of the typewriter and slightly to the right of the center of the keyboard.

Fingers. Keep the fingers well curved so that you can make the reach-strokes without a change of hand position and without a forward movement of the arm. Hold the wrists low.

Thumbs. Hold the right thumb above, not on, the space bar. The left thumb is not used in operating the keyboard; keep it out of the way of the fingers and the right thumb.

Illustration 15 — Correct Typing Posture

STATEMENT OF COMPLAINT

The plaintiff company, a Pennsylvania corporation with its principal office located at 4 East Main Street in the city of New Wilmington, Pennsylvania, claims of the defendant, Fred H. Morgan, who resides at 701 North Street in the city of Pulaski, Pennsylvania, and who operates a retail jewelry business at 10 Vine Street, Pulaski, Pennsylvania, the sum of Four Hundred Fifty Dollars ($450), with interest thereon at the rate of six (6) per cent per annum from August 1, 195__, which is justly due and payable to the said plaintiff by the defendant, and is the cause of an action, whereof the following is a statement:

The defendant, on August 1, 195__, in New Wilmington, Pennsylvania, made and delivered to the plaintiff his 90-day promissory note, a copy of which is attached hereto, made a part hereof, and marked "Exhibit A"; and also a conditional sales contract calling for three (3) monthly payments of One Hundred Fifty Dollars ($150) each, a copy of which contract is attached hereto, made a part hereof, and marked "Exhibit B."

The plaintiff states that it has demanded the payment of said obligation as evidenced by said note and conditional sales contract, but the defendant has not paid and refuses to pay any part thereof.

WHEREFORE, plaintiff prays for judgment against the defendant in said sum of Four Hundred Fifty Dollars ($450) with interest thereon at the rate of six (6) per cent per annum from the 1st day of August, 195__.

_____
Attorney for Plaintiff

STATE OF PENNSYLVANIA ⎱
COUNTY OF LAWRENCE   ⎰ ss.

Before me, the undersigned notary public, personally came the plaintiff, Robert M. Solomon, treasurer of the McNeeley Jewelry Company, who, being duly sworn according to law, deposes and says that he is familiar with the facts as stated, and that the allegations in the statement of complaint given above are true and correct.

_____

Sworn to before me and subscribed in my presence this _____ day of _____, 195__.

_____
Notary Public

My commission expires
(Use date two years hence.)

SKILL MAINTENANCE 283 — 10 minutes

Directions. Use Timed Writing 280, page 322, for a 5-minute writing. *Type on the control level.* Determine your nwpm.

LESSON 284

CONDITIONING PRACTICE 284 — 5 minutes

	STROKES
Amazing as it is, we have liked Quebec for all the months except July.	70
We moved to 5826 Roberts Road after living at 4137 since January 1940.	70
Watch a better typist than you work, and try to become better than he.	70

PROBLEM TYPING 284 — 25 minutes

PROBLEM I—AFFIDAVIT OF DEFENSE

An affidavit of defense is a written statement setting forth the defense of a person in a lawsuit instituted against him, and sworn to by that person in the presence of a notary public.

Directions. Type the affidavit of defense given on the following page. Make a carbon copy. Use a date two weeks after the date on the statement of complaint typed as Problem 1 of Lesson 283, page 326, and type the caption in the form shown in Illustration 73, page 326. Prepare a backing sheet, type an endorsement similar to the one shown for the statement of complaint in Illustration 68, page 316, and bind the pages together.

SKILL BUILDING 5

Directions. Type each line as three 1-minute writings. Double-space between groups of sentences.

Technique Emphasis. Curve the fingers and poise them lightly on the keys. Hold the arms quiet as you type. Make the reach-strokes with the fingers and without arm movement.

	Strokes	Words * 60"	Words 30"
He likes to sing all the songs he hears.	40	8	16
It is right for all of us to do these drills.	45	9	18
All of us can use the lines of drill for learning.	50	10	20
Just do each of the lines of the drill again and again.	55	11	22
It is a fine thing for all of us to like to do these drills.	60	12	24

* If you type the first sentence once in 60 seconds, you will be typing at the rate of 8 words a minute, counting 5 strokes as one word. If you type the same sentence in 30 seconds, you will be typing at the rate of 16 words a minute. Read the rate for the other sentences in a similar manner.

DIRECT DICTATION 5

Directions. As your teacher dictates these words to you, close the book or cover the page as you type so that you can think the word instead of the letters of the word. If your teacher directs you to type without dictation, try to think each word and type it as you think it, or, if you are instructed to do so, say the word just before you type it.

```
he he he if if if he if or or or is is is or is he

to to to us us us to us do do do it it it do it to

go go go an an an go an of of of us us us of us an
```

LESSON 6

Machine Checkup and Adjustments

1. Check the placement of the paper guide, the paper-bail rolls, and the paper bail.
2. Set the stop for the left margin at 17 for a pica-type or at 25 for an elite-type machine; move the stop for the right margin to the end of the scale.
3. Set the line-space regulator for single spacing.
4. Set the ribbon lever for typing on the upper half of the ribbon.

RECALL PRACTICE 6

Directions. Type each line three times. Double-space after the third typing of the line.

```
ed uj rf ik tf hj gf nj cd ol of it or an if he is

for the ask ask jug did and can sir all all can and

I can go.  I can go for John King.  I can see Jack.

Donald told us of the nine houses he has for rent.
```

period the net profit or the net loss after salaries have been allowed is to be shared equally. (P) SEVENTH: No partner is to withdraw assets in excess of his share of the profits without the written consent of the other partners. (P) EIGHTH: During the operation of this partnership, no partner is to become surety or bondsman for anyone without the written consent of the other partners. (P) IN WITNESS WHEREOF, the parties aforesaid have hereunto set their hands and affixed their seals on the day and in the year first above written.

_____ (SEAL)
Louis D. Barrett

_____ (SEAL)
Clifton H. Leonard

_____ (SEAL)
James L. Quinn

Witnesses:

_____

_____

SKILL MAINTENANCE 282

10 minutes

Directions. Use the second paragraph of Timed Writing 280, page 322, for 1-minute writings. *Type on the skill-building level.* Determine your nwpm.

LESSON 283

CONDITIONING PRACTICE 283

5 minutes

STROKES

We save quite a sizable sum for Dick by paying the county tax in July.	70
They sold the house at 2957 Fox Chapel Road for $31,480 on January 26.	70
We can't afford to let down and allow things to take their own course.	70

PROBLEM TYPING 283

25 minutes

PROBLEM 1—STATEMENT OF COMPLAINT

A statement of complaint is a written assertion of rights, sworn to before a notary public, setting forth in legal form the complaint upon which a person is to have a lawsuit instituted.

Directions. Type the statement of complaint. Make a carbon copy. Use the current date, and type the caption similar to the form shown in Illustration 73. Prepare a backing sheet, type an endorsement similar to the one shown in Illustration 68, page 316, and bind the pages together.

```
   IN THE COURT OF COMMON PLEAS OF LAWRENCE COUNTY, PENNSYLVANIA

McNEELEY JEWELRY COMPANY,            )
a corporation                        )
New Wilmington, Pennsylvania         )     No. 7202
                       Plaintiff     )
                                     )
         vs.                         )
                                     )
FRED H. MORGAN,                      )     July Term, 195-
Pulaski, Pennsylvania,               )
                       Defendant     )

              STATEMENT OF COMPLAINT
```

Illustration 73 — Caption for Legal Papers Filed in a Lawsuit

IN THE COURT OF COMMON PLEAS OF LAWRENCE COUNTY, PENNSYLVANIA

McNEELEY JEWELRY COMPANY, a corporation, New Wilmington, Pennsylvania,   )
))))) No. 7202
    Plaintiff)
)
    vs.)
)
FRED H. MORGAN,) July Term, 195-
Pulaski, Pennsylvania,)
    Defendant)

v is controlled by the *f finger*
w is controlled by the *s finger*
y is controlled by the *j finger*

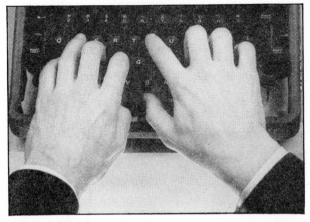

Illustration 17 — Reaches to w and y

1. Illustration 16 shows the reach to *v*, made with the *f finger*. As you touch *vf* lightly, hold the other fingers in their typing position. Make the reach direct to *v*; avoid twisting the hand or the elbow. Watch your fingers as you type **vf** a few times.

Illustration 16 — Reach to v

2. Illustration 17 shows the reach to *w*, made with the *s finger*; and the reach to *y*, made with the *j finger*. As you touch *ws* lightly, hold the *a finger* in its position, lift the *d* and *f* fingers slightly, and strike *w* with the *s* finger extended. As you touch *yj* lightly, make the reach without moving the hand or the fingers from their typing position. Watch your fingers as you type **ws yj** a few times.

Directions. Type each line three times. Double-space after the third typing of the line.

Start to type immediately.

```
ws yj ws yj way say why vf yj vf very five very
work work very with give away work with give away
I can work; I can work well; I can work well now.
You work very well.  You can work very well today.
```

Throw the carriage quickly.

DIRECT DICTATION 6   *7 minutes*

Directions. The purpose of this direct dictation is to speed up your stroking. *Think the word* and let your fingers work out a pattern of stroking for the word. Speed up your stroking a little each day, but do not attempt to make great gains in speed at one time as this may tie your fingers in muscular knots. Relax; hold the hands and arms quiet; let your fingers do the work.

```
or or for for or for for he he the the he the he the
an an and and an and and it it fit fit it fit it fit
I can.  I can go.  I can go to work.  I can go now.
```

MEASUREMENT SENTENCE 6   *5 minutes*

Directions. Use the sentence for three 1-minute writings.

STROKES WORDS

```
It is right for all of us to do all the work well.
```
50   10

In the presence of:

_____ _____

_____ _____

_____ _____

STATE OF **WISCONSIN,**
MILWAUKEE COUNTY, ss.

This day, before me, a **notary public** in and for said county, personally came **Walter**

C. Stone and Alma N. Stone, husband and wife, and Howard D. Fisher, the parties to the foregoing Lease, and acknowledged the signing thereof to be their voluntary act.

Witness my hand and official seal this _____ day of _____, A. D. 195___.

_____

Notary Public

SKILL MAINTENANCE 281 ⟶ *10 minutes*

Directions. Use the first paragraph of Timed Writing 280, page 322, for 1-minute writings. *Type on the skill-building level.* Determine your nwpm.

LESSON 282

CONDITIONING PRACTICE 282 — *5 minutes*

	STROKES
May Jack explain the quiz before we go on doing several of the stunts?	70
On May 26, 1952, we paid $37,480 for the house at 361 Sulgrave Street.	70
A loafer on the job may be worse than having no one on the job at all.	70

PROBLEM TYPING 282 — *25 minutes*

PROBLEM I—ARTICLES OF COPARTNERSHIP

Directions. Type these articles of copartnership on legal paper, following the directions for legal documents given on page 316. Make one carbon copy. Use the current date.

Arrange the lines for the signatures of the witnesses and partners in a manner similar to that shown in Illustration 71.

ARTICLES OF COPARTNERSHIP

This contract, made and entered into on this _____ day of _____, 195___, by and between **LOUIS D. BARRETT,** of Atlanta, Georgia, **CLIFTON H. LEONARD,** of Decatur, Georgia, and **JAMES J. QUINN,** of Atlanta, Georgia, (P) **WITNESSETH:** That the said parties have on this day formed a copartnership for the purpose of engaging in and conducting a wholesale grocery business under the following stipulations, which are made a part of this contract: (P) FIRST: The said copartnership is to continue for a term of five years from the date hereof. (P) SECOND: The business is to be conducted under the firm name of North Georgia Wholesale Grocery Company, at Eighth and Peachtree Streets, Atlanta, Georgia. (P) THIRD: Each partner to this agreement shall, at the signing of these presents, pay into the copartnership the sum of Fifty Thousand (50,000) Dollars in cash. (P) FOURTH: Each partner is to devote his entire time and attention to the business and is to engage in no other business enterprise without the written consent of the other partners. (P) FIFTH: Louis D. Barrett will have general supervision of the business; Clifton H. Leonard will have charge of the sales, credits, and collections; and James L. Quinn will have supervision of the buying and of the accounting records. In addition, each partner is to attend to such other duties as shall be deemed necessary for the successful operation of the business. (P) SIXTH: Each partner is to receive a salary of Four Thousand Eight Hundred (4,800) Dollars a year, payable in installments of Four Hundred (400) Dollars in cash on the last business day of each month. At the end of the annual fiscal

LESSON 7

Machine Checkup and Adjustments

1. Check the placement of the paper guide, the paper-bail rolls, and the paper bail.
2. Set the stop for the left margin at 17 for a pica-type or at 25 for an elite-type machine; move the stop for the right margin to the end of the scale.
3. Set the line-space regulator for single spacing.
4. Set the ribbon lever for typing on the upper half of the ribbon.

RECALL PRACTICE 7

7 minutes

Directions. Type each line three times. Double-space after the third typing of the line.

ed uj rf ik gf hj cd nj ws yj vf ik ws yj vf ik

day how day how say way work with very very work

> Space once after a semicolon.

He can work; he can work well.   He works very well.

Vera will work well with Harry and Harvey Vincent.

REACH-STROKE PRACTICE 7—*q, m, x*

20 minutes

q is controlled by the *a finger*

m is controlled by the *j finger*

x is controlled by the *s finger*

1. Illustration 18 shows the reach to *q*, made with the *a finger*; and the reach to *m*, made with the *j finger*. As you touch *qa mj* lightly, hold the elbows steady. Make the reach to *q* by straightening the *a finger*; make the reach to *m* without moving the other fingers from their typing position. Watch your fingers as you type   *qa mj*   a few times.

Illustration 18 — Reaches to q and m

Illustration 19 — Reach to x

2. Illustration 19 shows the reach to *x*, made with the *s finger*. As you touch *xs* lightly, lift the *d* and *f* fingers slightly to give freedom of movement to the controlling *s finger*. Make the reach-stroke direct to the letter *x*; avoid twisting the elbow or the wrist. Keep the fingers curved. Watch your fingers as you type *xs*   a few times.

LESSON 281

CONDITIONING PRACTICE 281

5 minutes

	STROKES
We expect to fly from Quebec to Brazil in July to visit with Don King.	70
The bid on Louisville Electric is 93 5/8, but it is offered at 94 1/4.	70
Think of how you can serve the company and not what it can do for you.	70

PROBLEM TYPING 281

25 minutes

PROBLEM I—LEASE

The agreement that establishes the relation of landlord and tenant is known as a *lease*; consequently, the landlord is often called the *lessor*; and the tenant, the *lessee*.

Directions. Type the following lease. If a printed form is not available, type the complete form, arranging the copy in approximately the same manner as that shown in Illustration 72. Use the current date.

THIS LEASE WITNESSETH:

THAT **Walter C. Stone and Alma N. Stone, husband and wife,** Hereby Lease To **Howard D. Fisher** the premises situate in the **City** of **Milwaukee** in the County of **Milwaukee** and State of **Wisconsin,** described as follows: **Dwelling house to be used as a funeral home located at 2001 East Main Street, Milwaukee, Wisconsin,** with the appurtenances thereto, for the term of **ten (10) years** commencing **October 1, 195-,** at a rental of **One Hundred (100)** dollars per **month** payable **monthly.**

Said Lessee Agree**s** to pay said rent, unless said premises shall be destroyed or rendered untenantable by fire or other unavoidable accident; to not commit or suffer waste; to not use said premises for any unlawful purpose; to not assign this lease, or underlet said premises, or any part thereof, or permit the sale of **his** interest herein by legal process, without the written consent of said lessor**s**. Upon nonpayment of any of said rent for **ten** days, after it shall become due, and without demand made therefore; or if said lessee or any assignee shall fail to keep any of the other covenants of this lease, it shall be lawful for said lessor**s**, **their** heirs or assigns, into said premises to re-enter, and the same to have again, re-possess, and enjoy, as in **their** first and former estate; and thereupon this lease and everything herein contained on the said lessor**s'** behalf to be done and performed, shall cease, determine, and be utterly void.

Said Lessor**s** Agree (said lessee having performed **his** obligations under this lease) that said lessee shall quietly hold and occupy said premises during said term without any hindrance or molestation by said lessor**s**, **their** heir or any person lawfully claiming under them.

Signed this _____ day of _____, A. D. 195___.

Illustration 72 — Lease

Directions. Type each of the first four lines three times. Double-space after the third typing of the line. Use the last two sentences for three 1-minute writings each.

```
qa qa quick quickly quire require acquired quickly

mj mj sum rum gum ram home more much whom some whom

xs xs mix six fix say mix lax tax six fox mix six

I move quickly.  Most tax laws are not much liked.
```

	STROKES	WORDS
This is the kind of work that he can do very well.	50	10
Most of us take far too much time to do so little.	50	10

Use for 1-minute writings.

MANIPULATION—TABULATOR-KEY CONTROL

12 minutes

The use of the tabulator mechanism enables you to indent quickly and accurately to the place at which you are to begin to type.

Before setting the tabulator stops, clear all previous settings to eliminate false stops. To do this, depress and hold down the tab clear key (No. 31) and move the carriage in one motion from left to right. A single stop may be cleared by tabulating to the stop and pressing down the tab clear key. (Special instructions for clearing the tabulator stops are given for the Smith-Corona machine on page VII and for the IBM electric machine on page IX.)

To set tabulator stops, move the carriage so the writing position indicator (No. 33) is at the desired stop position; then depress the tab set key (No. 23). Repeat this operation to set as many tabulator stops as are needed. The tabulator bar or key is then used to move from one stop to the next.

Directions. You are to type the word *them* in four columns. Adjust the margin and tabulator stops as follows:

	PICA	ELITE
Margin stop for left margin	17	25
First tabulator stop	33	41
Second tabulator stop	49	57
Third tabulator stop	65	73

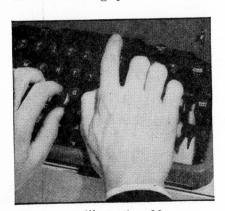

Illustration 20
Reach to Tabulator Bar

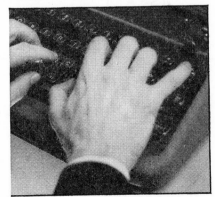

Illustration 21
Reach to Tabulator Key

Use the right forefinger to control the tabulator bar or the right little finger to control the tabulator key. Make the reach to the bar or the key by stretching the controlling finger; do not move the hand from its home position. Study Illustration 20 or 21; learn to operate the tabulator mechanism efficiently and add to the ease and speed with which you type.

Type the word *them* at the left margin. Depress and hold down the tabulator bar or key until the carriage stops moving; then type the word *them* again. Depress and hold down the bar or key until the carriage has moved to the third column; then type the word *them* again. Do the same for typing the word in the fourth column; then return the carriage and continue typing.

```
them               them               them               them
```

Checkup. If you failed to have all words correctly placed in columns, you are probably not holding the tabulator bar or key down until the carriage has stopped moving.

PROBLEM 1—PROXY

A proxy is a written form by means of which a person is given the authority or the power to act for another.

Directions. Type this proxy on regular typewriting paper with double spacing. Make one carbon copy, and use the current date.

PROXY

Know All Men by These Presents, That I, the undersigned, do hereby constitute and appoint Paul J. Davis to be my true and lawful attorney to represent me at the special meeting of the stockholders of The American Manufacturing Company, to be held on (one week from current date), and for me, and in my name, place, and stead, to vote at the said meeting upon stock standing in my name on the records of the said company at the time of the said meeting; and I do hereby grant to my said attorney all the powers that I should ordinarily possess if I were present in person. (P) IN WITNESS WHEREOF, I have hereunto set my hand and seal this _____ day of _____ one thousand nine hundred and _____.

_____ (SEAL)

Witness:

_____

PROBLEM 2—POWER OF ATTORNEY

A power of attorney is a formal written document in which an agent is appointed.

Directions. Type this power of attorney on legal paper, following the directions for legal documents given on page 316. Make one carbon copy, and use the current date.

POWER OF ATTORNEY

Know All Men by These Presents, That I, Martha L. Marshall, of the city of Hartford, county of Hartford, state of Connecticut, have made, constituted, and appointed, and by these presents do make, constitute, and appoint, Herbert P. Wagner, of the city of New Rochelle, county of Westchester, state of New York, my true and lawful attorney, for me and in my name, place, and stead, to sign my name to any and all checks drawn on the Merchants Bank and Trust Company against my deposits in the same, for the purchase of the property situate at the corner of Pomeroy Avenue and West Fork Road, known as the Bentley property; and I hereby ratify and confirm all that my said agent or attorney will lawfully do, or cause to be done, in connection with this purchase. (P) IN WITNESS WHEREOF, I have hereunto set my hand and seal this _____ day of _____ in the year of our Lord one thousand nine hundred and _____.

_____ (SEAL)

Witnesses:

_____

_____

State of Connecticut ⎫
County of Hartford ⎬ ss.
                    ⎭

The above-signed authority, Martha L. Marshall, personally appeared before me on the _____ day of _____ in the year of our Lord one thousand nine hundred and _____, and in due form acknowledged the attached instrument to be her act and deed and declared that it may be recorded as such.

_____
Notary Public

SKILL MAINTENANCE 280

Directions. Use the rough-draft sentence for 1-minute writings as time permits. Determine your nwpm.

	STROKES	WORDS
The party *of the second part* agrees to pay ~~the sum of $600.~~ *Six Hundred Dollars ($600).*	70	14

LESSON 8

Machine Checkup and Adjustments. Use the uniform pattern of preceding lessons. *3 minutes*

RECALL PRACTICE 8 *5 minutes*

Directions. Type each line three times. Double-space after the third typing of the line.

Center the typing ac- tion in the fingers.

```
xs yj vf uj tf nj xs yj ed mj cd ik ws .l qa ol qa
vim who yet for ask can lag and sum quit just next
Quick finger motions may cause me to excel them.
Make an extra effort to work as quietly as you can.
```

REACH-STROKE PRACTICE 8—*b, p, ,* (Comma) *20 minutes*

b is controlled by the *f finger*
p is controlled by the *; finger*
, is controlled by the *k finger*

1. Illustration 22 shows the reach to *b*, made with the *f finger*, and to the letter *p*, made with the *; finger*. Make the reaches without moving the elbows outward or the hands out of their typing position. Watch your fingers as you type   bf p;   a few times.

Illustration 22 — Reaches to b and p

Illustration 23 — Reach to , (comma)

2. Illustration 23 shows the reach to , (comma), made with the *k finger*. As you touch *,k* lightly, lift the *j finger* slightly. Move the *k finger* downward and slightly to the right without twisting the wrist or the elbow. Watch your fingers as you type   ,k   a few times.

Directions. Type each of the first four lines three times. Double-space after the third typing of the line. Use the last two sentences for three 1-minute writings each.

Space once after a comma.

Use for 1-minute writings.

	STROKES	WORDS
`bf bf bag but big fob p; p; pay pad map cup but box`		
`bay rob bay rub dip rub dip map box but map big pay`		
`Paul quit his job, but Robert expects to keep his.`		
`It is quite possible, I think, to excel in typing.`		
`The first thing for me to do is to type with ease.`	50	10
`I can now type the short and simple words quickly.`	50	10

Directions. Use the sentence for 1-minute writings. Determine your nwpm.

	STROKES	WORDS
If you want to excel in your job, be both a fine and a capable person.	70	14

LESSON 280

CONDITIONING PRACTICE 280   *5 minutes*

	STROKES
Frank will be amazed by the explicit answer John gave to the question.	70
In 1870, Philadelphia had a population of 674,022; in 1950, 2,064,794.	70
Do not try to think and work just as you thought and worked last week.	70

TIMED WRITING 280   *8 minutes*

Directions. Type for 5 minutes *on the control level*. Determine your nwpm; or correct each error as you type, if this is approved by your teacher.

Each paragraph has every letter of the alphabet and a syllable intensity of 1.40.

	STROKES	
	PARA.	TOTAL
There are many ways to build typing skill and no one best way for all	70	
of us. Each of us can discover the right way to type so that maximum power	146	
will be realized in the least possible time. Learning to type is a very	219	
individual problem. If you want to reach out into new speed areas, just	292	
push yourself into more rapid fingering patterns when typing for a minute.	368	
You will know when you are pushing yourself too rapidly. If you type with	443	
continuity, you are using the right stroking pattern for you. When you	515	
feel considerable tension in your typing practice, that will be the cue	587	
for a change in the purpose as well as the procedure of practice. A short	662	
writing under time is a good device for forcing your typing pattern to	733	
change to a quite rapid one, but it is not a measure of your typing power.	807	
It appears extremely simple when you think about what has to be done	69	876
to type well. The copy is placed in the usual position; the typewriter	141	948
is the one you have been accustomed to using; you read the copy and type	214	1021
what you read. That is the simple truth, but it is not exactly the	282	1089
unadulterated truth. There wouldn't be any more to it than the very simple	358	1165
statement that you just type what you see if it were not for the signi-	428	1235
ficant fact that each of us is a human being. While many of us generally	502	1309
do things in somewhat the same way, each of us frequently does things in	575	1382
a vastly different way. That is why we are so human. We frequently fail	649	1456
to realize the significance of this statement.	695	1502

Directions. As your teacher dictates the material to you, type each line three or four times; then at the conclusion of the drill, type the last two sentences of the preceding reach-stroke practice as 1-minute writings.

```
by by me me us us to to if if so so an an it it

he he the the or or for for an an and and for the

I can type.  I can type well.  I can type very well.
```

PARAGRAPH TYPING   *7 minutes*

Directions. Use double spacing and a 5-space paragraph indention. As the left margin is set at 17 for a pica- or 25 for an elite-type machine, the tabulator stop will be set at 22 or 30 for the paragraph indention. Type the paragraph two or three times.

```
Depress the tab bar or key to indent for the

beginning of a paragraph.
```

LESSON 9

Machine Checkup and Adjustments. Use the uniform pattern of preceding lessons.   *3 minutes*

RECALL PRACTICE 9   *5 minutes*

Directions. Type each line three times. Double-space after the third typing of the line. All letters taught are used in each line of the drill.

```
rfmj vfuj ed,k cdik ws.l xsol tfnj bfyj qap; fghj

had for was map can lay vex box jug kit pay but quit

work them quit next pave fact days just glad both

Please pack my box with five jugs of liquid veneer.
```

SKILL BUILDING 9   *15 minutes*

Directions. Set the machine for double spacing. The stop for the left margin has already been set at 17 for a pica- or at 25 for an elite-type machine. Set the tabulator stop for a 5-space paragraph indention (pica-type machine, 17 plus 5 = 22; elite-type machine, 25 plus 5 = 30). Type the paragraph twice. All the letters that have been taught are used in this paragraph.

	STROKES	WORDS
I can learn to type if I will do my best work	46	9
each day. It is not enough just to make my fingers	98	20
move; they must make quick and exact strokes. If I	150	30
do each thing well, my typing skill will grow.	196	39

Hold your eyes on the copy as you throw the carriage.

LESSON 279

CONDITIONING PRACTICE 279

STROKES

My liking for frozen juices explained why we have a big quantity here. 70
They offered to sell 1260# of sugar @ 8½¢ a pound for prompt delivery. 70
You can do the drill well when the outcome is known to be worth while. 70

PROBLEM TYPING 279

25 minutes

PROBLEM 1—AGENCY CONTRACT

An agency contract is a written instrument setting forth the terms of an agreement whereby one person or company is empowered to act as the agent of another.

Directions. Type this agency contract on legal paper, following the directions for legal documents given on page 316. Make one carbon copy, use 10-space paragraph indentions, and use the current date. The closing lines are shown in Illustration 71.

AGENCY CONTRACT

This agreement, made and entered into on this, the _____ day of _____, 195__, by and between **THE ACME PRODUCTS CORPORATION,** a corporation of Tulsa, Oklahoma, the party of the first part, and **ANDREW F. FOGARTY,** of San Antonio, Texas, the party of the second part, (P) **WITNESSETH:** That, whereas, the party of the first part is about to open a branch office, to be located in San Antonio, Texas, for the sale of its products, the said party of the first part hereby engages the services of Andrew F. Fogarty, the party of the second part, as manager of that office. (P) The party of the first part hereby agrees to pay to the party of the second part a monthly salary of Five Hundred Dollars ($500), payable on the last day of every month, for a period of one year from the date of this contract. (P) The party of the first part hereby agrees to pay all reasonable office expenses, including rent and salaries of such help as shall be agreed upon from time to time between the parties hereto. (P) The party of the second part agrees to give his undivided time and attention to the business of the party of the first part and not to engage in any other business or occupation while in the employ of the party of the first part. (P) The party of the second part also agrees that he will be governed at all times by the instructions of the party of the first part with regard to all contracts entered into with third persons for the party of the first part; that he will render a report of each and every sale at the time of such sale, giving a detailed account of the products sold, the prices, and the terms of the sale; and that he will submit each month to the party of the first part an itemized list of office expenses. The party of the second part agrees also to make all collections for products sold by his office and to make remittances of funds on hand as directed by the party of the first part from time to time. (P) **IN WITNESS WHEREOF,** The parties have hereunto affixed their hands and seals on the day and in the year first above written.

THE ACME PRODUCTS CORPORATION

_____ (SEAL)
President
Party of the First Part

_____ (SEAL)
Party of the Second Part

Witnesses:

_____

_____

Illustration 71 — Closing Lines of an Agency Contract

z is controlled by the *a finger*

Illustration 24 — Reach to z

Illustration 24 shows the reach to *z*, made with the *a finger*. As you touch *za* lightly, move the controlling finger to *z* without moving the other fingers from their typing position. Watch your fingers as you type   **za**   a few times.

Directions. Use single spacing. Type each of the lines three times. Double-space after the third typing of the line.

     za za lazy hazy size This is the size.   He is lazy.

     Robert can win a prize.   Robert has a lot of zeal.

     If you have zeal for your work, you can do much.

Alphabetic sentence.   Pack my box with five dozen jugs of liquid veneer.

MEASUREMENT SENTENCES 9   *10 minutes*

Directions. Use each sentence for two 1-minute writings.

Mark each writing on the basis of correct words per minute (called cwpm). To do this, draw a circle around each word in which an error appears; then proceed as follows:

a. To the number of strokes in complete lines, add the strokes typed for a part of a line. This will give the gross strokes typed.

b. Divide by 5 to get the gross words.

c. From the gross words, deduct 1 for each error to get the number of correct words.

d. Divide by the time of the test (1 minute in this case) to determine the correct words per minute (cwpm).

Gross Strokes ÷ 5 = Gross Words — Errors = Correct Words ÷ Time = cwpm.

	STROKES	WORDS
It is fine for all of us to do the work well.	45	9
We can learn to do well anything we want to learn.	50	10
Know what you are to do; then do it as well as you can.	55	11

Backspacing. At times you may need to backspace one or more times. To do this, depress the backspace key (No. 30) once for each space required to bring the carriage to the desired writing position. Depress the backspace key with the finger that will call for the shortest possible reach and yet will be strong enough to depress the backspace key with easy control. (If you find the little finger strong enough for backspacing, use it and avoid moving the hand from its typing position; otherwise, use the *s* or the *d finger* to depress the backspace key.) When it is necessary to backspace a third of a line or more, it is quicker and therefore better to move the carriage by hand rather than to use the backspace key.

Illustration 70 form (left column, image of the printed form):

STATE OF PENNSYLVANIA } SS.
COUNTY OF ALLEGHENY

Personally came before me, Nelson C. King, Notary Public
in and for said county, the following named persons, viz: T. J. Moorhead and James A. Dilworth
............who, being duly sworn, do depose and say that they, at
the request of Union National Bank............Executor-Adm'r ..c. t. a.
whose P. O. Address is Wilkinsburg, Pennsylvania............will well and truly
and without prejudice or partiality, value and appraise the goods and chattels, rights and credits, which were of............
Robert A. Kunkel,............deceased
and in all respects perform their duties as appraisers to the best of their skill and judgment.

Sworn and subscribed before me
this 18th day of September, 195-.

INVENTORY AND APPRAISEMENT

of the goods and chattels, rights and credits, which were of Robert A. Kunkel, late of 1424 Guffey Place Street, Wilkinsburg City 4th Ward Boro Twp. Pennsylvania, taken and made in conformity with the above deposition.

NOTE—Appraisers should sign inventory at the end thereof.

	Dollars	Cents
Savings Account Book #4342, of the Union National Bank of Wilkinsburg, Pennsylvania, balanced to 8/8/5-	2,250	00
Interest on the above Savings Account to 8/8/5-	9	50
Checking Account Book #2067, of the Union National Bank of Wilkinsburg, Pennsylvania, balanced to 8/8/5-	1,125	30
1,000 shares Penn Building & Loan Association, Wilkinsburg, Pennsylvania, @ $10, Certificate #632425	10,000	00
15 Bonds, par value $1,000 each, of the City Gas & Electric Company, Wilkinsburg, Pennsylvania, and numbered A44225 to A44239 inclusive	15,000	00
Accrued interest on the above bonds to 8/8/5-	182	00
5 $500 United States Savings Bonds purchased July, 1950; January, 1951; July, 1951; December, 1951; and April, 1952	1,902	50
	30,469	30

APPRAISERS

Illustration 70 — Inventory and Appraisement

Appraisers

STATE OF PENNSYLVANIA } SS.
COUNTY OF ALLEGHENY

Personally came before me, **Nelson C. King, Notary Public** in and for said county, the following named persons, viz: **T. J. Moorhead and James A. Dilworth** who, being duly sworn, do depose and say that they, at the request of **Union National Bank** Adm'r **c. t. a.** whose P. O. Address is **Wilkinsburg, Pennsylvania,** will well and truly and without prejudice or partiality, value and appraise the goods and chattels, rights and credits, which were of **Robert A. Kunkel,** deceased, and in all respects perform their duties as appraisers to the best of their skill and judgment.

INVENTORY AND APPRAISEMENT
of the goods and chattels, rights and credits, which were of **Robert A. Kunkel, late of 1424 Guffey Place** Street, **Wilkinsburg** City **4th** Ward **Pennsylvania,** taken and made in conformity with the above deposition.

	Dollars	Cents
Savings Account Book #4342, of the Union National Bank of Wilkinsburg, Pennsylvania, balanced to 8/8/5-	2,250	00
Interest on the above Savings Account to 8/8/5-	9	50
Checking Account Book #2067, of the Union National Bank of Wilkinsburg, Pennsylvania, balanced to 8/8/5-	1,125	30
1,000 shares Penn Building & Loan Association, Wilkinsburg, Pennsylvania, @ $10, Certificate #632425	10,000	00
15 Bonds, par value $1,000 each, of the City Gas & Electric Company, Wilkinsburg, Pennsylvania, and numbered A44225 to A44239 inclusive	15,000	00
Accrued interest on the above bonds to 8/8/5-	182	00
5 $500 United States Savings Bonds purchased July, 1950; January, 1951; July, 1951; December, 1951; and April, 1952	1,902	50
	30,469	30

APPRAISERS

SKILL MAINTENANCE 278

Directions. If time permits, use the sentence for 1-minute writings. Determine your nwpm.

	STROKES	WORDS
Loaf if you want to, but then you can't collect the wages of a worker.	70	14

SECTION 2. Continuity Typing

Purpose. The lessons of this section are organized to build appropriately rapid and continuous stroking of the keys when simple sentence and paragraph material is being typed.

Pattern of Lessons. The lessons in this section are one in purpose, one in pattern, and vary but little in the timing. Each lesson logically builds basic skills needed for your satisfactory growth in typing power. Portions of the lessons are given identifying headings that indicate the purpose of the practice. Know the purpose of the learning materials as well as the practice procedures you are to use. You will make the best progress if you do not vary the pattern of these lessons except at the direction of your teacher.

Finger Gymnastics. A minute or two of finger-gymnastic practice each day will help you to develop good control of your fingers. Some gymnastic drills are illustrated and described on the inside front cover of this book. Refer to these drills at the beginning of each period and practice one or two of them briefly. This will be a uniform daily assignment even though it will not be repeated with the instructions in each lesson.

General Directions. Use a full-size sheet of paper, 8½ by 11 inches. Type your name at the top of each sheet of paper you use in typing the lessons. Separate the portions of the lesson (conditioning practice, pace writing, skill building), when they are typed on the same page, by operating the line-space lever twice.

Machine Checkup and Adjustments. 1. Check the placement of the paper guide, the paper-bail rolls, and the paper bail.

2. Set the stop for the left margin at 12 for a pica-type or at 20 for an elite-type machine; move the stop for the right margin to the end of the scale.

3. Set the ribbon lever for typing on the upper half of the ribbon.

4. Use single spacing for drills and double spacing for paragraphs.

5. Set the machine for a 5-space paragraph indention.

These directions are to be used in typing each lesson of this section.

Conditioning Practice. The way to type the conditioning practice is to begin at an easy, controlled rate. The purpose of the practice is implied by the word "conditioning"—you are to condition yourself to the control of yourself; then you can control the typewriter. Type this first work of each lesson with controlled, continuous stroking.

Pace Writing. Type each sentence as a 1-minute writing to "feel out" the rate (or the pace) you want to maintain when you type the paragraphs of the skill building which follows. Check each writing for cwpm (correct words per minute, explained on page 17). Do not try to type at your fastest possible speed, but type with continuity—just keep on typing without pausing or letting the carriage stop its movement.

LESSON 10

CONDITIONING PRACTICE 10

5 minutes

Directions. Type each line three times, or more if time permits. Double-space after the third typing of the line.

STROKES

rf mj vf uj tf nj bf yj ed ,k cd ik ws .l xs ol qa p; za p;   59

Alphabetic sentence. Jack Gwin quietly planned for the visit to Mexico or Brazil.   60

Type as rapidly as you can type with a feeling of real ease.   60

That deponent is a resident of Pennsylvania, residing at **Wilkinsburg, Pennsylvania,** a Citizen of the United States, and respectfully petitions the Register to admit said will to probate and grant letters of administration cum testamento annexo on said estate.

Sworn and subscribed before me.

August 11, A. D., 195-.

_____

Register

UNION NATIONAL BANK

By _____

Trust Officer

ALLEGHENY COUNTY, ss:

I, **Clark Fulton,** do swear that, as I verily believe, the above-named **Robert A. Kunkel**

died on the **8th** day of **August,** A. D. **195-,** at **10 A.** M., and I do further swear that, as the Administrator cum testamento annexo of the estate of the said decedent **Union National Bank** will well and truly administer the goods and chattels, rights and credits of said deceased according to law, and also will diligently and faithfully regard and well and truly comply with the provisions of the law relating to inheritance tax.

Sworn and subscribed before me this **11th** day of **August,** A. D. **195-,** and letters of Administration cum testamento annexo granted unto **Union National Bank of Wilkinsburg.**

_____

Register

_____

Assistant Clerk

_____

SKILL MAINTENANCE 277   *10 minutes*

Directions. Take a number of 1-minute writings on the second paragraph of Timed Writing *276,* page 315. Select a goal that is 5 to 7 words faster than your five-minute nwpm. You will be guided by the call of "Half," and "One." Adjust the goal to challenge you to type at your maximum rate with appropriate control. *Type on the skill building level of practice.*

LESSON 278

CONDITIONING PRACTICE 278   *5 minutes*

STROKES

Ben said the July seizure excuse was quite vague and may lack support.	70
Wilbur Parks flew more than 6,500 miles to get to Alabama by April 26.	70
That man who learns to love his work will always have work to be done.	70

TIMED WRITING 278   *8 minutes*

Directions. Type for five minutes *on the control level,* using the material of Timed Writing 276, page 315. Determine your nwpm; or correct each error as you type, if this is approved by your teacher.

PROBLEM TYPING 278   *25 minutes*

PROBLEM I—INVENTORY AND APPRAISEMENT

Two appraisers, who are named by the administrator, appraise the assets at their value on the day of the death of the decedent and execute a form listing the assets known as an *inventory and appraisement.*

Directions. Prepare the inventory and appraisement. Use the current date. If a printed form is not available, type the complete form, arranging the copy in approximately the same manner as that shown in Illustration 70.

PACE WRITING 10

5 minutes

Directions. Type each sentence as a 1-minute writing. Type with easy, continuous stroking.

	STROKES	WORDS
Let no one tell you that you cannot do well in all the work.	60	12
It is up to you to know how to do the work in the right way.	60	12

SKILL BUILDING 10

20 minutes

For this lesson you are expected to type at a rate of 10 to 15 cwpm. If you type faster than 15 cwpm and are making errors, pace yourself at a slower rate. If you do not type a minimum of 10 cwpm, build a slightly more rapid stroking pattern.

Directions

1. a. Type the first paragraph for ½ minute.
   b. Set a new goal 5 strokes beyond the end of your first typing.
   c. Type two or three ½-minute writings attempting to reach this goal.
2. a. Type for 1 minute.
   b. Set a new goal 10 strokes beyond the end of this typing.
   c. Type two or three 1-minute writings attempting to reach this goal.
3. Use the second paragraph in the same way that you did the first.
4. If time permits, take one or more 2-minute writings.

	STROKES PARA.	TOTAL
This is a new kind of work for me and a new way for me	55	
to learn to type. I know that I can learn to type well if I	116	
will do all the work each day just as well as I can.	168	
Hit one key at a time. That is what you are to do when	56	224
you type. Do not pause after you hit the key. Turn loose of	118	286
it; then hit the next key. That is the way to type.	170	338

DIRECT DICTATION 10

10 minutes

Directions. As your teacher dictates this material to you, close the book or cover this page. Think the word and type the word as a unit.

is is of me of me to do to do for for for the the for the

well well work work kind work type work will type well know

I will work. I can learn to type. I can learn to type well.

of it of it at that what what you are what you are it hit hit

Hit one key. Hit one key at a time. Turn loose of it.

Take another 1-minute writing on each of the paragraphs in the preceding skill building and check the cwpm to determine possible gains through this organized practice on words that appear in those paragraphs.

LESSON 277

CONDITIONING PRACTICE 277

5 minutes
STROKES

Give them a big prize for quickly answering Judith's expert questions.	70
The stenographer's attention was called to the attorney's exact words.	70
A man can't expect to collect the wages of a worker if he is a loafer.	70

PROBLEM TYPING 277

25 minutes

PROBLEM 1—PROBATE OF WILL

If the will of the decedent does not specify a personal representative to execute the duties relevant to closing his estate, the attorney for the estate prepares a form, known as a *probate of will*, requesting the register of wills to issue letters of administration for the appointment of an administrator.

Directions. Prepare an application for the probate of a will. In the copy given below, the material to be typed on a form similar to that in Illustration 69 is printed in bold face. If a printed form is not available, type the complete form, arranging the copy in approximately the same manner as that shown in the illustration.

The Latin expression *cum testamento annexo* used in the Probate of Will means *with the will annexed*. The abbreviation *ss.* is for the Latin word *scilicet,* which means *namely*. This abbreviation may be written either in capitals or lower case.

IN RE PROBATE OF THE WILL OF **Robert A. Kunkel,** late of **Wilkinsburg, Pennsylvania,** deceased, and Grant of Letters of Administration, cum testamento annexo.

REGISTER'S OFFICE
ALLEGHENY COUNTY. ss.

Before the Register of Allegheny County personally appeared **Clark Fulton, Trust Officer of the Union National Bank of Wilkinsburg, Pennsylvania,** who being duly sworn, says that **Robert A. Kunkel,** being at the time a resident of **Wilkinsburg,** Allegheny County, and a citizen of **Pennsylvania,** died at **Wilkinsburg, Pa.,** on **August 8, A. D. 195-,** at **10 A. M.,** having first made **his** last will and testament, dated **January 20, 195-.**

That Testat**or** was possessed of personal estate to the value of **$30,000.**

That said Testat**or** was survived by a spouse and was **not** survived by children born to or adopted by Testat**or** after the execu-

tion of the Will offered for probate; that the said Decedent's heirs and next of kin (including heirs by adoption) are as follows:

	Relationship	Residence
Mary Chase Kunkel	Wife	1424 Guffey Place Wilkinsburg, Pa.
James David Kunkel	Son	11 Lane Terrace Pittsburgh, Pa.
Donald Paul Kunkel	Son	1424 Guffey Place Wilkinsburg, Pa.
Ruth Kunkel Main	Daughter	1347 Valley Drive Philadelphia, Pa.

Illustration 69 — Probate of Will

LESSON 11

The pattern of procedures for this and the following lessons of this section was given at the beginning of the section. Set the stop for the left margin at 12 or 20; move the right margin stop to the end of the scale. Use a 5-space paragraph indention; use single spacing for drills and double spacing for paragraph writings.

CONDITIONING PRACTICE 11   *5 minutes*

Directions. Type each line three times, or more if time permits.

STROKES

rfvf mjuj edcd ,kik tfbf njyj wsxs .lol qaza p;p; gfbf hjyj 59

Alphabetic sentence. Robert quickly realized that jumping was very fine exercise. 60

Basic skills in typing will be improved by right daily work. 60

PACE WRITING 11   *5 minutes*

Directions. Type each sentence as a 1-minute writing.

STROKES WORDS

Work can be done with ease if it is known what must be done. 60   12

It takes time to learn to do right that which is to be done. 60   12

SKILL BUILDING 11   *20 minutes*

Directions. Follow the procedure outlined on page 19. For this lesson you are expected to type at a rate of 11 to 16 cwpm.

STROKES
PARA. TOTAL

Hit the key with a quick blow to the center; then pull   55

the finger back without letting it follow the key. Make the   116

stroke with the finger, and hold the hand and arm still.   172

I can learn to type well if I want to learn and if I   53   225

will work to learn. Good skill in typing comes through the   113   285

right kind of daily work. I shall keep on working as well   172   344

as I can, and good typing skill will come to me.   220   392

DIRECT DICTATION 11   *10 minutes*

it it hit he the the hit the if to an an and can the if it

with with then then work work with then work will work well

I can learn. I can learn to type. I can learn to type well.

I want to learn. I will work to learn. I shall keep on.

Take another 1-minute writing on each of the paragraphs in the preceding skill building and check the cwpm to determine possible gains through this organized practice on words that appear in those paragraphs.

Preparation of the Backing Sheet. 1. At the top of the backing sheet make a fold of approximately an inch. 2. Bring the bottom edge of the backing sheet even with the top edge. Crease the fold neatly. 3. Place the bottom edge of the last fold even with the top of the sheet and crease. 4. Type on the fold facing you. To do this, unfold the last fold, insert the backing sheet into the typewriter, and type the endorsement.

Place the typed pages under the inch fold at the top of the backing sheet, and bind them, placing an eyelet at each side, about a half inch from the top and an inch from the sides.

PROBLEM I—TYPING A WILL

Directions. Type the following will with double spacing on plain paper. Add two lines at the bottom of the will for the names and addresses of the witnesses. Prepare a backing sheet, type an endorsement similar to the one shown in Illustration 68, page 316, and bind the pages together.

	STROKES
LAST WILL AND TESTAMENT	24
OF	27
ROBERT A. KUNKEL	44

I, Robert A. Kunkel, of the city of Wilkinsburg, county of Allegheny, and state of Pennsylvania, being of sound mind and memory, do hereby make, publish, and declare this to be my last will and testament, hereby revoking any will or wills heretofore made by me. — 77, 107, 141, 173, 204, 241, 277, 307

First. I direct that all my just debts and funeral expenses be fully paid and satisfied, as soon as conveniently may be, after my decease. — 341, 377, 411, 448

Second. I give, devise, and bequeath unto each of my three children, James, Donald, and Ruth, the sum of five thousand dollars ($5,000). In the event that any one of said children shall predecease me, then the sum which would otherwise have been paid to such decedent shall be paid to the children of such decedent in equal shares. If any of said children, James, Donald, and Ruth, shall not be living at the time of my death and shall not have left descendants, then the sum which would have been paid to such deceased child — 479, 512, 547, 587, 621, 656, 691, 727, 765, 802, 839, 877, 914, 944, 977

shall be paid to my surviving children in equal shares. — 1011, 1034

Third. I give, devise, and bequeath to my wife, Mary Chase Kunkel, all the rest, residue, and remainder of my estate, both real and personal, of every kind and description, wheresoever situate, which I may own or have the right to dispose of at the time of my decease. In the event my said wife shall predecease me, I give, devise, and bequeath the portion of my estate which she would have taken, if living, to my surviving children in equal shares. — 1064, 1097, 1131, 1167, 1202, 1237, 1269, 1305, 1340, 1374, 1406, 1445, 1479, 1488

In Witness Whereof, I, Robert A. Kunkel, the testator, have set my hand and seal hereto this twentieth day of January in the year of our Lord one thousand nine hundred and fifty-three (1953). — 1518, 1555, 1591, 1625, 1656, 1681

_____(Seal) — 1718

Signed, sealed, published and declared as and for his last will and testament by Robert A. Kunkel, the above-named testator, in the presence of us, who, at his request and in the presence of him and of each other, have subscribed our names hereto as witnesses on the day and year last aforesaid. — 1750, 1786, 1821, 1854, 1890, 1925, 1958, 1993, 2013

SKILL MAINTENANCE 276

Directions. If time permits, take some 1-minute writings on the first paragraph of Timed Writing 276. Select a goal that is 5 to 7 words faster than your five-minute nwpm. You will be guided by the call of "Half," and "One." *Type on the skill-building level of practice.*

LESSON 12

Set the stop for the left margin at 12 or 20; move the stop for the right margin to the end of the scale. Use a 5-space paragraph indention; use single spacing for drills and double spacing for paragraph writings.

CONDITIONING PRACTICE 12   *5 minutes*

Directions. Type each line three times, or more if time permits.

STROKES

bf tf vf uj yj mj sx ws qa ik nj yj quiz very next quiz ring 60

Alphabetic sentence. Have Peter get four dozen quarts of lime juice by next week. 60

Hold your hands and arms quiet; let the fingers do the work. 60

PACE WRITING 12   *5 minutes*

Directions. Type each sentence as a 1-minute writing.

STROKES WORDS

It is well for all of us to try to do a lot more than we do. 60 12

A man can be just about anything that he really wants to be. 60 12

SKILL BUILDING 12   (For 1- and 2-minute writings)   *20 minutes*

Directions. Follow the procedure outlined on page 19 except that you will omit the ½-minute writings and type each paragraph first for 1 minute and then for 2 minutes. For this lesson you are expected to type at the rate of 12 to 17 cwpm.

	STROKES PARA.	TOTAL
Hold the hands and arms low so your fingers can flick	54	
the keys and get away quickly. Let the fingers rest very	112	
lightly on the keys, and they will make the reaches with a	171	
speed and sureness that will add much to your typing skill.	232	
A light stroke is an aid to good typing.	272	
Do more than you say you will do. This is the way to	54	326
grow in the power to do things. It is true that words have	114	386
power; but words must be backed with the zeal to do or your	174	446
chance to grow is lost. Do more than you say you will do;	233	505
this is a good plan to follow all the time.	276	548

DIRECT DICTATION 12   *10 minutes*

do do is is to to be be on on it it so so in in be be is is
the the and and can can and can the and can the say say but
low low say get and get you add you add but all but all all
Do more. Do more than you say. Hold the hands and arms low.
This is the way. This is the way to grow in power to do.

Take another 2-minute writing on each of the paragraphs in the preceding skill building. Contrast the cwpm with the earlier writings.

thrown away by the student before improvement in quality or in rate of   1265

work is typed with figures in the wrong column, total

[with stroke markers 255, 260, 265]

work is shown. Reports are typed with figures in the wrong column, total   1339

[270, 275, 280]

unchecked, and other errors made that will never be permitted in business.   1415

[285, 290, 295]

Some businessmen feel that the beginning worker is a liability for some   1487

[300, 305, 310]

months. You can make your first work easier if you will learn to find and   1562

[314]

correct your errors.   1582

PROBLEM TYPING 276   *25 minutes*

Legal Documents. Many legal documents have become standardized in form and may be obtained as printed copies to be filled in. This study must be limited to a few special forms that show the general arrangement of typical legal documents.

Most legal papers are typed with double spacing on legal paper 8½ by 13 or 15 inches with left and right ruled margins. Type within these vertical lines, leaving two or more spaces between the ruled line and the typing. If the paper does not have vertical rulings, set the margin stops for a 1½-inch left margin and a ½-inch right margin. The first line of typing should begin about 2 inches from the top of the paper. The first page is usually not numbered, but subsequent pages are numbered in the center at the bottom of each page.

The Endorsement. Legal documents may be bound in a manuscript cover or backing sheet, a sheet usually slightly heavier and about 1 inch wider and 1½ inches longer than the sheet on which the document is typed. On the cover is typed information concerning the contents of the document. Frequently a printed form of endorsement is used that has all general information printed on the back of the last sheet and that provides blanks for inserting the specific information necessary to distinguish the instrument from similar instruments.

Illustration 68 — Endorsements of Legal Forms

LESSON 13

Set the stop for the left margin at 12 or 20; move the stop for the right margin to the end of the scale. Use a 5-space paragraph indention; use single spacing for drills and double spacing for paragraph writings.

CONDITIONING PRACTICE 13

5 minutes

Directions. Type each line three times, or more if time permits.

STROKES

qa p; vf p; qa vf p; xs xs p; za qa vex six zip zoo six quiz 60

Alphabetic sentence. Jack Downey began to save money quickly for this next prize. 60

You must practice to get the fingers under complete control. 60

PACE WRITING 13

5 minutes

Directions. Type each sentence as a 1-minute writing.

STROKES WORDS

Each one can learn to hold his mind on the work he is doing. 60 12

You can make your fingers go just where you want them to go. 60 12

SKILL BUILDING 13 (For 1- and 2-minute writings)

20 minutes

Directions. Follow the procedure outlined on page 19 except that you will omit the ½-minute writings and type each paragraph first for 1 minute; then use each paragraph for 2-minute writings. For this lesson you are expected to type at a rate of 13 to 18 cwpm.

STROKES
PARA. TOTAL

Think and work. Work and think. It takes time to do 54

either, but you will save time in doing your work if you try 115

to think about it and plan for it before you do it. Know the 177

work you are to do and how you are to do it. Not until then 238

are you ready to begin to do it. 270

You need to have faith in yourself if you are to do the 56 326

work well. Faith is a magic that will help you to do what 115 385

you have to do. To try to type when you doubt your ability 175 445

to type well, is like trying to win a race with your feet in 236 506

a sack. Faith sets you free. Have faith in yourself. 290 560

DIRECT DICTATION 13

10 minutes

and you and you try try for try for and how and how and how

work work help help have have what what help help with with

Know the work. Know the work you are to do. Think and work.

Work and think. Faith is a magic. Faith sets you free.

You need to have faith. You need to have faith in yourself.

Take another 2-minute writing on each of the paragraphs in the preceding skill building. Contrast the cwpm with the earlier writings.

SPECIALIZED TYPING
SECTION 50. Legal Typing
LESSON 276

CONDITIONING PRACTICE 276 — 5 minutes

	STROKES
We are expecting them to require an adjustable desk of this very size.	70
Joe Roberts agreed to pay the sum of Three Hundred Ten Dollars ($310).	70
This expression "and/or" is used to denote both or one of two factors.	70

TIMED WRITING 276 — 8 minutes

Directions. Type for five minutes *on the control level*. Determine your nwpm; or correct each error as you type, if this is approved by your teacher.

Each paragraph has every letter of the alphabet and a syllable intensity of 1.40.

	STROKES
Learn to proofread with exactness. Know when your work is right and	69
when it must be corrected. Businessmen are too busy to have to correct	143
every piece of work done, yet this is frequently necessary if they want	215
to be sure that the material is accurate. Speed in production typing is	288
needed, of course; but the ability to find and correct errors and to know	362
that the work is right or wrong is much more important than high speed.	435
There will be a direct relation between your production rate and the size	509
of your pay check. You are now establishing work habits and building	579
typing skills that will determine the salary you will get when you go to	652
work in an office. Be certain that you establish the habit of proofreading	728
all of your work carefully. Don't be just half right—always know that	800
your work is entirely right.	830
Some students fail to realize that they must proofread their class	897
typing just as they will proofread their office typing. The habit of being	973
exact in this does not come just because the office situation demands it,	1047
especially if it has been the practice in the classroom to overlook errors.	1124
All too often work is marked by the teacher, discussed in class, then	1194

LESSON 14

Set the stop for the left margin at 12 or 20; move the stop for the right margin to the end of the scale. Use a 5-space paragraph indention; use single spacing for drills and double spacing for paragraph writings.

CONDITIONING PRACTICE 14   *5 minutes*

Directions. Type each line three times, or more if time permits.

STROKES

box zip six rub cap big six boy may par pay but mix vim quit   60

Alphabetic sentence. Jack Ziegler and Bart Quiegley have swamped the four experts.   61

Have faith; expect much; work with zeal; be just; and do good.   62

PACE WRITING 14   *5 minutes*

Directions. Type each line as a 1-minute writing.

STROKES WORDS

Hit the key with a sharp blow; then lift the finger at once.   60   12

I want to do the work as well as I can. I like this typing.   60   12

SKILL BUILDING 14   (For 2- and 3-minute writings)   *20 minutes*

Directions. Use the uniform practice procedure except that you will type for 2 minutes; then, for 3 minutes. For this lesson you are expected to type at a rate of 14 to 19 cwpm.

STROKES

Sit back in the chair. Hold your shoulders up, but not   56

rigid. Keep your feet on the floor. Let your body position   117

help you to type well. Hit the key with a sharp blow; then   177

lift the finger at once. Try to get rid of all motions that   238

are not needed in good typing, and grow in typing power.   294

TIMED WRITING 14   *10 minutes*

Directions. Take two 3-minute timed writings. Determine your cwpm. Note the improvement in skill—the increase in stroking rate, the decrease in errors, or both. Record your rate so that you can compare it with your rate in later lessons.

STROKES WORDS

When you read, you see words that make sense to you; so   56   11

you read meaning and give no thought to the letters that are   117   23

in the words. This is the way you are to learn to type. It   178   36

is not easy at first to think the word and type the word, but   240   48

it is the way you will learn to type with best typing power.   300   60

JOB 7—SKILL BUILDING IN TYPING A TABULATED DRILL

Directions. Determine the horizontal placement of the columns and type the problem as a 5-minute writing. The time required for planning the report and making the machine adjustments is included in the 5 minutes. The more skillful you are in determining the correct machine adjustments for this simple tabulated drill, the higher will be your production rate.

							STROKES
8392	5103	2715	6392	2651	9201	5192	35
195	102	268	163	740	100	602	70
92	83	40	75	62	30	15	105
5819	5619	7192	9162	3791	6593	2104	139

Skill Building Procedures. 1. You will be timed for 5 minutes. Clear the tabulator rack; set the machine to type the first 5 columns of figures given above; and type the problem as many times as you can until time is called.

2. You will be timed for 5 minutes. Clear the tabulator rack; set the machine to type the first 3 columns of figures given above; and type the problem as many times as you can until time is called.

JOB 8—PRACTICE COMPARISON ON TYPING A TABULATED REPORT

Directions. Type Job 6 as a 5-minute writing. Compare your nwpm on this writing with that made when you typed the material before for 5 minutes.

JOB 9—TIMED WRITINGS ON PROBLEM SENTENCES

Directions. Take a series of 1-minute writings on each sentence. Compare your typing skill as shown in cwpm to discover the kind of practice material that reduces your production output. Practice those sentences on which your score is relatively low; then repeat the 1-minute writings to see if you have made improvement through your intensive practice.

SENTENCES FOR TIMED WRITINGS

	STROKES	WORDS
Joe's highest quiz marks excelled Frank's low marks by several points.	70	14
The May 29 check is for $583.27. Order #14650 for "B" stock is ready.	70	14
The $1,000 $3\frac{1}{2}\%$ bonds (Series Y-2) were sold to Moore & Lynch, of York.	70	14
Think of the bigness of small men and not of the smallness of big men.	70	14
Do not be afraid to go on higher. Take a step at a time. Move on up.	70	14
~~Frank~~ *John* Miller's article, "Have You Grown in *Typing* ⁁Power," is ~~fine.~~ *very good.*	70	14
The ⁁*interest* rate ~~will be~~ *is* 6½ %. He wrote ⁁*or* perhaps telephoned ⁁*yesterday.* ~~this morning.~~	70	14

SECTION 49. Production Measurement Comparison

LESSONS 271 TO 275

Type Section 46, beginning on page 302, for the next five lessons. This use of the materials already typed will approximate the office experience of typists who type problems similar in form and in content day after day. It is one way to increase your production rate. Compare your production rate on this writing with the rate made when you typed these lessons as Section 46. Before starting to type, KNOW what you are to do and how you are to do it. Type with continuity but without hurry.

SECTION 3. Learning to Type Figures and Symbols

General Directions

1. Use a full-size sheet of 8½ by 11 inch paper.

2. Type your name at the left on the first line. As soon as you have learned to type the needed figures, type the date on the line with your name, but at the right of the paper.

3. Space the paper forward approximately 9 lines. As there are 6 line spaces to a vertical inch, there will be a space of 1½ inches between the name line and the first line of the lesson.

4. Separate the various parts of the lesson by 3 or 4 spaces.

5. Make the reaches to the figure keys with the fingers; avoid changing the hand position.

Machine Checkup and Adjustments

1. Check the placement of the paper guide, the paper-bail rolls, and the paper bail.

2. Set the stop for the left margin at 12 for a pica-type or at 20 for an elite-type machine; move the stop for the right margin to the end of the scale.

3. Set the line-space regulator for single spacing.

4. Set the ribbon lever for typing on the upper half of the ribbon.

These directions will not be given in full for each lesson, but the same procedure is to be followed throughout this section (Lessons 15-20).

LESSON 15

CONDITIONING PRACTICE 15 *5 minutes*

Directions. Type each line twice. Double-space after the second typing of the line. Use the fourth line for one or more 1-minute writings.

All letters of the alphabet are used in each of the first two lines.

STROKES

work quiz such jobs live paid them form they glad next with 59

Space once after a semicolon. James can get very few boxes of this size opened so quickly. 60

Think clearly; work quickly; be experts in your use of time. 60

Faith that we can do well is needed by all of us to do well. 60

REACH-STROKE PRACTICE 15—3-#, 7-& (Ampersand) *25 minutes*

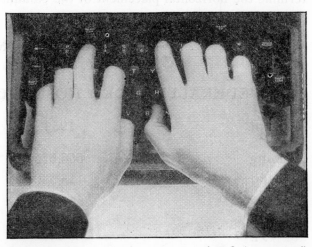

Control 3-# with the *d finger*

Control 7-& with the *j finger*

1. The figure *3* is above *e*; the # (number sign) is the shift of *3*. The *d finger* controls the *3-#*, as shown in Illustration 25. As you touch *de3d* lightly two or three times, lift the *f* finger slightly to give the *d finger* freedom to make the reach.

2. The figure *7* is above *u*; the & (ampersand) is the shift of *7*. The *j finger* controls *7-&*, as shown in Illustration 25. As you touch *ju7j* lightly two or three times, make the reach by straightening the *j finger*. Hold the other fingers in their typing position.

Illustration 25 — Reaches to 3-# and 7-& (ampersand)

JOB 5—ROUGH DRAFT LETTER

Directions. You will be timed for 5 minutes beginning NOW. Set the machine for a 60-space line. Type an original and six carbon copies. Use the modified block style of letter with no indentions for paragraphs and with mixed punctuation. Use the current date.

	STROKES	WORDS
Mr. G. E. Billings *Mr. Joseph W. Wharton*	36	7
Mr. Ralph T. Flynn *Mr. Alex C. Young*	55	11
Mr. Albert C. Riley *Mr. John E. Young*	75	15
Gentlemen:	145	29
~~At the present time~~ We are revising/the copy of ~~the~~ *our* A to Z *[as]*	184	37
Quick-Check Lubrication Guide. ~~Since~~ you are in contact with	243	49
our attendants who use this guide, you may hear suggestions	303	61
from time to time for ~~improving it.~~ ~~As~~ We want to send the	363	73
revised copy of this guide to press soon. We shall appreciate *therefore,*	438	88
receiving any suggestions you may be able to give us for	495	99
changes in the following items:	528	106
1. A TO Z LUBRICATION, *page 1.* *its improvement*	561	112
Does this procedure cover every step?	600	120
2. GENERAL A TO Z INSTRUCTIONS, *pages 2-7.*	645	129
Are the subjects listed in the correct order?	692	138
3. SPECIAL SERVICES, *pages 8-10.*	727	145
Any other special services you wish given?	771	154
4. SERVICE HINTS THAT SELL, *pages 11-15.*	814	163
This page is to be revised completely.	854	171
Go over the Guide carefully and let us have your suggestions	915	183
for its improvement by the end of the coming week.	967	193
1 space # Very truly yours,	985	197
3 spaces # Training Supervisor	1005	201
AKRoss:jb	1014	203

(margin note at left of items: indent 5 spaces / double-space)

JOB 6—TABULATED REPORT

Directions. You will be timed for 5 minutes beginning NOW. Clear the tabulator rack; determine the horizontal placement of the columns and type the problem as a 5-minute writing.

				STROKES	WORDS
ENROLLMENT				11	2
IN				14	3
FEDERALLY AIDED HOME ECONOMICS CLASSES				53	11
Type	1952	1951	Increase	76	15
Evening	666,676	606,938	59,738	113	23
Part-Time	115,370	107,275	8,095	151	30
All-Day	647,711	614,308	33,403	187	37
All Types	1,429,757	1,328,521	101,236	224	45

Directions. Type each line three times. Double-space after the third typing of the line. Do not space between the # and the following figure; as #73.

Use the small letter l for the figure 1

de3d 3d 3d ju7j 7j 7j 3d 7j 37 37 He is 37.   The page is 73.

I am 17.   Jack is 37.   Joe is 13.   Ned was born on March 13.

3d #d 3d #d Bill #13 7j &j 7j &j Hall & Marks paid Bill #13.

Invoice #137 is dated March 7.   Check #73 is dated March 31.

I had 37 stamps.   I need 13 more.   Pay Bill #137 on April 7.

The sum of 7 and 13 and 17 is 37.   Jack still owes 73 cents.

SKILL MAINTENANCE 15 *10 minutes*

You are expected to type simple sentence and paragraph material at the rate of 15 to 20 cwpm for the lessons of this section. Because of the nature of the practice materials used for learning the control of figures and symbols, you are not expected to increase your stroking rate much, if any; but you are expected to maintain your stroking rate. This is the purpose of the skill maintenance portion of the lessons in this section.

Directions. Use each sentence for two 1-minute writings.

STROKES WORDS

It is easy to see that it pays to hold the eyes on the copy.   60   12

There are a good many ways in which we can use typing skill.   60   12

You are not asked to do more than it is right for you to do.   60   12

LESSON 16

CONDITIONING PRACTICE 16 *5 minutes*

Directions. Type each line twice. Double-space after the second typing of the line. Use the fourth line for one or more 1-minute writings.

STROKES

3d 7j 37 37 Sue is 37.   I read 73 pages.   We used 37 stamps.   60

3d#d #d Bill #73 is paid.   7j&j &j Lang & May paid Bill #73.   60

Alphabetic sentence. Ajax and Kingsley have a few more prizes to be sold quickly.   60

Know that you have a mind; then make it get to work for you.   60

	STROKES	WORDS
for you. Use your creative imagination to surround your work with the | 1259 | 252 |
interest that comes from doing it well. | 1298 | 260 |

There is work for you to do. Your job is to get ready for it. Low-level positions paying low wages call for low-level ability. If you have exercised much thought and devoted much energy to building in your mind and your spine right work habits, useful office skills, and sound personal qualities, you will find your right place in business when you are ready for it. Be prepared to meet the exacting demands of office work, and you will grow in usefulness and value to the business. To meet these demands, you must have physical energy, mental alertness, and a strong faith in your ability to measure up to the responsibilities. Know what you can do now and determine what you must do in the remaining period of your training so that you will be ready to take your place as an efficient worker in a business organization.

STROKES	WORDS
1366	273
1440	288
1507	301
1578	316
1650	330
1720	344
1789	358
1858	372
1933	387
1996	399
2069	414
2125	425

JOB 2—STATISTICAL TYPING

Directions. Take 1-, 2-, and 3-minute writings. Contrast your nwpm with the nwpm on the 5-minute writing on Job 1. You should be able to type this simple statistical material at 85 to 90 per cent of your straight-copy nwpm.

	STROKES	WORDS
It is estimated that capital requirements of the air transportation | 68 | 14 |
industry will reach $750 million in the next ten years. The industry earned | 145 | 29 |
29 per cent on investment before taxes and 14 per cent net on investment | 218 | 44 |
in the year ended December 31. During a ten-year period, fares went from | 292 | 58 |
an average of 5.07 cents to 5.56 cents a passenger mile, a rise of less than | 369 | 74 |
10 per cent. Last year, first-class rail passenger fares averaged 42 per | 443 | 89 |
cent and rail coach 48 per cent over the 1940 levels. In this same period | 518 | 104 |
the index of consumer prices increased 88 per cent; wholesale prices, 127 | 592 | 118 |
per cent. | 601 | 120 |

JOB 3—SKILL BUILDING IN TYPING FIGURES

Directions. Use each sentence for 1-minute writings with the appropriate call of the guide, or type each sentence five times.

Strokes		Words 15"	Words 12"	Words 10"
53	The sleeve of the coat can be shortened 2 7/8 inches.	42	53	64
55	Invoice #758 gives the list price of the book as $1.20.	44	55	66
57	The postage on a special delivery letter is now 20 cents.	46	57	68
60	Joe Wood used 15 gallons of white paint and 3 quarts of oil.	48	60	72
63	Her address was 5906 Fifth Avenue, Pittsburgh 13, Pennsylvania.	50	63	76
65	Sam walks less than a half mile to work, but Frank walks 4 miles.	52	65	78
67	A week-end round trip by air coach to Paris will cost them $202.50.	54	67	80
70	It is approximately 20 to 25 miles from here to the West & Long plant.	56	70	84

JOB 4—PRACTICE COMPARISON ON STATISTICAL TYPING

Directions. Type Job 2 as a 3-minute writing. Compare your nwpm on this writing with that made when you typed the copy before for 3 minutes.

Control *5-%* with the *f* finger

Control *9-(* with the *l* finger

Illustration 26 — Reaches to 5-% and 9-(

1. The figure *5*, above and to the right of the letter *r*, is controlled by the *f finger*; the shift of the *5* is *%*. Stretch the *f finger* to the *5* key without moving the other fingers from their typing position, as shown in Illustration 26. Touch *f5f* lightly two or three times and watch to see that the *f finger* is straightened and that the reach is made without a forward movement of the hand.

2. The figure *9* is above *o*; the shift of *9* is *(*, the left parenthesis. This key is controlled by the *l finger*. As you touch *lo9l* lightly two or three times, hold the *; finger* near the typing position and lift the *k* and *j fingers* slightly to give freedom to the controlling *l finger*.

Directions. Type each line three times. Double-space after the third typing of the line. Do not space between the figure and *%; as 5%*.

Use the small letter l for the figure 1.

f5f 5f 5f 191 91 91 59 159 He read page 159.   Joe is 15 now.

Max is 19.   I am 15.   My uncle is 59.   Don was born on May 5.

5f %f 5f %f The rate is 5%.   91 (l 91 (l He paid on March 19.

The 5% note is dated March 15, 1951.   You owe Harry 95 cents.

Sam paid the 5% note on August 9.   Add 5 and 9 and 31 and 75.

The sum of 5 and 9 and 3 is 17.   Add 39 and 57 and 13 and 17.

SKILL MAINTENANCE 16   *15 minutes*

Directions. The purpose of this practice is to build sustained typing power.

Use double spacing. Type two 5-minute writings with the carriage throw called at the end of each minute. When the throw is called, return the carriage, indent, and start to type again from the beginning of the paragraph. You will do this for each minute of writing. At the end of each 5 minutes, check the different writings to see how uniform you are in the number of words you type each minute.

	STROKES	WORDS
Keep the fingers flying, but keep them flying to the	53	11
right keys. Hold the hands quiet. Do not let the elbows	111	22
move in or out. A change of hand position means a change	169	34
in the feel of the reach to the key.	205	41

SECTION 48. Production Practice Jobs

You will not know until you begin your first day's work just what will be the nature of your typing jobs; but you will be expected to correct all errors expertly and to do a full day's work every day. To be able to measure up to standards of job competence for which typing standards have been set, build high skill on the production practice jobs of this section.

It is impossible to say how many times you should type a practice job. Your teacher will help you to make the most efficient use of these materials and the wisest use of your practice time. Make each day's work show measurable improvement in these basic production skills.

LESSONS 266 TO 270

CONDITIONING PRACTICE FOR LESSONS 266 TO 270 · *5 minutes*

	STROKES
There is evidence that the quiz was partially blocked by Judge Moxley.	70
A loan of $37,500 at 5¼% interest has been made to Germaine & Company.	70
The need today is for men and women who will learn to love their work.	70

PRODUCTION PRACTICE JOBS 266 TO 270 · *35 minutes each period*
JOB 1—STRAIGHT-COPY MEASUREMENT

Directions. Type three 5-minute writings. For each writing determine your net words per minute (nwpm). Net words per minute are found as follows: Total strokes — 50 strokes for each error = net strokes ÷ 5 = net words ÷ time = nwpm.

If your teacher directs you to do so, neatly erase and correct each error. No penalty will be charged for an error satisfactorily corrected.

Record the score for your best writing. Let this be the basis for the comparison of your skill on the production practice jobs provided for lessons 266 to 270.

Each paragraph has every letter of the alphabet and a syllable intensity of 1.40.

	STROKES	WORDS
Work right. This is important. Some day you will find that the size	70	14
of your monthly pay check will be fixed to a large extent by the way	139	28
you work. Of course, what you are—the person you are—is just as	206	41
important as anything else even when it comes to getting and holding	275	55
an office position. The good old qualities of mind and heart and soul—	347	69
dependability, loyalty, intelligence, and the ability to get along with	419	82
others—are still in demand in business. Without these qualities, even a	493	99
good worker finds it hard to fit into the life of a busy office.	557	111
Right work habits are made up of many small things. You must be	622	124
prompt in assembling your work materials. You must plan your work	689	138
before you try to type it. You need to develop the power to visualize	760	152
the finished job so that you can check on the adequacy of your plans.	831	166
These things will help to make the right work habits. In addition, the	903	181
right kind of creative imagination will be a help to you. You should	973	195
not expect all of your work to be inherently interesting. Typing a long	1046	209
tabulated report may not have any interest for you; but do your job	1114	223
well. No matter what the job is, it should have a great deal of interest	1188	238

LESSON 17

CONDITIONING PRACTICE 17 *5 minutes*

Directions. Type each line twice. Double-space after the second typing of the line. Use the fourth line for one or more 1-minute writings.

STROKES

Read page 59.   He paid 3% interest.   Al was born on March 9.   60

I paid Bill #73.   Order #591 is from Ziegler & Hay, of York.   60

_{Alphabetic sentence.} Jackson and Quigley, wax importers, have this size of boxes.   60

It is a good thing to learn to do some one thing quite well.   60

REACH-STROKE PRACTICE 17—2-", 0-) (Right Parenthesis) *20 minutes*

Control *2-"* with the *s finger*

Control *0-)* with the *; finger*

1. The figure *2* is above *w*; the shift of *2* is the *"* (quotation mark). The key is controlled by the *s finger*. As you touch *sw2s* lightly two or three times, hold the *a finger* near the typing position; lift the *f* and *d fingers* slightly to give freedom to the controlling *s finger*.

2. The *0* (zero) is above the letter *p*; the shift of the *0* is *)*, the right parenthesis. This key is controlled by the *; finger*. As you touch *;0;* lightly two or three times, stretch the *; finger* and move it forward to the key, keeping the other fingers as close to the home keys as possible.

Illustration 27 — Reaches to 2-" and 0-)

Directions. Type each line three times. Double-space after the third typing of the line. Do not space between the quotation mark and the word quoted.

Line 3: The colon is the shift of the semicolon.
Line 3: Type the quotation mark after the period.

s2s 191 2s 91 2s 91 29 29 The sum of 12 and 50 and 31 is 93.

Rob is 20.   Jack is 5 ft. 10 in. tall and weighs 150 pounds.

2s "s He said, "Come at 2:30."   He wrote, "Ten (10) is right."

To type those words in all capitals, depress the SHIFT LOCK.

He said, "Read pages 20 to 29."   I spoke on "Uncommon Men."

Add 7 and 2 and 9 and 3 and 5.   The sum of 75 and 20 is 95.

LESSON 265

CONDITIONING PRACTICE 265

5 minutes

STROKES

How do you expect quick results from just being so very free and lazy?   70

Mr. Paul N. McMullen lives at 4902 Roberts Avenue, Denver 7, Colorado.   70

You can learn much from those you like and from those you do not like.   70

PRODUCTION TYPING 265

25 minutes

MEASUREMENT OF TYPING A FORM LETTER AND INDEX CARD

PROBLEM 1

Directions. As you type the copy for the form letter, make the necessary insertions of the material listed below. Use the style of letter and form of punctuation you prefer. Add an appropriate salutation to each letter. Address an envelope for each letter.

To: **Dr. Myron T. Caldwell**
      615 East Dale Avenue
      Seattle 6, Washington

Royalty of: 8
Total Amount: $10,650.20
Amount Paid: $7,987.65
Date Paid: March 15
Balance Due: $2,662.55
Date of Final Payment: September 10

PROBLEM 2

Directions. Type the form letter given above with the following changes.

To: **Professor Lester Knox Heron**
      University Preparatory School
      Missoula, Montana

Royalty of: **10**
Total Amount: $39,647.20
Amount Paid: $29,735.43
Date Paid: **March 15**
Balance Due: $9,911.77
Date of Final Payment: **September 10**

FORM LETTER TO AUTHORS

STROKES

(P) Soon after the close of our fiscal 35
year on June 30, we always report 69
to each author the total amount of 104
royalty earned by his publications. 140
(P) Your contract calls for a royalty 174
of   per cent of the net dollar volume 209
of sales of your books. The 242
total amount thus earned in the year 279
just closed is $, of which 315
$ was paid to you on   , 354
leaving a balance due you of $. 395
A check for this balance of $ 433
will be sent to you not later than 468
    . (P) It is very gratifying 505
to be able to make such a favorable 541
report to you. There is every reason 579
to believe that the sales will continue 613
to be high during the coming 648
year. Cordially yours William Watson 682
son Smith, President 702

PROBLEM 3

Directions. Type index cards for Problems 1 and 2. Type the surname first, then the address, total amount of royalty, amount paid and date, and the balance due.

TIMED WRITING 265

10 minutes

Directions. Type for 5 minutes, using the timed writing on pages 296 and 297. Use the remainder of the period for 1-minute writings. *Type on the control level of practice.*

Directions. Use double spacing. Build sustained typing power through typing two 5-minute writings with the carriage throw called at the end of each minute. When the throw is called, return the carriage, indent, and start to type again from the beginning of the paragraph. You will do this for each minute of writing. At the end of each 5 minutes, check the different writings to see how uniform you are in the number of words you type each minute.

STROKES WORDS

	STROKES	WORDS
You should be typing with more ease now than you did a	55	11
day or so ago. If so, you can know that you are growing in	115	23
the power to type. Move the finger quickly to the center of	176	35
the key; hit the key with a quick blow.	215	43

LESSON 18

CONDITIONING PRACTICE 18   *5 minutes*

Directions. Type each line twice. Double-space after the second typing of the line. Use the fourth line for one or more 1-minute writings.

STROKES

	STROKES
2s"s I wired, "Meet me at 2:50." They wrote "Quiz Experts."	60
91(1 0;); 0;); Bill #920 (of May 5) must be paid by June 29.	60
Alphabetic sentence. Kefour, New Jersey, and Cruz, Mexico, have quite big plants.	60
A good way to type is to think the word and not the letters.	60

REACH-STROKE PRACTICE 18—*4-$, 8-'* (Apostrophe)   *20 minutes*

Control *4-$* with the *f finger*

Control *8-'* with the *k finger*

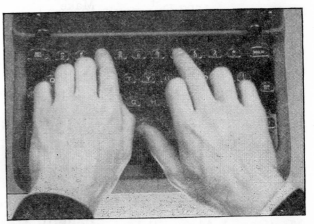

1. Study Illustration 28, which shows the reaches to *4-$* and *8-'* (apostrophe). The *f finger* controls *4-$* (dollar sign). As you touch *fr4f* lightly two or three times, make the reach with a direct finger movement and without change of hand or elbow position.

2. The *k finger* controls *8-'* (apostrophe). As you touch *ki8k* lightly two or three times, lift the *j finger* slightly to give the *k finger* freedom to make the reach.

Illustration 28 — Reaches to 4-$ and 8-' (apostrophe)

Make a pencil notation of the pages on which the mailing lists will be found. Stack 30 envelopes at the left of the typewriter to be chain fed into the typewriter, as directed on page 268. Address an envelope to each person listed. Use a line guide for accuracy in reading the names and addresses. Stack the envelopes face down after they are typed.

SKILL MAINTENANCE 263
10 minutes

Directions. Use the paragraph for 3-minute writings. *Type on the control level.*

	STROKES	WORDS
Standards of work are set by some organizations. One company does not	71	14
hire a typist, for example, unless she can type at least 1,200 envelopes	144	29
a day, or at the rate of 150 an hour. Expert typists can do from 1,500 to	219	44
1,800 envelopes in a day. Either the No. 6 3/4 or the No. 10 commercial	292	58
envelope can be used with equal facility. In order to be able to type	363	73
envelopes at the rate set by this company, you would need a speed of 60 to	438	88
75 words a minute and the skill to type figures rapidly and with control.	511	102

LESSON 264

CONDITIONING PRACTICE 264
5 minutes

	STROKES
The tax prober quickly vowed to seize the map of the housing projects.	70
Date my letter April 26, my check April 29, and mail both on April 30.	70
Stick to a problem until it is solved; that is the way to win success.	70

PRODUCTION TYPING 264
25 minutes

PROBLEM 1—SKILL BUILDING IN TYPING A FORM LETTER

Directions. Type Style Letter 8, page 290, with the following changes. Make a pencil copy of these changes and keep it on your desk as you type the letter.

Address to: **Mr. Regis L. Cheswick**
1602 Dunmoyle Place
Covington, Kentucky
Omit: First and final paragraphs
Policy No. in Paragraph: 163749
Amount of Policy: $5,000
Amount Due: $279.80   (Type 2 spaces below reference initials)

PROBLEM 2—SKILL BUILDING IN TYPING A FORM LETTER

Directions. Type Style Letter 8, page 290, with the following changes.

Address to: **Mrs. Margaret H. Norton**
850 McMurray Road
Cincinnati 4, Ohio

Omit: First and final paragraphs
Policy No. in Paragraph: 195036
Amount of Policy: $7,000
Amount Due: $325.75

SKILL MAINTENANCE 264
10 minutes

Directions. Use each sentence for 1-minute writings. *Type on the control level of practice.*

	STROKES	WORDS
Many hundreds of hungry men are hunting here in the Huntington jungle.	70	14
Stretch the first finger straight to make a good stroke in striking 6.	70	14
Martin and Alan will be in Atlantic City, New Jersey, in April or May.	70	14

Directions. Type each line three times. Double-space after the third typing of the line. Do not space between the $ and the number. Use the apostrophe (') in typing contractions.

```
4f 4f 14 Sue is 14.   Jim has 40 books.   Add 40 and 74 and 14.
Read pages 48 to 50.   I have 14 copies of "Typing Champions."
4f $f $f He owes me $14.   8k 'k 'k He won't pay the $14 bill.
Joe's pay was $40 a week.   Jack's bill is for $84.   I owe $8.
Their check isn't for $140.   Howe & Lang's check is for $284.
The total of 4 and 9 and 3 and 8 and 85 and 37 and 12 is 158.
```

Type the quotation mark after the period.

SKILL MAINTENANCE 18 — *15 minutes*

Directions. Use double spacing. Type two 5-minute writings with the carriage throw called at the end of each minute. When the throw is called, return the carriage, indent, and start to type again from the beginning of the paragraph. At the end of each 5 minutes, check the different writings to see how uniform you are in the number of words you type each minute.

	STROKES	WORDS
Take time to type it right, of course; but also take	53	11
time to type it in the right way. One thing all of us must	113	23
learn is the value of good form in typing. Good form is the	174	35
only basis on which fine typing skill can be built.	225	45

LESSON 19

CONDITIONING PRACTICE 19 — *5 minutes*

Directions. Type each line twice. Double-space after the second typing of the line. Use the fourth line for one or more 1-minute writings.

	STROKES
4f 8k 48 48 148 Study page 48. He works 84 hours. I am 18.	60
4f $f 8k 'k 'k Harry's age is 28. His week's pay is $48.50.	60
Alphabetic sentence. Jules Dawson began quickly to save money for the next prize.	60
I am sure that you can learn to do this work with some ease.	60

REACH-STROKE PRACTICE 19—6-_ (Underscore), - (Hyphen), * (Asterisk) — *20 minutes*

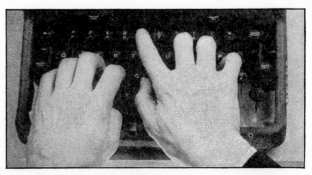

Control 6-_ (Underscore) with the *j finger*
Control - and * with the *; finger*

1. Illustration 29 shows the reach to *6-_* (underscore), made with the *j finger*. As you touch *j6j* lightly two or three times, stretch the *j finger* until it is straight. Keep your wrist low. Make the reach with the least possible hand movement.

Illustration 29 — Reach to 6-_ (underscore)

LESSON 262

STROKES

We drop many exercises which lack objectives for pupils facing a quiz.   70
They quoted on 95 pounds @ 28¼¢ a pound. (This is a very good price.)   70
Slow down the muscles of your body and speed up your mind all you can.   70

PRODUCTION TYPING 262   *25 minutes*

Directions. Use the form letter of Lesson 261, page 307, for each problem, filling in the appropriate information as you type, except that you will omit the paragraph beginning "If you wish to discuss. . ."

PROBLEM 1—SKILL BUILDING IN TYPING LETTERS WITH FILL-INS

To: H. L. Webster
     26958 Brighton Road
     Detroit 30, Michigan

Amount of Check Received: **$104.80**

Dated: **March 10**

Received: **March 14**

Balance Due: **$10.48**

From: **W. R. Fisher, Credit Manager**

PROBLEM 2—SKILL BUILDING IN TYPING LETTERS WITH FILL-INS

To: Mrs. L. Murray Hill
     58192 Morrowfield Road
     Detroit 6, Michigan

Amount of Check Received: **$74.30**

Dated: **March 9**

Received: **March 12**

Balance Due: **$7.43**

From: **W. R. Fisher, Credit Manager**

PROBLEM 3—SKILL BUILDING IN TYPING INDEX CARDS

Directions. Type ruled index cards for Problems 1 and 2. Type the surname first; place the address on succeeding lines. List the balance due below the address.

SKILL MAINTENANCE 262   *10 minutes*

Directions. The sentences provide practice in making awkward or difficult reaches. Type each sentence five times; or, if your teacher so directs, use each sentence for 1-minute writings.

STROKES WORDS

Bart Barrington brought both bread and butter from my brother's place.   70   14
Cecil Edwards decided to check each certified and each canceled check.   70   14
Many a man years younger than you does too much worrying and hurrying.   70   14

LESSON 263

CONDITIONING PRACTICE 263   *5 minutes*

STROKES

He worked with zeal for right objectives and may expect quick results.   70
Order #740-Y was shipped on April 26, wasn't it? The date was May 26.   70
What you think and do count most in life—not what you say you can do.   70

PRODUCTION TYPING 263   *25 minutes*

PROBLEM 1—LEARNING THE NATURE OF THE PROBLEM

Directions. A mailing of circular material is to be sent to the 30 persons listed on the mailing lists given on pages 292, 294, and 295. Large envelopes will be required.

2. Illustration 30 shows the reach to the - (hyphen), which is above the letter *p* and is controlled by the *; finger.* The shift of this key is the * (asterisk).

(On some typewriters the shift of the hyphen is a special key instead of the asterisk.)

As you touch *;-;* lightly two or three times, stretch the little finger to the key. Do not move the elbow outward. Move the hand slightly forward by bending the other fingers; but move only the *; finger* from typing position.

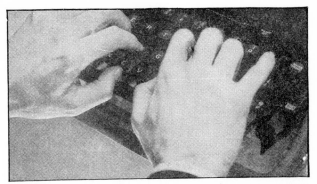

*Illustration 30 — Reach to - (hyphen) and * (asterisk)*

Directions. Type each line three times. Double-space after the third typing of the line. Do not space before or after the hyphen.

To Underscore: Depress the backspace key (No. 30) to the first letter of the word to be underscored and strike the underscore once for each letter. If an entire line is to be underscored, type the line; move the carriage back to the first letter; depress the shift lock (No. 29); and strike the underscore key once for each letter in the words to be underscored. The use of the shift lock makes it unnecessary for you to hold the finger on the shift key. To release the shift lock, depress the shift key. (On some typewriters, you have to depress the shift key opposite from the shift lock to release it.)

Spell each word as you strike the underscore. Underscore the words but not the spaces between words or the marks of punctuation.

Line 4: Type the dash with two hyphens without space before or after the dash.

```
6j 6j 26 36 46 56 Alan is 26.   I shall be 26 on May 6, 1962.

6j_j To underscore a word, hit the key once for each letter.

DON'T underscore punctuation marks or the space between words.

-; -; Know what you are to do--and just how you are to do it.

He has 63 first-class letters.   I need 26 three-cent stamps.

Use a - (hyphen) in a compound; * (asterisk) for a footnote.
```

SKILL MAINTENANCE 19   *15 minutes*

Directions. Use double spacing. Type the paragraph for 3 minutes. Determine your cwpm. Then practice the words that have awkward or difficult typing patterns, such as *sequence, realize, shortest.* After you have practiced the words that may be speed traps for your fingers, take additional 3-minute writings on the paragraph as time permits.

This paragraph uses all letters of the alphabet and has a syllable intensity * *of 1.25.*

	STROKES	WORDS
Have a goal for your daily work. It does very little	54	11
good just to type without knowing why you are typing. The	113	23
goal may be the raising of your speed so many words a minute	174	35
or the setting up of a new and improved way of typing some	233	47
hard sequence of strokes. Fix your goal in mind; then work	293	59
for it in such a way that you will realize the goal in the	352	70
very shortest possible time.	380	76

* Syllable intensity is determined by dividing the total number of syllables by the total number of words of the paragraph.

SECTION 47. Form Letters with Fill-Ins

LESSON 261

	STROKES
Who very quickly rejected the plan for making the tables a fixed size?	70
Ninety-seven men worked on eight-hour shifts for the three-day period.	70
He can send us a copy of the education program for the May 29 meeting.	70

PRODUCTION TYPING 261   *25 minutes*

PROBLEM 1—LEARNING THE NATURE OF THE PROBLEM

Directions. Copy the form letter, but make the appropriate insertions from the information given below. Use the style of letter and form of punctuation you prefer as long as you are consistent in their use.

To: Ford G. Raymond
       621 North 56th Street
       Detroit 9, Michigan

Amount of Check Received: $358.29

Dated: March 17

Received: March 19

Balance Due: $3.58

Call: Charles N. Martin

From: W. R. Fisher, Credit Manager

	STROKES
Your check for $, dated	30
, was received on .	67
We thank you for this payment,	98
which has been credited to your account.	132
count. There is still an unpaid balance due of $	168
ance due of $.	188
Our Discount Plan applies to accounts paid by the tenth of each	219
counts paid by the tenth of each	252
month. Complete details of this	285
plan were sent to you at the time	319
you opened your account. Perhaps	353
you overlooked the discount date at	389
the time you mailed your check.	422
If you wish to discuss the Discount Plan, please call Mr. .	452
count Plan, please call Mr. .	494
Please send us your check for the	528
balance due of $ and plan to	561
take advantage of the discount plan	597
next month by sending your check	630
before the discount date has passed.	668
Yours very truly	713

PROBLEM 2—SKILL BUILDING IN TYPING LETTERS WITH FILL-INS

Directions. Retype the letter given in Problem 1. For this problem make the insertions indicated below.

To: Mrs. Dorothy C. Harrington
       650 Van Nuys Boulevard
       Grosse Point, Michigan

Amount of Check Received: **$47.65**
Dated: March 20
Received: March 25
Balance Due: $4.77
Call: Charles N. Martin
From: W. R. Fisher, Credit Manager

PROBLEM 3—SKILL BUILDING IN TYPING INDEX CARDS

Directions. Type ruled index cards for Problems 1 and 2. Type the surname first; place the address on succeeding lines. List the balance due below the address.

SKILL MAINTENANCE 261   *10 minutes*

Directions. Use each sentence for 1-minute writings. *Type on the control level of practice.*

	STROKES	WORDS
A man who knows that he has a great mind and can make it work does so.	70	14
Have faith in yourself, of course; but above all know what you can do.	70	14

LESSON 20

CONDITIONING PRACTICE 20

5 minutes

Directions. Use double spacing. Type the paragraph twice.

All letters of the alphabet are used in the paragraph.

	STROKES	WORDS
Henry Mill, an English engineer, is said to be the first	57	11
man to have had the amazing idea of the typewriter. No model	119	24
of his machine is known to exist; yet on January 7, 1714, he	180	36
was granted a patent by Queen Anne.	215	43

PACE WRITING 20

2 minutes

Directions. Type the sentence for 1 minute at a rate that you can maintain with ease.

	STROKES	WORDS
Now is the time to make a close check of your typing skills.	60	12

TIMED WRITING 20

5 minutes

Directions. Use double spacing and a 5-space paragraph indention. Type for three minutes. Determine your cwpm. Contrast the rate made on this writing with that recorded for the timed writings of Lesson 14. *Goal:* To type with ease and continuity.

This paragraph uses every letter of the alphabet and has a syllable intensity of 1.25.

	STROKES	WORDS
Take it easy. Do not try too hard. You cannot be lazy	56	11
and learn to type with ease, of course; but there is such a	116	23
thing as trying too hard. Just keep the carriage moving	173	35
steadily. Fix your eyes on the material you are typing and	233	47
hold them there. Keep your wrists low. Hold your hands and	294	59
arms quiet and let your fingers do the work. If you will	352	70
type in this way, you can be certain that you will develop	411	82
the power to type exceedingly well.	446	89

REACH-STROKE PRACTICE 20—/-?, ½-¼, ¢-@

20 minutes

Control /-? with the ; *finger*
Control ½-¼ with the ; *finger*
Control ¢-@ with the ; *finger*

1. Illustration 31 shows the reach to the /-?. The / (diagonal) is below the ; key and is controlled by the ; *finger*. The shift of the / is ? (question mark). As you touch ;/; lightly two or three times, make the reach with a direct movement of the ; *finger* and without changing the hand position.

Illustration 31 — Reach to / (diagonal) and ?

PROBLEM 11—TABULATED REPORT

Directions. Arrange the report on a full sheet of paper. Double-space the body of the report.

			STROKES
center □ *all caps* summary of customers, amount of sales			21
	Total Sales	*Balance Due*	45
Baker *+ Marshall*	$ 429.50	$ 275.62	86
Bennøington Sales *Company*	1,524.93	1,014.93	130
Chadwick, Chester & Smith	2,906.40	*956.83*	165
□Davidson Manufacturing Co.	857.40	500.00	237
Endicott Corporation	1,010.50	□750.75	267
Exeter – Martin Company	*259.65*	*259.65*	307
Garvin & Fisk*³her*	692.00	575.75	341
Holmes, Mitchell *+ Norton*	5,250.00	*3,175.85*	385
] Longstaff-Barth Company	626.65]	490.00	418
O'Donovan Furniture Company	1,260.49	895.65	464
Upshaw Steel Company	*6,250.00*	*4,590.00*	503
Winlock & Bryant	~~1,000.32~~ 956.20	~~450.00~~ 730.00	538

PROBLEM 12—TELEFAX MESSAGE

Directions. Type the Telefax message, using Illustration 52, page 216, as a model.

	STROKES
BLZ NL PD Memphis, Tennessee Current Date	46
Gibson Fire Extinguisher Company Fifth Avenue at Logan Road	106
Knoxville, Tennessee Need 200 dry-chemical extinguishers, 2½-pound	173
capacity, for apartments just completed. When can you ship, and at	241
what price? Be specific. Colonial Renting Agency CRB:mh 200 2½	305

PROBLEM 13—INTEROFFICE CORRESPONDENCE

Directions. Type this interoffice memorandum, arranging the copy similar to Illustration 53, page 217.

		STROKES
To: James A. Maxwell	Date: Current	45
From: William T. Rhodes	File: PR 15-B-209	89
Subject: Processing Future Orders		124

Because of recent regulations governing the allocation of steel for non- 195
military purposes, all orders now being placed must be reviewed and ad- 265
justed in terms of Government directives. Priority ratings must be assigned 342
and contracts must be re-examined. It is important that each order be given 419
a preference status. (P) The urgency of the present situation suggests the 491
need for careful, unbiased treatment of all future orders. Personnel in charge 571
of processing new orders must be thoroughly familiar with the content of 644
Government directives affecting their particular activities. Supervisors 718
must be alert to the fact that greater detail in supervision is necessary. 794
(P) Will you, therefore, acquaint your staff with the problem at hand and 864
take whatever steps are necessary to ensure the expeditious handling of all 940
orders received after January 15. mh 977

2. Illustration 32 shows the reach to $\frac{1}{2}$-$\frac{1}{4}$. The $\frac{1}{2}$ is to the right of the letter p; the shift of the $\frac{1}{2}$ is the $\frac{1}{4}$. This key is controlled by the ; finger. As you touch ;$\frac{1}{2}$; lightly two or three times, make the reach directly from the ; key without going through the position for the letter p. Remember to shift for $\frac{1}{4}$.

In typing "made" fractions (fractions for which there are no special keys) use the /. In typing 1/2 or 1/4 with other fractions that must be made, such as 2/3, type all in a uniform manner with the /.

Illustration 32 — Reach to ½-¼

3. The ¢ (cent or cents) symbol is to the right of the ; key. The shift of the ¢ is @ (at). This key is controlled by the ; finger. As you touch ;¢; lightly two or three times, make the reach by moving the ; finger to the right. Hold the other fingers in typing position.

These symbols are used in typing invoices, market quotations, and statements.

Illustration 33 — Reach to ¢-@

Directions. Type each line twice. Double-space after the second typing of the line.

Line 1: Space twice after a colon used as a mark of punctuation.

Type "made" fractions in the following way: 2/3 and 3/4.

In typing several carbons, use 1/2 and 1/4 and not $\frac{1}{2}$ and $\frac{1}{4}$.

Are the symbols ¢ and @ used in typing market quotations?

Space between whole numbers and "made" fractions; as, 9 3/8.

Be uniform in typing fractions; as, $\frac{1}{4}$ and $\frac{1}{2}$ or 1/4 and 1/2.

Did this store change the price from 75$\frac{1}{2}$ cents to 85$\frac{1}{4}$ cents?

SKILL MAINTENANCE 20

8 minutes

Directions. The purpose of typing this drill is to learn to handle the tabulator mechanism efficiently and to type figures skillfully. Type the drill as many times as you can in the time allowed for this portion of the lesson.

Machine Adjustments. Clear the tabulator rack. Then set the stops as follows:
Pica-type machines: Left margin, 10; tabulator stops at 20, 30, 40, 50, 60, 70.
Elite-type machines: Left margin, 20; tabulator stops at 30, 40, 50, 60, 70, 80.

| 37 | 48 | 50 | 29 | 36 | 12 | 62 |
| 58 | 49 | 36 | 20 | 51 | 39 | 50 |

PROBLEM 8—TELEGRAM

Directions. Prepare the message as a full-rate telegram.

	STROKES
Charge to **Automotive Supplies Company, Inc.** Johnstown, Pennsylvania	58
(Current Date) Independent Tire and Rubber Company 1562 Somerset Boule-	114
vard Akron, Ohio State availability 4-ply black side-wall tires, sizes 6.00-16,	194
6.50-16, and 7.00-15. State possible time of shipment from warehouse and	268
method of transportation to be used. Also state credit terms possible for	343
orders over 200 tires. Automotive Supplies Company, Inc. 3408 North Hamil-	417
ton Avenue crb	431

PROBLEM 9—PERSONAL-BUSINESS LETTER

Directions. Prepare the letter in the style shown in Style Letter 1, page 43. Address an envelope.

	STROKES
319 Rebecca Street Sacramento 5,	33
California Current date Mr. Samuel	72
A. McConaghie Association of Re-	104
search and Statistics 3409 North	137
Brandon Street Newark 7, New	166
Jersey Dear Mr. McConaghie (P)	193
Within the next three weeks, I shall	230
be preparing an itinerary for a tour	267
of business organizations participat-	303
ing in our research project. As has	340
been my custom in the past, I shall	376
plan to visit only those companies	411
engaged in activities pertinent to the	450
phase of the project assigned to me.	488
By concentrating my energies solely	524
in those areas, I shall be able to col-	562
lect the type of information that will	601
be most relevant in the development	637
of this project. (P) Inasmuch as	667
you have been directly affiliated	701
with many of the places I plan to	735
visit and have worked in the areas I	772
plan to cover, I should like to have	809
you suggest some things you think	843
I should do to make my visits most	878
profitable. I realize that you may	914
feel hesitant about making specific	950
suggestions for fear of limiting my	986
activities, but I assure you that I	1022
shall be grateful for a list of just a	1061
few items you consider to be par-	1093
ticularly important. (P) If things	1125
go as planned, I shall have my part	1161
of the study ready for publication	1196
by the end of this year. As the study	1235
progresses, I am looking forward to	1271
its completion with much anticipa-	1304
tion. I am confident that it will aid	1343
greatly in streamlining work in our	1379
production activities. (P) As always,	1414
I want you to know that I appre-	1445
ciate the help and encouragement	1478
you have given me in this most im-	1511
portant undertaking. Yours very	1544
sincerely Robert A. Millar	1570

PROBLEM 10—ANNOUNCEMENT

Directions. Arrange this message on a half sheet of paper.

	STROKES
All caps → Announcing	11
Annual Picnic and Get Together	42
Thursday Evening, June 17, 195-	74
Community Park, McKeesport, Pa.	106
Games, Dancing, and Entertainment	140
Ticket Sale Begins June 5	166
Price $2.50 Per Couple	189
All Employees are Urged to Attend	223
Plan Now for a Wonderful Evening	255

THE IMPROVEMENT OF TYPING SKILL

Major Techniques of Typing. There are a number of major techniques in learning to typewrite that must be brought to as high a level of control as possible. Up to this time, you have been too conscious of the numerous details of learning to type for you to keep these techniques in mind; but beginning with this instructional block, techniques will be emphasized one at a time. Build into your fingering the best use of these basic techniques. In this way you will grow rapidly in typing power.

Finger Gymnastics. At the beginning of each practice period, use a finger gymnastic drill for a short period. (See the inside of the front cover of this book.) This practice will aid you in acquiring fingering facility.

Bonus Typing. Learners type at different rates. Bonus typing is therefore suggested as a means of adapting the materials to individual needs. If you complete a lesson before the end of a period, you may type the sentences on page 50 for extra credit.

SECTION 4. Speed Emphasis

Machine Checkup and Adjustments

1. Check the placement of the paper guide, the paper-bail rolls, and the paper bail.
2. Set the stop for the left margin at 12 for a pica-type or at 20 for an elite-type machine; move the stop for the right margin to the end of the scale.
3. Set the line-space regulator for single spacing for drills and for double spacing for paragraphs.
4. Set the tabulator for a 5-space indention.
5. Set the ribbon lever for typing on the upper half of the ribbon.

The machine checkup and adjustments will not be given in full for each lesson, but the same procedure is to be followed throughout this section (Lessons 21 through 25).

LESSON 21

CONDITIONING PRACTICE 21   *5 minutes*

Typing the Conditioning Practice. The way to type the conditioning practice is to type at an easy, controlled rate. This is the time you are to condition yourself to the control of yourself as well as to the control of the typewriter. Test out your position at the typewriter; check to see that you are using just the right power in returning the carriage, the exact reach to the tabulator bar or key, the easy and sure reach to the shift keys; and condition your fingers to give a swift and sure stroke to the center of the key, with a minimum of hand or arm movement and with a low finger reach.

Type each line three to five times. Double-space between the groups of lines.

STROKES

Alphabetic sentence. Jack Gwinn quietly planned for the visit to Brazil or Mexico. 61

Alvin is 15. Max is 29. Robert lives at 4736 Center Street. 61

We swam the river. The six men expect quite a lot of prizes. 61

PROBLEM 4—MAILING LIST

Directions. Type the mailing list on a full sheet of paper, double spacing the body of the tabulation.

Subscription List

Subscriptions to be Renewed by June 30

			STROKES
Mr. Howard J. Hartman	5826 Wightman Street	Madison 5, Wisconsin	121
Mr. William R. Houston	4709 Virginia Avenue	Camden 7, New Jersey	186
Mr. Vincent C. Jansen	1823 Mifflin Street	Pontiac 8, Michigan	248
Mr. Norman R. Killian	5672 Wharton Avenue	New Haven 3, Connecticut	315
Mr. John S. Latimer	4308 Bartlett Street	Oakland 2, California	379
Mr. Edward C. Manning	2916 Hawthorn Blvd.	Dallas 9, Texas	437
Mr. Charles E. Murray	5843 Hillcrest Street	Tacoma 5, Washington	502
Mr. Ernest J. Olson	7020 Denniston Avenue	Omaha 7, Nebraska	562
Mr. George C. Reinhart	1386 Meade Street	Paterson 8, New Jersey	626
Mr. Robert L. Ritchey	5472 Dunlap Avenue	Roanoke 10, Virginia	688
Mr. Glenn A. Sampson	6350 Kincaid Blvd.	Columbia 9, South Carolina	755
Mr. Albert R. Schaffer	8192 Prospect Street	Flint 11, Michigan	718
Mr. Paul J. Stroman	7460 Bayard Avenue	Mobile 6, Alabama	775
Mr. Joseph L. Verner	5231 Hatfield Street	Memphis 5, Tennessee	841
Mr. Lester C. Wissner	4807 Burrows Street	Buffalo 7, New York	902

PROBLEM 5—INDEX CARDS

Directions. Prepare index cards for each person on the mailing list in Problem 4. At the bottom of each card type in all caps the following notation: SUBSCRIPTION TO BE RENEWED BY JUNE 30.

PROBLEM 6—CHAIN FEEDING ENVELOPES

Directions. Address a small envelope for each person on the mailing list in Problem 4. Use the chain-feeding technique described on page 268.

PROBLEM 7—FREIGHT BILL

Directions. Prepare a freight bill for the Wilshire Transportation Company in a form similar to that shown in Illustration 60, page 229.

To **The McKeown Construction Company** 2106 South Lexington Avenue   61
Philadelphia 9, Pennsylvania Date 11/23/5— Shipper **The Continental**   115
Supply Company 5834 North Washington Avenue Youngstown 7, Ohio   178

No. Pieces	Description	Weight	Rate	Collect	
					221
					264
12 crts.	3/4 H. P. Piston-Type Paint Sprayers	970	.85	8.50	328
75 kegs	Fed. Spec. FF-N-191 Steel Nails	7587	.80	60.80	386
50 ctns.	#30-K-9346 Paint Undercoat	3450	.95	33.25	440
35 drs.	Fiber Roof and Foundation Coating	17500	.95	166.25	500
125 bdls.	Gov. Spec. SSR-421 Asphalt Shingles	10500	.75	78.75	563
60 rolls	Rosin Sheathing Paper—36 in. wide	1800	.75	13.50	625
25 bxs.	Assorted Pipe Fittings, Iron & Steel	1625	.80	13.60	688
					695
				374.65	702
	3% Federal Tax			11.24	709
					716
				385.89	722

How to Read the Copy. You have been typing much of your work on the stroke (or letter) level of response. You type on this level of response when you see, think, and type letter by letter.

In typing short, simple words, *think the word,* not the letters. For example, instead of thinking and typing *h-e,* think the word *he.* The right sequence of letters will be noted by your eyes without conscious effort on your part.

Directions. Type each line three times. Think the words, not the letters.

(The lines may be dictated to emphasize the word-recognition level of response.)

	STROKES
or for for for he the the the for the for the an and and and	60
He is to go. He is to go for them. He is to go for them now.	62
I did the work. I did the work well. I did all the work well.	63
Did he go? Did he go with them? Did he go with them too much?	63
I like to type. I like to type this. I like to type this way.	63

SKILL BUILDING 21

1. Paragraphs for 1-Minute Writings   *10 minutes*

Directions. (1) Type the paragraph as a 1-minute writing. Determine your cwpm. (2) Type the paragraph a second time and determine the cwpm. (3) Average the two writings. The result will be your base typing rate. Remember this rate for use in the skill building.

	STROKES
This is the day for me to do things. There is no need	55
for me to wait until next week or next year to do good work.	117
I shall do all that I have to do as well as I can. This is	177
my purpose for each day.	201

Skill-Building Procedures. Select a goal that is 1 or 2 words more than your base rate. Take 1-minute writings until you are able to type your goal. Eliminate the waste motions. Advance your goal another word, and take additional minute writings as time permits.

2. Sentences for Calling the Guide   *10 minutes*

Directions. You are to type each of the following sentences for 1 minute on the 30-second call of the guide. At the end of 30 seconds, your instructor will say "One."

If you complete the sentence before the guide is called, throw the carriage and continue typing but pace your typing a little more slowly. If you have not completed the sentence when the guide is called, increase your speed of stroking slightly.

When you have typed the sentences at the rate called for by the 30-second guide, type them with the guide called each 20 seconds. If time permits, also type the sentences with the guide called each 15 seconds. Use the stroke level of response in typing these sentences.

The first column at the right of the sentences shows the number of strokes in each line; the second column shows the number of words written a minute if the sentence is typed once each 30 seconds; the third column shows the number of words typed a minute if the sentence is typed once each 20 seconds; the fourth column shows the number of words typed a minute if the sentence is typed once each 15 seconds.

	Strokes	Words 30"	Words 20"	Words 15"
Add 8 and 4 and 29 and 14 and 36 and 50.	40	16	24	32
The sum of 5 and 2 and 9 and 6 and 4 is 26.	43	17	26	34
Chester is 16 years 9 months and 10 days old.	45	18	27	36

the cost of carbon paper is influenced 1395
somewhat by the weight selected; 1428
and, when making purchases, buy 1460
several different weight types. (P) 1493
In the near future, will you examine 1530
the carbon needs of your organiza- 1563

tion and let us have the pleasure of 1600
helping you meet those needs satis- 1634
factorily as well as economically. 1670
Sincerely yours, UNIVERSAL PA- 1699
PER COMPANY Ralph S. Brown- 1725
ing Sales Manager crb 1746

PROBLEM 2—TABULATED REPORT

Directions. Arrange the report on a full sheet of paper, double-spacing the body of the report.

Annual Subscription Report
by
Selected States

State	Representative	New Subscribers	Expired Subscriptions	Active Subscriptions	STROKES
					27
					30
					46
					188
					268
					339
Alabama	Cooper	386	72	4,137	371
California	Zeller	1,850	275	12,758	406
Connecticut	McDonald	956	102	2,013	444
Florida	Young	802	42	1,906	475
Georgia	Hunter	732	105	3,170	507
Kentucky	Levinson	63	39	809	542
Michigan	Kennedy	2,014	308	10,159	576
Pennsylvania	Matthews	3,859	216	13,062	615
Washington	Robertson	901	85	5,129	653
					723

PROBLEM 3—NOMA SIMPLIFIED LETTER

STROKES

Directions. Type this letter in the form recommended by NOMA illustrated in Style Letter 7, page 265. Prepare an appropriate envelope.

STROKES

Current date **Mr. Gerald A. Robin-** 36
son 1925 Washington Street Knox- 67
ville 5, Tennessee STATUS OF 96
WELDING ROD STOCKS (P) 115
During the past few months we have 150
had numerous requests for welding 184
rod from customers in Kentucky, 216
Tennessee, and North Carolina. 248
These requests have totaled far 280
greater quantities than we have been 317
able to supply. As a result, we are 354
faced with the problem of recheck- 387
ing our inventories in an attempt to 424
locate sources of supply that, per- 458
haps, have been overlooked. (P) It 490
is essential that you determine the 526
stocks of welding rod in the ware- 559
houses within your district. Stock 595
control records on file in the home 631

office indicate that substantial re- 665
serves are available in outlying 698
warehouses. If those records are 732
correct, steps must be taken imme- 765
diately to redistribute those surplus 803
stocks. (P) Within the next ten 832
days, then, will you arrange to do 867
the following: 1 Conduct a personal 904
inspection of all warehouses within 940
your district 2 Prepare an inven- 972
tory of all welding rod stocks on 1006
hand 3 Determine the amount of 1037
stock already obligated to previous 1073
orders 4 Submit immediately a de- 1105
tailed report of your findings. (P) 1138
If, during the course of your investi- 1175
gation, you discover irregularities in 1214
our storage records, notify the home 1251
office at once. Our facilities are 1287
available to you for preparing your 1323
report. GAZA A. KATONA crb 1351
Mr. Walter A. Greenwood Mr. Nor- 1382
man J. Connelly Mr. Robert K. 1412
Selfridge 1421

LESSON 22
CONDITIONING PRACTICE 22

5 minutes

Directions. Type each line three to five times.

STROKES

Alphabetic
sentence.

A report was quickly given to an amazed audience by John Fox. 61

They wrote, "Policy #846295 for $7.000 is due May 27, 1958." 60

It is good to take pride in what you do and in what you are. 60

TECHNIQUE STUDY 22

12 minutes

Directions. Type each line three times; then double-space. Use the stroke level of response for all lines except the sentences. Type the sentences on the word-recognition level of response.

Stroke Technique for the Upper Row of Keys. *Use* a "low" finger stroke; lift the finger high enough to move with the shortest and most direct reach to the center of the key. Return the finger to typing position by pulling it slightly toward the palm of the hand. Hold the hands and arms quiet.

rf p; tf ol ed yj ws ik qa uj fur old the was play quit wish

Stroke Technique for the Lower Row of Keys. Direct a quick stroke to the center of the key; then pull the finger upward and toward the typing position.

vf ?; bf .l cd nj xs mj za ,k fun gum rub cad six big size

Put your improved technique to work. Use the right stroke as well as the right reach.

STROKES

with work quit paid lake girl rush they pair quit wish they 59

cashed murmur barber hungry exist zealot vivify breath zeal 59

I can and I will hold my eyes on the copy while I am typing. 60

I think that I work as well as I know how to work right now. 60

SKILL BUILDING 22

I. Paragraph for Guided Writings

13 minutes

Directions. Type a 1-minute writing. Determine your cwpm. Half of this will be your half-minute base rate.

The figures in the copy indicate the number of 5-stroke words.

STROKES

If you want to grow in the power to do things, find the 56

work to which you can give your finest thought and effort. 116

Study it until you learn all you can know about it; then 173

study it some more. This is the way the power to do things 233

will come to you. 250

Skill-Building Procedures. 1. Place a small, easily erased check mark* at a point in the above paragraph that indicates your half-minute base rate *plus 1* word (5 strokes) and a similar check mark to indicate your minute base rate *plus 2* words (10 strokes).

2. Type for a half minute, attempting to reach your half-minute goal. Repeat the half-minute writing, attempting to reach the same goal set for the first writing.

3. Now type for 1 minute, attempting to reach your half-minute and minute goals. The guides will be called as "Half," "One." Repeat the 1-minute writing.

4. If time permits type the paragraph for two minutes.

---

*If you are instructed not to mark your textbook, note the half-minute and the minute goals mentally.

SECTION 46. Production Unit

LESSONS 256 TO 260

General Directions. In each lesson, you are to type for 30 minutes on the problems designated. Correct all errors as you type; uncorrected errors will be penalized. At the end of the fifth lesson, you will compute your stroking rate per minute. You will receive credit for each stroke typed. If you finish typing all problems before the end of the fifth lesson, go back to the beginning and retype as many problems as possible in the time remaining. Follow the specific directions given for each job. Prepare one carbon copy for each problem.

DAILY OUTLINE FOR LESSONS 256 TO 260

Conditioning Practice ....5 minutes   Assembling Materials .... 5 minutes
                                                    Production Typing ....30 minutes

CONDITIONING PRACTICE 256 TO 260
5 minutes

Directions. In each lesson, type each line twice. Double-space after the second typing of the line. Retype the lines as often as time permits.

	STROKES
Next to quick wit, brevity is most highly prized by Franklin Johnston.	70
That buyer will examine 153 coats, 276 hats, 84 gloves, and 90 purses.	70
The things one does are more important than those he would like to do.	70

PRODUCTION TYPING 256 TO 260

PROBLEM 1—BUSINESS LETTER

Directions. Type the business letter in modified block style with indented paragraphs and with mixed punctuation. Address an appropriate envelope and mark it AIR MAIL, SPECIAL DELIVERY.

	STROKES
Current date The Smithfield Sales	38
Company 4109 East Homewood	65
Avenue Shreveport 10, Louisiana	97
Attention Mr. Wilson A. Peterson	130
Gentlemen: Subject: Selection of	165
Carbon Paper (P) Are you aware of	195
the fact that office costs may be	229
greatly exaggerated because of the	264
type of carbon paper used in various	301
offices? Are your typists, stenog-	335
raphers, and secretaries using car-	369
bon paper selected scientifically, or	407
are they consuming costly supplies	442
without regard to the appropriate-	475
ness of the materials being used?	510
Think it over, and investigate the	545
possibility of reducing your operat-	580
ing costs through an adjustment in	615
carbon paper purchases. (P) You	644
will find that the weight of a carbon	682

	STROKES
sheet, as well as the finish, influ-	717
ences the quality of work obtained.	754
It is recommended that you con-	784
sider your selections in terms of	818
established carbon paper weights.	853
Choose the types of carbon paper	886
from the following: (P) (1) Light	918
weight, for manifolding where many	953
copies at one writing are required	989
(P) (2) Medium weight, for mani-	1016
folding where fewer copies are de-	1049
sired at one writing (P) (3) Stand-	1080
ard weight, for general correspond-	1114
ence work, or where from one to four	1151
copies are required (P) (4) Heavy	1182
weight, for one-copy correspondence	1218
work or for billing or bookkeeping	1253
work where the machine has a heavy	1288
stroke and where durability is im-	1321
portant. (P) Realize, of course, that	1356

2. Sentences for Calling the Guide

10 minutes

Directions. Type each line for 1 minute on the appropriate call of the guide; then type with the guide called for the next higher speed indicated.

	Strokes	Words 30″	Words 20″	Words 15″
Paul owes Norton & Jones a balance of $725.	43	17	26	34
Sue raised $129.50 for the Student Loan Fund.	45	18	27	36
The teacher said, "Think right and type right."	47	19	28	38
Check #859 is for $3,465. It is dated January 20.	50	20	30	40

LESSON 23

CONDITIONING PRACTICE 23

5 minutes

Directions. Type each line three to five times. Double-space between the groups of lines.

STROKES

Alphabetic sentence. F. J. Hibbs is spending a week quietly in Vera Cruz, Mexico.   60

2s 91 2s91 129 129 5f 0; 5f0; 150 150 6j 2s 6j2s 162 162 162   60

Carl is 26. I am 15. The date is March 29. Read page 506.   60

TECHNIQUE STUDY 23

12 minutes

Stroking. A quick, sure, controlled stroke is made with the finger directed to the center of the key and with little arm or hand movement.

Place the fingers in typing position, curved so that the reach to *y* can be made without any forward arm movement. Move the finger in the shortest and most direct way to the key. "Snap the key" after the finger touches it to give a quick blow directed to the center.

Directions. Type each line twice. Double-space after the second typing of the line. If time permits, retype selected lines.

Type the first four lines on the stroke level of response. As you type the fifth line, think the word; and type the sixth line on the combination level of response using the word-recognition level for short and simple words and the letter level for typing the long words.

STROKES

uj u ed e ue duel duel rf r ik i ri right right yj y yj year   60

tf t ol o to told told qu q quit quit p; paid paid quit paid   60

mj m za z maze maze nj n xs x next next cd c cd cad cad next   60

bf b .l . He has a fob. vf v van van six jam and ham cad an   60

if if he is to go on and and or for for the the and for them   60

The way he sticks to this work makes for success or failure.   60

SKILL BUILDING 23

I. Paragraph for Guided Writings

13 minutes

Directions. Type the paragraph for two 1-minute writings. Determine the cwpm for each writing. Average the two writings to find the base rate. You are expected to type approximately 20 to 25 words a minute on these writings.

PROBLEM 6—LETTER OF APPLICATION

Directions. The letter of this problem was written by an applicant for a position as typist and general clerk. Type the letter in the form you think most appropriate. Use your own return address and pen signature. As this is a personal letter, reference initials should not be used.

Direct the letter to the Excelsior Paper Company, 5916 Westhope Avenue, Savannah 8, Georgia, and call it to the attention of Mr. Wilber B. Parker. Use an appropriate salutation.

At this morning's conference with 34
you in regard to a position with your 72
company as typist and general clerk, 109
you asked that I send a written ap- 143
plication and submit complete per- 176
sonal and professional information 211
concerning my preparation for office 248
work. I enclose a data sheet on 281
which information is given concern- 315
ing my training and part-time work 350
experience. I have also listed the 386
names of four references who have 420
expressed willingness to answer 452
questions concerning me. (P) I was 484
graduated from the Senior High 515
School in June. In my class of 158, 552
I ranked ninth. While in school, I 588
participated in student activities and 627
was treasurer of our Future Business 664
Leaders of America Club. (P) If 693
the results of the test I took and 728
the impression made in the inter- 760
view warrant your offering me a 792
position, I shall be glad to begin 827
work immediately. You will find me 863
eager to take advantage of every 896
opportunity to grow in usefulness to 933
you. Sincerely yours Enclosure 965
(159)

PROBLEM 7—PERSONAL DATA SHEET

Directions. Type a data sheet to enclose with the letter typed in Problem 6. Arrange it in a form similar to that used in Lesson 122, page 173. The information you give should be based upon yourself and your own activities. It should be listed under the headings given below.

PERSONAL
Name:
Address:
Telephone No.:
Nationality:
Weight:
Height:
Age:

EDUCATION
High School:
Rank in Class: Use the information given in the letter typed in Problem 6.

Leadership Activities:
Technical Skill: **Typewriting Speed**
Shorthand Dictation Speed
Transcription Rate
Include these last two items only if you have studied shorthand.

WORK EXPERIENCE
List all types of work experience you have had during your high school life. Examples of desirable work experience are (1) selling papers, (2) store sales work, (3) stenographic work in the school principal's office, (4) general office work for school, teachers, church, or community organizations.

REFERENCES (by Permission)
List three or four, but do not use members of your family.

PROBLEM 8—LONG LETTER OF APPLICATION

Directions. Combine into one long letter the letter and the data sheet typed as Problems 6 and 7. Make necessary changes in the wording of the first paragraph of the letter. Use the outline form in the body of the letter to list the information from the data sheet. Use the form of letter and style of punctuation you consider appropriate.

	STROKES
There is a lot of fun in learning to do things very	52
well. It is when we do things only halfway that we find	109
ourselves low in mind and wishing to change to something	166
else. If you have work to do, be sure that you do it well;	226
you will then know that you can learn to do well anything	284
you need to do.	299

Skill-Building Procedures. Use the same skill-building procedures that you used in Skill Building 22, page 35.

2. Sentences for Calling the Guide   *10 minutes*

Directions. Type each sentence for 1 minute on the call for the appropriate guide; then type the sentences with the guide called for the next higher speed indicated.

	Strokes	Words 30"	Words 20"	Words 15"
Alan Spaulding will move to Texas on April 4.	45	18	27	36
The check for $937.50 was mailed on October 28.	47	19	28	38
Paper that is 11 inches long has 66 writing lines.	50	20	30	40
Charles Jackson is 26 years 7 months and 12 days old.	53	21	32	42

LESSON 24

CONDITIONING PRACTICE 24   *5 minutes*

Directions. Type each line three to five times. Double-space between the groups of lines.

STROKES

Alphabetic sentence.   Frank and I won just by expecting more zeal and quick service. 62

5f%f 9l(l The rate is 3%. 0;); The rate (on JL Bonds) was 2%. 62

Each of us can learn to work well. He can type very well now. 62

TECHNIQUE STUDY 24   *12 minutes*

Shifting for Capitals. Here is the identification of two common faults in shifting for capitals, followed by the suggested corrective measures. Keep in mind *the right way to shift* for capitals as you type.

1. If a capital letter is typed slightly above the line of writing, the shift key was not depressed firmly or it was released too quickly.

2. If the reach to the shift key causes the hand to move far from the typing position, hold the arms in their normal typing position and stretch the little finger. Do not move the elbow as you make the reach.

ℛ HOTEL
ℛEGIS-PLAZA

RALPH HARVEY
MANAGER

THIRTY-FOURTH STREET
AT BROADWAY

NEW YORK 5

February 13, 19--

	STROKES	WORDS
February 13, 19--	18	4

	STROKES	WORDS
Mr. Wilbur B. Parker	39	8
Excelsior Paper Company	63	13
5916 Westhope Avenue	84	17
Savannah 8, Georgia	104	21
Dear Mr. Parker	120	24
Our room reservations are so heavy at this time and	172	34
for the next four months, we are concerned that	220	44
we may not be able to take care of our regular	267	53
customers unless they notify us some weeks in	313	63
advance of their proposed trip to New York.	358	72
As you have used our hotel for some of your sales	408	82
conferences, this letter is sent to ask that	453	91
you let us know just as soon as possible when	499	100
you expect to hold another conference here.	544	109
We hope that you will make our hotel your head-	590	118
quarters for your next conference, as you have	637	127
done for some years.	659	132
The enclosed rate sheet shows the new schedule of	709	142
prices for rooms at the Regis-Plaza. These	753	151
prices will not apply to long-time customers	798	160
such as the Excelsior Paper Company if reserva-	844	169
tions are made by March 1.	872	174
If you will let us know your plans for using the	921	184
facilities of our hotel within the next month,	968	194
we shall be able to see that adequate space is	1015	203
reserved for you.	1034	207
Cordially yours	1050	210
Ralph Harvey		
Ralph Harvey, Manager	1072	214
hs	1075	215
Enclosure *(Words in body of letter, 172)*	1084	217

Style Letter 9 — Inverted Style Letter With Open Punctuation

Directions. Type each line twice.   If time permits, retype selected lines.

Paul and I met Jack and Harry Pinza in Mexico on January 26.	60
Carl and Alan Walker were at the Algonquin Club on April 30.	60
Elvin and Clint are in Algiers, but James is in Mexico City.	60
James and Albert met in Mexico City in March or early April.	60
Karl lives in Dallas, Texas; but Sam moved to New York City.	60

SKILL BUILDING 24

1. Paragraph for Guided Writings
13 minutes

Directions. Type the paragraph for two 1-minute writings. Determine the cwpm for each writing. Average the two writings to find the base rate. You are expected to type approximately 21 to 26 words a minute on these writings.

	STROKES
Hit the right key. Do not let the fingers move around	55
from key to key without knowing where they are to go. When	115
you want to tell the fingers to make strokes, think the word	176
you want to type and they will know what they are to do. You	238
will type with speed and with control if you will type with	298
ease and without pausing after a stroke has been made.	352

Skill-Building Procedures. Use the same skill-building procedures that you used in Skill Building 22, page 35.

2. Sentences for Calling the Guide
10 minutes

Directions. Type each line for 1 minute on the call for the appropriate guide; then type the lines with the guide called for the next higher speed indicated.

	Strokes	Words 30″	Words 20″	Words 15″
The $1,500 note bears interest at the rate of 4½%.	50	20	30	40
The room is 20 by 30 feet. The rug is 15 by 26 feet.	53	21	32	42
"You can do anything," she said, "that you want to do."	55	22	33	44
The box is 4 feet by 8 feet and weighs 275 to 290 pounds.	57	23	34	46

LESSON 25

CONDITIONING PRACTICE 25
5 minutes

Directions. Type each line three to five times. Double-space between the groups of lines.

STROKES

Alphabetic sentence. J. V. Brown will quickly explain the things made for prizes. 60

His son-in-law is 36. Nat weighs 140 pounds. I owe him $7. 60

Andy Cole met Mark and Ned in Mexico City in March or April. 60

PROBLEM 4

Directions. Before starting to type the following rough draft, read it through and note the corrections indicated. Use a 60-space line, a 5-space paragraph indention, and single spacing.

NOTE: The letters *l.c.* written in the margin indicate that any letter through which a diagonal has been drawn in the same line is to be written in lower case, that is, as a small letter.

It ~~would~~ seem from the report of the Company that almost all of our *l.c.*
branch Offices have operated at a profit this year. ~~that has just~~ *l.c.*
~~passed.~~ This was not the situation last year, ~~too.~~ Although we understand that conditions have changed ~~greatly~~ somewhat during the past year,
~~still~~ this increase has been ~~gratifying~~ amazing, but, Never~~the~~less, ~~it has~~ *l.c.*
~~been~~ ~~pleasing~~ gratifying to the officers of the company.

The following ~~table~~ data, compiled from the detailed report presented to
the directors at their last meeting, January 2, will be of interest to you: ~~is illuminating.~~

Do not spread heading

O F F I C E S	Sales	Cost of Operation
Pennsylvania:		
Pittsburgh--	$300,243	$225,457
Harrisburg--	130,090	100,301
Scranton--	65,708	51,197
West Virginia:		
Wheeling--	98,724	92,165
Maryland:		
Cumberland--	76,289	54,231
Ohio:		
Columbus--	210,134	234,135
Toledo--	101,163	115,136
Cincinati--	178,361	
	177,451	
New York:		
Albany--	32,189	34,134

Omit dashes after all city names

Have 7 spaces between columns

Drop these figures one line

This report ~~points out~~ shows that a few branch offices have not had
a ~~profitable~~ satisfactory year. An analysis of the ~~points~~ factors involved in each
case will show that ~~the~~ local conditions ~~in each locality~~ in the territory served by the branch office have had ~~something~~ a great deal to do with the
poor showing this year.

PROBLEM 5

Directions. Type an original and two carbons of the letter shown as Style Letter 9, which is typed in the inverted paragraph form.

Tabulator-Key Control and Carriage Throw. The purpose of typing this tabulated report is to increase your skill in handling the tabulator mechanism and in typing figures. Type the report as many times as you can in the time allowed for this part of the lesson.

Machine Adjustments. Clear the tabulator rack. Then set the stops as follows:
Pica-type machines: Left margin, 10; tabulator stops at 20, 30, 40, 50, 60, 70.
Elite-type machines: Left margin, 20; tabulator stops at 30, 40, 50, 60, 70, 80.

Technique Guides. 1. Hold the tabulator bar or key down until the carriage has completed its movement. If you release the bar or key too quickly, you may have figures out of alignment in the column.

2. Make the carriage throw with a quick wrist movement. Return the hand to typing position immediately and start typing without hesitating.

							STROKES
841	481	148	731	317	137	847	28
621	261	126	951	159	591	956	56
206	307	401	508	209	301	506	83

SKILL BUILDING 25

I. Paragraph for Guided Writings   *13 minutes*

Directions. Type the paragraph for two 1-minute writings. Determine your cwpm. Average the two writings. You are expected to type at 20 to 25 words a minute.

All letters of the alphabet are used in this paragraph. The syllable intensity of the paragraph is 1.25.

	STROKES
Start to type at an easy pace. There is no need to rush	57
or hurry or worry. Just keep on typing. Skill comes when you	120
get rid of the pauses in typing. You do not need to make the	182
fingers go so much more rapidly, but you do need to keep them	244
moving from key to key at a uniform pace. Hold the hands and	306
the arms quiet--almost motionless. Let the fingers do the work	370
for you. This is the way to improve in expertness. This is	431
the way to realize the most from your typing periods.	484

Skill-Building Procedures. Use the same skill-building procedures that you used in Skill Building 22, page 35.

2. Sentences for Calling the Guide   *10 minutes*

Directions. Type each line for 1 minute on the call for the appropriate guide; then type the lines with the guide called for the next higher speed indicated.

	Words 30"	Words 20"	Words 15"
This plane gets in at 10:25 p.m. It leaves at 10:40.	21	32	42
It is about 40 to 50 miles to the New Kensington plant.	22	33	44
Is Karl's Policy No. 912583? It expires on May 27, 1958.	23	34	46
Pica type has 10 spaces and elite type 12 spaces to an inch.	24	36	48

PROBLEM 1—LETTER WITH TABULATED REPORT

Directions. You are asked to type the following letter for Mr. Wilber B. Parker, Sales Manager, Excelsior Paper Company, of 5916 Westhope Avenue, Savannah 8, Georgia. Because of the tabulated report, use a 60-space line and use the letter style and form of punctuation you think appropriate.

	STROKES
s. j. weymouth, director of purchases, stratton publishing company, 2171	88
south 16th street, houston 8, texas dear mr. weymouth	142

in accordance with your telegram received this morning, we are making	212
shipment via continental truck of the materials listed below at the prices	287
quoted in our letter of april 25:	322

3M	#H95 Envelopes	$15.90 M	348
2M	#H83 Envelopes	13.98 M	373
2M	#10-28 Postage Saver Envelopes	2.52 M	414
4M	Sheets 22 x 34 Rising Bond	21.75 cwt.	455
5M	" 28 x 42 Champion Lexicon	8.50 cwt.	501
2M	" 22 x 24 20# S & W Cover	8.75 cwt.	546

thank you for this order. we are sure the quality of the materials shipped	626
will be entirely satisfactory for even the most exacting customer.	694
yours truly	705

PROBLEM 2

Directions. Type an index card for the Stratton Publishing Company to whom a shipment was made as confirmed in the letter written as Problem 1. After typing the company name and address, list the director of purchases.

PROBLEM 3

TABULATED REPORT

Directions. Type this report with double spacing.

	STROKES
Payroll for Sales Department	29
November 28, 195-	47

Worker	Days Worked	Monthly Salary	Gross Amount	Income Tax Withheld	O.A.B. Tax	Net Amount	STROKES
							136
Adams	20	$320.00	$320.00	$31.50	$4.80	$283.70	187
Bosworth	19	400.00	380.00	53.80	5.70	320.50	231
Burris	20	360.00	360.00	6.10	5.40	348.50	273
Denton	19	250.00	237.50	3.20	3.56	230.74	315
Ford	18	300.00	270.00	20.30	4.05	245.65	355
Harris	20	250.00	250.00	6.00	3.75	240.25	397
Horton	20	180.00	180.00	14.20	2.70	163.10	439
Jessup	17	420.00	357.00	60.10	5.36	291.54	481
Maggard	18	360.00	324.00	20.40	4.86	298.74	524
Winlock	20	320.00	320.00	9.20	4.80	306.00	566

SECTION 5. Fixation Practice and Personal-Use Typing

The purposes of the lessons in this section are (1) to fixate the control of the reach-strokes and (2) to provide experience in typing simple problems of a personal-use nature. The pattern of procedure changes but slightly from that used in the preceding section. Typing readiness is the same for all sections of work—machine checkup and adjustments; brief finger gymnastics; conditioning practice. Typing readiness is largely a matter of right mind-set toward the work and an orderly procedure in pre-typing activities and in typing the conditioning practice.

Machine Checkup and Adjustments for Section 5, Lessons 26 to 30

1. Check the placement of the paper guide; set the paper-bail rolls; adjust the paper bail against the paper; and set the ribbon lever for typing on the upper half of the ribbon.
2. Except for problems where you are given other instructions, set the left margin stop at 12 for a pica- or at 20 for an elite-type machine. Move the stop for the right margin to the end of the scale. Set a tabulator stop for a 5-space paragraph indention when typing paragraph material.
3. Use single spacing unless otherwise directed.

LESSON 26

CONDITIONING PRACTICE 26   5 minutes

Directions. Type each line three to five times. Double-space between the groups of lines.

Begin the typing of a conditioning practice at a slow and controlled rate with marked emphasis on getting the right "feel" of the reach-strokes. Condition yourself to the control of the machine; recall the exact power needed to control the operative parts, such as the carriage return, the space bar, and the shift keys. Gradually increase the speed with which you type; never push yourself in this practice for your fastest speed. This is the *best way* to condition yourself for exact control of the typewriter.

STROKES

a; a;sl a;sldk a;sldkfj a;sldkfjgh a;sldkfjghfj a;sldkfjghfj   60

Alphabetic sentence. Mary said the box was packed with five dozen jugs of liquid.   60

What is the sum of 36 and 27 and 49 and 150 and 264 and 318?   60

FIXATION PRACTICE 26   10 minutes

Fixation practice offers an opportunity for concentrating on a specific reach-stroke without neglecting other reach-strokes. This practice is similar to the practice of scales in the study of piano. These "typing scales" are designed to improve the control of specific reach-strokes. Type them on the stroke level of response at approximately 20 words a minute.

Directions. Type each sentence two or more times. Double-space between the groups of lines. Retype selected sentences if time permits.

Drill for   STROKES

a Alan gave days to analyzing all legal data for their papers.   60

b Robert Brooks bought books about the subject of big bridges.   60

c Claire called the cashier to check on these canceled checks.   60

d Did Don expect to direct a rapid check of the device I made?   60

e Every effort to get speed and accuracy should be made by me.   60

f Fred suffered from the effects of his fourth fearful defeat.   60

	STROKES	WORDS

First of all, be ready for the interview. Realize just how you should `823` `165` dress for the occasion. Loose and sporty school styles are not quite suit- `897` `179` able for office wear. Avoid extremes in style. You can do this without `970` `194` looking dowdy or old-fashioned. Above all, be absolutely certain that `1041` `208` your clothes are clean and pressed and your shoes shined. Suitable groom- `1114` `223` ing for applicants includes hat, gloves, and purse for the women; and `1184` `237` coat, collar, tie, and hat (that must be removed from the head when enter- `1257` `251` ing the reception office) for the men. Dress the part of a business worker. `1333` `267`

Employment tests are coming into greater use to determine an appli- `1399` `280` cant's fitness for work. In some cases the tests are harder than the `1469` `294` office work. If you learn the technique of taking a test, you can reduce `1543` `309` the factor of nervousness. The best way to learn to take a test is to do `1617` `323` office work on a part-time basis. The experience of having to produce `1688` `338` usable work is just the thing to make you realize the great need of being `1762` `352` accurate in all you do. When you apply for a position in person, take your `1838` `368` notebook, pen, eraser, and eraser shield with you. Employers are impressed `1914` `383` with those who can get to work with a minimum of wasted time. `1975` `395`

Be sure to reconstruct your technical skills before you go to the `2041` `408` interview. Never put yourself in the position of having to apologize for `2115` `423` poor work because you are out of practice. Get acquainted with the `2183` `437` operative parts and the touch of the typewriter before you try to use it. `2258` `452` You will not be expected to type at your highest rate. Hold yourself to a `2333` `467` controlled speed. Employers will be impressed with your power to control `2407` `481` yourself as well as your machine. Speed in typing is important just so `2479` `496` long as it is speed with control. Do not forget that a poorly typed `2548` `510` piece of work is almost valueless. If you erase, be sure that the erasure `2623` `525` is neat and complete and that your page is free of fingerprints. `2687` `537`

It is sometimes difficult to know just when to end an interview. Be `2756` `551` alert to catch the first hint of a desire on the part of the interviewer to `2832` `566` terminate the call. For example, if the man says, "Well, we will let you `2906` `581` know," rise promptly and quietly, and make as composed an exit as you `2976` `595` can. Remember to thank the interviewer for his time. End the interview `3049` `610` with a brief mention of your desire to work with that organization. `3118` `624`

When you get a position, be sure that you live up to your responsi- `3184` `637` bilities as an office worker. Get to work on time or ahead of time. If `3257` `651` the office closes at five o'clock, work right up to closing time. Don't be `3333` `667` a clock watcher. If overtime work is required, you will be expected to `3405` `681` adjust your own affairs on short notice and without protest so that you can `3481` `696` carry your share of such work. "The work must go out" is the demand of `3553` `711` modern business. Some companies do not permit overtime work, but in `3622` `724` many offices it is necessary to ask workers to stay at peak periods in the `3697` `739` month in order to get the work out. If you realize that overtime work is `3771` `754` the rule rather than the exception, you will realize that you have no cause `3847` `769` to resent the call for this additional service. `3894` **`779`**

Personal Note. You are ready to put your typing skill to use. Type the personal note on a half sheet of paper without address but with a salutation and complimentary close. Later, you will type personal letters and address envelopes with complete addresses.

Machine Adjustments. *For a pica-type machine* set a tabulator stop at 42 for the complimentary close; set a stop at 55 for the date. *For an elite-type machine* set a tabulator stop at 50 for the complimentary close; set a stop at 60 for the date.

Typing Directions. Space down approximately 1½ inches (9 lines) from the top of the page; tabulate to the second stop and type the date to end near the right margin. Leave 4 spaces between the date and the salutation. Type the salutation to begin at the left margin.

Tabulate to the first stop to type the complimentary close. Type the note twice, using a half sheet of paper for each writing. Sign your name to the note with pen and ink.

	STROKES	WORDS
October 13, 195-	17	3
Dear Bob:	28	6
You need not try to argue with me any more about the social	88	18
acceptance of the typed letter. I read an article by Emily	148	30
Post in which she says, "All letters may be typewritten today	210	42
except the most formal or the most private." Who wins now?	271	54
I've found a lot of fun in learning to type. I am making use	333	67
of the skill, too. What do you think of this letter as a	391	78
sample of my "good" typing?	420	84
Yours,	426	85

Directions. Use each sentence for two 1-minute writings. Be guided by the 20-second call. If time permits, type the sentences on the 15-second call of the guide.

	Strokes	Words 20"	Words 15"
Curve the fingers; place them lightly on the keys.	50	30	40
How I sit at the machine has much to do with my work.	53	32	42
Nothing worth having ever comes without some hard work.	55	33	44

LESSON 27

CONDITIONING PRACTICE 27   *5 minutes*

Directions. Type each line three to five times. Double-space between the groups of lines.

	STROKES
a; a;sl a;sldk a;sldkfj a;sldkfjgh a;sldkfjghfj a;sldkfjghfj	60
Alphabetic sentence. Fred Brown expects the lazy dog to jump quickly over a gate.	60
What is the sum of 83 and 72 and 94 and 250 and 162 and 103?	60

INSTRUCTIONAL BLOCK 21

TYPING PROBLEMS

SECTION 45. Taking an Employment Test

Classroom work in applying for a position can give you some understanding of interview techniques and types of problems used in employment tests. The problems of this section provide some materials that are similar to test materials used by employment managers. Work as efficiently as possible. Proofread all work before you hand it in. Speed of production is important; but speed *with* accuracy is the goal. In typing the problems, you will be expected to correct all correctible errors. Make neat erasures and keep each page free from fingerprints.

This work on applying for a position is given early in the semester so you can identify your areas of typing weakness and utilize every possible opportunity throughout the remainder of the semester to build job competence.

General Directions. At the beginning of each class period, type the conditioning practice until you are directed to begin the problem typing. You will type under employment test timing for 30 minutes in each lesson of this section. When you have completed one problem, begin the next unless you are otherwise directed. Work rapidly, but do not work hurriedly. Emphasize steady, continuous typing at all times.

LESSONS 251 TO 255

CONDITIONING PRACTICE 251
5 minutes

	STROKES
They have awarded a plaque to Judge Burt Mazur for his excellent work.	70
The terms are 2% in 10 days, or 30 days net. Make the check for $768.	70
If you really want to go to work, you will be able to find work to do.	70

FIVE-, TEN-, OR FIFTEEN-MINUTE TIMED WRITING

Directions. Employment tests differ in length, but most straight-copy tests are timed for 5 or 10 minutes, although some companies use the 15-minute test to determine the applicant's ability to stand up under pressure. Your teacher will tell you whether this test is to be typed for 5, 10, or 15 minutes. *Type on the control level of practice.* A usable speed of 60 words a minute is acceptable; higher rates with control are, of course, preferred and tend to set you apart as above average for beginning office workers. Any rate lower than 60 words a minute with accuracy places you in the average or below-average group of beginning office workers. If your first timing is for 10 or 15 minutes, use selected paragraphs for 5-minute writings in later lessons.

Each paragraph has every letter of the alphabet and a syllable intensity of 1.40.

	STROKES	WORDS
Give some thought now to the right way to apply for a position. It	68	14
may not be long until you will be called for an interview. The outcome of	143	29
that interview may fix your work life for some years. You cannot prepare	217	43
for all possible questions that may be asked in an interview, but you can get	291	58
the right understanding of how you should dress, how you should behave,	367	73
and the kind of test you may be expected to take. It is your job to make	441	88
a good impression on the employer. Many men make snap judgments	506	101
as to an applicant's fitness for work. Such decisions are not always based	582	116
on the fullest utilization of school records or test results. All too	653	131
often they are based on some intangible thing that impresses the employer	727	145
favorably or unfavorably.	752	150

FIXATION PRACTICE 27

Directions. Type each sentence two or more times. Double-space between the groups of lines.

Drill for		STROKES
g	Grants from the government gave Guy his growth to greatness.	60
h	Has Harry Hart shown just how the authors vary their themes?	60
i	I think Jim Martin justified his initiative in this inquiry.	60
j	Judge Johnson could not justify the injustice to Jim Jasper.	60
k	Knocks and kicks by his kinsfolk may make Karl leave Keokuk.	60
l	Little talk, less idleness, and more work; then skill comes.	60
m	Mayor Mumford said his message must be marked by moderation.	60

PROBLEM TYPING 27

Personal Letter. Directions. Use a full sheet of paper in typing the problem at the top of the following page. For this problem, which uses a 50-space line, set the stops as follows:

For a pica-type machine set the left margin stop at 17. Set a tabulator stop at 22 for the paragraph indention; at 37 for the complimentary close; and at 50 for the return address.

For an elite-type machine set the left margin stop at 25. Set a tabulator stop at 30 for the paragraph indention; at 45 for the complimentary close; and at 55 for the return address.

Space down approximately 10 lines from the top of the page; tabulate to the third stop; and type the return address and the date. Leave 10 spaces between the date and the address.

For the complimentary close tabulate to the second stop. Type the name 4 spaces below the complimentary close.

Type the letter twice.

SKILL MAINTENANCE 27

Directions. Use double spacing and a 5-space paragraph indention. Type the paragraph for 3 minutes. Practice words that may be speed traps for your fingers, such as *doubt, necessary, exact, reader, realize;* then take a second 3-minute writing and record the cwpm. You are expected to type at the approximate rate of 25 to 27 cwpm. (Note that this paragraph, like the other drill material in this section, is to be typed with the left margin at 12 for a pica- or at 20 for an elite-type machine.)

This paragraph uses every letter of the alphabet and has a syllable intensity of 1.25.

	STROKES	WORDS
If you want to be able to write good letters, learn to	55	11
say what you need to say in such a way that the reader will	115	23
never be in doubt as to your meaning. Your letters will be	175	35
good or bad as the selection of words to convey your meaning	236	47
is carefully or carelessly made. It is quite necessary that	297	59
you know the use of words just as a good workman knows the	356	71
use of the tools with which he works. In truth, words are	415	83
the tool of the writer of letters. Realize this now; then	474	95
learn to use words with an understanding of the exact shades	535	107
of meaning that many of them possess.	572	114

PROBLEM I—MEASUREMENT OF FILL-INS

Directions. When you completed Problem 1 of Lesson 241, you were told to keep the extra copies of the mimeographed letter for later use. You have used 20 of the 30 letters run off. Fill in the appropriate information for the remaining 10 letters, using the information given below. (To the stroke count given with the list add 35 strokes for each date line and salutation.)

STROKES

Name	Address	Policy No.	Amount of Policy	Amount Due	
Professor J. D. Long, Jr.	2630 Martin Drive Cincinnati 9, Ohio	147582	$20,000	$425.75	83
Gordon B. McParland	261 West Tenth Street Covington, Kentucky	261409	5,000	103.50	169
T. J. Parkinson	2985 Wilson Place Newport, Kentucky	193501	3,000	93.25	245
Dr. R. B. Richards	Trenton, Ohio	243678	2,500	87.00	297
W. B. Robertson	West Chester, Ohio	542906	5,000	75.00	355
Mrs. Alice M. Underwood	R. D. 4 Hamilton, Ohio	621507	10,000	237.50	422
Miss Mary H. Whitmer	429 Bennington Avenue Cincinnati 10, Ohio	482105	3,500	92.50	505
S. C. Yates	Princeton, Ohio	120586	1,500	42.75	556
Thomas B. Yeakel	Trenton, Ohio	362591	2,500	57.25	611
Wallace R. Young	Princeton, Ohio	502613	7,500	127.50	667

PROBLEM 2—MEASUREMENT OF ADDRESSING ENVELOPES

Directions. Address an envelope for each person whose name and address are given in Problem 1. Place the letter completed as Problem 1 under the flap of its envelope; then fold and insert the letter into its envelope. (The stroke count is that given with the list minus 20 for each envelope.)

PROBLEM 3—MEASUREMENT OF TYPING INDEX CARDS

Directions. Type an index card for each name given in Problem 1. Use the form practiced in the two preceding lessons. (The stroke count is that given with the list plus 55 for each card.)

SECTION 44. Production Measurement Comparison

LESSONS 246 TO 250

In an office, there would often be similarity of problems to be typed. You would not have a new form to be learned each day. This familiarity with the setup and with the nature of the materials to be typed obviously increases the production rate of the typist. For this reason, office typists frequently show marked improvement in production rate after a few weeks of experience.

To approximate the office experience a beginning typist would have, you are to use the lessons of Section 42 beginning on page 284 as the materials to be typed for the next five lessons. Type these materials just as you did when you typed them the first time. Compare your production rates on the different kinds of problems. Before starting to type, KNOW what you are to do and how you are to do it. Organize your desk and work materials. Type with continuity but without hurry. You should show some improvement in your production score when typing this material this second time.

	STROKES	WORDS

Begin the writer's return address about 10 line spaces from the top of the page. 2958 Elkins Street — 19 — 4

Jamestown, New York — 39 — 8

October 7, 195- — 55 — 11

For this short letter have 10 line spaces between the date and the letter address.

Mr. William E. Harrison — 79 — 16

Harrison Insurance Agency — 105 — 21

2746 Eighth Street — 124 — 25

Erie, Pennsylvania — 143 — 29

Double-space before and after the salutation. Dear Sir — 152 — 30

My father, Mr. Charles F. Wilson, was called — 197 — 39
to Chicago yesterday. He asked me to let you know — 248 — 50
that he cannot meet you on Wednesday of next week — 298 — 60
as planned. — 311 — 62

As soon as my father returns, he will get in — 356 — 71
touch with you to arrange for another appointment. — 408 — 82

Capitalize the first word of the complimentary close. Sincerely yours — 424 — 85

Frances Wilson

Type the signature 4 line spaces below the complimentary close. Miss Frances Wilson — 443 — 89

In this letter no mark of punctuation is used at the end of any of the special lines, such as the address, the salutation, and the complimentary close, unless a line ends with an abbreviation. This form of punctuation is known as *open punctuation.*

Style Letter 1 — Personal Business Letter with Open Punctuation

LESSON 28

CONDITIONING PRACTICE 28

5 minutes

Directions. Type each line three to five times. Double-space between the groups of lines.

STROKES

rfvf mjuj tfbf njyj edcd ,kik wsxs .lol qaza /;p; gftf njhj — 59

Alphabetic sentence. He quickly realized that jumping was very excellent for Bob. — 60

What is the sum of 50 and 83 and 94 and 827 and 462 and 103? — 60

PROBLEM 1—SKILL BUILDING IN FORM FILL-INS

Directions. Fill in the necessary information to complete 10 of the mimeographed letters prepared as Problem 2, Lesson 241. This problem is similar to Problem 1 of the preceding lesson.

Name	Address	Policy No.	Amount of Policy	Amount Due	STROKES
					52
Genevieve G. Herman	2552 Hudson Avenue	231177	1,000	33.93	112
	Cincinnati 16, Ohio				132
Frances A. Hewitt	4825 Central Boulevard	222334	2,000	56.22	194
	Cincinnati 12, Ohio				214
Mrs. Mary H. Hilton	3466 Trimble Avenue	101417	5,000	165.05	275
	Cincinnati 19, Ohio				295
Frances M. Johnson	483 Upton Place	418629	2,000	65.88	351
	Hamilton, Ohio				366
Dr. Lionel V. Judson	812 Commercial Building	331684	5,000	128.00	432
	Cincinnati 5, Ohio				451
Mrs. Anna B. King	3435 Bevis Avenue	189821	3,000	92.16	507
	Cincinnati 17, Ohio				527
Lester L. Knapp	843 Oliver Road	100481	7,500	230.25	580
	Cincinnati 13, Ohio				600
Mrs. Agatha T. Knight	101 Lilac Drive	384524	25,000	981.75	659
	Cincinnati 18, Ohio				679
Victor S. Lyall	2609 Adams Street	268506	20,000	598.00	734
	Ft. Thomas, Kentucky				755
Gordon P. Mack	2486 Arbor Avenue	200156	10,000	345.80	809
	Cincinnati 10, Ohio				828

PROBLEM 2—SKILL BUILDING IN ADDRESSING ENVELOPES

Directions. Address an envelope for each letter completed in Problem 1. Fold and insert each letter into its envelope.

PROBLEM 3—SKILL BUILDING IN TYPING INDEX CARDS

Directions. Type an index card for each name given in Problem 1. Type the surname first, followed by a comma and the given name and/or initials with the title (if any) typed last and enclosed within parentheses. Type the address on the succeeding lines. Two or three lines below the address, type at the left margin the Policy No.   and at the right of the same line type the Amount of Policy $. On the next line, beginning at the left margin, type the Amount Due $, followed immediately by the present date typed in figures.

LESSON 245

CONDITIONING PRACTICE 245
5 minutes

STROKES

Jim and I have been expecting to work quite zealously for the schools.   70

We bought General Utilities 5s at 101 5/8 and Groton Co. 4s at 47 7/8.   70

Always think through your problem before you begin to work through it.   70

TIMED WRITING 245
8 minutes

Directions. Use a 70-space line and a 5-space paragraph indention. Type the material of Timed Writing 244, page 293, for a 5-minute writing.

FIXATION PRACTICE 28

10 minutes

Directions. Type each sentence two or three times. Double-space between the groups of lines. Retype selected sentences if time permits.

Drill for

STROKES

n	Never think you can learn this unless the work is well done.	60
o	Opportunity comes most to those who know how to do the work.	60
p	Place the piano properly for the performance of the pianist.	60
q	Querulous women quickly answered those queer quiz questions.	60
r	Right work marked all his career, for he abhorred all wrong.	60
s	Sessions of Congress often last as long as the last session.	60
t	That story merits very little of your interest or attention.	60

PROBLEM TYPING 28

25 minutes

Directions. 1. Type Style Letter 1 on page 43 according to the directions on page 42.

2. Type the following letter using the same machine adjustments and spacing that you used for Style Letter 1. If time permits, type the letter twice.

Type your own name in the signature position 4 spaces below the complimentary close where the name *Donald T. Earle* is shown in the copy. A woman may type "Miss" or "Mrs." before her typed name in the manner shown in Style Letter 1. A man's name is typed without a personal title.

	STROKES	WORDS
Senior High School	19	4
Eaton, Kentucky	35	7
October 14, 195-	52	10
Mr. Ronald Paulson, President	82	16
Paulson Manufacturing Company	112	22
Louisville 12, Kentucky	136	27
Dear Mr. Paulson	153	31
The members of our Future Business Leaders of	199	40
America Club look forward with interest to the talk	251	50
you are to give us at 7:30 on Friday evening of next	304	61
week.	311	62
The meeting will be held in Room 385.	350	70
Sincerely yours	366	73
Donald T. Earle	381	76

PROBLEM 3—LEARNING THE NATURE OF THE PROBLEM

Directions. Type an index card for each name given in Problem 1. Use ruled cards, and use the variable spacer to adjust the machine to type on the lines of the card. Have the typed material close to the line without letting the line cut through any of the letters.

Type the surname first, followed by a comma and the given name and/or initials with the title (if any) typed last and enclosed within parentheses: as Worthington, Homer C. (Dr.). Type the address on the lines below the name. Two or three lines below the address, type at the left margin the Policy No.   and at the right of the same line type the Amount of Policy $. On the next line, beginning at the left margin, type the Amount Due $, followed immediately by the present date typed as illustrated: 4/26/52 (for April 26, 1952).

LESSON 244
CONDITIONING PRACTICE 244

5 minutes

STROKES

Jack V. Baxter has quite a large group of women and boys in your zone.	70
The check is for $1,590.28. Bill #731-A is for $2,816.40. I owe $10.	70
"Mind over matter" is more than just a clever phrase. Mind has power.	70

TIMED WRITING 244

8 minutes

Directions. Type a 5-minute timed writing in this lesson. Use a 70-space line and a 5-space paragraph indention.

Each paragraph has every letter of the alphabet and a syllable intensity of 1.40.

	STROKES	WORDS
If you were to apply for an office position now, what skills do you	68	14
possess that would cause a businessman to want to employ you? What can	140	28
you do reasonably well, and what can you do exceedingly well? You must	212	43
judge your abilities in terms of office standards. The question is not	284	57
what you want but what you can do. If your typewriting production rate	356	71
is high, that is one office skill that you should emphasize when you	425	85
apply for a position. Think now of the probable demands that will be	495	99
made upon you in your very first office experience, and undertake to build	570	114
the skills in your fingers and the qualities in your mind and heart that	643	129
will make for easy and quick occupational adjustment.	698	140
One of the first things asked an applicant for a position is about	765	153
his experience. This is very true when trained workers exceed the number	839	168
of positions. At such a time the pattern seems to be that there is no	910	182
work without experience, yet no experience without work. Not all firms	982	196
insist on work experience when taking on new office help; but most men	1053	211
realize that experience adds to the skill of the employee. For one thing,	1128	226
work habits grow on the job. More, some of the job adjustments that	1197	239
must be made are taken care of through a few months of good hard work.	1269	254
So work experience has come to be required for some jobs and found	1336	267
desirable for others that call for competence and judgment.	1395	279

LESSON 29

CONDITIONING PRACTICE 29 *5 minutes*

Directions. Type each line three to five times. Double-space between the groups of lines.

STROKES

4f$f 4f$f We owe $140.   5f%f 5f%f The rate is 3%.   4f$f 5f%f   60

Alphabetic sentence. John Pavlong saw the experts from Brazil drive away quickly. 60

2s"s 2s"s I said, "Can he type well?"   8k'k 8k'k Isn't it so? 61

FIXATION PRACTICE 29 *10 minutes*

Directions. Type each sentence two or more times. Double-space between the groups of lines. Retype selected sentences if time permits.

Drill for

STROKES

u Unusual though your plan is, you must question your success.   60

v Verbal vivacity never achieves over valid bravery and valor.   60

w When workers willingly use wisdom with their work, they win.   60

x Exert extra effort to excel when typing exercises or drills.   60

y Your young boy's very lovely play may make you justly happy.   60

z Zeal to learn and zest to work do not characterize the lazy.   60

PROBLEM TYPING 29 *15 minutes*
PROBLEM 1

Directions. Use a half sheet of paper; double spacing; and the current date typed $1\frac{1}{2}$ inches from the top of the paper. Have 4 or 5 spaces between the date and the salutation.

Members of FBLA

Mr. Ronald Paulson, of Paulson Mfg. Co., is to be the speaker at our Friday evening meeting. He is an interesting and dynamic speaker. You will enjoy hearing and meeting him.

Remember: Friday at 7:30. Room 385.

Ray Allison
President of FBLA

PROBLEM 2

Directions. Use a half sheet of paper. Set the machine for double spacing. Begin typing approximately $1\frac{1}{2}$ inches (9 spaces) from the top of the paper. Type the headings as given, beginning each heading at the left margin. Type the information called for, beginning the line 2 spaces after the colon.

Name:
Home Address:
Date of Birth:
Home Room:
Name of Typewriter Used:
Serial No. of Typewriter:
Present Typing Rate (cwpm):

LESSON 243

CONDITIONING PRACTICE 243

5 minutes

STROKES

Quite often, many quick students have justly won extremely big prizes. 70

Paul is 46 years 5 months and 19 days old; Jack, 37 years 28 days old. 70

There is great value in believing, but there is real magic in knowing. 70

TIMED WRITING 243

8 minutes

Directions. Use a 70-space line and a 5-space paragraph indention. Type the material of Timed Writing 241, page 289, as a 5-minute writing.

PRODUCTION TYPING 243

27 minutes

PROBLEM 1—LEARNING THE NATURE OF THE PROBLEM

Directions. Fill in the current date, the address, the salutation, the correct policy number, the amount of the policy, and the correct amount due on the mimeographed letters prepared as Problem 2, Lesson 241. Try to match the fill-ins both as to type and as to color of ribbon. You will have 20 extra copies of the letter that will be needed for later lessons.

Use a ruler or a sheet of paper placed underneath the address of the first person to whom a letter is to be addressed. When you have typed that information on the mimeographed letter, move the guide to the next name. Use the same kind of guide when typing envelopes from an address list containing a number of names.

STROKES

Name	Address	Policy No.	Amount of Policy	Amount Due	
					52
Howard L. Barker	526 Crest View	311479	$10,000	$323.70	109
	Ft. Thomas, Kentucky				130
Mrs. Joseph J. Beckley	4161 London Street	165383	3,000	108.24	193
	Dayton 6, Ohio				208
Cecil W. Clark	2843 Pendlay Road	111265	6,000	288.06	262
	Newport, Kentucky				280
Ellen E. Crockett	3641 Jefferson Street	161593	1,000	11.82	341
	Newport, Kentucky				359
Louis A. Daniels	2355 Montana Avenue	298411	15,000	460.50	417
	Ludlow, Kentucky				434
Dr. Arthur F. Duffy	417 West Fourth Street	86508	5,000	125.25	498
	Cincinnati 4, Ohio				517
David S. Dwight	Roselawn Apartments	151466	5,000	270.30	574
	615 Roselawn Place				593
	Dayton, Kentucky				610
Thomas A. Ellis	1916½ Gilpin Avenue	201423	2,500	79.78	667
	Cincinnati 9, Ohio				686
Sylvester U. Fisher	R. D. 2	99216	2,500	135.15	735
	Mt. Healthy, Ohio				753
Marian Henderson	123 Overlook Place	257123	2,000	39.24	810
	Cincinnati 5, Ohio				828

PROBLEM 2—LEARNING THE NATURE OF THE PROBLEM

Directions. Address an envelope for each letter completed in Problem 1.

Directions. Type for 3 minutes. Record your cwpm. Practice words that may be speed traps for your fingers, such as *fingers, control, errors, worry, sureness*; then take a second 3-minute writing and record the cwpm. You should type at the approximate rate of 25 to 28 cwpm.

This paragraph uses every letter of the alphabet and has a syllable intensity of 1.25.

	STROKES	WORDS
You now have all the skill you need to begin to type as	56	11
you think. Your fingers will type the words as you think if	117	23
you know just what it is that you want to say. The first	175	35
thing, obviously, is to have something to say and to know	233	47
the words you need to use to express yourself. If you make	293	59
some errors in your typing, do not let them worry you. In	352	70
time you will develop the power to type with the ease and	410	82
the continuity that will make typing useful to you. Type	468	94
as you think, and quite certainly think as you type. This	527	105
is the way to realize big dividends from your typing power.	586	117

LESSON 30

CONDITIONING PRACTICE 30   *5 minutes*

Directions. Type each line three to five times. Double-space between the groups of lines.

STROKES

Sam's policy for $10,000 is #938261. It will expire in 1958.   61

Alphabetic sentence. We quickly rejected the use of five dozen more packing boxes. 61

Robert Stephens is exactly 16 years 4 months and 7 days old.   60

FIXATION PRACTICE 30   *10 minutes*

Directions. Type each line two or more times. Double-space between the groups of lines.

Reach-Stroke Techniques. Control the figures and symbols by stretching the finger to the key. Move the finger straight to the key without moving the elbow or changing the hand alignment with the keyboard. Keep the wrists low, the arms quiet, and the fingers curved, except the controlling finger, which should be straightened for the reach-stroke.

STROKES

Paul owes me $7.25. Study pages 39-68. He gets $40 a week.   60

Type the dash with two hyphens--and use the * for footnotes.   60

Ford & Owen's order (dated May 2) must be shipped by May 29.   60

Don't pay 6%. They wrote, "Think and type; type and think."   60

Order #84 is for $200. Alfred moved to Alabama on April 27.   60

PROBLEM I—LEARNING THE NATURE OF THE PROBLEM

Directions. Type Style Letter 8, shown on page 115, as a master copy from which a stencil is to be prepared. Omit the date, the address, and the salutation, but leave space for them so that they can be filled in on the stenciled copies. Use 10-space paragraph indentions. In the third paragraph, leave enough blank spaces after No. and after $ so that you will be able to fill in the figures later. Omit the figures for the amount due at the bottom of the letter.

To make it possible to type the amount due on the same line as the name of the dictator, begin the complimentary close a little to the right of the center of the page. When a long letter is being crowded onto one page, such variations from standard procedure may be made.

PROBLEM 2—LEARNING THE NATURE OF THE PROBLEM

When your master copy has been approved for form, prepare a stencil, sign Mr. Rolph's name with a stylus, and run off 30 copies. If you must await your turn to use the mimeograph, continue the work on the following problems.

LESSON 242

CONDITIONING PRACTICE 242 *5 minutes*

	STROKES
Many amazing and explicit questions have been asked of Judge Worthing.	70
This library has 492 first editions, 180 plays, and 736 rare records.	70
Some beginning workers have to learn that they must do all work right.	70

TIMED WRITING 242 *8 minutes*

Directions. Use a 70-space line and a 5-space paragraph indention. Type the material of Timed Writing 241, page 114, as a 5-minute writing.

PRODUCTION TYPING 242 *27 minutes*

PROBLEM I—LEARNING THE NATURE OF THE PROBLEM

Directions. Prepare a master copy for the request for a reinstatement of a lapsed policy. Center the first three lines; begin the address and date lines about the center of the page.

After the master copy has been approved, prepare a stencil and run this form on the back of the letter completed as Problem 1, Lesson 241.

	STROKES
REQUEST FOR REINSTATEMENT	26
OF	29
LAPSED POLICY NO._____	61
Address_____	96
_____	131
Date_____	166
Central Equitable Life Insurance Co.	203
Cincinnati 4	216
Ohio	221
It is my desire to provide for the	256
continuance of my insurance policy.	293
I am enclosing my remittance for	326
$ to cover the amount now	358

	STROKES
due with interest in order to have	393
my lapsed policy reinstated.	423
I hereby certify that the following	459
is a complete statement of all my	493
illnesses and/or injuries in the past	531
twelve months and of all physicians,	568
surgeons, and/or practitioners whom	604
I have consulted in the past twelve	640
months:	646

					STROKES
					684
Illness or Injury	Month	Year	Duration in Weeks	Name and Address of Physician, Surgeon, Practitioner	784
					819
					854
					889
					924
					959
					994
					1028
Signature of Policyholder					1145

Directions. Type the following letter twice with the same spacing and arrangement that you used in Style Letter 1, for which directions are given on page 42.

Use your own return address and the current date. Type your signature 4 spaces below the complimentary close.

NOTE: The title of a book should be underscored or typed in all capital letters.

```
South-Western Publishing Company
634 Broadway
Cincinnati 2, Ohio

Gentlemen

        Please send to me one copy of your publication
entitled Effective Communication in Business, by
Aurner.  I understand that the list price of this
is $4.50.  My check will be sent to you as soon as
I receive your bill.

        My instructor in typewriting is Mr. R. F. Carter.
It was he who suggested that I write to you.

                    Yours very truly
```

TIMED WRITING 30   *10 minutes*

Directions. Use double spacing and a 5-space paragraph indention. Type the paragraph as a 5-minute writing. Record your cwpm. Contrast your cwpm on this 5-minute writing with your record made on 3-minute writings.

This paragraph uses every letter of the alphabet and has a syllable intensity of 1.25.

	STROKES	WORDS
The boy in my class who always had the highest typing	54	11
speed and the best control told me one day that he had gained	116	23
his skill through typing the same short and simple paragraph	177	35
over and over. He would type the same copy time after time,	238	48
pausing only long enough to think of how to improve his tech-	298	60
niques. He said he realized it would help him to type the	357	71
same material fifty to a hundred times and that he was going	418	84
to do so as soon as he could learn to hold his mind on what	478	96
he was doing. It will help you to type a drill, exercise, or	540	108
timed writing several times if it is done in just the right	600	120
way.	604	121

CENTRAL EQUITABLE LIFE INSURANCE COMPANY
CINCINNATI 4, OHIO

STROKES WORDS

May 12, 19--   13   3

Mr. Howard L. Barker   34   7
526 Crest View   49   10
Ft. Thomas, Kentucky   70   14

Dear Mr. Barker   86   17

     All of us realize that the really worth-while things   139   28
in life are usually secured at some cost. Too often, however,   202   40
we pay for advantages that seem important at the moment but   262   52
that later cause regrets.   289   58

     Of all the things that it is possible for a person   340   68
to acquire, none is so valuable, so dependable, or so secure   401   80
as Life Insurance, and it rests with the individual alone to   462   92
add permanency. Frequently this calls for careful budgeting,   524   105
perhaps for many years, but in no other manner can you maintain   588   118
and enjoy the feeling of security, the peace of mind, and the   650   130
satisfaction that adequate insurance provides.   698   140

     You had all these advantages in mind when you decided   752   150
to purchase your Policy No. 311479 for $10,000. The policy now   831   166
stands lapsed, and the protection that you planned so thought-   895   179
fully is without effect. Is it to remain so, or will you send,   958   192
us your remittance and arrange for reinstatement?   1009   202

     For your answer to this question we have prepared   1059   212
on the reverse side of this letter a form that you should sign   1122   224
and return properly completed in order to reinstate your lapsed 1185   237
policy.   1194   239

     If you do not wish to have your policy reinstated,   1245   249
please file this letter with the policy so that, in case of   1305   261
your death, those to whom this insurance would mean so much   1365   273
will know that the policy has no value. We often have cases   1426   285
where a request for payment is made under the assumption that   1488   298
a policy is effective, and it is a most unpleasant duty to have 1552   310
to inform the beneficiary that there is nothing payable.   1610   322

     We are ready and willing to assist you in every possi-   1663   333
ble way to restore the feeling of security that only an insur-   1724   345
ance policy, in good standing, can provide.   1769   354

                  Sincerely yours   1785   357

Richard S. Rolph

RR/1 Amount due, $323.70   Richard S. Rolph, Secretary   1837   367

(Words in body of letter, 301)

Style Letter 8 — Long Letter Typed on One Page

SECTION 6. Building Sustained Typing Power

PRACTICE LEVELS

There are three levels of practice appropriate for use in building typing power:
1. Exploration (forced speed) level.
2. Skill-building level for building sustained typing power.
3. Control level for typing material to be used or handed in for marking.

When the purpose of the writing is to force you into a new speed area, use the *exploration level of practice*. The appropriate mood is experimental; you are "feeling out" a new area. Errors in such typing are simply cues for less tension and more attention.

The *skill-building level of practice* should be used when the purpose of the typing is to build sustained typing power. This is the intermediate level of practice that calls for a rate that is lower than the exploration (or forced speed) level. This drop-back in speed will enable you to give attention to the improvement of your stroking patterns.

The *control level of practice* should be used in typing problems to be handed in to be marked. When typing on the control level, drop back 10 to 15 words below your *exploration level*. This drop-back in speed will add to the ease with which you will type. When typing on this level, your goal is to produce work at a *suitable rate and with a high degree of accuracy*.

Machine Checkup and Adjustments
1. Check the placement of the paper guide, the paper-bail rolls, and the paper bail.
2. Set the stop for the left margin at 12 for a pica-type or at 20 for an elite-type machine; move the stop for the right margin to the end of the scale.
3. Use single spacing for drills and double spacing for paragraphs.
4. Use a 5-space paragraph indention.
5. Set the ribbon lever for typing on the upper half of the ribbon.

LESSON 31

CONDITIONING PRACTICE 31   5 minutes

Directions. Type the paragraph twice.

All letters of the alphabet are used in the paragraph.

	STROKES	WORDS
It is quite easy to place some dates. America refused	55	11
to be subject to England in 1775; Clark explored the way to	115	23
the great Northwest in 1779; and "Old Hickory" seized Florida	177	35
in 1814. These dates in history have meaning for all of us.	237	47

PROGRESSION TYPING 31   10 minutes

Directions. Type for a half minute with the goal of errorless work. The next timing will be for 1 minute. If you typed without error, type for 1 minute; but if you made an error in the first writing and therefore failed to make progression, type again for only a half minute.

The third timing will be for 2 minutes. If you have typed the half-minute and the minute writings without error, you will double your progression time. The call of the half-minute guide will be given as "Half," "One," "Half," "Two." You can begin to type for a half-minute progression at any call, and for a minute progression when the call of "One" is given.

The fourth timing will be for 3 minutes with the call of the half-minute guide given so that you can start at any call to type a half-minute progression; and you can start at the call of "One" or "Two" to type for a minute progression; or you can start at the call of "One" to type for a 2-minute progression, as the timing is for 3 minutes. *Type on the control level of practice.*

SECTION 43. Stenciling and Form Fill-In

LESSON 241

CONDITIONING PRACTICE 241 · 5 minutes

	STROKES
He quickly expressed prejudice about moving from Washington to Brazil.	70
Martin & James owe $738. Isn't the check for $645? This is the 29th.	70
Build right skills in your fingering and right attitudes in your mind.	70

TIMED WRITING 241 · 8 minutes

Directions. Type a 5-minute timed writing in this and each of the following two lessons. Use a 70-space line and a 5-space paragraph indention.

Each paragraph has every letter of the alphabet and a syllable intensity of 1.40.

	STROKES	WORDS
In many offices typists must make multiple carbons of their work.	67	13
Those who use carbons quite often learn by experience just how to avoid	139	28
getting carbon smudges on their fingers and then transferring these	207	41
smudges to the paper. One way in which to handle carbons without	273	55
getting the fingers smeared is to fold back the corners of the carbon	343	69
sheet so that it can be held without the carbonized surface being touched.	419	84
If the corners are folded back, it is relatively easy to remove the carbon	494	99
sheets from the pack of papers by taking hold of the papers at a corner	566	113
and gently shaking the carbon sheets free. The carbon sheets can also	637	127
be shaken from the pack of papers if the corners of the carbons are cut	709	142
off. The carbon sheets can also be inserted between the paper after the	782	156
paper has been rolled into the machine just enough for the feed rolls to	855	171
grip it, with the ends of the carbon sheets extending below the paper.	927	185
The carbon sheets can then be removed by pulling them out at one time.	999	200
When you insert a pack made up of sheets of paper and carbons, you	1066	213
can put it in evenly if you will place it under the flap of an envelope.	1140	228
Quite often a thick pack of carbons and paper will cause one or more of	1212	242
the carbons to wrinkle and thus will make many streaks on the copies	1281	256
that are next to the carbonized surfaces. One way to avoid this is to	1352	270
depress the paper-release lever just after the pack is inserted into the	1425	285
typewriter and before it is twirled all the way around the platen. When	1498	300
the paper-release lever is depressed, the feed rolls release the grip on	1571	314
the paper and the pressure is evenly distributed after the release lever	1644	329
is returned to its normal position.	1679	336

All letters of the alphabet are used in the paragraph.

	STROKES	WORDS
If you want to type, you can do so. Tell your fingers	55	11
just what they are to do, and they will do it. It is not a	115	23
question of chance. Your fingers are strong and flexible,	174	35
but they have to be told what they are to do. Do each day's	235	47
,work as well as you can do it, and you will be amazed at the	296	59
way your typing skill will grow. This is your part in this	356	71
work of winning the prize of good typing power. You dare not	418	84
do less than your best work at all times.	459	92

TECHNIQUE STUDY 31

10 minutes

Quiet, Almost Motionless, Hands and Arms. When the hands or arms move excessively, your typing skill is lowered and your fatigue is increased. The expert types with the fingers and holds the hands and arms quiet—almost motionless. The purpose of this technique study is to help you to feel the ease of stroking that comes when the hands are correctly positioned and when the typing is done with the fingers, with little hand or arm movement.

Directions. Type each line three times, pausing briefly after each line to think of ways to improve your stroking and to reduce hand or arm movement. Have the fingers curved, wrists low, elbows free of your body, and the shoulders erect but relaxed. *Type on the control level.*

	STROKES
aid man can got own but big may buy say six rub tub ask fix	59
such ever cent much many quiz both give deck very wish like	59
check money river bother bright hungry except switch prized	59
quote hinder brothers realize coverage excessive emphasized	59

SKILL BUILDING 31

15 minutes

Directions. The purpose of your next typing is to build sustained typing power. Type for 1 minute; then when your instructor says "Throw; indent; type," start at the beginning of the paragraph and type for another minute. Do this for five minutes without pausing between the writings. Strive for easy, continuous typing. *Type on the skill-building level.*

	STROKES	WORDS
Hold your eyes on the copy as you type. This will help	56	11
you in typing smoothly and without pauses. It is the pause	116	23
that kills speed. Get rid of it by just keeping on typing.	175	35

Skill-Building Procedures. You will take several additional 1-minute writings using the paragraph above. Your instructor will call the guide for the carriage throw as follows:

1. The first writing will be on the 30-second call of the guide. You will type the first line in a half minute and the second line by the end of the minute, a speed of 23 words a minute.

2. When you have typed for one minute at the rate called for by the 30-second guide, type with the guide called each 20 seconds, a speed of 35 words for a minute. Take repeated writings until you can build your skill to this 35-word rate.

PROBLEM 10—BUSINESS LETTER

Directions. Prepare in block style with open punctuation. Type the notation on the *carbon copy only.* Address an appropriate envelope.

STROKES

Current Date Dr. John A. Eaton — 35
School of Business Syracuse Uni- — 66
versity Syracuse 8, New York Dear — 100
Dr. Eaton (P) Under separate cover, — 132
I am sending you a copy of our lat- — 166
est publication, *Business Communi-* — 215
cation Problems. This book has just — 267
come from the press and will prob- — 300
ably be released within the next 60 — 336
to 90 days. (P) Examination of this — 369
unusual textbook will reveal many — 402
outstanding features never before — 436
included in a book dealing with cor- — 471
respondence as well as other types — 506
of business writing. In a style most — 544
interesting and in a tenor especially — 582
appealing, the authors have dealt — 616
with the most important communi- — 647
cation problems. (P) Will you, at — 678

your convenience, read through this — 714
complimentary copy and comment — 745
on its contents. I shall be especially — 785
eager to learn your reaction, since — 821
you played such an important part — 855
in helping us plan the items to be — 890
included. (P) I am enclosing a — 918
stamped, self-addressed envelope — 951
which I should like to have you use — 987
in sending me your comments. — 1017
Please feel free to discuss the book — 1054
without reservations. Your unbiased — 1091
appraisal will do much to help us — 1125
evaluate it effectively. Very sin- — 1159
cerely yours UNIVERSAL PUB- — 1185
LISHING COMPANY Sales Man- — 1210
ager AMRoberts/crb Enclosure — 1239
Notation: A copy autographed by — 1261
the authors has been sent. — 1287

PROBLEM 11—BUSINESS LETTER—ADDITIONAL COPIES

Directions. Write the same letter that you used in Problem 10 to **Mr. Wayne J. Whitfield** **1492 Morrison Street Sacramento 5, California;** and **Mr. Thomas M. Burton 985 Brashear Avenue Toledo 6, Ohio.** Do not make carbon copies. Address an appropriate envelope for each.

PROBLEM 12—ANNOUNCEMENT

Directions. Prepare on a full sheet of paper.

STROKES

You are cordially invited to attend a reception honoring — 57
Professor Emeritus Thomas Burke Craver — 96
on — 99
Thursday, the third day of November — 135
between the hours of four and six o'clock — 177
at the — 184
National University Art Center — 215
This will also mark the opening of a comprehensive exhibition — 277
of Professor Craver's paintings — 309
to be held in — 323
The Fine Arts Gallery — 345
from this date through November 15 — 379

BONUS TYPING

Whenever you complete a lesson before the period ends, use the opportunity to practice for higher levels of skill. The sentences given below are to be used for bonus typing. You may use the sentences (1) for 1-minute writings, (2) for calling the guide, or (3) for repetitive practice, typing each sentence five or more times. *Type the sentences on the exploration level.*

	Words 30"	Words 20"	Words 15"
Do as well as you can all you are told to do.	18	27	36
Big things are built on small things well done.	19	28	38
To do anything well, keep yourself out of the rut.	20	30	40
Learn how much you can do in a given time--and do it.	21	32	42
Always use right typing techniques to build good speed.	22	33	44
Most of us show our true worth by the way we do our work.	23	34	46
Luck seems always to favor the man who does not count on it.	24	36	48
When typing "made" fractions, use the /.	16	24	32
There are 6 line spaces to a vertical inch.	17	26	34
The * (asterisk) is often used for footnotes.	18	27	36
Do you have a first-class bond selling at $750?	19	28	38
You should sit 8 to 10 inches from the typewriter.	20	30	40
"Do your best," he said, "and good will come to you."	21	32	42
Figure 10 pica or 12 elite spaces to a horizontal inch.	22	33	44
Place the paper-bail rolls approximately 3½ inches apart.	23	34	46
Don't space between #, %, or ¢ and the figure typed with it.	24	36	48

LESSON 32

CONDITIONING PRACTICE 32
5 minutes

Directions. Type the paragraph twice.

All letters of the alphabet are used in the paragraph.

	STROKES	WORDS
It is quite necessary for you to learn how to express	54	11
numbers correctly. Just a few items can be given here; but	114	23
know these well. Use figures to state dimensions, weights,	174	35
temperature, and page numbers, regardless of size.	224	45

PROGRESSION TYPING 32
10 minutes

Directions. Use the following paragraph for half-minute progressions. The purpose of this practice is to type without error. When you have typed for a half minute without error, type for 1 minute without error; then 2 minutes; then 3 minutes. If other students are typing for longer progressions, repeat your progression two or more times. At the conclusion of this typing, note the progressions you have made and begin typing at the next progression in the succeeding lesson.

PROBLEM 8—FREIGHT BILL

Directions. Use this information to complete a freight bill for the Wilshire Transportation Company. Refer to Illustration 60, page 229.

Refer to Illustration 60, page 229.

		STROKES
To **The Woodlawn Nurseries, Inc. 1901 Murrayhill Avenue Williams-**		60
port 12, Pennsylvania Date 12/15/5— Shipper **The Garden Supply**		109
Company 3197 Frankstown Avenue Schenectady 12, New York		165

No. Pieces	Description	Weight	Rate	Collect	STROKES
					208
					251
50 bags	Shurgrow Organic Fertilizer	5100	1.09	55.59	304
12 crts.	5-shovel Garden Cultivators	720	1.23	9.84	358
15 rolls	42 in. Steel Lawn Fence	1890	.95	18.05	408
10 bxs.	16 gal. Wheelbarrow Sprayers	1032	1.20	13.20	462
6 drums	All-Purpose Weed Killer	1350	1.17	16.38	513
15 bxs.	Heavy Duty Garden Wheelbarrow	1080	1.15	12.65	568
20 bxs.	Assorted Garden Tools—Steel	1910	1.10	22.00	622
					629
				147.71	636
	3% Federal Tax			4.43	643
					650
				152.14	656

PROBLEM 9—LETTER WITH TABULATED REPORT

Directions. Type this letter in modified block style with no indentions for paragraphs. Use mixed punctuation. Address an appropriate envelope and mark it SPECIAL DELIVERY.

	STROKES
Mr. Joseph A. McGovern 1492 West Baden Drive Atlanta 6, Georgia	64
Dear Mr. McGovern: (P) We appreciate your letter of October 15 in which	132
you enclosed an order for photographic equipment and supplies. It is	202
always a pleasure to hear from you; it is a double pleasure to be able to	276
serve you. At this time, however, it is impossible for us to furnish all of	353
the supplies you requested because of shortages in our local stocks.	423
These shortages exist because of the diversion of photographic materials	496
for military purposes. You realize, of course, the problem involved. (P)	567
We are sending you, therefore, the following items:	620

Quantity	Item	Amount	STROKES
			641
			662
3 ea.	Homestyle Enlarger 89 mm. f:6.3 lens	$156.75	715
6 ea.	Trimming Boards, 12-in.	41.00	753
5 ea.	Enlarging Easels, 11 x 14 in.	52.25	797
15 ea.	Developing Trays, 8 x 10 in.	14.95	840
2 ea.	Acme Print Dryer 110-120 volt AC-DC	25.00	890
			898
	Total	$289.95	912

	STROKES
(P) Enclosed is a stamped, self-addressed envelope which we should like	985
to have you use in directing us concerning the portion of your order as	1057
yet unfilled. Shall we obligate future stocks for you, or is it your desire	1134
to cancel the remaining part of the order? A prompt reply will be greatly	1209
appreciated. **Cordially yours, NATIONAL CAMERA SUPPLY COM-**	1266
PANY H. A. Backstrom Sales Manager mh Enclosure	1313

All letters of the alphabet are used in the paragraph.

	STROKES	WORDS
It is well to note the way you type even more than how	55	11
much you type. The key to good work is quite often found in	116	23
some little thing that is not being done just as it should be	178	36
done. The expert does things expertly. He realizes that it	239	48
takes only a little more skill to build much more speed. He	300	60
knows that the way to add this little more skill is to learn	361	72
to do well all that has to be done. This is why you need to	422	84
note the way you type even more than the number of words you	483	97
type. Build a little more skill and have much more speed.	541	108

TECHNIQUE STUDY 32

10 minutes

Shift-Key Control. Stretch the finger to the shift key. Make this reach without moving the elbow in or out and without changing the arm position. Hold the shift key down firmly, release it quickly after the capital letter has been typed, and return the controlling finger to its typing position immediately.

Directions. Type each line twice. Double-space after the second typing of the line. *Type on the control level.*

	STROKES
Max and Jane will sail for Italy in March. Is Mark in Maine?	61
Al and Alan went to Alaska in April. Ed Speers is in Algiers.	62
James, Max, and Ned go to Hawaii before going to Puerto Rico.	61
Alan Black and Clay Evans will be in Austin, Texas, in April.	61
Jack and Elvin met Sam Marshall in Mexico City late in March.	61

SKILL BUILDING 32

15 minutes

Directions. Type for 5 minutes with the call of the throw at the end of each minute of typing. *Type on the skill-building level.*

	STROKES	WORDS
Take a look at the way you get ready to type. Note the	56	11
things you do that can be done better; then learn to do them	117	23
better. You should plan your work and always work your plan.	178	36

Skill-Building Procedures. 1. Take a 1-minute writing with the 30-second call of the guide. This will give you a speed of 23 words a minute. *Type on the skill-building level.*

2. Type the paragraph with the 20-second call of the guide. Take repeated writings until you can type at this 36-word rate. *Type on the exploration level.*

BONUS TYPING

Use the sentences of Lesson 31, page 50, for bonus typing.

PROBLEM 4—ANNOUNCEMENT

Directions. Arrange this notice on a half sheet of paper. Material to go on one line is indicated by extra spaces in the type.

	STROKES
The President and The Board of Trustees of Richmond University	63
and The Residents of Men's New Halls	100
Announce an Open House and Guided Tours Sunday, November 20, 195—	166
Two until four o'clock The public is cordially invited	221
1500 East Tenth Street Richmond, Virginia	263

PROBLEM 5—TABULATED REPORT

Directions. Prepare a tabulated report for the membership list given. Arrange it on a full sheet of paper.

MEMBERSHIP LIST

	Name	Street and Number	City and State	STROKES
				16
				54
				92
1.	Alden, John H.	604 Madison Street	Mishawaka, Indiana	149
2.	Campbell, Howard	1801 West Grant Boulevard	Lexington 6, Kentucky	217
3.	Daily, Helen T.	1822 Vassar Avenue	Paris, Illinois	272
4.	Delaney, Jesse S.	1620 Indiana Street	Louisville 5, Kentucky	337
5.	Gordon, Rita	1133 Portage Avenue	Terre Haute, Indiana	395
6.	Ireland, Harry	1205 Pico Boulevard	Akron 8, Ohio	448
7.	Marshall, Grace	722 Park Avenue	South Bend 12, Indiana	507
8.	Moran, Jane	3383 Fairfield Avenue	Fort Wayne 9, Indiana	567
9.	Neff, Paul	1201 Sixteenth Street	Jeffersonville, Indiana	628
10.	Nesbitt, Clyde	950 University Avenue	Cincinnati 10, Ohio	690
11.	Owens, Milton	304 North Liberty Street	Dayton 6, Ohio	749
12.	Porter, Melvin J.	270 Madison Avenue	Elkhart, Indiana	818
13.	Regan, Stephen J.	216 North Street	St. Louis 6, Missouri	870
14.	Starr, Louis	308 West Seventh Street	Greencastle, Indiana	934
15.	Weaver, Leonard	634 Broadway	Cincinnati 5, Ohio	986

PROBLEM 6—FILL-IN FORM

Directions. Use a sheet of ruled paper. Type the tabulation used in Problem 5.

PROBLEM 7—TELEGRAM

Directions. Send the message as a full-rate telegram. Use the current date.

	STROKES
Send to: Mr. Glenn A. Overman	48
1569 Craighead Street, Boston, Massachusetts.	95
Charge to: Metal Products Company, 142 South Boulevard;	153
Message: Need report of sales in Central Territory for September.	221
When will figures be available? Wire immediate reply.	277
W. A. Kennedy	290

LESSON 33

Directions. Type the paragraph twice.

All letters of the alphabet are used in the paragraph.

	STROKES	WORDS
In 1492 Columbus set sail into the vast unknown, there	55	11
to find a new land. He never received much reward for his	114	23
amazing trip, but what of that? He had conquered fear; he	173	35
had experienced the "joy of discovery."	212	42

PROGRESSION TYPING 33   *10 minutes*

Directions. When you typed the preceding lesson, you noted the progressions you made. Begin with the next progression and type the following paragraph. As the length of time you have to type for each added progression adds to the chances of making errors in typing, you will need to control yourself as well as your typewriter with great care. Remember that the purpose of progression typing is *errorless typing on the control level.*

All letters of the alphabet are used in the paragraph.

	STROKES	WORDS
Organize your desk for typing. If you have extra books	56	11
or papers that are not to be used just now, put them out of	116	23
your way. See that the work tools are in the right place so	177	35
that you can move the hands to them quickly and pick them up	238	48
without having to look for them. Be orderly in all you do.	299	60
This is one way to add to your speed without typing faster.	360	72
In fact, speed in typing is not gained so much by making the	421	84
fingers go faster as it is by doing each thing as well as it	482	96
can be done. Gain speed by being orderly in all that you do.	543	109

TECHNIQUE STUDY 33   *10 minutes*

Equalized Stroking Power. If your typed copy has some light letters because the keys were faintly struck, you need to give attention to equalizing your stroking power. The corrective measure for unequal stroking power is to pace your typing at a controlled rate and to think the word forcefully enough to give a positive typing impulse to the controlling fingers.

Directions. Type each line twice. Double-space after the second typing of the line. Type at a rate that is much slower than your highest speed; give positive direction to the fingers for swift, sharp, sure strokes. Let the *r* and *u* strokes become patterns for good stroking.

	STROKES
yes but may pay why six wax pin red mop tag you tab him quiz	60
were only card jump dear mill case lump text hill ever pull	59
Relax the arms. Relax the arms and let your fingers work.	58
This is not hard to do. This is not hard to do when I try.	59

	STROKES		STROKES
the latest reports and commentary	1153	turn it to us immediately? We	1393
on major issues confronting modern	1188	should like to have the pleasure of	1429
businessmen—all written by compe-	1221	entering your name on the mailing	1463
tent authors with deep insight and	1256	list of this worthwhile publication.	1500
keen understanding. (P) While this	1288	Very sincerely yours UNIVERSAL	1531
special offer is fresh in mind, won't	1326	PUBLISHING COMPANY Sales	1556
you fill in the enclosed card and re-	1362	Manager AMRoberts/crb Enclosure	1588

PROBLEM 2—INTEROFFICE CORRESPONDENCE

Directions. Type in appropriate style, using single spacing.

		STROKES
To: William I. Kennedy	Date: (Current)	48
From: Austin R. Lucas	File: GS-Thayer 201.3	94
Subject: Test of Metal Polishes		127

	STROKES
We are now ready to receive bids for the supply of metal polish for the	199
next fiscal year. Suppliers have been requested to submit estimates, together	278
with samples of the products on which they are bidding. (P) You are hereby	350
directed to make tests of the samples. You should test the tarnish removal	426
ability of each, the degree of abrasiveness, the tendency to scratch exces-	500
sively, inflammability, acidity, the tendency to stain, and what, if any, poison-	580
ous cyanides or oxalates are present. (P) Your report should be ready by	650
January 15.	661

PROBLEM 3—TABULATED REPORT

Directions. Arrange this report on a full sheet of paper, making the necessary corrections indicated.

	STROKES
all caps — western conference	19
enrollment statistics	41
Center From the Educational Directory	72
The United States Office of Education	110

School	*Location*	No. of *Students*	*No. of Teachers*	158
Minnesota	Minneapolis, Minn.	32,205	2,154	200
[Illinois	Champaign, *Ill.*	[30,215	3,011 *144*	238
Ohio State	Columbus, Ohio	28,048]	2,060	277
Wisconsin	Madison, Wisconsin	25,514	1,955]	319
Michigan	ann arbor, mich.	22,876	1,025	358
Indiana	*Bloomington, Ind.*	*15,802*	458 *693*	397
Purdue #	Bloomington, Ind.	15,784	1,260	433
Michigan State	*East Lansing, Mich.*	15,444]	1,386	481
Iowa	Iowa City, Iowa	10,999	561 *601*	515
[Northwestern	*Evanston, Ill.*	10,200	*2,043*	555

Lafayette

Directions. Type for 5 minutes with the call of the **throw** at the end of each minute of typing. *Type on the skill-building level.*

	Strokes	Words
Pace yourself at a speed that you can handle. Build skill	59	12
by keeping the carriage moving along at a smooth and steady rate.	126	25
Get control of yourself first; then learn to control the machine.	191	38

Skill-Building Procedures. 1. Take a 1-minute writing with the 30-second call of the guide. This will give you a speed of 25 words a minute. *Type on the control level.*

2. Type the paragraph with the 20-second call of the guide. Take repeated writings until you can type at this 38-word rate. *Type on the exploration level.*

BONUS TYPING

Use the sentences from page 50 for bonus typing as time permits.

LESSON 34

CONDITIONING PRACTICE 34 *5 minutes*

Directions. Type each line three times. Double-space after the third typing of the line.

STROKES

Alphabetic sentence. The five jugs of liquid will be packed in my box for prizes. 60

Is Joe 27? I am 15. The date is January 9. Read page 384. 60

The check is for $150. Hart & Hunt's 4% note is due May 29. 60

PROGRESSION TYPING 34 *10 minutes*

Directions. The purpose of this typing is to build control in typing figures and symbols. You can expect a drop in your typing rate. That does not need to worry you. It is not even necessary to check your rate of typing, but the material shows the stroke and word count so that you can do so if you wish. Just keep the carriage moving steadily, and you will have all the speed you need. Begin with a half-minute writing. When you have typed a half minute without error, type for 1 minute; then for 2 minutes; and then for 3 minutes. *Type on the control level.*

	STROKES	WORDS
There are 10 pica or 12 elite spaces to a horizontal inch	58	12
and 6 lines to a vertical inch. A sheet of paper 8½ by 11	117	23
inches has 66 lines, therefore, and each line has 85 pica or	178	36
102 elite spaces. Don't space between #, $, or % and a figure	241	48
typed with it. These are details all of us must know.	295	59

INSTRUCTIONAL BLOCK 20

PRODUCTION MEASUREMENT

SECTION 42. Production Unit

LESSONS 236 TO 240

General Directions. In each lesson, you are to type for 30 minutes on the problems designated. Correct all errors as you type; uncorrected errors will be penalized. At the end of the fifth lesson, you will compute your stroking rate per minute. You will receive credit for each stroke typed. If you finish typing all problems before the end of the fifth lesson, go back to the beginning and retype as many problems as possible in the time remaining. Follow the specific directions given for each job. Prepare one carbon copy for each problem.

DAILY OUTLINE FOR LESSONS 236 TO 240

Conditioning Practice ....5 minutes   Assembling Materials .... 5 minutes

Production Typing ....30 minutes

CONDITIONING PRACTICE 236 TO 240   *5 minutes*

Directions. Type each sentence three times, or more if time permits. Double-space after the second typing of the line. Start writing slowly and increase your stroking rate gradually with each repetitive typing.

STROKES

Elvin or Lyle Maxwell quizzed both sections on kinds of jumping frogs.   70

That country had 73 canals, 68 inclines, 295 bridges, and 104 tunnels.   70

The man who knows where he wants to go has no trouble finding his way.   70

PRODUCTION TYPING 236 TO 240

PROBLEM I—BUSINESS LETTER

Directions. Type in modified block style with indented paragraphs; use open punctuation. Address an appropriate envelope and mark it AIR MAIL.

	STROKES
Current Date Prof. Woodie L.	33
Tucker School of Business North-	64
western University Evanston, Illi-	97
nois Dear Prof. Tucker (P) A per-	125
sonal library is a sound investment.	163
When selected with care and dis-	194
crimination, it is a valuable source	231
of vital information to the progres-	266
sive educator. Wouldn't you like to	303
add to your library the most out-	335
standing reference volume to come	369
off the press this year? (P) *Busi-*	403
ness, an internationally famous pub-	442
lication specializing in foreign and	479

	STROKES
domestic commerce, is one you	509
should have readily accessible. In	545
Business, you will find stimulating	589
articles on challenging and contro-	623
versial issues of our day written in	660
appealing style by outstandingly	693
successful journalists. Its subject	730
matter is authentic; its presentation,	769
attractive. It is unique among all	805
current business literature. (P) To	838
help you appraise this unusual pub-	872
lication, the publishers of *Business*	909
will send you at a special educators'	947
rate 12 issues of this wonderful mag-	983
azine for only $7.50—a rate $5 less	1010
than the regular subscription price	1046
of $12.50. At this greatly reduced	1082
price, you will receive for one year	1119

Tabulator-Key Control. Hold down the tabulator bar or key until the carriage completes its movement; then release the bar or key quickly.

Directions. You are to type columns of words and figures. You will set the machine to have 6 spaces between columns; therefore, after you clear the tabulator rack, make the following adjustments.

Steps. 1. Check the adjustment for the left margin.

2. Test the accuracy of your adjustments by depressing the tab bar or key and indenting to the columns 2 to 7. (You know that the first column is typed at the left margin and no tabulator stop is required for this column.)

3. Type the problem twice, using single spacing. Double-space after the first typing of the problem.

	PICA	ELITE
Left Margin	10	20
First Tabulator Stop	20	30
Second Tabulator Stop	30	40
Third Tabulator Stop	40	50
Fourth Tabulator Stop	50	60
Fifth Tabulator Stop	60	70
Sixth Tabulator Stop	70	80

Technique Emphasis. Hold the tab bar or key down until the carriage has stopped its movement.

								STROKES
they	6419	next	5720	them	7385	part		35
such	6310	play	7129	tell	9350	your		70
seem	7240	path	6184	than	6120	paid		105
well	9392	paid	3028	many	6280	hope		139

SKILL BUILDING 34 — *15 minutes*

Directions. Type for 5 minutes with the call of the throw at the end of each minute of typing. *Type on the skill-building level.*

	Strokes	Words
Right stroking is needed for speed and control. Use a	55	11
quick stroke. Center the action in your fingers. Equal power	118	24
in strokes will avoid having some letters light and some dark.	180	36

Skill-Building Procedures. 1. Take a 1-minute writing with the 30-second call of the guide. This will give you a speed of 24 words a minute. *Type on the skill-building level.*

2. Type the paragraph with the 20-second call of the guide. Take repeated writings until you can type at this 36-word rate. *Type on the exploration level.*

BONUS TYPING

Use the sentences from page 50 for bonus typing as time permits.

LESSON 35

CONDITIONING PRACTICE 35 — *5 minutes*

Directions. Type each line three times. Double-space after the third typing of the line.

		STROKES
Alphabetic sentence.	James quickly packed five more boxes with good frozen quail.	60
	3d#d 7j&j Knox & Hazard paid Bill #738. 2s"s 91(1 Joe is 29.	61
	Plan to work hard. Do all the work well. You can type well.	61

used; but, although it is no longer recommended, it is still used occasionally. Begin the subject notation at the left margin.

STROKES

In Re Education Convention 196

(d) Type the suggested titles of the talk in tabulated form. Omit the comma following the title. (This mark of punctuation is included to indicate to you the exact end of a title for the talk.)

STROKES

I shall be very glad to appear on 230
your program as the representative 265
of business to discuss the general 300
problems of education for better 333
business behavior. You may select 368
one of the following topics: Educa- 403

STROKES

tion and Business Leadership, Edu- 436
cation for the Improvement and 467
Preservation of Democracy, Educat- 500
ing the Future Business Leaders of 535
America, Education for Better Busi- 569
ness Behavior. Please inform me as 605
to the time I shall be scheduled to 641
speak, the place of the meeting, and, 679
if possible, the approximate number 715
expected in the audience. Cordially 752
yours a. r. horton 770

(e) Type your initials as the reference line but have the initials show on the carbon copy of the letter only. Refer to page 266 for directions for typing on the carbon copy only.

PROBLEM 2

STROKES

Directions. Use the modified block style of letter with no indentions for paragraphs. Use mixed punctuation. Type the "scrambled" address and closing lines in correct form. There are no errors to be corrected in the body of the letter.

STROKES

SUBJECT: all-risk insurance 29

mrs. raymond t chesterton 816 plaza 66
building san francisco 9, california 103
dear mrs. chesterton A few years 137
ago you needed fourteen policies for 174
adequate insurance coverage. To- 206
day, a householder normally needs 240
no more than four policies. This is 277
because of our All-Risk Insurance 311
plan, which has the "put-in" feature 348
—the policyholder names what is to 384
be covered in the policy. (P) Three 417
all-risk type insurance policies that 455
you should carry are: 478

Comprehensive Fire, Theft, 505
and Collision 519
Comprehensive Liability 543
Personal Property Floater 569

(P) For adequate coverage, the 596
DWELLING POLICY, which is 622

STROKES

not yet available on an all-risk basis, 662
is also needed. Even though this is 700
not an all-risk policy, it now pro- 734
tects against the hazards listed 767
below: 775

Fire, Lightning, and 796
Windstorm 806
Explosion (except steam 830
boilers) 838
Motor Vehicle and Aircraft 866
Damage 873
Water Damage (leaky roof, 899
broken pipes, etc.) 918
Vandalism and Malicious 942
Mischief 951

(P) Enclosed are three pamphlets 980
that will give you detailed informa- 1015
tion about our All-Risk Insurance. 1051
A personal representative of the 1084
company will be glad to call to dis- 1119
cuss your insurance needs if you will 1157
return the enclosed postage-free 1190
card indicating a convenient time 1224
for you to see him. (P) Thank you 1255
for your inquiry. Cordially yours 1290
robert w. jenkins, general agent 1322

PROBLEM 3

Directions. Use the remainder of the period for retyping Problem 2 as directed.

Directions. Begin with a half-minute writing. When you have typed a half minute without error, type for 1 minute; then for 2 minutes; and then for 3 minutes. *Type on the control level.*

	STROKES	WORDS
The pay for beginning typists varies quite a lot. It	54	11
ranges from $130 to $190 a month. When there are more workers	117	23
than jobs, the pay may drop to $120 a month. In good times	177	35
the good beginner will earn $140 to $160 and some will earn	237	47
$175 to $180 a month.	258	52

TECHNIQUE STUDY 35 *10 minutes*

Relaxation. Begin to type at a controlled, rhythmic rate; deliberately pace the typing at a speed that is slower than your best. Gradually increase your speed of stroking as your feeling of ease and certainty increases. If you make a misstroke, drop back to the slower rate.

Directions. Type each line three times, using the following practice procedures:

1. Type the word once as you say or think each letter. Relax the finger after each stroke.
2. Type the word the second time at an increased speed. Relax the finger after each stroke.
3. Say or think the word (not the letters) and type it the third and fourth time on the word-recognition level of response. Make the spacing a part of the rapid stroking of the word.

	STROKES
he he he he if if if if or or or or an an an an do do do do	59
me me me me to to to to us us us us of of of of it it it it	59
for for for for and and and and the the the the sir sir sir sir	63

TIMED WRITING 35 *15 minutes*

Directions. Type for 5 minutes. Determine the cwpm.

	STROKES	WORDS
That study educates that gives you the power to do, the	56	11
power to think, and the power to feel. You must have power	116	23
to do things; that is how you will carry your share of the	175	35
work of the world. You must have the power to think things,	236	47
for only in that way can you grow. You must have the power	296	59
to feel things, for feeling is life itself. Do all you can	356	71
to grow in the power to do, to think, and to feel. You will	417	83
grow in the power to do things, to think things, and to feel	478	96
things as you use these powers day by day, for we learn to	537	107
do by doing, to think by thinking, and to feel by feeling.	595	119

Skill-Building Procedures. Practice the difficult words, such as *educates, power, itself*; then take a second 5-minute writing and note the improvement.

Directions. Set the machine for a 60-space line and single spacing. Type the number of each problem 4 spaces outside the left margin.

1. Type the address and salutation in block form with open punctuation.

	STROKES
mr. joseph d. ellsworth	24
president, ellsworth & west	52
st. louis 6, missouri	74
dear mr ellsworth	91

2. Type the address given as Problem 1, but address the letter to the company and call it to the attention of Mr. Ellsworth. Add an appropriate salutation.

3. Make needed corrections as you type the address and opening lines of the letter. Use close punctuation and the block style.

	STROKES
Messrs. Campbell Products Company,	35
2,351 East 51st Str.	57
St. Paul, 16, Minnesota	81
Dear Mr. Campbell:	99
Your letter of the 16th has been re-	134
ceived. Order #2,390 will be shipped on	174
or about the 22d. of the month.	204

4. Make needed corrections as you type. Use open punctuation and the indented style.

	STROKES
Dr. E. J. Brown, M. D.	23
1207—1209 Terrace Plaza Building	57
Jacksonville 2, Florida	91
My Dear Dr. Brown	108

5. Type the correct salutation for a letter addressed to a man and a woman.

6. Type the correct salutation for a letter addressed to a company made up of women.

7. Insert another sheet of paper and type a second-page heading for the letter of Problem 1.

8. Type the concluding line of a paragraph and the lines of the tabulated report:

			STROKES
below show how fast your dollars will			38
add up in a few years:			62
Weekly	Two-Year	Four-Year	108
Deposit	Total	Total	
$10	$1,040.00	$2,080.00	131

9. Type the closing lines for a letter to be signed by E. O. Paulson, Credit Manager of the McCloskey-MacArthur Company. Add the appropriate reference line and an enclosure notation itemized to show two enclosures — Check for $500 and Form of Agreement.

LESSON 235

CONDITIONING PRACTICE 235   *5 minutes*

	STROKES
How did they know about the quizzing of the experts on juvenile crime?	70
My check for $136.50 is dated May 27. Order #849 can go out on May 2.	70
It is in the minds of men that the defense against wars must be built.	70

PROBLEM TYPING 235—MEASUREMENT   *35 minutes*

PROBLEM I

Directions. The various parts of this problem will, when completed, make up a letter. Type the parts on one sheet of paper. Make a carbon copy.

(a) Use a 60-space line, open punctuation, and the block form of letter. Type the current date at the left margin. On a line with the date and typed to end near the right margin, type the following copy:

	STROKES
In reply please refer to	25
File No. 469-Y	39

(b) Use the block form. As the personal title is unusually long, it may be placed on two lines in the address.

	STROKES
dr. fred c. overton associate su-	71
perintendent and director of per-	103
sonnel board of education arlington,	140
illinois my dear dr. overton	169

(c) The notation "In Re" or "re" is sometimes used in place of the word "Subject." This expression means "in the matter of" or "concerning." It was once commonly

INSTRUCTIONAL BLOCK 3

PROBLEM TYPING

Problem typing is not new to you, but the problems in the lessons of this instructional block will be appropriately different from those you have typed in former lessons. Type each problem at an easy rate so that you can think as you type.

Bonus Typing. As the goal of your typing practice is the power to type problems of different kinds and of varying difficulty, extra practice on selected problems should be done as time permits. Extra credit may be allowed for additional typing of the problems.

SECTION 7. Problem Typing

Machine Checkup and Adjustments

1. Check the placement of the paper guide; paper-bail rolls; paper bail; and see that the ribbon indicator is set for typing on the upper half of the ribbon.
2. Unless otherwise directed, set the stop for the left margin at 12 for a pica-type machine or at 20 for an elite-type machine. Set a tabulator stop for a 5-space paragraph indention. Use single spacing for drills and double spacing for paragraphs.

These directions will be used in each lesson of this section except where other directions are given, as with the problem typing. Follow these directions even though they are not repeated.

LESSON 36

CONDITIONING PRACTICE 36   *5 minutes*

Directions. Type the paragraph twice.

Line 5: The dash is typed with two hyphens without spacing between it and the preceding or the following word.

All letters of the alphabet are used in this paragraph.

	STROKES	WORDS
We often say that there isn't time enough in which to do	57	11
all the things that must be done. We evade, pretend, bluff,	118	24
or just muddle on. A great hurry has seized us. We have an	179	36
excess of motion, but not quite enough sense of direction.	239	48
As a result, we get nowhere. We don't blame ourselves--we	298	60
must have a scapegoat; so we blame luck.	338	68

THINGS TO REMEMBER WHEN CENTERING   *5 minutes*

You will need to remember:

1. Full-size sheets of paper are 11 inches long.
2. There are 6 lines to a vertical inch; therefore, a full-size sheet of paper has a total of 66 writing lines.
3. A horizontal inch of elite type has 12 spaces.
4. A horizontal inch of pica type has 10 spaces.
5. The paper is $8\frac{1}{2}$ inches wide and has 102 elite or 85 pica spaces across the page.
6. A half sheet has the same horizontal line of 102 elite or 85 pica spaces, but a half sheet has only 33 vertical lines (half of the 66 writing lines for a full-size sheet of paper).

the following is a report of the number of years our present tenants have lived in our property and the monthly rents received under the terms of our alamo rental contract:

name of tenant	yrs. tenant has lived in property	monthly rents	STROKES
			179
			215
			250
			283
			320
			383
j. m. watson	2½	$132.50	408
daniel jones	1	98.00	430
cecil morris	1½	76.00	453
w. o. green	2	87.50	474
wm. nichols	5	47.50	495
homer cobb	3½	92.00	516

(e) Remove your paper and insert another sheet as you would if you were typing a two-page letter. Type a second-page heading, properly placed, to correspond with the address given in item (a). Leave the correct number of spaces between the second-page heading and the first line of writing. Type the following closing lines of the body of the letter.

	STROKES
we are enclosing with this letter	550
blueprint no. 40-y and a copy of the	587
specifications for the improvement	622
of our property in the alamo sub-	654
division.	665

(f) Type the closing lines in correct order blocked at the complimentary close position. Use your initials in the reference notation. List the items of the enclosures under the word "Enclosures" with each item indented 5 spaces from the left margin. This is one way to indicate enumerated enclosures.

	STROKES
very truly yours	683
hartwell-morton co., inc.	709
lester g. hartwell	729
general secretary and treasurer	761
enclosures	772
blueprint no. 40-y	791
specifications	805

PROBLEM 2—SKILL BUILDING

Directions. Take 1-minute writings on parts of Problem 1 attempting to add to the ease and the speed with which you can type difficult portions of the problem.

Let the first test begin with the date and type through as much of the address, salutation, and subject line as possible. Start the next test with the first paragraph of the letter and type as far as you can. Then start a 1-minute writing with the tabulated copy for which you have the machine adjustments already made. Use the closing paragraph and the closing lines for another 1-minute writing.

Repeat the difficult portions of the problem in 1-minute writings as skill-building practice that will increase production rate.

SKILL MAINTENANCE 233   *10 minutes*

Directions. Use each line for two 1-minute writings. Make needed corrections as you type the second and third lines. Determine the cwpm for each writing.

	STROKES	WORDS
Build right skills in your fingering and right attitudes in your mind.	70	14
200 is what he paid. They sold 290 sheep and sixty-three hogs.	70	14
i saw the book, *profile of a typist,* but not *ready for the typing job.*	70	14

LESSON 234

CONDITIONING PRACTICE 234   *5 minutes*

	STROKES
The Fox Quick Frozen Foods proved to be just as good as Wymetal Foods.	70
I typed the following drill: he 36 so 92 if 58 or 49 up 70 and by 65.	70
If you make an error, pause; then begin typing without hurry or worry.	70

VERTICAL CENTERING

1. Count the lines in the problem.

2. Subtract the total lines required to type the problem from the available lines (66 lines for a full sheet or 33 lines for a half sheet).

3. Divide the remaining number of lines by 2 to get the top and bottom margins. If the result contains a fraction, disregard it.

HORIZONTAL CENTERING

Use the backspacing method of centering in these first problems irrespective of the typewriter you are operating. This method of centering is very exact provided you work from the center of the paper.

Turn to the illustration of the typewriter you are using, pages V to IX, and read the directions for adjusting the paper guide and determining the centering point.

1. Check the placement of the paper guide.

2. Clear the tabulator rack.

3. Move the carriage to the centering point. Set a tabulator stop.

4. Backspace once for each two spaces in the line to be centered. If there is one letter left, do not backspace for it. Begin to type at the point where the backspacing is completed.

5. Tabulate to the centering point; backspace to center the next line; and type.

PROBLEM TYPING 36   *25 minutes*

PROBLEM I

Directions. Use a half sheet of paper. Center the problem vertically so that you will have equal top and bottom margins. Center each line horizontally. Use double spacing.

Carl van der Voort & Company

announce the removal of their offices to the

PLAZA BUILDING

on January 9

ANALYSIS OF VERTICAL CENTERING

Lines on half sheet, 8½ by 5½ inches	33
Lines to be used in typing the drill	7
Lines to be divided between top and bottom margins	26

26 ÷ 2 = 13

Therefore: top margin, 13 lines
             bottom margin, 13 lines

Proof: 13 + 13 + 7 = 33

What would be the top and bottom margins for this same problem if the announcement were typed on paper 8½ by 11 inches?

PROBLEM 2

Directions. This second problem in centering is to be typed on a half sheet of paper in double-spaced form. Center the problem vertically; center each line horizontally. The first two lines when centered will look as follows:

Business Arithmetic

Bookkeeping

Type the entire problem in a similar manner. Follow the steps for vertical and horizontal centering.

Business Arithmetic
Bookkeeping
Consumer Business Education
Economics
General Business
Office and Secretarial Practice
Shorthand
Transcription
Typewriting

(c) When the typed company name consists of a company name and a division name, the two names may be typed on two lines, each line centered from the middle point of the complimentary close. The name of the dictator and his title are then typed as usual below the division name, and they are also centered from the middle point of the complimentary close. (See Illustration 67.)

	STROKES
Very truly yours RALPH LANDE &	930
SONS, INC. Division Office Equip-	962
ment Mfrs. Ralph Lande, Manager	993

Very truly yours

RALPH LANDE & SONS, INC.
Division Office Equipment Mfrs.

Ralph Lande, Manager

Illustration 67 — Company Name and Division Name Typed on Two Lines, Centered from the Middle Point of the Complimentary Close

PROBLEM 2—SKILL BUILDING 232

Directions. Make pencil corrections in the letter typed as Problem 1, if corrections are needed. Retype the letter as directed.

SKILL MAINTENANCE 232   *10 minutes*

Directions. Use each sentence for two 1-minute writings. Make needed corrections as you type the third line. Determine the cwpm for each writing.

	STROKES	WORDS
The right kind of practice can improve your typing skill a great deal.	70	14
They will find the quotation in Volume VII, Section 23, pages 198-205.	70	14
joe smiths birthday is on january 9 and he will be exactly seventeen.	64	13

LESSON 233

CONDITIONING PRACTICE 233   *5 minutes*

	STROKES
Lew and Buck have failed to report the tax quiz to County Judge Smith.	70
What is the sum of 48 and 295 and 374 and 260 and 501 and 205 and 936?	70
You need to know what you really know as well as what you do not know.	70

PROBLEM TYPING 233   *25 minutes*

PROBLEM I

Directions. Use a 60-space line, single spacing, close punctuation, and the modified block form with the closing lines blocked at the complimentary close position. Type the current date placed to end approximately at the right margin. Use paragraph indentions of 10 spaces. Make needed corrections.

(a) Type the address on the seventh space below the date line.

	STROKES
attention mr. ralph b. murray	33
worthington real estate company	66
san antonio 2, texas	89
496-498 edgeworth street	114

(b) Type the correct salutation for the address given as item (a).

(c) Type the subject heading in the correct position for a letter with indented paragraphs.

	STROKES
subject: alamo rental contract	146

(d) Type the opening paragraph of the letter with a 10-space paragraph indention. Type the tabulated copy to follow the paragraph and use 7 spaces between columns. Center each column heading above its column.

PROBLEM 3

Directions. Up to this lesson you have been typing line for line as the copy has been arranged and have not, therefore, needed the bell as a warning for the line ending. You must now learn to use the right margin stop and to listen for the ringing of the bell so that you will be able to type from unarranged copy and yet have an acceptable right margin.

Set the margin stops at 12 and 77 for a pica- or at 20 and 85 for an elite-type machine. These adjustments will provide a 60-space line with 5 spaces added at the right margin. On most typewriters the bell rings 7 or 8 spaces before the stop for the right margin. Your bell should, therefore, ring 2 or 3 spaces before the place where you want the line to end.

The sentence you are to type on one line is longer than the 60-space line for which the typewriter is set. When the bell rings, type on until the carriage locks; then depress the margin release key (No. 25) and type the remainder of the word. This is the way to type outside the right margin. Type the sentence five times, using double spacing.

NOTE: On the Underwood typewriter, you will have 4 more spaces to use after the line lock has been released when you depress the margin release key. On other typewriters, the margin release key releases the line lock entirely and you can type to the end of the paper.

	STROKES
Every day you should wipe or brush the dust off your typewriter.	64

SKILL MAINTENANCE 36   *5 minutes*

Directions. Use each sentence for two 1-minute writings. Think the *word,* and *type on the exploration level.*

	Strokes	Words 20″	Words 15″
If I use time wisely, I may have more time to use.	50	30	40
Now is the time to make a close check of typing habits.	55	33	44

NOTE: If time permits, type each sentence for 1 minute with the appropriate call of the guide. Your teacher will tell you whether to use the 20- or the 15-second call for the guide.

LESSON 37

CONDITIONING PRACTICE 37   *5 minutes*

Directions. Type each line twice. Double-space after the second typing of the line. If time permits, retype all or selected lines.

	STROKES
Karl Byes was just hoping for a quiet day in Vera Cruz, Mexico.	63
2s ”s Howe & Hays wrote, “Ship 27 cars of 4/4 Oak by March 30.”	63
A check is for $839.61. Isn’t a $50 bond (Class I) due May 27?	63

PROBLEM TYPING 37   *25 minutes*

PROBLEM 1

Directions. Center the problem vertically and center the heading horizontally on a half sheet of paper. Triple-space between the heading and the first line of the problem.

	STROKES	WORDS
CHARACTERS NOT ON THE KEYBOARD	31	6
EXCLAMATION POINT. Type the apostrophe; backspace, and	87	17
type the period.	105	21
SPACING RULE. Space once after an exclamation point	158	32
typed within a sentence; twice, at the end of a sentence.	217	43
Example: You must think! and work! Work hard!	270	54

Directions. 1. Use the paragraph for a 1-minute writing; then set a goal of 2 or 3 words more than you typed and take another 1-minute writing.

2. Type for 2 minutes; then set a goal of 2 or 3 words more than you typed and take another 2-minute writing.

3. Type additional 1 or 2-minute writings as time permits.

	STROKES
Keep them flying. Make those fingers go where you want them to go and	71
at the speed you want them to make. Relax the shoulders and arms; hold	143
the hands quiet and do not let the elbows weave in and out. Throw that car-	218
riage with a swift wrist and finger movement. Let the power flow smoothly	293
to the fingers so the typing will be without jerks. Emphasize the release	368
of the key through the swift stroke of poised fingers held lightly on the	442
keys. Keep them flying—but keep them flying to the right keys.	506

LESSON 232

CONDITIONING PRACTICE 232   *5 minutes*

	STROKES
He will very quickly excel in typing and amaze just about all of them.	70
Invoice #912736 for $28,147.50 is subject to a 2% discount in 10 days.	70
It is not so much what they can get as what they can give that counts.	70

PROBLEM TYPING 232   *25 minutes*

PROBLEM I—LEARNING THE NATURE OF THE PROBLEM

Directions. The various parts of this problem will make up a complete letter.

(a) Use a 60-space line, single spacing, open punctuation, and the modified block form. Type the current date placed to end approximately at the right margin. Begin the address 5 spaces below the date line. Note the salutation for a firm composed of a man and a woman.

	STROKES
John and Ruth Williams Commer-	30
cial Artists 2916 Main Street Spring-	66
field, Ohio Dear Sir and Madam	97

(b) Type the paragraphs with single spacing and a 5-space paragraph indention. Paragraph and capitalize the letter.

	STROKES
thank you for your letter inquiring	133
about the types of furniture we	165
would recommend for your new	194
office. we are enclosing with this	230
letter two folders that illustrate the	269
various types of office furniture that	308
we believe would be suitable for your	346
needs. the folders also give the	380
prices quoted by the dealer in your	416
city. you will want to be in personal	455
touch with the dealer so that he can	492
give you the best possible attention.	531
we are writing him today to call you	568
for an appointment. if he can see the	607
exact size and arrangement of the	641
rooms for which the furniture is	674
needed, he will be better able to sug-	711
gest the most desirable equipment.	747
we greatly appreciate your interest	783
in our line of office equipment. we	820
hope that you will be able to find	855
just what you need in our large	887
selection.	899

PROBLEM 2

Directions. Center the problem vertically and center the heading horizontally on a half sheet of paper.

	STROKES	WORDS
CHARACTERS NOT ON THE KEYBOARD	31	6

FRACTIONS NOT ON THE KEYBOARD. In typing "made"	80	16
fractions, use the / with the figures. In typing $\frac{1}{2}$ or $\frac{1}{4}$	137	27
with other fractions, use the / for typing all fractions	194	39
uniformly.	206	41
SPACING RULE. Space between the whole number and the	260	52
"made" fraction; but if you use a fraction key for $\frac{1}{2}$ or $\frac{1}{4}$,	319	64
do not space between the whole number and the fraction.	376	75
Examples: The rug is 15 3/4 by 18 1/2 feet.	422	84
The room is $24\frac{1}{2}$ feet long.	448	90

ACTION TYPING 37   *5 minutes*

In this action typing, you will not copy the material as it appears in the book; instead you will read the directions and type what you are told to type.

Directions. Use double spacing. Read direction 1, and type what you are directed to type; then read direction 2, and type what you are directed to type; follow the same procedure for 3 and 4. Do not number the problems as you type.

1. Center your name $1\frac{1}{2}$ inches (9 spaces) from the top of the paper.
2. Center the date below your name.
3. Type the sentence below, beginning at the left margin; but type the dash instead of the word *dash* and end the sentence with an exclamation point.

He can think well <u>dash</u> but so can I

4. In typing the sentences below, change the words for the whole numbers and fractions into figures.

John is <u>six</u> <u>and</u> <u>a</u> <u>half</u> feet tall.

The rug is <u>twelve</u> <u>and</u> <u>three</u> <u>quarters</u> feet long.

SKILL MAINTENANCE 37   *5 minutes*

Directions. Set the machine for single spacing. Use each sentence for two 1-minute writings. Think the *word,* and *type on the exploration level.*

	Strokes	Words 20″	Words 15″
Keep on trying to do well, and you will do very well.	53	32	42
Each day you can pace your typing just a little faster.	55	33	44

SECTION 41. Sampling Letter Problems

LESSON 231

CONDITIONING PRACTICE 231

STROKES

Peter may have to make two quick flights to Mexico and Brazil in June.   70
Six of the 469 fourth-semester students typed for 35 minutes at 72 cwpm.   70
Jane would not come down town for a new gown to take to the big party.   70

PROBLEM TYPING 231

25 minutes

You must learn to adapt letter styles to forms acceptable in different offices. The problems in the lessons of this section represent a sampling of many of the fundamental techniques and the related knowledge taught in earlier portions of this book. Some of the problems show new or modified forms you should note. As you type the problems, make the necessary corrections so that the work will be usable. If you do not know the correct form for a problem, use the table of contents or the index to this book and find the illustrations and instructions in earlier lessons that will give you an understanding of the way the problem should be typed.

PROBLEM I—LEARNING THE NATURE OF THE PROBLEM

Directions. The various parts of this problem will, when completed, make up a letter. Type the parts on one sheet of paper as you are instructed in items (a) to (d).

(a) Use a 60-space line, open punctuation, and the modified block form of letter. Type the current date placed to end approximately at the right margin. Type the address in single-spaced form on the seventh space below the date line. Note the salutation used in a letter addressed to a firm composed of women.

STROKES

mary and june barth 914 east main   34
street cincinnati 6, ohio ladies   67

(b) A combination of single spacing for the address and double spacing for the body of the letter may be used for short letters. This gives another variation of the modified block form of letter inasmuch as the address will be typed in blocked form.

Use a 10-space paragraph indention and double spacing.

Add needed capitals and divide the letter into two or more paragraphs.

STROKES

thank you for returning to us the   101
application for a charge account. we   139
have checked the references you   171
listed in the application and have   206
found them to be highly satisfac-   238
tory. we shall therefore be glad to   275
open an account for you. our usual   311
credit terms are 2 per cent within   346
10 days, net 30 days. we shall be   381
happy to take care of your orders on   418
these terms.   432

(c) Type the closing lines of the letter blocked at the complimentary close position. Note the form of the typed company name when lower case letters must be used.

STROKES

yours very truly   449
McCreery-McIntosh Stores, Inc.   480
D. O. Wilson, Credit Manager   508

(d) If the letter is placed too high on the page, you can give it length by typing the reference initials 4, 6, or even 8 spaces below the dictator's name.

PROBLEM 2—SKILL BUILDING

Directions. Make pencil corrections in the letter typed as Problem 1, if corrections are needed. Type the letter a second time, but make a carbon copy. Erase and correct all errors. Address an envelope. Arrange the completed letter in form for pen signature.

LESSON 38

5 minutes

Directions. Type the paragraph twice or use the paragraph for three 1-minute writings with a goal of easy, continuous typing.

All letters of the alphabet are used in the paragraph.

	Strokes	Words
Keep on typing! There is no need to rush or to hurry.	56	11
Hit the key and turn loose of it. To excel, don't hurry--just	119	24
keep on typing! Your skill will grow as you learn to keep the	182	36
carriage moving quite evenly. This skill is the prize to be	243	49
sought in each day's practice.	273	55

PROBLEM TYPING 38 *30 minutes*

PROBLEM I

The purpose of this tabulated report of 7 columns is to provide practice in the control of the tabulator mechanism and the carriage throw and to speed up your typing of figures.

Directions. Clear the tabulator rack. Set the stop for the left margin at 8 for a pica- or at 10 for an elite-type machine; move the stop for the right margin to the end of the line. The first column will be typed at the left margin. Set the tabulator stops as directed:

	PICA	ELITE
First tabulator stop	19	23
Second tabulator stop	30	36
Third tabulator stop	41	49
Fourth tabulator stop	52	62
Fifth tabulator stop	63	75
Sixth tabulator stop	74	88

Center the problem vertically with triple spacing between the heading and the first line of the problem. Type the heading centered horizontally.

STROKES

TABULATOR CONTROL AND CARRIAGE THROW

for	the	and	use	sir	did	pay	
for	the	and	use	sir	did	pay	65
key	aid	fit	own	rid	man	lay	93
841	481	148	731	317	137	847	121
621	261	126	951	159	591	956	149
had	has	one	any	day	say	lay	177
was	him	are	mop	fed	lip	bar	205
361	471	580	650	741	831	921	233
206	307	401	508	209	301	506	260

(heading strokes: 37)

PROBLEM 2

Directions. Use Problem 1 as a 5-minute writing. Type the problem in the same way you typed it before, but type under time. If you complete the typing of the problem before time is called, repeat as much of the body of the problem as you can but do not type the heading in this repeated typing. *Type on the skill-building level.*

Score this timed writing of the tabulated problem as you would score a similar typing of a paragraph. Contrast this score with that you have made when typing a paragraph.

ACTION TYPING 38 *5 minutes*

Directions. In Problem Typing 38, you had the machine set for seven columns. Use the same adjustments for this action typing. Type the lines as directed below:
   a. Type the figures 830 in each of the seven columns.
   b. Type the figures 26 in each of the seven columns, remembering to space once to align the figures correctly.
   c. Type the figure 9 in each of the seven columns.

LESSON 230

CONDITIONING PRACTICE 230 — 5 minutes

	STROKES
James Knox was very brief, which is a quality prized by good speakers.	70
The 4½% note for $950 is dated June 29. Policy #268913 is for $7,500.	70
Be sure that you know when you are right; then go on and do your work.	70

TIMED WRITING 230 — 20 minutes

Directions. Use a 70-space line, a 5-space paragraph indention, and double spacing. Type three 5-minute writings. *Type on the control level.* Choose the best writing to be handed in for record.

Each paragraph has every letter of the alphabet and a syllable intensity of 1.40.

	STROKES	WORDS
Office work is not "cut and dried"—work that must be borne for the	68	14
sake of a small wage. An office is a place where you can work out your	140	28
business future, mature in personal qualities, and serve the public as	211	42
well as any other citizen. Many office jobs require constant work under	284	57
pressure. If you have not really learned how to stand up under the	352	70
demand of maximum production, put yourself to that test without delay.	424	85
In an office, employers usually rate workers on the basis of how much	494	99
they can do plus the kind of persons they are. Expert copying speed is	566	113
just a means to an end, and the end is the ability to transfer this speed	640	128
to the typing of business forms, such as letters, invoices, and reports.	714	143
Production is what counts when it comes to the measurement of your work;	787	157
but your character traits enter into the extent of your fitness for quick	861	172
promotion. Do not minimize skill, but do not overlook the need of a poised	930	186
and balanced personality.	964	193
Businessmen declare that the typist must be able to do a day's work	1032	206
judged by business standards. The size of the salary check will depend on	1107	221
how much, as well as how well, the typist does. It is not always true that	1183	237
the champion speed typist is the champion office worker. When other con-	1255	251
siderations are equal, though, the worker who has expert skill in typing	1328	266
will be able to command a better place in the business world than the	1398	280
worker who has just average skill. Nowhere is speed more needed than in	1471	294
business, but there must be accuracy with the speed. Business does not	1543	309
forgive quickly the one who fails to correct his work.	1597	319

SKILL BUILDING 230 — 10 minutes

```
     1    2    3    4    5    6    7    8    9   10   11   12   13   14
You will walk a mile by taking one step at a time.  Begin to step now.
By hitting one key at a time, I can type as rapidly as I need to type.
Know that you can type well.  Then type with ease and with confidence.
     1    2    3    4    5    6    7    8    9   10   11   12   13   14
```

SKILL MAINTENANCE 230 — 5 minutes

	STROKES	WORDS
We are all not a ble to work at the same rate of speed.	70	14

LESSON 39

Directions. Use a 70-space line; that is, set the margin stops for pica type at 7 and 82 or for elite type at 15 and 90. Type each line twice. Double-space after the second typing of the line. If time permits, retype all or selected lines.

	STROKES
Jack Goff would have been quite happy for a month in Texas or Arizona.	70
Cedric cashed the check. Robert Browne brought the baggage to Boston.	70
This is not hard to do. This is not hard to do when I want to do it!	71

THE BELL AND THE RIGHT MARGIN STOP

When material is not to be typed line for line, you must set the stop for the right margin and listen for the bell so that you will know when to throw the carriage. As is explained on pages VI *to* IX, the centering point is 42 for a pica- and 50 for an elite-type machine. Therefore, a 40-space line should be written between 22 and 62 on a pica-type machine and between 30 and 70 on an elite-type machine. As the bell usually rings 7 or 8 spaces before the machine locks, the stop for the right margin should be set 5 spaces after the desired right margin. It is possible, then, to have a line about the length desired. Note the chart at the right.

As you are typing each line, listen for the ringing of the bell to indicate that you are approaching the end of the line. When the bell rings, complete the word you are typing and throw the carriage. If the carriage should lock before the word is completed, operate the margin release and complete the word.

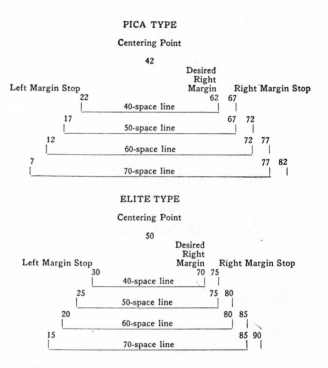

PROBLEM TYPING 39   *25 minutes*

PROBLEM I

Directions. Type the following paragraph three times: First, with a 70-space line; second, with a 60-space line; and third, with a 50-space line.

As you type, listen for the ringing of the bell to guide you in throwing the carriage.

	STROKES	WORDS
Do you like to read? You can share the lives of others through books.	72	14
You can get away from the gloom of any dark day that comes your way	140	28
if you have some good books at hand and will lose yourself in them. Chase	215	43
away the gloom of a dark day with a good book.	261	52

PROBLEM 2

Directions. Type the following short theme on a half sheet of paper with a 60-space line, double spacing, and a 5-space paragraph indention. Center the problem horizontally. Type the title on the ninth line from the top of the page, and leave 2 blank lines between the title and the paragraph. Listen for the ringing of the bell to guide you in throwing the carriage.

If time permits, repeat the writing of this paragraph.

Directions. Type two 3-minute writings to reconstruct your skill in typing a tabulated report. Refer to page 146 if you need detailed instructions on setting up the problem.

			STROKES
Total Sales and Balance Due			28
Daniels Manufacturing Co.	$294,150	$3,768	72
Harrison Sales, Inc.	82,735	946	107
Winlock + Hatcher	9,284	1,305	138

LESSON 229

CONDITIONING PRACTICE 229   *5 minutes*

STROKES

Five boys played quiet games that were extra puzzling to Jack and Ned.   70

Tom read pages 139-476 of *Economic Foundations* between 8:30 and 12:15.   70

Try not to make errors. But if you do so, find them and correct them.   70

TYPING FOR CONTROL 229   *20 minutes*

Directions. Use the paragraphs of TYPING FOR CONTROL 226, pages 272 and 273, as directed. You should be able to type this material with greater ease and control than when you practiced it before.

SKILL BUILDING 229   *10 minutes*

Directions. Type each line as two 1-minute writings with the 12- or the 10-second call of the guide. If you cannot type the entire line at the rate called for by the guide used, select an appropriate portion of the line that will keep you typing at your maximum rate.

```
          1      2      3      4      5      6      7      8      9     10     11     12     13     14
It is worth while to try for that which is worth while.  Work and win.
Know what to do and how to do it:  Work, and do not doubt the outcome.
Each of us must believe in something.  We must have faith in the good.
          1      2      3      4      5      6      7      8      9     10     11     12     13     14
```

SKILL MAINTENANCE 229   *5 minutes*

Directions. Type each sentence as a 1-minute writing, making needed corrections in capitalization and punctuation.

	STROKES	WORDS
the principals talk to the girls group was on principles of justice.	70	14
i am sure that you Mr. Long will agree with our general conclusions.	70	14

RAIN

	STROKES	WORDS
	5	1

The sounds of the night were stilled, like a frightened child, with held
breath, unexpectedly alone in an unlighted room. Several quick flashes of
lightning zigzagged into the jet blackness of the night as big drops of
rain splashed on the ground. I leaned far out a window and saw, by the
light of the great streaks of lightning, the bed of wilted tulips lift their
petals to the cool freshness of the rain.

STROKES	WORDS
78	16
153	31
225	45
297	59
374	75
415	83

SKILL MAINTENANCE 39   *10 minutes*

Directions. Use each sentence for three 1-minute writings. Think the word, and *type on the exploration level.*

	Strokes	Words 20″	Words 15″
I am sure that you can learn to do this with some ease.	55	33	44
Try to get out of the rut before you lose the power to grow.	60	36	48
They worry too much about the things that mean little or nothing.	65	39	52

LESSON 40

CONDITIONING PRACTICE 40   *5 minutes*

Directions. Type each line two or three times. Double-space between groups of lines. If time permits, retype all or selected lines.

	STROKES
The lamp Joe and Barry have is not quite the size for the Klug Wax Co.	70
Mr. Kane must be in Atlantic City, New Jersey, on July 12 by 9:45 a.m.	70
Jack owes us $15, doesn't he? Is Paul's bill 75 cents? We owe $6.30.	70

PROBLEM TYPING 40   *20 minutes*

Directions. Use a 70-space line and single spacing. Type the problem twice. Center each writing vertically on a full sheet of paper.

Type the sentences on the control level, using the stroke-level of response.

		STROKES
(1)	Express percentage and decimals in figures.	43
(2)	He will pay 4½% interest for the $500 loan.	
(3)	Type words to state approximate age in years.	45
(4)	Robert Barton is nearly thirty-six years old.	
(5)	Invoice and order numbers are typed in figures.	47
(6)	The Harris & Long Invoice #612 is dated May 28.	
(7)	Express measures, weight, and distance in figures.	50
(8)	Joe used 6 quarts of oil on his trip of 821 miles.	
(9)	Type fractions not on the keyboard with the diagonal.	53
(10)	Be uniform in typing fractions; as ¼, ½, or 1/4, 1/2.	
(11)	Type even sums of money without the decimal or ciphers.	55
(12)	Joe's policy for $6,000 is #846392; it expires in 1957.	
(13)	Type numbers used at the beginning of a sentence in full.	57
(14)	Two hundred seventy-six men were lost on that expedition.	

(This problem is completed on the following page.)

LESSON 228

CONDITIONING PRACTICE 228

STROKES

Judge Forker was very puzzled by the excitement of the men questioned.   70

The $800 note dated March 24, 1967, bears interest at the rate of $3\frac{1}{2}\%$.   70

Look at the record of your work and let it tell how well you now type.   70

TYPING FOR CONTROL 228   *15 minutes*

Progression Typing for Control. Type a 1-, a 2-, and a 3-minute writing. *Type on the control level of practice.*

Guided Writing with the Line Endings Called. Type for 1 minute with the guide for the line ending called each 15 seconds, which will give a speed of 45 words. Type for 2 minutes with the 15-second call of the guide, which will give an average speed of 49 words a minute.

Selected-Goal Typing. Select a goal that is 1 or 2 words faster than you have been typing in this lesson. Check the half-minute and minute goals. Use a 70-space writing line. Your teacher will call "Half," and "One." Repeat the writing, increasing the goal by 1 or 2 words.

STROKES

When you apply for your first position, it will help   53

you to be able to point to a successful work experience   109

even if it has been gained on a part-time job. On a job   166

you will measure up to your office standards of performance   226

or someone else will take your place. Try to have some office   289

experience now. Do work for your teachers or for your father or   354

brother if you cannot get work after school. The pay you may earn   421

will mean less to you than the learning experience that will be yours.   492

SKILL BUILDING 228   *5 minutes*

Directions. Type each line as two 1-minute writings with the 12- or the 10-second call of the guide. If you cannot type the entire line at the rate called for by the guide used, select an appropriate portion of the line that will keep you typing at your maximum rate.

Dust the typewriter each day; keep the desk clean; be a good "duster."

Brush the type with a forward and backward motion. Brush it each day.

Make up your mind what you want. Hold this in mind until you have it.

(15) Use figures in stating exact age in years, months, and days.   60
(16) Margaret Marvin is exactly 17 years 2 months and 9 days old.
(17) Spell the hour in full when "o'clock" is used for stating time.   63
(18) Mr. Robertson will be in his office at eleven o'clock tomorrow.
(19) Type distance in figures except when indicating less than a mile.   65
(20) It is 220 miles from Annapolis, Maryland, to Lynchburg, Virginia.
(21) Type policy numbers without a comma between hundreds and thousands.   67
(22) Policy #104836 for $7,000 has been issued to Albert Richard Speers.
(23) When two numbers immediately follow each other, spell out the smaller.   70
(24) Elvin bought 275 two-cent stamps and 195 three-cent stamped envelopes.

ACTION TYPING 40   *7 minutes*

In preceding lessons you have typed outside the right margin. You will now learn how to type outside the left margin.

For All Typewriters Except the Underwood: To move the carriage outside the point at which the stop for the left margin is set, depress the margin release key (No. 25) and move the carriage (or backspace) to the point at which the typing is to begin.

For the Underwood Typewriter: To move the carriage outside the point at which the stop for the left margin is set, depress the left margin release latch (No. B) and move the carriage to the point at which the typing is to begin. On this typewriter, the keyboard margin release key is to be used when it is necessary to type beyond the right margin, and the left margin release latch must be used to move the carriage outside the left margin.

Directions. Set the margin stops for a 60-space line (12 and 77 for a pica- or 20 and 85 for an elite-type machine). Type the sentence five times, each time on a single line. Begin each line 5 spaces to the left of the point at which the stop for the left margin is set.

STROKES

Each of us must learn to handle the typewriter mechanism with great skill.   74

TYPING FOR CONTROL 40   *8 minutes*

Directions. Type the paragraph for a 5-minute timed writing with a 60-space line. *Type on the control level* as your purpose is to demonstrate your ability to produce usable copy, not to set a new speed record. Keep the carriage moving steadily; avoid the pause that interrupts skill. Your typed lines will be shorter than the lines in the paragraph. Listen for the ringing of the bell to guide you in throwing the carriage.

This paragraph has every letter of the alphabet and a syllable intensity of 1.25.

	STROKES	WORDS
Take good care of your typewriter. It will render you far better service	74	15
when it is kept free from all dust and dirt. Rub the carriage rods well	147	29
with an oiled cloth, but do not oil the machine except when you are in-	217	43
structed to do so by your teacher. Too much oil will prove injurious quite	293	59
as much as too little oil. Use an oiled cloth to remove the dust from the	368	74
surface and from the parts of the machine. Wipe or brush the dust off	439	88
every day, and brush the type with a stiff brush when you finish your	509	102
work each day. The importance of a clean typewriter cannot be empha-	577	115
sized too much.	592	118

Progression Typing for Control. Type for a minute, a minute and a half, two minutes, two and a half minutes, and three minutes. Start at the beginning of the paragraph for each writing. Goal: Errorless typing. Record the number of errorless writings you make. *Type on the control level of practice.*

Guided Writing with the Line Endings Called. Type for 1 minute with the guide for the line ending called each 15 seconds. This will give you a typing speed of 43 words a minute. Type for 2 minutes with the guide for the line ending called each 15 seconds. As the second minute of writing will be at the rate of 51 words, your average for the two minutes of writing will be 47 words a minute. Goal: Appropriate speed with appropriate control.

Selected-Goal Typing. Select an appropriate goal to type a 1- and a 2-minute writing. Place a small check mark to indicate each half-minute and minute goal. You will use the full 70-space writing line in this typing. Your lines of typing will thus be longer than the first lines in the copy. Your teacher will call "Half," "One," etc., to guide you in typing at your selected goal rate.

	STROKES
How much would you pay yourself if you had to pay	50
the bill for the work you do? You will say you want	103
to earn a big salary, but do you realize that the word	158
"earn" is the important word in that statement? The work	216
you do now should help you to acquire the job competence you	277
need for job security. You can acquire this competence if you	340
will take stock of what you can do well and what you should learn	406
to do better. Direct your effort toward raising the level of your	473
typing performance so you will have job competence when it is needed.	542

SKILL BUILDING 227   *10 minutes*

Directions. Type each line as two 1-minute writings with the 12- or the 10-second call of the guide. If you cannot type the entire line at the rate called for by the guide used, select an appropriate portion of the line that will keep you typing at your maximum rate.

```
     1     2     3     4     5     6     7     8     9     10    11    12    13    14
They have all the time there is, and that is time enough for any work.
Stand up and be counted with all who work and who fight for the right.
To do big things, think as a big man would think.  Think big thoughts.
     1     2     3     4     5     6     7     8     9     10    11    12    13    14
```

SKILL MAINTENANCE 227   *5 minutes*

Directions. Use the sentence for three 1-minute writings. Determine your cwpm.

	STROKES	WORDS
Give thought to the way to apply for a position.	65	13

(handwritten corrections: "now" above "thought", "best" above "to the", "for you" above "way")

SECTION 8. The Business Letter

Learn to set up letters in acceptable form. The letter style you will use in typing your own letters will be determined by your personal preference, but your letters must conform to the basic elements of accepted letter styles. If you work as a typist, the style of letter to be used will be determined by office custom or the employer's preference.

GENERAL DIRECTIONS

1. Check the placement of the paper guide; paper bail; paper-bail rolls; and the ribbon indicator.

NOTE: If you are using an Underwood typewriter with the colored diamonds on the front scale, slide the paper guide so that the left edge of the guide is at 8½ to have paper of standard size (8½ by 11 inches) centered when it is inserted into the typewriter. From now on, adjust the paper guide at this point, and center titles as directed on page VI.

2. Set the machine for a 70-space line and single spacing to type the conditioning practice. Set a tabulator stop for a 5-space paragraph indention and use double spacing and a 70-space line when typing the straight-copy timed writing. Specific directions are given for the machine adjustments to be made for typing the problems of each lesson.

3. Type each line of each conditioning practice two or three times in single-spaced form with double spacing between groups of sentences.

LESSON 41

CONDITIONING PRACTICE 41
5 minutes

STROKES

Jack and Elvin met Sam in Mexico City late in March or early in April. 70

The sum of 48 and 37 and 26 and 59 and 72 and 84 and 93 and 50 is 469. 70

When we know how to do our work right, we can always earn our own way. 70

PROBLEM TYPING 41
25 minutes

Directions. Set the margin stops for a 50-space line. Type Style Letter 2, page 65. Type the current date beginning at the left margin as follows:

a. If a letterhead is used similar to that in Style Letter 2, type the date on the second line below the address line.

b. If plain paper is used, type the date approximately 2 inches from the top.

The initials in the lower left corner are the initials of the typist and are known as reference initials. Type your own initials in this position. (As will be shown in later style letters, the initials or the name of the dictator may be typed immediately before the initials of the typist.)

Before removing the letter from the typewriter, proofread it and encircle all errors, unless you are otherwise directed.

SKILL BUILDING 41

Directions. Use Style Letter 2 for three 1-minute writings. Type in the following way:

1. Type for 1 minute beginning with the date and spacing down 8 to 10 times for the address. Type as far as you can.

2. Double-space after typing the first 1-minute writing. Type a second 1-minute writing, beginning with the salutation and typing as much of the first paragraph of the letter as you can.

3. Double-space. Type a third 1-minute writing, beginning with the second paragraph of the letter.

4. Determine your cwpm for each minute of writing; then identify the slowing up portions of the letter and practice them several times.

60-stroke lines.

Learn to judge the amount of work that you can do in a given	61	590
time. It is fine to be willing to do all you can, but it is	122	651
foolish to take on more work than you can possibly get done	182	711
in the time you have. In judging your output per hour, do	241	770
not forget to include the time needed for planning the work.	303	832

65-stroke lines.

A great deal of work in an office has to be done under pressure	64	896
although no one will be standing with a stop watch in hand to see	130	962
that you turn out page after page in record time. The mail must	195	1027
go out, and an extra rush of important mail will often come close	261	1093
to the end of the day. This is when good work habits repay you.	327	1159

70-stroke lines.

Build into your fingers and into your mind the right way of typing,	68	1227
for your mind has much more to do with how you type than your fingers.	140	1299
Type with ease and with the feeling of sure control. You can usually	210	1369
do whatever you think you can do, and you will almost surely make the	280	1439
work harder to do if you let yourself fear that you cannot do it well.	352	1511

SKILL BUILDING 226   *10 minutes*

Directions. Type each line as two 1-minute writings with the 12- or the 10-second call of the guide. If you cannot type the entire line at the rate called for by the guide used, select an appropriate portion of the line that will keep you typing at your maximum rate.

   1   2   3   4   5   6   7   8   9   10   11   12   13   14

Know what a drill is to do for you. Type with a purpose. Type right.
Do things in the same right way day after day. Use right work habits.
You learn to do by doing and to think by thinking. Think and do more.

   1   2   3   4   5   6   7   8   9   10   11   12   13   14

SKILL MAINTENANCE 226   *5 minutes*

Directions. Use the line for three 1-minute writings. Determine your cwpm.

STROKES   WORDS

Employers ~~pay~~ *rate* worker *s* on *a* the ~~plan~~ *basis* of ~~checking~~ what *#* they do *and what they are.*   70   14

LESSON 227

CONDITIONING PRACTICE 227   *5 minutes*

STROKES

A tax rebate of some size was given to the Quincy and Jackson Lamp Co.	70
The $1,000 bonds (Series Y) of Martin & Owens are due on May 25, 1968.	70
You can build good office typing skill if you will use good technique.	70

BAXTER RADIO COMPANY

3650 EAST UNIVERSITY PLACE • MORGANTOWN, WEST VIRGINIA

	STROKES	WORDS

Type the date 2 spaces below the address line. November 16, 195—

18 4

Have 8 to 10 line spaces between the date and the address in typing this short letter.

Mr. R. J. McKillips, Manager 47 9
Television-Radio Division 73 15
General Electronics, Inc. 99 20
Newark 6, New Jersey 120 24

Double-space before and after the salutation.

Dear Mr. McKillips: 141 28

What is the retail price of a Model S7-30 CLEARVU 191 38
custom-built console in mahogany veneer with two 240 48
full-length doors and with a 20-inch screen? 286 57

We have Model S6-29, which has the 17-inch screen, 337 67
but our customer wants the larger screen and a 384 77
console in mahogany veneer. 413 83

How soon can delivery be made of Model S7-30? 460 92

Capitalize the first word of the complimentary close.

Yours very truly, 478 96

James C. Baxter

James C. Baxter, President

Type the dictator's name 4 spaces below the complimentary close. 505 101

Type the reference initials 2 spaces below the dictator's name.

mos 508 102

In this letter a colon is used after the salutation and a comma is used after the complimentary close. No mark of punctuation is used after the other special lines unless a line ends with an abbreviation, as does the third line of the address of this letter. The form of punctuation used in this letter is commonly known as *mixed punctuation*.

Style Letter 2 — Block Letter with Mixed Punctuation

WORK EXPERIENCE

INSTRUCTIONAL BLOCK 19

THE IMPROVEMENT OF BASIC SKILLS

SECTION 40. Building Sustained Typing Power

Before you begin your production typing on this work experience level, bring your basic skills for typing to as high a degree of perfection as possible. You need not work for great speed in stroking; rather, work for continuity of stroking at a rate that is within your range of control except when you are specifically directed to use the exploration level of practice to push out into a new speed area.

LESSON 226

CONDITIONING PRACTICE 226   *5 minutes*

Directions. Type each sentence three times, or more if time permits. Start writing slowly and increase your stroking rate gradually with each repetitive typing. This will be the uniform assignment for typing the conditioning practice for all lessons in this section.

	STROKES
It required two to move the large size icebox for Joe's party in Kane.	70
Albert Speers lived at 4759 North 36th Street until February 18, 1952.	70
Skill in typing is the sum total of doing many small things very well.	70

TYPING FOR CONTROL 226   *20 minutes*

Directions. 1. Type each paragraph for 1 minute with the guide for the line ending called each 15 seconds (unless your teacher directs otherwise). *Type on the control level of practice.* Type the copy line for line.

2. Type each paragraph for 1 minute with the guide for the line ending called each 12 seconds. *Type on the exploration level of practice.* Type the copy line for line.

3. Use the paragraphs for a 5-minute writing. Use a 70-space line. The lines of your typing will not be the same as the lines of the copy. *Type on the skill-building level of practice.*

	STROKES	
	PARA.	TOTAL
50-stroke lines.		
Use a quick stroke in typing, but type with exact	50	
timing of your strokes. This means that you must	100	
pay attention to how you type just as much as to	149	
what you type. Emphasize right work habits in all	200	
of the work you do for improvement in typing power.	253	
55-stroke lines.		
Begin the work without wasting time. Be quick to get	54	307
started. This is one good way to excel in any kind of	109	362
work and especially in typing, as the typist who begins	165	418
to type when the signal is given is the one who can do	219	472
the work without worrying about how well she is typing.	276	529

Directions. Use the machine adjustments as directed for Problem Typing 41. Type Style Letter 2 for 5 minutes. If you complete the typing of the letter before time is called, use the back of the paper (or insert another sheet) and start to type the letter a second time. De-termine your cwpm. Contrast your rate of typing the style letter with your 5-minute paragraph writing speed. Use the remainder of the period for skill-building practice on difficult parts of the style letter.

LESSON 42

CONDITIONING PRACTICE 42   *5 minutes*
STROKES

Vera Jackson will be requested to fix some things for your door prize.   70

Has Policy #163592 for $10,000 been issued to Robert Graves, of Salem?   70

The way you work has a lot to do with how much of the work you can do.   70

HOW TO ADDRESS AN ENVELOPE   *5 minutes*

Insert the envelope into the typewriter so the left edge will be against the paper guide.

If you are using the ordinary business envelope, 3⅝ by 6½ inches, type the first line of the address approximately 1 line above the vertical center. If the lines of the address are not long, begin typing approximately at the horizontal center; but when the lines of the address are long, begin typing approximately 5 spaces to the left of the horizontal center.

Use exact placement for the first practice in addressing envelopes. As soon as you have addressed a few envelopes by exact placement, learn to twirl the envelope to the right position without counting the spaces. To do this, you must get a mental picture of the correct placement of the address on an envelope and then use "eye measurement" to determine how far to twirl the envelope into the typewriter for the placement of the address.

Spacing of the Address. Always use at least three lines for an envelope address. If no street address is given, type the names of the city and the state on separate lines. A three-line address for the envelope should be typed with double spacing even though the letter is single spaced. This practice makes for greater accuracy in the handling of mail by postal workers. When four or more lines are used for the envelope address, it is permissible to use single spacing.

If you do not have an envelope, cut paper to the right size and use this "made" envelope.

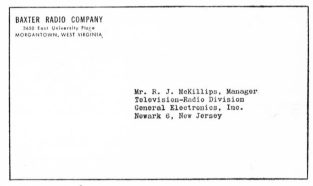

BAXTER RADIO COMPANY
3650 East University Place
MORGANTOWN, WEST VIRGINIA

Mr. R. J. McKillips, Manager
Television-Radio Division
General Electronics, Inc.
Newark 6, New Jersey

Illustration 34 — An Addressed Envelope

PROBLEM TYPING 42   *30 minutes*
PROBLEM I

Directions. Refer to Style Letter 2, page 65, and note the form used and the placement of special parts, such as the title in the address, the closing lines, and the reference initials.

NOTE: The title in an address may be placed on the line with the company name; but as this would make the second line disproportionately long, the title is here typed on the line with the personal name, separated from the name by a comma.

Use a 50-space line; single spacing; current date; 6 to 8 spaces between the date and the address; and your initials as the reference initials, typed 2 spaces below the dictator's name. Type the problem letter given at the top of page 67 in a form similar to Style Letter 2, using the block style and mixed punctuation. Before removing the letter from the typewriter, proofread it; and encircle all errors, unless you are otherwise directed.

Address an envelope. Place the letter under the flap of the envelope, address side up.

INSTRUCTIONAL BLOCK 18

PRODUCTION MEASUREMENT

SECTION 38. Production Measurement Review

LESSONS 216 TO 220

DAILY OUTLINE FOR LESSONS 216 TO 220

Conditioning Practice ....5 minutes   Assembling & Organizing Materials. 5 minutes
                                               Production Typing ....30 minutes

PROBLEM TYPING—MEASUREMENT REVIEW   *30 minutes*

General Directions. For each lesson in this section, you will type for 30 minutes on problems included in previous measurement lessons. The list of lessons to be used is indicated below. USE ONE LESSON ONLY EACH DAY.

First use the Conditioning Practice for the assigned lesson. Then when your teacher directs you to begin, start typing on the problems. Follow the directions given. Proofread each problem carefully; all errors must be corrected. Uncorrected errors will receive a 10-word penalty. If you finish typing all problems in a given lesson before time is called, go back to the beginning and retype as many as possible in the time remaining. At the end of each 30-minute writing, compute your stroking rate per minute. *Type on the control level.*

Lesson	Assignment	Lesson	Assignment
216	Lesson 165, page 219	219	Lesson 185, page 241
217	170, 225	220	190, 247
218	175, 230		

SECTION 39. Production Measurement Comparison

LESSONS 221 TO 225

DAILY OUTLINE FOR LESSONS 221 TO 225

Conditioning Practice ....5 minutes   Assembling & Organizing Materials. 5 minutes
                                               Production Typing ....30 minutes

PROBLEM TYPING—MEASUREMENT COMPARISON   *30 minutes*

Directions. In this section you will use the Conditioning Practice and the problems of Section 33, pages 253 to 258. Each day you will type for 5 minutes on the Conditioning Practice of Section 33. Then you will type for 30 minutes on the problems in this section. Start with the first problem in the section and type the problems in the order in which they are given. Proofread each problem carefully and correct all errors. Uncorrected errors will receive a 10-word penalty.

If you finish all problems before time is called, go back to the beginning and retype as many as possible in the time remaining. You will receive credit for each stroke typed.

At the end of each 30-minute writing, compute your stroking rate per minute. *Type on the control level.*

Mr. R. J. McKillips, Manager Tele- 49
vision-Radio Division General Elec- 83
tronics, Inc. Newark 6, New Jersey 118
Dear Mr. McKillips: Your telegram 153
has just been received stating a de- 188
livery date of six weeks after the 223
receipt of order and quoting a retail 261
price of $392.50, less 25% discount to 300
dealers, on Model S7-30 CLEARVU 332
custom-built console in mahogany 365
veneer with full-length doors and 399
with a 20-inch screen. (P)** Please 430
enter the order for shipment at the 466
earliest possible date. (P) If you 498

have any printed material on align- 532
ment and servicing, with informa- 564
tion on antennas and transmission 598
lines and with directions on how to 634
diagnose, locate, and correct com- 667
mon troubles in FM and television 701
receivers, please send this to me for 739
the use of our Service Department. 775
Yours very truly, James C. Baxter, 810
President 819

_____

*In counting the total strokes, 16 strokes for the date are added in the letters unless the actual date is shown, as in a style letter.

**When this sign is used, begin a new paragraph.

PROBLEM 2

Directions. Use the directions given for Problem 1, but have 10 spaces between the date and the address.

STROKES

Dr. Albert C. Blackburn 837 Molli- 49
son Place Essexville, West Virginia 85
Dear Dr. Blackburn: The manufac- 117
turer of the CLEARVU television 149
sets has notified me that shipment 184

STROKES

of your Model S7-30 console in ma- 217
hogany veneer with a 20-inch screen 253
will be made within the next four to 290
six weeks. (P) The cost of this 319
Model S7-30 is $392.50, less 10% pro- 355
fessional discount. Very truly yours, 394
James C. Baxter, President 420

LESSON 43

CONDITIONING PRACTICE 43

5 minutes

STROKES

We have just been making a quiz of tax reports filed with this county.   70

Is the rate on "E" bonds ($1,000 series) changed from 2 3/8 to 1 3/4%?   70

I know that typing power will come if I can add a stroke or two a day.   70

HOW TO ERASE

The efficient typist strives for a usable first copy. When errors are made, however, they must be corrected. Skill in making these corrections will help to offset loss of time. Study carefully the following steps in erasing:

1. Move the carriage to the right or the left before erasing. This will prevent erasure waste from falling into the typewriter mechanism.

2. Use an eraser shield to protect the writing that is not to be erased.

3. If the erasure is to be made on the upper two thirds of the paper, turn the cylinder forward. If the correction is to be made on the lower third of the paper, turn the cylinder backward so that the proper alignment of the type will not be disturbed.

NOTE: Your teacher will tell you whether or not you are to erase and correct the errors made in typing the problems of this and the following sections of this instructional block.

Production schedules for next year 1158
must be completed soon, and we 1189
must know the contracts to which 1222
we are committed. (P) Will you 1260
write me at your earliest convenience 1288
and tell me what disposition has 1321
been made of our various bids? If 1356
no final action has been taken as yet, 1395
will you indicate the approximate 1429
date on which we may expect a re- 1461
port from you? O. S. EBERSOLE 1492
Mr. John A. Matthews Mr. Edgar 1523
Eaton Mr. John Stover *(241)* 1544

PROBLEM 2

Directions. Type the following letter in modified block style with no indentions for paragraphs and with mixed punctuation. Type the special notation on *the carbon copy only.*

STROKES

Mrs. Ralph H. Winslow Chief Die- 48
tician Albany Municipal Hospital 81
Albany 5, New York Dear Mrs. 110
Winslow: Are you interested in im- 144
proved meal service with less help, 180
in enriched diets at reduced costs? 216
If so, we have an unusual proposi- 249
tion for you—one that will guarantee 287
those results. (P) For breakfast, 318
why not serve the exceptionally 350
popular dry cereal, Vimix, instead of 388

costlier, less nutritious ones? Vimix 427
is a new cereal, sensationally differ- 464
ent from all others on the market. 500
It combines irresistible flavor with 537
vitamin-packed ingredients in an at- 572
tractive, immensely appetizing form. 610
Adults, as well as youngsters, en- 643
joy this health-building, easy-to-eat, 682
simply prepared, breakfast food. (P) 716
Service problems are at a minimum 750
with Vimix; it is packed in indi- 782
vidual cartons ready for the break- 816
fast table or hospital tray. It re- 851
quires no special handling and no 885
extra preparation. (P) When you 914
serve Vimix, operating costs dwin- 947
dle. This new, wholesome cereal is 983
available to public institutions at a 1021
price well below that of competing 1056
brands. It is designed for the budget 1095
—maximum nourishment at mini- 1124
mum cost. (P) Our sales representa- 1155
tive, Mr. Conley, will call on you 1190
soon to discuss the possibilities of 1227
using Vimix in your hospital. May 1262
we have the pleasure of serving you 1298
in the near future? Yours very sin- 1333
cerely, THE AMERICAN FOOD 1359
PRODUCTS COMPANY Presi- 1381
dent JAMatthews/crb *Notation:* 1411
Copy sent to Mr. Conley with a 1442
suggested date, January 9. *(190)* 1468

PROBLEM 3

Directions. Address as many envelopes as possible in the time remaining. Add the mailing notations as indicated.

STROKES

Mr. Frank C. Hartman	819 Fordham Avenue	Portland 7, Oregon	59
Mr. William R. Johnson	5703 Bouquet Street	Stockton 5, California	125
*Mr. Watson J. Knepper	7468 Prospect Boulevard	Sioux City 11, Iowa	200
Mr. Forrest C. Lessner	3012 Hawthorne Drive	Lincoln 12, Nebraska	265
**Mr. George J. Marquis	1439 Edgewood Avenue	St. Joseph 5, Missouri	357
Mr. Walter O. Nicholas	2847 Heathmore Place	Mobile 6, Alabama	419
*Mr. Raymond J. Osterman	5016 Rivermont Street	Columbia 9, South Carolina	501
Mr. Edward W. Portman	4928 Woodward Boulevard	Paterson 12, New Jersey	571
Mr. Webster R. Ramsey	3157 Warrington Avenue	Dayton 11, Ohio	632
Mr. Elmer O. Turnbull	6029 Anderson Street	Alexandria 7, Louisiana	698

*Mark Envelope Air Mail
**Mark Envelope Air Mail, Special Delivery

TYPING CARBON COPIES

Most business offices require a carbon copy of each outgoing letter. Often it is necessary to make eight to ten or more carbon copies of typed material.

To type a carbon copy, place a sheet of carbon paper with the glossy side against a plain sheet of paper. The letterhead sheet or paper for the ribbon copy is then placed on top of the carbon paper, and all sheets are inserted into the typewriter so that the dull back of the carbon sheet is toward the typist.

Handle the carbon sheets with care. One way to avoid streaks or smeared places on carbon copies is to insert the assembled papers far enough for the feed rolls to grip the papers; then operate the paper-release lever to release the pressure on the papers. Return the lever to its normal position and twirl the papers into the typewriter.

PROBLEM TYPING 43   *25 minutes*

PROBLEM 1

Directions. Type the following letter with a carbon copy. Use the form and arrangement that was used in Style Letter 2, page 65. Use the current date and your own initials as the reference initials. *Type on the skill-building level.*

	STROKES
Mr. R. J. McKillips, Manager Tele-	49
vision-Radio Division General Elec-	83
tronics, Inc. Newark 6, New Jersey	118
Dear Mr. McKillips: A short time	152
ago I made an installation of a True-	188
tone AM-FM console. For the FM	220
antenna, I put a folded dipole with	256
director on the peak of the roof, ori-	293
enting it toward Pittsburgh. (P) A	324
letter recently received from the	358
customer indicates the need for im-	392
proved selectivity of this FM set, but	431
I do not know just what to do to get	468
this improvement. Any suggestions	503
you can give me will be greatly ap-	537
preciated. Yours very truly, James	573
C. Baxter, President	593

PROBLEM 2

Directions. Type this letter in the same manner that you typed Problem 1. The address and the signature are the same as those used in that problem.

	STROKES
	139
Earlier today we wrote you about	172
a complaint about the selectivity of	209
a Truetone AM-FM console. Since	242
writing we have again talked to the	278
customer, Mr. J. Lester Marshall,	312
and have found that signals from	345
several Pittsburgh stations come	378
through satisfactorily but on one of	415
them there is a lot of co-channel in-	451
terference. Two stations are affected	491
—one on the low-frequency side of	524
the carrier wanted and another on	558
the high-frequency side. (P) Can	588
anything be done within the set to	623
help improve the rejection of the un-	659
wanted signals?	676
	720

TIMED WRITING ON PROBLEM TYPING 43   *7 minutes*

Directions. Type Problem 1 for 5 minutes. *Type on the control level.* If you complete the typing of the letter before time is called, use the back of the sheet (or insert another page) and start to type Problem 2.

SKILL MAINTENANCE 43   *3 minutes*

Directions. Use the following sentence for 1-minute writings. *Type on the exploration level* and try to push your writing rate to a new speed by typing a stroke or two more in each successive minute writing.

	STROKES	WORDS
If you do your best every day, you need never worry about making good.	70	14

LESSON 214

CONDITIONING PRACTICE 214

5 minutes

STROKES

Lewis Zimmer quietly helped Felix Jacks plan a volleyball game Friday. 70
Our store had 403 cards, 275 books, 86 magazines, and 19 office files. 70
Alert office workers try to keep pace with important business changes. 70

PROBLEM TYPING 214—SKILL BUILDING

35 minutes

Directions. Make pencil notations on a piece of note paper of the problems listed below, and place the paper on the desk near your textbook so that you can refer to it as you complete the typing of each problem. You will be timed for 30 minutes. Correct all errors; uncorrected errors will receive a 10-word penalty. If you complete the typing of the problems before time is called, retype as many of them as possible. Compute your stroking rate.

Page 264, Problem 2, type with one carbon copy.
Page 266, Problem 1, type with two carbon copies.
Page 268, Problem 2, address as many envelopes as possible.

LESSON 215

CONDITIONING PRACTICE 215

5 minutes

STROKES

Proxies for Vinylite were made quickly by just some of the organizers. 70
Our warehouse stored 205 tables, 183 chairs, 69 lamps, and 47 mirrors. 70
A skillful typist will be concerned with the condition of his machine. 70

PROBLEM TYPING 215—MEASUREMENT

35 minutes

Directions. You are to type for 30 minutes on the problems given below. Proofread carefully and correct all errors. Uncorrected errors will receive a 10-word penalty. If you complete all problems before time is called, go back to the beginning and retype as much as possible in the time remaining. At the end of the 30-minute writing, compute your stroking rate per minute. *Type on the control level.*

PROBLEM 1

Directions. Type the following letter in the NOMA Simplified Letter Style. Prepare one carbon copy.

STROKES

Mr. John R. Demmler, Treasurer 48
The Union Supply Company 1623 78
North Meridian Avenue Bridgeport 111
12, Connecticut DISPOSITION OF 142
ANNUAL BIDS (P) On Septem- 163
ber 1, you requested that all bids for 202
manufactured articles be submitted 237
by September 15. You instructed us 273
to prepare separate bids for each 307
different item on which we were in- 341
terested in bidding. On September 376
8 we prepared bids for the following 413
items: 1 #91 Multivane grinders 447
with arbor extensions 2 #1004-C 479

STROKES

Terminal blocks with cover and lock 515
washers 3 #617, Drawing #A-418, 546
Test Switches with card inserts. 580
Those bids were mailed to you, Reg- 614
istered, on September 9 Postal Re- 647
ceipt of Delivery was dated and 679
signed on September 12. (P) To 707
date, November 30, we have heard 739
nothing from you concerning the 771
awarding of contracts on bids sub- 804
mitted. Needless to say, we are 837
anxious to know which, if any, bids 873
were acceptable, as well as the num- 908
ber of contracts awarded to us. (P) 941
Because of material shortages and 975
production demands on our facilities, 1013
it is important that we know within 1050
the next few weeks just what to ex- 1084
pect in terms of orders from you. 1119

LESSON 44

CONDITIONING PRACTICE 44

STROKES

A report was quickly given to an amazed audience by John and Mary Fox. 70

Is Mr. Lynn's Policy #830416 for $7,500? It expires on June 29, 1958. 70

It is up to me to dig in and do this work just as well as I can do it! 72

PROBLEM TYPING 44

25 minutes

PROBLEM 1

Directions. Type the letter in the form used in Style Letter 2, page 65, the block style with mixed punctuation. Use a 50-space line; single spacing; current date; 6 to 8 spaces between the date and the address; and your initials as the reference initials, typed 2 spaces below the dictator's name.

Before removing the letter from the typewriter, proofread it and erase and correct all errors, unless you are otherwise directed.

Address an envelope. Place the letter under the flap of the envelope, address side up.

STROKES

	STROKES
Mr. Charles G. Nelson County Su-	47
perintendent of Schools Morgan-	77
town, West Virginia Dear Mr. Nel-	109
son: Some information about the	142
use of tape recordings of educational	180
programs for use in schools not now	216
served by the radio outlets in our	251

	STROKES
state has just reached me. This in-	286
formation forces me to realize that	322
I have a personal responsibility to	358
help you with the work of our public	395
schools. Until now the only thing	430
I have done to help you has been to	466
trust you. Perhaps I can now do	499
more to strengthen your educational	535
program. (P) In Minnesota, I am	564
told, in the first seven months after	602
a tape-recording program of educa-	635
tional value was started, 125 schools	673
were served with a total of 2,004	707
tape recordings. (P) I should like	739
to talk over the problem with you.	775
I shall be glad to come to your office	814
at your convenience to talk about a	850
positive program of action. Sin-	882
cerely yours, James C. Baxter, Presi-	918
dent	922

PROBLEM 2

Directions. Type a copy of the following summary of a telephone conversation. Use a 2½-inch top margin, a 60-space line, and single spacing. Double-space between single-spaced paragraphs. Center the heading horizontally.

STROKES

	STROKES
Telephone Conversation	23
with	28
Dr. A. W. Spaulding, University of West Virginia	77
1. *Tape recordings of educational programs can be under*	134
University sponsorship.	159
2. *A conference with Mr. Nelson (County Superintendent)*	216
will be arranged by Dr. Spaulding.	252
3. *Information as to programs in other states should*	306
be ready for the conference.	**334**

CHAIN FEEDING ENVELOPES

Letter shops that make a business of preparing form letters for business houses have established a standard of 150 envelopes an hour for their typists. To hold their positions, workers MUST produce this minimum number of envelopes; therefore, in order to meet these requirements, typists "chain feed" the envelopes.

To chain feed envelopes, insert into the typewriter the next envelope to be typed before removing the first. As you turn the cylinder to remove one envelope, you automatically turn the next envelope into position to be typed. Prepare a chain of three envelopes before typing the first.

Set up exact hand movements to economize on time and effort. Stack the envelopes on the left, flap down. Insert the envelope with the left hand, twirl the right cylinder knob with the right hand, and when the envelope has been addressed, remove it with the right hand and stack it FACE DOWN on the right of the desk while *at the same time* the left hand grasps another envelope and brings it to the cylinder for insertion. Practice these movements slowly at first. The necessity for turning the envelope over or twisting the hand around to place the envelope properly for insertion proves a lack of organization for this work.

PROBLEM 2—LEARNING THE NATURE OF THE PROBLEM

Directions. Use the addresses below for timings on addressing envelopes. Your teacher will time you for 5 minutes; at the end of the writing, count the number of envelopes you have addressed. Compare your results with the quota indicated above. Take as many 5-minute writings as time permits. Use five large envelopes and five small envelopes for this writing practice.

See Illustration 66 for the correct placement of special notations on envelopes. Always allow at least 7 lines at the top of an envelope for the placement of stamps.

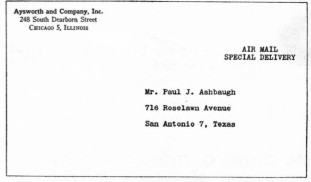

Illustration 66 — Special Envelope Notations

			STROKES
Mr. Robert P. Milligan	9481 Lexington Avenue	Minneapolis 12, Minnesota	71
*Mr. Samuel M. Rothrock	3955 Maplewood Boulevard	Sacramento 17, California	154
Mr. Edgar S. Williamson	6207 Mulberry Boulevard	Richmond 15, Virginia	224
**Mr. Paul J. Ashbaugh	716 Roselawn Avenue	San Antonio 7, Texas	312
Mr. Ralph C. Becker	3015 Munson Street	Bridgeport 9, Connecticut	377
*Mr. Robert M. Fontana	326 Winterburn Avenue	Syracuse 10, New York	452
Mr. Albert R. Gardner	7408 Hawthorn Street	Pontiac 9, Michigan	515
Mr. Daniel E. Gregory	3286 Brodhead Boulevard	Pasadena 7, California	584
**Mr. Leonard A. Malcolm	1293 Downing Avenue	Huntington 11, West Virginia	682
Mr. John D. Richardson	4618 Sterling Place	Kansas City 8, Missouri	748

*Mark Envelope Air Mail
**Mark Envelope Air Mail, Special Delivery

SKILL MAINTENANCE 213   *5 minutes*

Directions. Use the following sentence for 1-minute writings; make the necessary corrections.

STROKES

As one acquires more speed he will use it for his personal use.   70

Directions. Use the sentences for several 1-minute writings. *Type on the exploration level.*

	STROKES	WORDS
You should learn to work up to your highest capacity for doing things.	70	14
When you let your fingers linger on the keys, you hold your rate down.	70	14

LESSON 45

CONDITIONING PRACTICE 45   *7 minutes*

Directions. Use a 70-space line, a 5-space paragraph indention, and single spacing. Type the paragraph twice. Type on the *control level.*

Every letter of the alphabet is used in this paragraph.

	STROKES	WORDS
If you make a letter say just what you want it to say in such a way	68	14
that the reader will understand the message, it has served its purpose.	141	28
If it is also typed in a form that appeals to the reader, it has a double	215	43
value. The letter must be right—quite as right in form as in words. Re-	288	58
alize that you cannot expect a shabby letter to serve you well.	351	70

TIMED WRITING 45   *8 minutes*

Directions. Use a 70-space line, a 5-space paragraph indention, and double spacing. Type for 5 minutes. Compare your cwpm with the record of the 5-minute writings taken with Lesson 40. *Type on the control level.*

This paragraph has every letter of the alphabet and a syllable intensity of 1.25.

	STROKES	WORDS
Everyone loves to win. It is a fine feeling to be on top, to be first	71	14
in whatever we try to do. Often the prize is not worth the effort, but	143	29
still we want to win. Perhaps this desire to win, fostered in all who	214	43
enter competition, is the best prize of all. In games, only one can be	286	57
best; there is only one first prize. In life, each one can win; there is	360	72
a place for each of us and a work for us to do. The next time you	427	85
question this, just look around you and see the great things that re-	495	99
main to be done. The winner must achieve his victory; it cannot be	563	113
bestowed on him. If you will develop superior ability in the doing	631	126
of one thing, you, too, can be a winner.	671	134

PROBLEM TYPING 45   *25 minutes*

Type Style Letter 3, page 71, with a carbon copy. Use a centered date line and block the closing lines five spaces to the left of center. Use a 50-space line, single spacing, the current date, 6 spaces between the date and address, and your initials as the reference initials. If time permits, type the letter again on a separate sheet of paper.

PROBLEM 2—LEARNING THE NATURE OF THE PROBLEM

Directions. Type the letter in modified block style with no indentions for paragraphs. Use mixed punctuation. Make two carbon copies. At the end of the letter type the following notation on the *carbon copies only:* **Copies promised in Knoxville by January 15.** Follow the directions given above for handling the slipsheet.

SKILL MAINTENANCE 212   *5 minutes*

Directions. Use the following sentence for 1-minute writings; make the necessary corrections.

		STROKES
~~Special~~ F letters may loss forms ~~will~~ avoid ~~waste~~ of time and money in ~~sending~~ writing some ~~special~~ answers.		70

LESSON 213

CONDITIONING PRACTICE 213   *5 minutes*

STROKES

He exerted his influence quite well on Vera Zachary and Jacob Kemptag.   70

The auto dealer moved 395 tires, 64 rims, 82 wheels, and 107 hub caps.   70

A typist can improve his skill regardless of his level of performance.   70

PROBLEM TYPING 213—TYPING "COPY" LETTERS AND ADDRESSING ENVELOPES *30 minutes*

PROBLEM 1—LEARNING THE NATURE OF THE PROBLEM

Directions. The following letter was received earlier this week. A copy of this letter (exactly as it was received) is to be sent as an enclosure with another letter you will write later in the business day. This letter, then, must have the word "Copy" typed at the top of the page to distinguish it from an original letter. Type this letter in modified block form with no indentions for paragraphs and with mixed punctuation. Begin 1½ inches (9 lines) from the top of the page and center the word C O P Y in all capitals.

	STROKES
December 20, 195— Mr. Edward R.	32
Moorehead National Advertising	63
Agency 1956 North Michigan Ave-	93
nue Chicago 12, Illinois Dear Mr.	127
Moorehead: On March 15 we expect	161
to introduce to the public a new	194
breakfast cereal. This new-type ce-	229
real is an entirely different product	267
which has just been developed by	300
our research specialists. From all	336
preliminary reports, we expect it to	373
be a highly popular breakfast item.	410
(P) I should like to have your	437
agency take care of the advertising	473
for the launching of this new prod-	507

	STROKES
uct. I am anxious to have extensive	544
circulation through the newspapers,	580
radio, and television; and I should	616
like to have selected circulation	650
through nationally known maga-	679
zines. (P) Will you submit to me,	710
at your earliest convenience, a list	747
of recommendations for handling	779
this advertising program. Will you	815
include in your report a list of the	852
media you propose to use as well as	888
the extent to which each shall be	922
utilized. Include, too, an estimate of	962
the total cost of handling the entire	1000
promotional campaign. I hope it will	1038
be possible for you to have your re-	1073
port available within the next 30	1107
days. (P) Inasmuch as we are com-	1136
mitted to an ambitious advertising	1171
plan, we shall be receptive to any	1206
suggestions or ideas you wish to	1239
offer for our further consideration.	1277
Yours very sincerely, THE AMER-	1307
ICAN FOOD PRODUCTS COM-	1328
PANY President JAMatthews/crb	1357
(193)	

Radio Service Shop

1246 Harrison Avenue

HAMILTON, OHIO

December 16, 195-

STROKES WORDS

18   4

Mr. Ford G. McClintic   40   8
Princeton   50   10
Ohio   55   11

Dear Mr. McClintic   74   15

It has occurred to me that some of your friends may   126   25
be glad to know of a place where they can take their   179   36
radios with full assurance that repair work will be   231   46
done carefully and expertly. Won't you tell them   281   56
of the RADIO SERVICE SHOP?   309   62

A great many people do not know that the SERVICE   358   72
SHOP has a force of expert servicemen on duty at all   411   82
times. Your friends will thank you for giving them   463   93
this information, for they can call for service day   515   103
or night and be sure of prompt and efficient work.   567   113

As we have had the pleasure of taking care of all   617   123
your radio repairs during the past three years, we   668   134
hope you will tell your friends about our work.   717   143

Thanks ahead of time for anything you can do to make   770   154
the SERVICE SHOP known to your friends. Thanks,   819   164
too, for the business you have given us.   861   172

                    Sincerely yours   877   175

                    Thomas O. Powell

                    Thomas O. Powell   894   179
                    Manager   902   180

jb   904   181

Style Letter 3 — Modified Block Letter with Open Punctuation

LESSON 212

CONDITIONING PRACTICE 212

5 minutes

STROKES

Julie quit teasing Max about Ken and Cora Ziner while Vic played golf.	70
The Play House bought 286 masks, 103 caps, 54 vests, and 79 odd suits.	70
It is important to be able to type business letters in various styles.	70

TYPING SPECIAL NOTATIONS

5 minutes

On Original Copy Only. Special notations (references) are often typed after the last item in a letter. To type the notation on the original without having an impression on the carbon copy, (a) turn the platen backward a few inches; (b) place a sheet of paper between the carbon sheet and the onionskin copy; (c) align the original letter to the point where the message is to be typed; (d) type the message; (e) remove the slipsheet.

On Carbon Copies Only. When notations intended for the carbons only are desired, (a) turn the platen backward a few inches; (b) place a sheet of paper back of the paper pack; (c) turn the platen forward to the point where the message is to be typed; (d) type the message; (e) remove the slipsheet.

PROBLEM TYPING 212—TYPING SPECIAL NOTATIONS

25 minutes

PROBLEM I—LEARNING THE NATURE OF THE PROBLEM

Directions. Type the following letter in modified block style with no indentions for paragraphs and with open punctuation. After the enclosure notation, type the message on the original copy only; follow the procedures outlined above. (See Illustration 65 for the placement of the notation.)

STROKES

Dr. John R. McClelland Depart-	46
ment of Commerce The University	78
of Tennessee Knoxville 10, Tennes-	111
see Dear Dr. McClelland It is	141
always a pleasure to hear from edu-	175
cators who have been using our pub-	209
lications as source materials in their	248
classes. It is especially gratifying to	289
have your comments concerning our	323
publication BUSINESS TRENDS.	353
I am happy you found each issue so	388
helpful in your economics classes.	424
(P) Because of unprecedented de-	451
mands throughout the country for	484
copies of BUSINESS TRENDS, we	514
are again offering at special student	552
rates yearly subscriptions to this	587
very outstanding and most popular	621
business magazine. Subscriptions	655
will run for the calendar, rather	689
than for the academic, year. (P) I	721
am enclosing summary subscription	755
sheets on which you may enter the	789
names and addresses of those stu-	821
dents interested in this unusual op-	856
portunity to receive BUSINESS	886
TRENDS, beginning January 1, at	918

STROKES

our greatly reduced rate. (P) You	949
may remit one check to cover the	982
total of all subscriptions or you may	1020
forward each individual check and	1054
money order. Regardless of the	1086
method of payment you select, we	1119
shall verify each order by sending	1154
an Order Verification Card to each	1189
subscriber. (P) My best wishes to	1220
you and your students for another	1254
pleasurable year as you study BUSI-	1288
NESS TRENDS. Very sincerely	1317
yours UNIVERSAL PUBLISHING	1344
COMPANY Sales Manager AM	1369
Roberts/crb Enclosures *Notation*	1392
for the original copy: Copies should	1406
be received by January 15. *(186)*	1432

AMRoberts/crb

Enclosures

Copies should be received by January 15.

Illustration 65 — One Method of Showing Dictator's Name with the Typist's Reference Initials. Also a Special Notation Typed on the Original Copy Only

LESSON 46

CONDITIONING PRACTICE 46

STROKES

Fred and Jim will get very few boxes of this size opened that quickly.   70

Jack read pages 75 to 82 for the test which will be given at 9:30 a.m.   70

The aim is not to outdo another typist, but to improve your own skill.   70

FOLDING AND INSERTING LETTERS INTO ENVELOPES

Step 1

Step 2

Step 3

Illustration 35 — Folding a Letter and Inserting It Into a Small Envelope

Steps 1 and 2. Fold the lower edge of the paper to within a half inch of the top edge of the sheet.

Step 3. Fold from the right to the left, making the fold approximately one third the width of the sheet.

Step 4

Step 5

Step 4. Fold from the left to the right, making the fold slightly less than a third of the width of the sheet and leaving a half-inch margin at the right in order that the letter may be opened easily.

Step 5. Insert the letter into the envelope in such a way that it will be in its normal reading position when it is removed from the envelope. Note that in Step 5 the last fold of the letter is under the thumb and the left-hand creased edge is inserted into the envelope.

PROBLEM TYPING 46

30 minutes

Directions. A copy of Style Letter 3, page 71, is to be sent to each of a number of customers whose names appear on the advertising mailing list. Type the letters according to the directions given for Problem Typing 45, page 70. Make a carbon copy for the first letter, but for that letter only. Make the needed change in the salutation of the letter. Address an envelope; place the

THE WILLIAM C. WESTON COMPANY

1472 West Market Street
ST. LOUIS 15, MISSOURI

STROKES

Date on the extreme left. January 18, 195- 17

Inside address at least 3 lines below date.
Mr. Howard H. Whitfield 41
Director of Purchases 63
The Standard Supply Company 92
3105 Madison Avenue 112
Tulsa 7, Oklahoma 130

Omit salutation

Capital letters, 3 lines below address. SHIPMENT OF ORDER #195672 156

Begin 3 lines after subject line.
Your order of November 15 for special-type gauges 206
to be used in the Enterprise Building is now being 257
processed. The order should be ready for shipment 308
within another ten days. When the materials leave 359
our warehouse, you will receive notice of shipment. 412

When you placed your order with us, we indicated 461
that we would be able to meet the delivery-date 509
requirements included in your specifications. We 559
did so on the assumption that there would be no 607
disruptions in our production schedules. Unfor- 654
tunately, we were unable to foresee many disturbing 706
developments. 721

It has been impossible for us to fill your order for 774
three very specific reasons: 804

Indent listed items 5 spaces except when preceded by a number. No period after a number used in outline form.
1 Curtailment in production because of government 855
   regulations 870
2 Unanticipated shortages in critical materials 919
3 Problems of conversion from civilian to military 971
   production 985

We regret most sincerely the unavoidable delay in 1035
filling your much-appreciated order. It is our hope 1088
that we shall be able to get the gauges to you by 1138
January 30. 1151

Omit complimentary close.

O. S. Ebersole

Capital letters, 5 spaces below body. O. S. EBERSOLE 1166

Ones to receive carbon copies, 3 spaces below signature.
Robert P. Shane – William Matthews – Edward Bartholemew 1222

(Words in body of letter, 161)

Style Letter 7 — NOMA Simplified Letter

typed letter under the flap of the envelope (address side up) and present it to your teacher for approval, unless you are otherwise instructed. After your letter has been approved, use it for the copy for typing the letter to the other names on the mailing list given below.

You are not expected to complete all six letters in this lesson. Additional time is provided for these letters in Lessons 47 and 48.

NOTE: On the envelope a three-line address should be double spaced; an address of four or more lines may be single spaced.

1. Mrs. Robert Maynard
   R. D. 4, Box 1026
   Hamilton, Ohio

2. Mr. Larry H. O'Neil
   West Chester
   Ohio

3. Dr. James Blackburn
   Trenton
   Ohio

4. Mr. Howard M. Langley, Jr.
   961 Deep Valley Drive
   Oxford, Ohio

5. Messrs. Rutland and Witmer
   629 Highland Building
   Hamilton, Ohio

   NOTE: Use Gentlemen as the salutation.

6. Dr. Richard O. Parker
   Dean of Instruction
   University Preparatory School
   Oxford, Ohio

LESSON 47

CONDITIONING PRACTICE 47

5 minutes

STROKES

Cy and Jack type quite well for having but six months of zealous work.   70
The box is 6 2/3 by 9 1/2 feet long; it weighs from 375 to 400 pounds.   70
No good can come from putting off until tomorrow what can be done now.   70

PROBLEM TYPING 47

35 minutes

PROBLEM 1

Your employer, Mr. Powell, has been called to Washington for a conference. He will not return to the office until Tuesday of next week. A letter has been received from Dr. Richard O. Parker, Dean of Instruction, University Preparatory School, Oxford, Ohio, in which certain questions are asked that require Mr. Powell's personal attention. Make a carbon copy of the letter you write to Dr. Parker to tell him of Mr. Powell's absence from the office and the probable date of his return. In a second paragraph say that you will call the letter to Mr. Powell's attention as soon as he returns to the office. Sign the letter as "Secretary to Mr. Powell," as given in the illustration.

Yours very truly

Elizabeth Henderson
Elizabeth Henderson
Secretary to Mr. Powell

Illustration 36 — Signature of a Secretary

NOTE: If the first copy of your letter is not satisfactory, make pencil corrections and retype it. Address an envelope. Sign the letter with pen and ink. Fold the letter and insert it into the envelope.

PROBLEM 2

Directions. Type the letter given as Style Letter 3, page 71, to names on the address list of Problem Typing 46, for whom letters have not been typed. Address an envelope for each letter typed. *Type on the skill-building level.*

SECTION 37. NOMA Letter, Special Notations, Copy Letters, Chain Feeding

LESSON 211

CONDITIONING PRACTICE 211 *5 minutes*

Directions. Type each line twice. Double-space after the second typing of the line. Retype the lines as often as time permits. Increase your stroking rate with each repetition. This will be the uniform assignment for typing the conditioning practice in all lessons in this section.

	STROKES
Howard Zervos moved the extra jeeps quickly from Broadway and Manning.	70
Santa gave 265 guns, 87 horns, 143 dolls, and 90 pins to poor kiddies.	70
They could not believe it was possible to write so quickly and easily.	70

THE NOMA SIMPLIFIED LETTER *5 minutes*

The National Office Management Association through its Office Standards Committee has adopted a simplified letter for use in business correspondence. Study Style Letter 7, page 265, to learn its distinguishing characteristics.

PROBLEM TYPING 211—TYPING NOMA SIMPLIFIED LETTERS *25 minutes*
PROBLEM 1—LEARNING THE NATURE OF THE PROBLEM

Directions. Type the NOMA style letter on page 265. Proofread the letter carefully before removing it from the typewriter; then retype the letter.

PROBLEM 2—SKILL BUILDING IN TYPING A NOMA SIMPLIFIED LETTER

Directions. Type the following letter in the NOMA letter style.

In all letters where the date is not given, use the current date.

	STROKES
Mr. Wilbert A. Kennedy Transpor-	48
tation Supervisor West Park Man-	80
ufacturing Company 1856 North	110
Amberson Avenue Jacksonville 9,	142
Florida CLARIFICATION OF	167
ORDER #813902 (P) Your order	192
#813902, dated November 15, is some-	227
what confusing. Among the many	259
items listed, you requested a Cutter	296
Bar Assembly with a Classification	331
Number X-3002-13. Apparently, you	366
have misread the catalogue in which	402
the classification numbers are listed.	442
(P) We do not manufacture a Cut-	469
ter Bar Assembly in the X-3002 class	506
with a Specification Number 13. As	542
a matter of fact, we produce only	576
two assemblies in the X-3002 class.	613
One has a Specification Number 22;	648
the other, a Specification Number 57.	687
(P) Will you recheck the classifica-	718
tion numbers of the assemblies you	753
have in mind and notify us imme-	784
diately of the appropriate catalogue	821
designations? (P) If, for any reason,	856
you have difficulty in identifying the	895
Cutter Bar Assembly you need,	925
please send us a description of the	961
one you have been using and we	992
shall try to determine the specific	1028
assembly you have in mind. O. S.	1062
EBERSOLE *(164)*	1070

SKILL MAINTENANCE 211 *5 minutes*

Directions. Use the following sentence for 1-minute writings; make the corrections as indicated.

	STROKES
There is so much to~~ ~~do in ~~life~~ we shouldn't waste ~~motion.~~	70

(handwritten corrections: # — be done the world — # not — any time)

LESSON 48

CONDITIONING PRACTICE 48

5 minutes

All letters of the alphabet are used in the paragraph.

	STROKES	WORDS
Office workers learn to keep busy. When the desk work is done, they	69	14
realize that the filing must be completed, supplies stocked, and cata-	138	28
logues sorted. They exert every effort to do their work just as quickly	211	42
and easily as they can do it. Ease and speed make for good performance!	287	57
Are you working with ease and speed?	323	65

PROBLEM TYPING 48

35 minutes

PROBLEM 1

Write to Mr. Thomas O. Powell at the Essex-Sussex Hotel, Washington, D. C. Tell him that you have made an appointment for him for Tuesday afternoon of next week, but that you have kept the morning free of appointments as there are a number of letters that he will need to answer.

Type your name in the signature position, but do not add the line "Secretary to Mr. Powell." Make pencil corrections on your first draft if these are needed; then retype the letter.

PROBLEM 2

Directions. For Lessons 46 and 47 you were instructed to type a letter to the names on the mailing list given on page 73. If you have not typed the letter to all names on the address list, complete the work now. After all letters have been typed, insert the carbon copy of the letter and add the following notation:

This form letter has been sent to the names listed below:

(Type the names and address of all to whom letters have been sent.)

Note: Use the remainder of the period for improvement practice in typing numbers. Some good sentences for this practice will be found in Problem Typing 40, page 62.

LESSON 49

CONDITIONING PRACTICE 49

5 minutes

	STROKES
I have to be as quick as Jim to realize the expert way for doing this.	70
This rate of 4½% isn't too high. He said, "Pay Bill #15896 for $273."	70
Do all things well. Keep on working until you know you can type well.	70

PROBLEM TYPING 49

35 minutes

PROBLEM 1

Directions. Type the letter with a carbon copy. Use the modified block form similar to Style Letter 3, page 71, with open punctuation, a 50-space line, and single spacing. Instead of counting the spaces between the date and the address, twirl the knob to what you judge to be the correct place for typing the address. It is necessary for you to learn to place the letter by judgment (or eye measurement) instead of counting the exact spaces each time you type a letter. If you fail to place the letter acceptably by judgment, retype it.

Directions. You are to type for 30 minutes on the problems given below. Proofread each problem carefully and correct all errors. Uncorrected errors will receive a 10-word penalty. If you complete all problems before time is called, go back to the beginning and retype as much as possible in the time remaining. At the end of the 30-minute writing, compute your stroking rate per minute. *Type on the control level.*

PROBLEM 1

Directions. Type the following letter in modified block style with no indentions for paragraphs and with open punctuation. This letter will serve as the model from which you will prepare a stencil in Problem 2.

	STROKES
Mr. Carleton J. Ashley 3062 Lehigh	52
Avenue Paterson 7, New Jersey	82
Dear Mr. Ashley A house with only	116
half a roof wouldn't be much good,	151
would it? A wise home builder ob-	184
viously would be sure to cover his	219
entire building. It is incredible to	257
think that one would build a strong	293
foundation and then fail to provide	329
adequate over-all protection. Yet,	365
that very thing happens every day.	401
(P) Has it occurred to you that, in	433
the field of personal protection, your	472
insurance coverage may be just as	506
inadequate as that so-called partial	543
roof? Do you have only a founda-	575
tion of insurance coverage instead	610
of sound over-all protection? (P)	641
The Universal Insurance Company	673
specializes in analyses of individual	711
insurance coverage. Already thou-	744
sands of men throughout the coun-	776
try have benefited from private	808
consultations with members of our	842
specially trained staff of analysts.	880
May we have the pleasure of discuss-	915
ing with you some time soon the	947
adequacy of your insurance program?	984
Very sincerely yours UNIVERSAL	1015
INSURANCE COMPANY Wil-	1036
liam A. Hunter Sales Manager *(145)*	1064

PROBLEM 2

Directions. Use the model copy typed in Problem 1 to prepare a stencil master. Do not include in the stencil the date, the address, and the salutation; but do leave space for these parts. They will be inserted separately on the individual letters after they have been mimeographed.

PROBLEM 3

Directions. From the following addresses, prepare appropriate index cards. Number each card consecutively beginning with J-813256. Near the bottom of each card, type the notation "Revised Mailing List M-57." Save these cards for the next problem. (To the stroke count given with the list add 35 strokes for the number and notation on each card.)

			STROKES
Mr. Kenneth I. Armstrong	4270 Bellefont Avenue	Shreveport 10, Louisiana	72
Mr. Watson J. Coleridge	1020 Kennebec Drive	Charleston 15, West Virginia	145
Mr. Arthur M. Donaldson	3958 Merrimac Avenue	Milwaukee 13, Wisconsin	214
Mr. George K. Gustafson	6172 Winebiddle Avenue	Bridgeport 16, Connecticut	288
Mr. Melvin R. Humphries	4093 Sycamore Street	Winston-Salem 10, North Carolina	366
Mr. Curtis A. Kingsford	5184 Brereton Avenue	Elizabeth 14, New Jersey	436
Mr. Lester E. Lockewood	1805 Castlegate Street	Chattanooga 12, Tennessee	508

PROBLEM 4

Directions. Use letters mimeographed in Lesson 206 for this problem. From the information recorded on the index cards in the preceding problem, fill in the current date, the inside address, and an appropriate salutation for each addressee. (To the stroke count given with the list add 35 strokes for each date line and salutation.)

Make one change in the body of the letter. Change the date of November 8 to the exact date for Thursday of the week following the day on which this letter is typed. Sign Mr. Powell's name with pen and ink and add your initials below the signature to show that Mr. Powell did not sign the letter personally even though he dictated it. *Type on the skill-building level.*

	STROKES
Dr. Martin L. Appleton University	50
Preparatory School Oxford, Ohio	82
Dear Dr. Appleton As you have re-	114
quested, I shall install a Jewell Elec-	152
tric Radio in the general clubroom of	190
your school on Thursday of next	222

	STROKES
week, November 8. This radio will	257
be placed at your disposal for a week	295
—and longer if you so wish. (P) Mr.	329
Robert Harris, the foreman of our	363
Service Department, will install the	400
radio and will give you or your as-	434
sistant full information about its	469
operation. (P) I hope that you and	501
your students will enjoy the Jewell	536
Electric. It is a superior radio and	574
well suited for a room the size of	609
your general clubroom. Sincerely	643
yours Thomas O. Powell Manager	674

PROBLEM 2

Directions. Type the letter with a carbon copy. Use the same style and line length that you used for Problem 1. Make all corrections marked on the copy. *Type on the control level.*

	STROKES
Dr. Eric S. Dodds	34
124 Walnut Street	52
Franklin, Ohio	67
Dear Dr. Dodds	82
television	
A booklet is being ~~shipped~~ *mailed* to you describing several	134
models of ~~TV~~ sets that can be installed ~~quickly.~~ *promptly*	193
The prices quoted are for console models with the	243
17 rectangular filter glass tube.	283
—inch	
The regular professional discount of ~~15~~ *20*% will be	332
allowed on the list price of models 682, 856, and	382
861. If you ~~wish~~ *would like* to have me install one of these	438
sets for you, I can do so promptly.	475
Yours very truly	492
add 1 line space →	
Thomas O. Powell	509
Manger	517
jb	519

			STROKES
Mr. Charles O. Angstrom	6195 Susquehanna Street	Charlotte 12, North Carolina	77
Mr. Edgar H. Courtney	1713 Spring Garden Avenue	Jacksonville 10, Florida	150
Mr. Walter F. Drummond	3220 Piedmont Boulevard	Baltimore 15, Maryland	220
Mr. Donald R. Grundman	2812 East Overbrook Drive	Springfield 10, Massachusetts	299
Mr. Frank C. Hutchinson	3013 Metropolitan Street	Williamsport 9, Pennsylvania	377
Mr. Joseph L. Kauffman	5738 West Hawthorne Avenue	Kansas City 11, Missouri	452
Mr. Thomas W. Lundquest	7023 Coleridge Boulevard	Indianapolis 9, Indiana	525
Mr. William R. Moorhead	2023 Plainview Avenue	Los Angeles 15, California	598
Mr. Donald S. Rousseau	4961 Bevington Avenue	San Francisco 11, California	672
Mr. Oliver M. Waterman	7518 Margaretta Street	Schenectady 13, New York	742

PROBLEM 2—LEARNING THE NATURE OF THE PROBLEM

Directions. Using the letters mimeographed in Lesson 206 and the index cards typed in the preceding problem, fill in the current date, inside address, and an appropriate salutation for each person listed. (Personalize the salutations; that is, use Dear Mr. Angstrom, not Dear Sir.)

SKILL MAINTENANCE 208   *5 minutes*

Directions. Use the following sentence for 1-minute writings; make the corrections as indicated.

STROKES

I ~~will~~ try to learn how to ~~force~~ my fingers ~~to move~~ rapidly and accurately. 70

LESSON 209

CONDITIONING PRACTICE 209   *5 minutes*

STROKES

Zinc oxide was used by the garrulous corpsman, Jack, from Camp Glover.   70
The builder used 82 windows, 103 doors, 69 lights, and 547 new hinges.   70
Office workers should have access to various reliable reference books.   70

PROBLEM TYPING 209—SKILL BUILDING   *35 minutes*

Directions. Make pencil notations on a piece of note paper of the problems listed below, and place the paper on the desk near your textbook so that you can refer to it as you complete the typing of each problem. You will be timed for 30 minutes. Correct all errors; uncorrected errors will receive a 10-word penalty. If you complete the typing of the problems before time is called, retype as many of them as possible. Compute your stroking rate at the end of the 30-minute period.

Page 260, Lesson 206, Problem 2, prepare a stencil from the model copy.

Page 260, Lesson 207, Problem 2, prepare a hectograph master.

Page 262, Lesson 208, Problem 2, fill in the duplicated letters. (To the strokes given with the list add 35 strokes for each date line and salutation.)

LESSON 210

CONDITIONING PRACTICE 210   *5 minutes*

STROKES

A zoom in TV shares was quite unexpected by wily judges of the market.   70
Women examined 380 pearls, 74 rubies, 52 sapphires, and 169 onyx gems.   70
All of us should be sure that our actions agree with our declarations.   70

LESSON 50

	STROKES
Please have Raymond get four dozen quarts of lemon juice by next week.	70
Tom said, "Winlock & Summers want 38 cars of 2 5/8 inch oak flooring."	70
Try to rid yourself of all fear so that you can do your work with joy.	70

TIMED WRITING 50   *15 minutes*

Directions. Use a 70-space line, a 5-space paragraph indention, and double spacing. Type two 5-minute writings. *Type on the control level.*

This paragraph contains every letter of the alphabet and has a syllable intensity of 1.25.

	STROKES	WORDS
You must know when to type as rapidly as possible and when to type	67	13
on the letter level. Many of the short and simple words can be read as	139	28
word wholes and the typing will be quicker than when the words are	206	41
read letter by letter. Your eyes will see the word and your fingers will	280	56
make the right pattern of strokes except when you let some fear or other	353	71
distracting influence cause you to tense your muscles or take your atten-	425	85
tion from the copy. Just as soon as you come to a long word or a series	498	100
of difficult or unfamiliar words, you may have to make some change in	568	114
the way you type. Up to this point, you have typed many of the words	638	128
of this paragraph on a level that is at least that of grouped letters	708	142
rather than on the single letter level. The more you type with attention	782	156
to how you type the words, the more ease you will have in typing rapidly	855	171
and with accuracy. Once you realize this, you will know that the way you	929	186
read the copy is as much a part of how you type as is the way you make	1000	200
your fingers move.	1018	204

PROBLEM TYPING 50   *20 minutes*

Build your production skill through the improvement of your handling of materials as well as the handling of your typewriter. Study your hand motions and eliminate those that are unnecessary for the work you are to do. *Type on the skill-building level.*

Directions. Make pencil notations of the following directions for the timed production of letters. Keep the notations where you can read them easily.

1. Type Style Letter 2, page 65, with a carbon copy. Proofread; correct the errors. Address an envelope; place the letter under the flap.

2. Type Style Letter 3, page 71, with a carbon copy. Proofread; correct the errors. Address an envelope.

3. Fold and insert each letter into the appropriate envelope.

4. Retype Style Letter 3 if time permits.

THE OLD MILL THEATRE

Schedule of Productions

Summer, 195—

Opening Date	Play	Time	
			81
			104
June 16	Boy Meets Girl	8:30 p.m.	139
June 23	Yes, My Darling Daughter	8:30 p.m.	184
June 30	Winterset	8:30 p.m.	214
July 7	You Can't Take It With You	9:00 p.m.	261
July 14	Happy Birthday	9:00 p.m.	296
July 21	The Family Upstairs	9:00 p.m.	336
July 28	Three Men On A Horse	9:00 p.m.	377
August 4	Peg O' My Heart	9:00 p.m.	413
August 11	The Charm Kid	8:30 p.m.	447
August 18	The Voice of The Turtle	8:30 p.m.	491

Prices:

500

Season Tickets ....$25.00 ea. 559

Individual Performances ....$1.75 to $3.15 ea. 617

SKILL MAINTENANCE 207

Directions. Use the following sentence for 1-minute writings; make the corrections as indicated.

~~Your~~ letters ~~should~~ *must* not have long paragraphs or too many ~~very~~ *too many* short ones. STROKES 70

LESSON 208

CONDITIONING PRACTICE 208 *5 minutes*

STROKES

Gay flowers, phlox and ivy, made bouquets for Janice, Kate, and Zelda. 70

Our cupboard held 308 knives, 175 forks, 62 spoons, and 49 big ladles. 70

Coin cards should be used when coins are to be sent through the mails. 70

PREPARATION OF INDEX CARDS

Index cards serve many purposes in the business office. Mailing information, cross reference data, and other reference items are often recorded on 3 by 5 cards. The cards are filed for future use. Illustration 64 shows an index card used for recording mailing list information.

PROBLEM TYPING 208—COMPLETING DUPLICATED LETTERS FOR MAILING *25 minutes*

PROBLEM I—LEARNING THE NATURE OF THE PROBLEM

Directions. Using the mailing list on the following page, prepare an index card for each name given. Number each card consecutively beginning with S-195680. Add the notation "Season Ticket Holder 195—" using the current year. Save the cards for use in completing the duplicated letters in the next problem.

```
Angstrom, Charles O. (Mr.)            S-195680
    6195 Susquehanna Street
    Charlotte 12, North Carolina




Season Ticket Holder 195-
```

Illustration 64 — Index Card with Mailing Information

INSTRUCTIONAL BLOCK 4

THE IMPROVEMENT OF BASIC SKILLS FOR TYPEWRITING

No one can tell you exactly how to learn to type with maximum skill in a minimum of time. You have to discover this for yourself. This textbook provides a variety of materials for your use, and your teacher will help you to discover the appropriate procedures for you to use; but you must assume responsibility for your own growth in typing power. You cannot pass this responsibility to anyone else.

SECTION 9. Building Sustained Typing Power

Learning to type well is primarily a matter of learning to discard awkward and wasteful movements and to build into your fingers the best stroking pattern you can devise at the time.

General Directions. 1. Use a full-size sheet of paper for each lesson. (If your teacher approves, you may type the conditioning practice on drill paper.) Set the machine for a 70-space line, single spacing, and a 5-space paragraph indention. Type the lines of the conditioning practice and the technique emphasis in single-spaced form with double spacing between groups. Type the skill-building paragraphs with double spacing.

2. Type each line of the conditioning practice two or three times, or until you feel you have control of yourself and of your typewriter.

3. Type the technique study as directed, but take time to study your own techniques and to experiment with ways of improving them.

Bonus Typing. If you complete the assigned work before the end of the period, select for practice parts of the current lesson or parts of lessons from preceding sections of work.

LESSON 51

CONDITIONING PRACTICE 51   *5 minutes*

	STROKES
The puzzled judge soon became quite vexed at your wonderful knowledge.	70
What is the sum of 5 and 40 and 30 and 26 and 39 and 48 and 57 and 26?	70
You won't have time to find fault with others if you do your own work.	70

TECHNIQUE STUDY 51—STROKING   *10 minutes*

Directions. Read the technique emphasis; and as you type, put the suggestions for technique improvement to work. Type each line two or more times. Center the stroking in the fingers and hold the arms and wrists as motionless as possible. *Type on the stroke level of response.*

Technique Emphasis: 1. After striking a home key, lift the finger upward just enough to allow the key to return to its normal position without finger interference.

2. From the lower row of keys, pull the finger upward and forward to typing position; from the upper row of keys, pull the finger toward the palm of the hand except when the succeeding letter is in a nearby position, as in the word *art*. In this case, the finger should move from *r* to *t* without returning to the *f* position before striking *t*.

	STROKES
ask led old was big cad may man led was old may ask him has art buy	67
give much must many river truce bring light bright honey money brought	70
jungle hungry strong strength streets strict hundreds average beverage	70

	STROKES		STROKES
plans for this summer. (P) Season	548	seasons to date. Why not plan now	726
tickets will go on sale within six	583	to order your season tickets as early	764
weeks. From letters of inquiry	615	as possible? Very cordially yours	798
already received, predictions are that	654	George C. Lindell Business Man-	828
this will be the most popular of all	691	ager Enclosure	842

PROBLEM 2—LEARNING THE NATURE OF THE PROBLEM

Directions. From the model letter typed in Problem 1, prepare a stencil; follow the steps outlined in the "Check List" after the model copy has been checked.

Do not include in the stencil the date, the address, and the salutation; but do leave space for these parts. They will be inserted separately on the individual letters after they have been mimeographed.

When you finish the stencil, give it to your teacher for approval. She will then have 35 copies run for your use in subsequent lessons. (Save the model letter for use in Lesson 209.)

SKILL MAINTENANCE 206   *5 minutes*

Directions. Use the following sentence for 1-minute writings; make the corrections as indicated.

              seems   *one*   *critical*   STROKES

it often ~~appears~~ ~~to be~~ much easier for ~~you~~ to be ~~a critic~~ than to be tolerant.   70

LESSON 207

CONDITIONING PRACTICE 207   *5 minutes*

                                                STROKES

Job lots of galoshes sold quickly when zippers were made by Mr. Vixon.   70

The club had 140 plates, 83 cups, 62 saucers, and 597 napkins for use.   70

A useful method of folding a letter for mailing is most easy to learn.   70

CHECK LIST FOR HECTOGRAPH CARBONS   *5 minutes*

1. Prepare a model copy.
2. Clean the typewriter type.
3. Insert the hectograph master and carbon.
4. Type with a normal, staccato stroke.

5. To make corrections, the procedures to follow will depend upon the materials being used. Follow the directions of your teacher.

PROBLEM TYPING 207—PREPARING HECTOGRAPH MASTERS FOR DUPLICATING   *25 minutes*

PROBLEM 1—LEARNING THE NATURE OF THE PROBLEM

Directions. Type the announcement at the top of the following page on a full sheet of paper. You will use it as a model to be followed when preparing a hectograph carbon in the next problem. This announcement will be the enclosure referred to in Problem 1, Lesson 206, page 84.

PROBLEM 2—LEARNING THE NATURE OF THE PROBLEM

Directions. Prepare a hectograph master from the model typed in Problem 1. After the hectograph master has been approved by your teacher, run 35 copies; these copies will be enclosed with the letters duplicated in Lesson 206. (Save the model copy for use again in Lesson 209.)

Direct Dictation. In typing from direct dictation, *think the word or the sentence and do not think the letters* of each word. Do not follow the copy in the book as the dictation is given, but get the impulse to type from the dictation.

or for for he the the for the for the an and and and for the and for

He can. He can go. He can go for them. He can go to work for them.

SKILL BUILDING 51

25 minutes

Pace Writings. Use the sentence below for two or three 1-minute writings paced at the rate of a sentence each 20 seconds, which will give you a speed of 33 words a minute. If you can type at that rate with a feeling of ease, give attention to the sequence of letters and type for control. If you cannot type at 33 words a minute with ease, push yourself and ignore the errors temporarily.

	STROKES	WORDS
Not much can be done without faith in your power to do.	55	11

Paragraph for Guided Writing. Each paragraph in this skill building has approximately uniform line length within the paragraph. For example, each line of the first paragraph is approximately 50 strokes; of the second paragraph, approximately 55 strokes; of the third paragraph, approximately 60 strokes. This arrangement of the practice materials makes it possible to use the technique of calling the guide each 20 seconds (or whatever time your teacher decides is appropriate). *Type on the skill-building level of response.*

Directions. 1. Take a 5-minute timed writing, using the first paragraph. Determine the cwpm.

2. You will now build your skill by typing the first paragraph in the following way:

    a. Type for 1 minute with the call of the guide for the line ending each 20 seconds (unless your teacher decides otherwise). If you maintain this rate, you will be typing at the rate of 30 words a minute.

    b. Type for 2 minutes with the call of the guide each 20 seconds. Start at the beginning of the first paragraph.

3. Type for 3 minutes with the call of the guide each 20 seconds. Start at the beginning of the first paragraph.

4. Take a second 5-minute writing, using the first paragraph. Determine the cwpm. Contrast this rate with that made on the first 5-minute timing. You should show measurable growth in stroking speed or in improved control or in both.

NOTE: As you will type the copy line for line as it is given in the book, it is not necessary for you to reset the margin stops for the exact line length.

Each paragraph has every letter of the alphabet and a syllable intensity of 1.25.

		STROKES
		PARA. TOTAL
50-stroke lines.	In times of crisis, most of us will rise to the	48
	occasion in the truly heroic way. This is because	99
	the urgency of the times calls for the use of all	149
	the force we have within us. If we can learn to	198
	make use of all our resources each day as fully as	249
	we do in times of special need, we can soon join	298
	the cult of excellence. Few of us quite realize	347
	the full power of our inner strength; so we seldom	398
	achieve all we have the ability to achieve. We do	449
	not do big things, yet do not know why we do not.	498

MAKING DUPLICATE COPIES

SECTION 36. Preparation of Masters, Filling-In Items, Index Cards

LESSON 206

CONDITIONING PRACTICE 206
5 minutes

Directions. Type each line twice. Double-space after the second typing of the line. Retype the lines as often as time permits. Increase your stroking rate with each repetition. This will be the uniform assignment for typing the conditioning practice in all lessons in this section.

	STROKES
Hazel helped Vernon box eight crates of quart jugs for Mrs. Ward York.	70
Our garden yielded 273 carrots, 85 beets, 69 onions, and 410 potatoes.	70
Make sure that you type with quiet, almost motionless arms and wrists.	70

PREPARATION OF MASTER COPIES
5 minutes

For duplicating jobs, master copies are needed. Two commonly used types are mimeograph stencils and hectograph carbons. These "masters" are generally produced from model copies that the typist prepares and checks for content, format, etc., before using the special materials provided for duplicating purposes. To insure readable copy with clear-cut impressions, the typist should always have clean type and should use a normal, staccato stroke, striking all letters and characters with equal force.

CHECK LIST FOR STENCIL MASTERS

1. Prepare a typewritten model copy.
2. Clean the typewriter type thoroughly.
3. Adjust the ribbon lever for stenciling.
4. Insert the cushion sheet between the stencil sheet and the stencil backing.
5. Place the top edge of the model copy at the corner marks and determine how far down on the stencil the first line of copy should be typed.
6. Take the combination of backing sheet, cushion sheet, and stencil sheet, and place it in the typewriter.
7. Use a normal staccato stroke.
8. To make corrections, apply correction fluid as directed on the container. When rolling the platen, hold all sheets firmly to avoid wrinkling the stencil.

PROBLEM TYPING 206—PREPARING STENCIL MASTERS FOR DUPLICATING
25 minutes

PROBLEM I—LEARNING THE NATURE OF THE PROBLEM

Directions. Type the following letter as a model to be used in preparing a stencil. Use the modified block style with no indentions for paragraphs and with open punctuation.

	STROKES
Mr. Carleton J. Ashley 3062 Lehigh	52
Avenue Paterson 7, New Jersey	82
Dear Mr. Ashley Summer Stock	113
this season will be the greatest in	149
the history of our theatre! New	182

	STROKES
financial backers have provided gen-	217
erous support for much-needed im-	249
provements in the building; and new	285
talent, already signed, will provide	312
the type of acting heretofore impos-	347
sible to enlist. (P) I am enclosing	380
a list of our proposed productions	415
together with their tentative open-	449
ing dates. Look over the schedule	484
carefully and note the ambitious	517

55-stroke lines.

All of us will have had a time when we were in top form and did some one thing superbly. From this we may have caught just a glimpse of what we could do if we could extend our moment of superiority to an hour or a day or a month. There is a pattern that must be followed no matter what it is in which we want to excel. We must know what we want, of course. Then there must be the intense desire for it, the zeal that is like a burning flame that does not flicker out at the first opposing wind. There must be superiority of effort, too. Quick spurts of energy may push us ahead for the moment, but it is continuous driving that holds the gains.

PARA.	TOTAL
56	554
112	610
166	664
222	720
276	774
330	828
384	882
439	937
493	991
549	1047
604	1102
650	1148

60-stroke lines.

Make the question a personal one. Why do you not excel as a typist? What keeps you from doing much more work than you now do? List the hindrances to your excellence. Write them down on paper. Do not evade or pretend or lay any of them aside. In this listing, reject no hindrances no matter how small they may seem to you. The mere listing of the things which keep you from doing your best in each day's practice may help you to size up the task ahead. This you must do if you are to rise above the level of the average. Why be willing to settle for less than the best you know you can be?

PARA.	TOTAL
59	1207
120	1268
181	1329
240	1388
300	1448
360	1508
419	1567
480	1628
540	1688
597	1745

LESSON 52

CONDITIONING PRACTICE 52

5 minutes

STROKES

Paul Kerr carefully moved six dozen jugs of liquid to a big warehouse. 70

Our total expenses were $6,285.40, an increase of 7.5% over last year. 70

If there were no hard things to do, there would be no joy in our work. 70

TECHNIQUE STUDY 52—CONTROL OF THE SHIFT KEYS

10 minutes

Directions. Type each line two or more times. Center the stroking in the fingers and hold the arms and hands quiet—almost motionless. *Type on the stroke level of response.*

Technique Emphasis. 1. Stretch the finger to the shift key. Hold the hands in the correct typing position. Avoid moving the elbow in or out as you control the shift key. If the capital letter is out of alignment, you may be releasing the shift key too quickly.

2. The space bar is the most used machine part. Hold the thumb as near the bar as possible without having it rest on the bar. Hit the bar quickly after striking the final letter of a word; then release the bar just as quickly as possible and type the first letter of the next word without pausing. Even a slight improvement in this manipulative skill will show in your improved quality and quantity of typing.

3. *Type on the skill-building level of practice.*

STROKES

Frank and Bob were just spending the day quietly in Vera Cruz, Mexico. 70

Max went to Maine on May 30. Alan and Sue reached Alaska on April 26. 70

Albert, Jack, and Clay will be in Atlantic City, New Jersey, in March. 70

PROBLEM 12—TABULATED REPORT

Directions. Arrange the following report on a full sheet of paper; prepare one carbon copy. Make all the necessary corrections.

all caps — Hotels in the United States *by* Geographic Division

	Division	Hotels	Guest Rooms	Receipts	Payroll	STROKES
					(In thousands of dollars)	28 / 31 / 51 / 124 / 197 / 242 / 268 / 339
~~Total~~	United States	29,650	1,549,~~203~~ *823*	2,172,756	~~535,876~~ *660,004*	388
	New England	2,192	94,233	143,273	42,572	435
	Middle Atlantic ~~States~~	5,058	*342,628*	~~598,204~~ *610,165*	194,325	486
	East North Central	~~3,300~~ *4,545* 286,264		418,125	~~79,002~~ *131,221*	540
	West North Central	3,303	145,270	170,446	49,716	594
	South Atlantic	3,697	~~328,006~~ *187,590*	268,231	75,285	644
	East South Central	1,035	47,838	67,471	18,879	696
	West South Central	*2,705*	110,826	~~7,200~~ *132,472*	37,456	750
	Mountain	2,322	85,233	105,604	30,841	794
	~~Coast~~ *Pacific*	4,793	249,941	256,969	79,709	837
						909

INSTRUCTIONAL BLOCK 16

RECONSTRUCTION OF TYPING POWER

SECTION 34. Speed Emphasis

LESSONS 201 AND 202

Use the skill-building materials of Lessons 151 to 155, pages 204 to 208, for two periods of emphasis on improvement of your stroking rate. In each period type a conditioning practice until you feel that you have control of yourself and control of your typewriter; then use the materials for goal selection, calling the guide, and selected-goal writing as directed in the lessons. Omit the material on Correct It As You Type, unless your teacher directs otherwise.

Meaningful repetitive practice is one excellent way to build typing speed. In this practice of material that is somewhat familiar, you should be able to increase your stroking rate without sacrificing control.

SECTION 35. Control Building

LESSONS 203 TO 205

Use the skill-building materials of Lessons 156 to 160, pages 209 to 214, for three periods of emphasis on typing for control. In each of the three periods, type a conditioning practice until you feel that you have control of yourself and control of your typewriter; then use the materials for selected-goal writing as directed in the lessons. Omit the material on Correct It as You Type, unless your teacher directs otherwise.

Build control of yourself and of your typewriter. Learn to type with a high degree of accuracy with appropriate speed. This is the purpose of the three lessons of this section. Use this practice time wisely and you will show measurable improvement in accuracy WITH acceptable speed.

Pace Writings. Use the sentence for two or three 1-minute writings paced at the rate of a sentence each 20 seconds, which will give you a speed of 36 words a minute. If you can type at this rate with a feeling of ease, give attention to the sequence of letters and type for control. If you cannot type at 36 words a minute with ease, push yourself and ignore the errors temporarily.

	STROKES	WORDS
All the work is to be done without a sense of hurry or fear.	60	12

Paragraph for Guided Writing. Type the second paragraph of Skill Building 51 as directed on page 78. As the lines of this second paragraph are approximately 55 strokes each, you will be typing at the rate of 33 words a minute if the call of the guide is given each 20 seconds.

Use the remainder of the period for the practice of words from the first and second paragraphs that are "speed traps" for your fingers. Such words as *heroic, realize, superbly, excel,* and others may call for a special kind of fingering pattern that can be worked out through individual drill. After typing the difficult word, type it in a three-word group—include the preceding and the following words; as *truly heroic way.*

LESSON 53

CONDITIONING PRACTICE 53   *5 minutes*

	STROKES
Your quaint jokes would tax even the grave analyzer of chess problems.	70
Charles conceded that Chester Clark's chief characteristic is conceit.	70
Luck seems always to favor the man who does not count very much on it.	70

TECHNIQUE STUDY 53—EYES ON THE COPY   *10 minutes*

Directions. As you type, hold your eyes on the copy. Make a determined effort to do this in order to avoid the "traps" in reading the copy. Type the paragraph as two 3-minute writings. *Type on the skill-building level.*

	STROKES	WORDS
It doesn't pay to do things halfway. You want to learn to type;	65	13
learn to be the best typist you can be. This does not mean you must	134	27
learn to be a better typist than another in your class. What another	204	41
learns or does not learn is no concern of yours. After all, the thing	275	55
for which you are responsible is your own progress. It does not mean	345	69
you are not to pay attention to what others in the class do. It means	416	83
what others have been able to do, you can do when you work right. So,	487	97
learn to be the best typist you can be. This is your job.	545	109

Direct Dictation. Use the word-recognition level of response. Put all of your improved technique to work for you. *Type on the exploration level of practice.*

well tell call fall sell bell fell fill will till bill well tell call

He will call. He is well. He will sell the bell. He fell in the well.

I do this well. I do this very well. I will do this well. Did he call?

realize an accompanying increase in 2833   long strides toward improving the 3079
secretarial efficiency. (P) If, then, 2867   quality of secretarial performance 3114
you will first determine the ultimate 2906   and toward the even more important 3149
purposes for which the paper is to 2941   goal of reducing office costs. Sin- 3184
be used, and select from the kinds of 2979   cerely yours, UNIVERSAL PAPER 3214
paper recommended the type appro- 3011   COMPANY Ralph S. Browning, 3241
priate to each job, you will take 3045   Sales Manager *(499)* 3254

PROBLEM 10—BILL OF LADING

Directions. Type the following bill of lading. Refer to page *227* for an illustration of a bill of lading.

STROKES

Shipper's No. **419260**   Company **Chicago, Milwaukee, and St. Paul Railroad**   49
At **Chicago, Illinois**   From **The Midwest Farm Implement Company**   102
November 23, 195—   Consigned to **The State Farm Equipment Company**   153
Destination **Minneapolis 12,**   State of **Minnesota**   Route **Your Line**   189
Car Initial **PXD**   Car No. **320592**   200

Packages	Description	Weight	STROKES
			228
			256
5	112 gal. Electric Separators	880#	293
6	Power take-off Mowing Machines	4518#	332
2	3-wheel Side-delivery Rakes	1830#	368
4	10½ ft. Tandem Disc Harrow	5564#	403
3	3-bottom Manual Control Plows	3345#	441
7	Tractor-drawn Planters w/parts	2625#	480

Shipper **The Midwest Farm Implement Company**   Permanent address of   515
shipper **4102 North West Avenue Chicago 9, Illinois**   557

PROBLEM 11—INTEROFFICE MEMORANDUM

Directions. Type with one carbon the following message in an appropriate form.

STROKES

     To: Ralph I. Laymon, Office   29
        Manager   37
Date: Current   61
From: R. L. Matthews,   84
        Comptroller   96
File: FY 37-R-4892   116
Subject: Disposition of Records   149

Management must always con- 175
cern itself with items influencing 210
overhead. Its concern must be ac- 243
tive, critical, and impartial; and it 281
must be exercised repeatedly and 314
continuously. It is important that 350
you give some thought in the near 384
future to the problem of records as 420

they affect the offices of our organ- 456
ization. (P) To justify its invest- 487
ment in records, management must 520
realize gainful returns from their 555
use. Unnecessary forms, excessive 590
carbons, inadequate entries, cumber- 625
some files—all must be appraised in 662
terms of their usefulness to our 695
many offices. Those having outlived 732
their usefulness must be discarded; 768
and those in need of revision must 803
be changed. (P) During the next 832
six months, will you undertake to 866
discover the status of the records 901
currently in use. And, by September 938
15, will you submit a report to this 975
office, listing what, if any, changes 1013
you recommend. mh 1031

Pace Writings. Use the sentence for two or three 1-minute writings paced at the rate of a sentence each 20 seconds, which will give you a speed of 39 words a minute. If you can type at that rate with a feeling of ease, give attention to the sequence of letters and type for control. If you cannot type at 39 words a minute with ease, push yourself and ignore the errors temporarily.

	STROKES	WORDS
It is well for the men to do me a good turn, but will they do so?	65	13

Paragraph for Guided Writing. Type the third paragraph of Skill Building 51 as directed on page 78. As the lines of this third paragraph are approximately 60 strokes each, you will be typing at the rate of 36 words a minute if the call of the guide is given each 20 seconds.

Use the remainder of the period for the practice of words from the three paragraphs of Skill Building 51 that are "speed traps" for your fingers. Identify the word for practice; then after typing it once or twice to "feel out" the difficulty, type the word in a group of three words, beginning with the preceding and ending with the following word.

LESSON 54

CONDITIONING PRACTICE 54   *5 minutes*

STROKES

Please have Dorothy get four dozen quarts of lemon juice by next week.   70

Erie Public Service 6% bonds, due May 1, 1975, are ready for exchange.   70

Now is the time for me to learn to do this work with ease and control.   70

TECHNIQUE STUDY 54—EYES ON THE COPY   *15 minutes*

Directions. Type the three paragraphs of Skill Building 51, pages 78 and 79, for ten minutes. Use the 70-space line for which the machine is set. Your typed line will be longer than the lines in the copy.

Direct Dictation. Type the sentences as dictated. *Use the exploration level of practice.*

Do well! Do well all that you have to do. Learn to type with control.

The check is for $129.65. Date the letter April 30. He owes me $184.

TYPING FOR CONTROL 54   *20 minutes*

Pace Writing. Use the first paragraph for a 1-minute writing, paced at the rate of a line each 20 seconds, which will give you a speed of 30 words a minute. This will be an easy rate for you to maintain. *Type on the control level of practice.*

Paragraph for Guided Writing. 1. The lines of the first paragraph are approximately 50 strokes each. Take a 5-minute writing. Type at the rate of approximately 30 words a minute. You should be able to type with a high degree of control.

2. Build your control by taking two 1-minute writings with the goal of errorless typing. Try to maintain the approximate rate of a line each 20 seconds, but if it is necessary for you to sacrifice this exact speed in order to type with ease and control, type at the rate that is appropriate for your control practice level.

3. Type the first paragraph for two 2-minute writings with the goal of errorless typing. Your teacher will tell you whether this typing is to be done with or without the line guide called each 20 seconds.

4. Type the same paragraph for a 3-minute writing with the goal of errorless typing.

Type the dash with two hyphens without spacing before or after the hyphens.

PROBLEM 8—LETTERS WITH TABULATED REPORTS

Directions. Type two original copies without carbons of the Chamber of Commerce letter given in Problem 7. Send the first letter to **Mr. Robert S. Criswell 5915 Riverview Avenue Kansas City 9, Kansas**; and send the second letter to **Mr. William M. Mahaffey 1042 Madison Street Oklahoma City 5, Oklahoma.** Supply an appropriate salutation for each letter. Use the same style as that used in Problem 7.

PROBLEM 9—TWO-PAGE LETTER

Directions. Type the following two-page letter in modified block style with indented paragraphs and mixed punctuation. Use the current date. Prepare one carbon copy.

	STROKES
Mr. William H. McFalls, Office Man-	51
ager U. S. Refractories, Inc. 1492	86
South Avondale Drive Baton Rouge	119
11, Louisiana Dear Mr. McFalls:	152
Your letter requesting information	187
concerning the type of paper best	221
suited to effective secretarial work	258
has been referred to me. I am happy	295
to have the pleasure of writing you	331
about the problems raised in that	365
letter. (P) It seems evident from	396
your various statements that you	429
have been spending too much money	463
on high-grade paper. Much of your	498
work could be done—and should be	532
done—on paper that is less expen-	565
sive than that now being used. Ac-	599
tually, there is only a small volume	636
of work for which you need high-	667
quality paper; most of your needs	711
could be met effectively by using	745
paper of lower quality and costing a	783
great deal less than you have been	818
accustomed to paying. There is no	853
particular reason, for example, why	889
you should feel obligated to use ex-	924
pensive paper for jobs of a more or	960
less temporary nature—ones not re-	994
quiring permanent records. (P) The	1026
question concerning the type and	1059
quality of paper to be used in any	1094
business office, however, is not one	1131
that can be answered without some	1165
serious thought and investigation.	1201
The number of different kinds of	1234
paper available for office use is great;	1275
and the wide range in price for each	1312
particular kind is further complicat-	1352

	STROKES
ing. Office managers selecting pa-	1382
per, therefore, must make their se-	1416
lections in terms of many variables,	1453
all of which require exhaustive re-	1487
search into the needs, uses, and dis-	1523
position of materials throughout	1556
their respective organizations. (P)	1589
The selection of paper best suited to	1627
your organization has presented a	1661
number of difficulties, but we have	1697
several suggestions to offer which	1732
we think are worthy of your consid-	1766
eration. They are given here in the	1803
hope that they will serve as guides	1839
in directing your thinking the next	1875
time you are faced with the job of	1910
replenishing your paper supply. Af-	1945
ter you have had a chance to study	1980
them carefully, we shall be inter-	2013
ested in learning your reaction to	2048
them. (P) The first recommenda-	2075
tion, then, is that you conduct a	2109
thorough investigation to discover	2144
the actual paper needs of your or-	2177
ganization. Determine the adequacy	2213
or inadequacy of the materials now	2248
in use; and try to discover what,	2282
if any, advantages would accrue	2314
through a change in paper. (P)	2342
Our second recommendation is that	2376
you stock three different kinds of	2409
paper: (1) A permanent, high-	2440
quality paper for work requiring	2473
durability; (2) a semi-permanent,	2507
lower-quality paper for work where	2542
good appearance is desired; and (3)	2578
a temporary, low-quality paper for	2613
less important work. By insisting	2648
upon the proper use of appropriate	2683
paper for specific jobs, you will find	2722
the over-all cost of office operations	2761
reduced, and, in addition, you will	2797

Each paragraph has every letter of the alphabet and a syllable intensity of 1.25.

50-stroke
lines.

Look at your list of hindrances to typing skill as
squarely as you can. Check off those that you can
do something about. If you are right in all this,
you can quickly reduce the list. Do not deceive
yourself, though; you have just determined those
you think you can handle—you have really not done
much about them. You can't cross them off before
you have a plan of action for handling them. Note
those that are left. They may seem to be the ones
which you cannot handle by yourself. If they are,
talk them over with your teacher. It is then you
will realize the great help that your teacher will
give you in your efforts to excel in typing power.

PARA.	
51	
102	
153	
202	
251	
302	
352	
403	
454	
505	
555	
606	
656	

55-stroke
lines.

It is at this point that too many of us stop. We know
our hindrances, but we fail to draw up a plan of action
to get rid of them. If we stop with a listing of these
hindrances, we have to realize that we will surely join
the ranks of the average and not of the expert. It is
up to each of us to decide to quit pretending we want
to be superior and to take the next step that will lead
to a plan for action. If we will get rid of only one
hindrance today, we can do the same tomorrow—and we
can get rid of a third on the day after that. This is the
blueprint for superiority. It works. Try it.

PARA.	TOTAL
55	711
111	767
167	823
223	879
278	934
332	988
388	1044
442	1098
495	1151
554	1210
600	1256

NOTE: Use the remainder of the period for the practice of words from the first paragraph that are "speed traps" for your fingers. Identify the difficult or awkward word; then after typing it once or twice to "feel out" the difficulty, type the word in a group of three words, beginning with the preceding and ending with the following word.

LESSON 55

CONDITIONING PRACTICE 55

5 minutes

STROKES

I am expecting to be moved just for a week mainly because of the quiz.   70

Mrs. Richardson's daughter-in-law sent 126 pieces of first-class mail.   70

It is the way you stick to work that makes you a success or a failure.   70

TECHNIQUE STUDY 55—EYES ON THE COPY

10 minutes

Directions. Type the first paragraph of Typing for Control 54, given above, twice, using the 70-space line for which the machine is set. Your typed line will be longer than the lines in the copy.

Type on the exploration level of practice. Think the word. The purpose of this practice is to give experience in typing unarranged material. It is appropriate for you to ignore the errors temporarily in this work.

PROBLEM 6—UNRULED INVOICE

Directions. Type this invoice in a form similar to the illustration on page 221.

Sold to **The McKenna-Wellman Motor Company**   6195 West Noblestown   55
Boulevard Fort Wayne 6, Indiana   Terms **Net** 30 days   Date **November 1,**   111
195— Our No. **RJ 91570** Cust. Order No. **61581** Shipped Via **Freight Prepaid**   147

Quantity	Description	Unit Price	Amount	
				186
				225
5 ea.	15/16 Morse Speed Twist Drills	6.13	30.65	276
22 ea.	#3 Style 210 Cutting Tips	3.50	77.00	322
10 ea.	#4 Style 210 Cutting Tips	3.50	35.00	368
8 ea.	.030 Piston Ring Sets	6.88	55.04	410
50 lbs.	Newtype Automobile Wax	.91	45.50	454
135 ft.	5/16 Copper Tubing	.24	32.40	493
8 C	U. S. S. Cap Screws	2.00	16.00	531
25 ea.	8" Style B Casing Collars	.45	11.25	577
				583
			302.84	589

PROBLEM 7—LETTER WITH TABULATED REPORT

Directions. Type this letter in modified block style with no indentions for paragraphs and with mixed punctuation. Use the current date. Make one carbon copy.

Mr. Robert J. Winston 2806 Morningside Street Syracuse 10, New York   85
Dear Mr. Winston: When you come to Pittsburgh this June for the an-   152
nual meeting of office managers, you will be interested, I know, in enjoy-   225
ing some of the unusual attractions of our city. Near the top of the list,   301
I am sure, will be the fascinating experience of a sight-seeing trip by   373
incline up the steep slope of one of the many hills surrounding the city.   448
(P) There are many controversies as to which incline affords the out-   512
standing view; yet, all of them provide a treat you will not want to miss.   587
To aid you in finding these nationally known inclines, I am listing some   660
of the more important ones together with their locations and lengths.   731

Monongahela	East Townsend Street	640 ft.	775
Castle Shannon	Carson to Bailey	1,363 ft.	818
Pittsburgh	Bradish to Allentown	2,644 ft.	861
Duquesne Heights	Carson to Grandview	800 ft.	909
17th Street	Penn to Ridgeway	837 ft.	950

(P) Each of these inclines is accessible by all types of public transporta-   1020
tion. Each can be reached within a few minutes from the heart of the   1100
downtown business district. Why not include one of these long-to-be-   1159
remembered incline trips as part of your visit to Pittsburgh? Very truly   1233
yours, PITTSBURGH CHAMBER OF COMMERCE Thomas M.   1281
Williamson Publicity Chairman (209)   1310

Direct Dictation. Type each word as many times as you can until the next word is dictated. Try to work out an improved stroking pattern for the words controlled by one hand. *Type on the skill-building level of practice.*

we on as up at in be my ax in we on as up at in be my ax in my be no

We are eager to work. We paid him the minimum wage. We faced defeat.

TYPING FOR CONTROL 55 — *25 minutes*

Pace Writing. Use the second paragraph of Typing for Control 54, page 82, for a 1-minute writing paced at the rate of a line each 20 seconds, which will be at a speed of 33 words a minute. This will be an easy rate for you to maintain as some of your writing has been paced at a faster rate and much of your controlled typing has been at this rate of 33 words a minute.

Paragraph for Guided Writing. Use the second paragraph of Typing for Control 54, page 82, as directed on page 81.

NOTE: Use the remainder of the period for the practice of words from the second paragraph of Typing for Control 54 that are "speed traps" for your fingers.

LESSON 56

CONDITIONING PRACTICE 56 — *5 minutes*

	STROKES
Give lamps of bronze and zinc or jade if they are exquisitely wrought.	70
Jack Mason is 27 years 5 months and 18 days old and weighs 183 pounds.	70
No man can do the work for you no matter how much he may try to do so.	70

TECHNIQUE STUDY 56—CONTROL OF TABULATOR MECHANISM — *20 minutes*

Directions. Use a half sheet of paper; single spacing; and a 2-inch top margin. Use 6 spaces between columns. Type the tabulated report twice, with an extra space between the typings.

Determine the horizontal placement of the columns as follows:

1. Insert the paper so that it is centered.

2. Count the number of spaces used to type the longest line in each column.

3. Decide upon the number of spaces to be left between columns, usually 4, 6, 8, or 10.

4. Find the total number of spaces required.

5. Subtract the total number of spaces from 85 for pica type or 102 for elite type.

6. Divide the number of spaces found in Step 5 by 2. This is the space to be left for each of the margins. If an extra space remains, add it to the left margin. Set the stop at this point.

7. Set the tabulator stops for the columns:

a. Add to the left margin the number of spaces to be used in typing the longest line of the first column and the number of spaces to be left between the first and second columns. Set the first tabulator stop at the point that corresponds to this sum.

b. To the number representing the tabulator stop for the second column, add the number of spaces to be used in typing the longest line in the second column and the number of spaces to be left between the second and third columns. Set the tabulator stop at the point that corresponds to the sum.

c. Continue in this way until the tabulator stops for all columns have been set.

Technique Emphasis. 1. Hold the hands in typing position and stretch the finger to the tabulator bar or key. Make this a short, low, controlled motion.

2. Depress the bar or key down until the carriage has stopped its movement; then type; depress the bar or key; type; and so on to type all columns of the report. Remember to space in when necessary to keep the digits aligned at the right.

	STROKES
To: Donald C. Collins	23
Date: Current	36
From: William T. Patterson	64
File: LG 12-E-596	83
Subject: Reporting Automobile Expenses	116
	123

During the past quarter, it has been difficult to allocate properly costs for the Sales Department because of the manner in which the reports of the salesmen have been compiled. Since we are to follow a uniform policy throughout the organization, certain changes in handling expense slips must be made at once. (P) For those salesmen using their own cars, a total allowance of 8 cents a mile is permitted. To aid our record keeping, however, this total amount should be reported as two separate items. The first listing should be an entry of 5 cents a mile for actual operating expenses; and the second, 3 cents a mile for depreciation. At all times, the figures should be shown separately. As you know, the breakdown of the depreciation amount is essential to the establishment of an appropriate reserve. (P) Will you please notify all men under your jurisdiction to have their expense slips show two separate items for Automobile Expense in the future. tcr

Stroke counts: 155, 196, 229, 262, 296, 332, 364, 398, 432, 464, 507, 544, 578, 613, 652, 689, 724, 760, 796, 832, 864, 899, 933, 964, 999, 1033, 1065, 1090

PROBLEM 4—TELEFAX MESSAGE

Directions. Type this message with one carbon copy. Use the appropriate form. Refer to page 216 for an illustration of a telefax message.

	STROKES
BLZ DL PD Atlanta, Georgia Current date	44
Panhandle Oil Distributors Chamber of Commerce Building Raleigh,	110
North Carolina Instruct local agent to ship 1,000 drums crude oil from	181
Greensboro siding to Asheville Storage Depot. Notify home office of	250
compliance. National Oil Refineries, Inc. EHR:wak	301

PROBLEM 5—PURCHASE ORDER

Directions. Type this purchase order in a form similar to the illustration on page 51.

	STROKES
Order No. NB 61705 To Allied Electrical Manufacturers, Inc. 1407 Wold	57
Avenue Sioux City 9, Iowa Date 12/15/5-	92
Ship Via Transcontinental Lines, Inc.	121

Requisition	Quantity	Description	Price	STROKES
				160
				179
MO 61751	1500	Flush Mounted "On-Off" Switches	2175.00	232
MO 61751	1000	5 x 3 x 3½ in. hub. Receptacles	2890.00	286
NB 01624	2400	Welson Standard Plug Fuses	288.00	336
NB 92735	750	Porcelain Outlet Receptacles	275.00	387
RN 17038	3100	Two-toggle Switch Plates	805.74	435
RN 17038	1500	Combination Toggle Switch and Outlet	690.00	494
				502
			7123.74	509

2938	3015	5172	2936	1562	1029	2915	35
591	201	862	361	470	100	206	70
29	38	40	57	26	30	51	105
1958	1956	2971	2619	1973	3965	4012	139

Direct Dictation. Type figures on the stroke level of response; but you can quicken the response and increase your speed and control in typing figures if you will make the reach with a low finger movement without arching the wrist or making much change in the hand position.

1 4 14 141 141 4 7 47 147 147 2 9 29 129 129 3 8 38 381 381

6 2 62 162 162 3 7 37 371 371 4 8 48 481 481 5 9 59 591 591

He paid them $38. I owe 95 cents. Date the letter April 30, 1952.

SKILL BUILDING 56 *15 minutes*

Directions. Use the paragraphs of Typing for Control 54, page 82, for a 10-minute writing. *Type on the skill-building level of practice.* Keep the carriage moving. Continuity of typing is the goal of this practice.

LESSON 57

CONDITIONING PRACTICE 57 *5 minutes*

STROKES

Max amazes people by his very exact and adequate knowledge of jujitsu. 70

Is the sum of 92 and 73 and 61 and 84 and 50 and 62 and 39 and 7, 468? 70

If you know you can do a thing very well, you will do it without fear. 70

TECHNIQUE STUDY 57—CONTROL OF TABULATOR MECHANISM *15 minutes*

Directions. Type Technique Study 56 as directed, including the material for direct dictation.

SKILL BUILDING 57 *20 minutes*

Paragraph for Guided Writing. 1. Use the paragraph for a 5-minute writing. *Use the skill-building level of practice.* Determine your cwpm.

The paragraph has every letter of the alphabet.

	STROKES	WORDS
55-stroke lines. A few rules for typing numbers should be known by all	54	11
of us. Express weights and measures and sums of money	109	22
in figures; as, Jack won a prize of $24.75 with which	163	33
he bought 16 quarts of oil and 39 or 40 gallons of gas.	220	44
If a number comes at the beginning of a sentence, use	274	55
words and not figures even though the number is large	328	66
and must be typed in two or three words. Page numbers	383	77
and market quotations should be typed in figures; as,	437	87
The quotation on United 4s is given on page 89 or 90.	490	98

2. Build your skill in typing numbers by taking a 1-, a 2-, and a 3-minute writing on the paragraph with the guide called each 20 seconds. This will guide you to type at the rate of 33 words a minute as the lines of the paragraph are approximately 55 strokes each.

3. Use the remainder of the period for typing figures in context. Use Problem Typing 40, page 62.

SECTION 33. Production Measurement

LESSONS 196 TO 200

DAILY OUTLINE FOR LESSONS 196 TO 200

Conditioning Practice ....5 minutes   Production Typing ....30 minutes
Assembling & organizing materials. 5 minutes

CONDITIONING PRACTICE—LESSONS 196 TO 200   *5 minutes*

Directions. In each lesson, type each line twice. Double-space after the second typing of the line. Retype the lines as often as time permits. This will be the uniform assignment for typing the conditioning practice for all lessons in this section.

	STROKES
Just Melvin and Ezra will go quickly to view Paradise Beach next fall.	70
The chef made 405 tuna, 173 chicken, 69 lobster, and 82 shrimp salads.	70
Try to decide what you might do in order to improve your typing power.	70

PROBLEM TYPING—MEASUREMENT   *30 minutes*

General Directions. As you type the problems, correct all errors; uncorrected errors will receive a 10-word penalty. At the end of each 30-minute writing, compute your stroking rate per minute. Record your rates for future comparison.

Each problem should be typed according to the specific directions given. If you finish typing all problems, start with the first problem and retype as many as possible in the time remaining. You will receive credit for each stroke typed.

PROBLEM 1—TELEGRAM

Directions. Send the following message as a full-rate telegram. Charge it to the company sending the message. Make two carbon copies. Refer to page 215 for an illustration of a telegram.

	STROKES
Wheeling, West Virginia Current date National Camera Supply Com-	67
pany 1805-1809 Clark Building Scranton, Pennsylvania (P) Submit	128
prices and terms for three Press Cameras with 135 mm. lens and speeds	198
to 1/400 of a second. Must be equipped with flash units. State approxi-	270
mate delivery date. The Community Journal, Inc. 4103 Montgomery	335
Avenue CRB:mh	348

PROBLEM 2—TELEGRAM

Directions. Send the message in Problem 1 as a full-rate telegram to the **Universal Camera Supply Company** 1205-1207 Plaza Building Rochester, New York. Charge to the company sending the telegram. Make two carbon copies.

PROBLEM 3—INTEROFFICE MEMORANDUM

Directions. Prepare in correct form with a carbon copy the interoffice memorandum at the top of page 254. Refer to page 217 for an illustration of an interoffice memorandum.

LESSON 58

CONDITIONING PRACTICE 58

STROKES

The vase makers are greatly amazed by the excellent quality of jasper. 70

What is the sum of 94 and 83 and 72 and 50 and 62 and 31 and 49 and 6? 70

One hard thing to learn is that we must wait for growth to take place. 70

TECHNIQUE STUDY 58—STROKING

10 minutes

Directions. Type Skill Building 57, page 84, with the 70-space line for which the machine is set. Your typed line will be longer than the lines in the copy.

Technique Emphasis. Think each word and type as much of the copy as possible without thinking the letters of the word.

Direct Dictation. Type the dictation on the *exploration level of practice.*

for but but how but how lot can and all with drop back type must mind

I can! I can learn! I can learn to type! I can learn to type well.

I must learn how to type. I must learn how to type with good control.

TYPING FOR CONTROL 58

25 minutes

Progression Typing for Control. Use a 70-space line. Your line of writing will be different from the copy. Type two writings each, for a half minute, a minute, a minute and a half, and two minutes with the goal of errorless typing. Start at the beginning of the paragraph for each timing. Record the number of errorless writings you make for each time interval. *Type on the control level of practice.*

	STROKES	WORDS
It is right for me to push my stroking speed	45	9
to as high a level as I can. I should keep in	92	18
mind that I must learn how to type with control.	142	28
A lot of speed without good control is of little worth	197	39
in typing. I can learn to type rapidly and well; but after	257	51
a drive for speed, I must drop back in my typing rate until	317	63
I can type all of the copy with speed and with good control.	379	76
To type with speed and with control is the goal of this work.	440	88

Guided Writing with the Line Endings Called. Type the copy line for line. Type for 1 minute with the guide for the line ending called each 20 seconds, a rate of 28 words a minute. Type for 2 minutes with the guide for the line ending called each 20 seconds, a rate of $31\frac{1}{2}$ words a minute. As the line length increases, you will be guided to type with a gradual increase in speed. Start at the beginning of the paragraph for each timing. *Type on the control level of practice.*

Timed Writings for 1 and 2 Minutes. Take a 1-minute and a 2-minute writing with the goal of errorless typing. Use a 70-space line. *Type on the control level.*

PROBLEM 2

Directions. Use the report in Problem 1 for a series of 3-minute writings. Your goal will be to improve your skill in handling troublesome sections in an attempt to increase your production rate on tabulated reports.

LESSON 195

CONDITIONING PRACTICE 195   *5 minutes*

	STROKES
Ray explained how an amazing quirk of nature saved the King John Club.	70
They manufactured 359 locks, 408 keys, 62 safes, and 17 vaults for us.	70
A warm smile is often more valuable than great fame or untold fortune.	70

PRODUCTION TYPING 195—TYPING SHIPPING PAPERS   *35 minutes*

Directions. Type for 20 minutes using the freight bill given below; make one carbon for each bill typed. (If you do not have the printed form available, arrange the bill on a half sheet of paper.) As you type correct all errors on both copies; uncorrected errors will receive a 10-word penalty. If you finish before time is called, retype as much of the bill as possible in the time remaining. At the end of the 20-minute writing, compute your stroking rate, deducting 10 words for each uncorrected error. Compare this rate with the average rate on your writings in Lesson 192.

PROBLEM 1

	STROKES
To **U. S. Sporting Goods Company** 2006 William Penn Place Canton 12,	64
Ohio Date 11/27/5— Shipper Motor Boat Sales & Service Co.	109
1529 East Wabash Avenue South Bend 14, Indiana	156

No. Pieces	Description	Weight	Rate	Collect	STROKES
					199
					242
7 cs.	2½ h. p. Outdoor Motors—Single	259	1.15	3.45	297
6 cs.	16 h.p. Outdoor Motors—Twin	876	1.15	10.35	350
10 cs.	14 ft. Molded Plywood Boats	2200	1.60	35.20	401
25 bxs.	S. A. E. Outboard Motor Oil	2700	.97	26.19	453
20 crts.	Outboard Motor Accessories	649	.85	5.95	505
15 crts.	Stand For Motor	240	.85	2.55	546
19 crts.	Boat Trailer Assembly	1235	1.05	13.65	593
					599
				97.34	605
	3% Federal Tax			2.92	626
					632
				100.26	638

PROBLEM 2

Directions. Use the freight bill in Problem 1 for a series of 3-minute writings. Your goal will be to increase your production performance through increased rates on each timed writing.

LESSON 59

STROKES

Both of them realized I was extremely prejudiced against quick revolt.   70

This interest rate of $4\frac{1}{2}\%$ will be changed to $3\frac{1}{4}\%$ on your future loans.   70

He wrongs himself who thinks that he has no real work that he must do.   70

TECHNIQUE STUDY 59—MACHINE MANIPULATION   *10 minutes*

Use all of your techniques of machine manipulation in a pattern of efficient operation. The six operative parts that must be controlled with precision as you type are the carriage return lever, space bar, shift keys, tabulator mechanism, backspacer, and margin release.

Directions. Type Technique Study 56, page 83, as directed, including the material for direct dictation.

TYPING FOR CONTROL 59   *25 minutes*

Progression Typing for Control. Type for a minute, a minute and a half, two minutes, two and a half minutes, and three minutes. Start at the beginning of the paragraph for each timing. Goal: Errorless typing. Record the number of errorless writings you make. *Type on the control level of practice.*

	STROKES
A speed spurt made in a minute of typing does not	50
tell what you can do when typing a longer writing, but	105
it can be used to explore new areas of typing and to set up	165
new ways to type at higher speeds and with improved control.	227
Do all of your typing in the right way and the change from short	292
to long timings will not give more than the expected loss in speed	359
or in control. Use right techniques, and type with speed and control;	430
this is the way to type so that you can do the best work at all times.	500

Guided Writing with the Line Endings Called. Type for 1 minute with the guide for the line ending called each 20 seconds. This will give you a typing speed of 33 words a minute. Type for 2 minutes with the guide for the line ending called each 20 seconds. This will give you a typing speed of 36 words a minute. Start at the beginning of the paragraph for each timing. Goal: Appropriate speed with appropriate control.

Selected-Goal Typing. Select an appropriate goal to type a 1- and a 2-minute writing. Place a small check mark to indicate each half-minute and minute goal. You will use the full 70-space writing line in this typing. Your lines of typing will thus be longer than the lines in the copy. Remember to listen for the bell signal for the line ending. Your teacher will call "Half," "One," to guide you in typing at your selected goal rate. *Type on the skill-building level of practice.*

Timed Writings for 1 and 2 Minutes. Take a 1-minute and a 2-minute writing with the goal of errorless typing. *Type on the control level of practice.*

	STROKES		STROKES
your family on one of these cruises	923	will be sent to you upon request.	1066
especially designed for your comfort	960	Very truly yours, THOMAS	1091
and enjoyment. Additional informa-	994	TRAVEL AGENCY G. G. Green	1117
tion concerning any of these cruises	1031	Sales Manager *(189)*	1130

PROBLEM 2

Directions. Select for individual practice those sections of the letter in Problem 1 that proved troublesome during the 20-minute writing. Practice those sections repeatedly to gain increased skill in performance, or take a series of 1-, 2-, or 3-minute writings on these sections of the letter.

LESSON 194
CONDITIONING PRACTICE 194

5 minutes

STROKES

Jack and Max put the quietus on filming two visits to Trabzon, Turkey. 70

This spring I sold 304 rakes, 86 hoes, 172 spades, and 59 lawn mowers. 70

There is real personal satisfaction to be gained from doing work well. 70

PRODUCTION TYPING 194—TYPING TABULATED REPORTS

35 minutes

Directions. Type for 20 minutes making one carbon of each report typed. Use double spacing and a full-size sheet of paper. Center the report vertically. Assign the number of spaces between columns and determine the correct setting of the tabulator stops for the horizontal placement of the columns. As you type correct all errors on both copies; uncorrected errors will receive a 10-word penalty. If you finish the report before time is called, retype as much of it as possible in the time remaining. At the end of the 20-minute writing, compute your stroking rate, deducting 10 words for each uncorrected error. Compare this rate with the average rate on your writings in Lesson 192.

PROBLEM 1

COMPARISON OF SALES FOR THREE YEARS

Department	1950	1951	1952	STROKES
				36
				101
				166
				192
				267
Automobile accessories	$149,510	$163,200	$185,265	320
Bakery goods	27,503	31,260	37,810	357
Books and supplies	19,585	26,400	35,125	400
Cosmetics	102,560	110,380	121,837	434
Children's wear	56,297	65,380	79,105	474
Furniture	124,658	130,500	139,426	508
Groceries	106,890	114,525	153,019	542
Hardware	92,508	103,562	115,248	575
Ladies' wear	175,240	200,385	235,462	612
Men's wear	94,650	100,000	165,015	647
				711

LESSON 60

CONDITIONING PRACTICE 60

5 minutes

STROKES

Paul Schwartz and David Jacques went to the lake shore for my big box.   70

The check is for $750. Order #269-B is dated May 14. Paul owes $385.   70

Do not think too much about your own gains and how you will get ahead.   70

TECHNIQUE STUDY 60—EYES ON THE COPY

10 minutes

Directions. Use Technique Study 53, page 80, including the direct dictation. Type the material as directed.

TIMED WRITING 60

25 minutes

Directions. Type three 5-minute writings. Determine the cwpm. Average the three writings or record the three separate writings. *Type on the control level of practice.*

Each paragraph has every letter of the alphabet and a syllable intensity of 1.25.   STROKES WORDS

	STROKES	WORDS
The right kind of practice is that which is done with a purpose. You	70	14
have to know what you are expected to gain from typing a word, a line,	141	28
or a problem once or any number of times. It does no good just to fill the	217	43
paper with typed words. If you are typing for speed, make the fingers go	291	58
quite fast even if this means typing without entire control for the time	364	73
being. If you are typing for control, drop back to the speed at which you	439	88
can type with ease; then give the fingers right and definite directions,	512	102
and you will be amazed at your typing power.	558	112
Your fingers will do what you tell them to do. If you do not tell	625	125
them what you want them to do, they may fly all over the keyboard with	696	139
an excess of motion and without any gains in skill. You can usually keep	770	154
them flying with control when you realize just when to push yourself in	842	168
your typing and just when to drop back to get control. It may not be	912	182
quite so easy to keep the fingers flying where you want them to go, but	984	197
this can be done when you learn to type on the right practice level and	1056	211
when you use the appropriate typing techniques. Most of all, practice	1127	225
with a purpose. That is the kind of practice that builds power.	1191	238

NOTE: Use the remainder of the period for 1-minute writings with the throw called each 15 seconds. Use the sentences on page 50.

	STROKES	WORDS
Few offices have a standard of accuracy that is at all like the one	749	150
set for most schools. True, most employment tests still make use of the	822	164
timed writing as one part of the measurement of job competency; but	890	178
office skill is often measured in terms of how much usable work can be	961	192
turned out in a given time. At first some allowance is made for the	1030	206
nervousness of the inexperienced worker and for the learning that must	1101	220
be a part of the job. The usual instructions to the beginner are quite	1173	235
brief. It is taken for granted that one who is ready for a job will have	1247	249
the power to adapt himself to the office way of doing things. In spite of	1322	264
the fact that all studies of adjustments show that the new worker needs	1394	279
a great deal of help in getting started at his work, office managers have	1468	294
little organized help for him in his first job.	1515	303

LESSON 193

CONDITIONING PRACTICE 193 *5 minutes*

STROKES

Vick boxed amazingly at Madison Square, punishing Jack for two rounds. 70

These women ordered 97 hats, 154 gloves, 82 shoes, and 306 nylon hose. 70

If you would find the truth, do not blind yourself by bias and hatred. 70

PRODUCTION TYPING 193—TYPING LETTERS WITH TABULATED REPORTS *35 minutes*

PROBLEM 1

Directions. You are to type for 20 minutes making one carbon copy of the letter each time it is typed. Use the modified block style with no indentions for paragraphs and mixed punctuation. Set the machine for a 60-space line; use the current date. As you type correct all errors on both copies; uncorrected errors will receive a 10-word penalty. If you finish the letter before time is called, retype as much of it as possible in the time remaining. At the end of the 20 minutes, compute your stroking rate, deducting 10 words for each uncorrected error. Compare this rate with the average rate of your writings in Lesson 192.

	STROKES
Dr. Philip J. Montgomery 4013	46
Woodward Avenue Youngstown 7,	76
Ohio Dear Dr. Montgomery: Now	107
is the time to think about making	141
plans for that long-awaited summer	176
vacation. While there is still time to	216
make reservations for the type of	250

	STROKES
accommodations you prefer, you	281
should consider some of the unusual	317
travel opportunities we are making	352
available to our friends this year.	389
(P) A listing of some of the cruises	422
that may be of interest to you and	457
your family is given below. With	491
this list, too, is included the sailing	531
time, length of cruise, and minimum	567
cost per person. Note the variety of	605
enticing possibilities available at	641
such amazingly low cost.	667

Europe	April 26	41 days	$975	696
West Indies	Weekly	11 days	$270	728
Alaska	July 9, 23	20 days	$575	759
Mexico	Weekly	13 days	$265	786
South America	July 10	38 days	$975	821

(P) Study this list carefully and de-	853
cide now to enjoy the summer with	887

INSTRUCTIONAL BLOCK 5

TYPING FOR PERSONAL USE

The materials in this instructional block are designed to help you gain experience with typing typical personal problems. Bring to class and submit to your teacher for approval and suggestions personal material that you need to type. Start now to make personal use of the typing power you have already developed.

SECTION 10. Problems in Personal Typing

Directions. Use a 70-space line, single spacing, and type the lines of the conditioning practice twice each; then double-space.

With each section headed Related Learning, you will find explanatory statements keyed to specific sentences. Study the explanatory statement for the sentence; then type the sentence and think of the technical English used as you type.

Correct It as You Type or Direct Dictation provides the testing portion of your mastery of the related learnings taught. If the sentences are dictated, keep the book closed or the page covered so that you will get the impulse to type through the dictation. If you are instructed to type the sentences from the book, read through the sentence and mentally note the corrections that are to be made but do not make pencil corrections; then type the sentence or the line at a speed that is appropriate for the thoughtful work you are expected to do.

With the permission of your teacher, substitute your own materials for any problems given in the textbook.

LESSON 61

CONDITIONING PRACTICE 61	5 minutes
	STROKES
Maybe John Pavlick does expect to win the prize for his quiet singing.	70
Jane is 16 years 3 months and 20 days old; Carl, 18 years 15 days old.	70
Make a fine art of all your work if you want the secret of succeeding.	70

RELATED LEARNING 61	10 minutes

Directions. Study the explanatory statements; then type each line twice. Double-space after the second typing of the line. Retype selected lines if time permits.

Line 1: To form the possessive of a singular noun, add *'s*.
Line 2: Spell out a number used at the beginning of a sentence.
Line 3: In expressing a date within a sentence, set off the year with commas.
Line 4: The title of a book printed in italics may be underscored or typed in all capitals.
Line 5: All numbers in a connected group should be expressed in the same manner.

	STROKES
Mr. Johnson's daughter was offended by the hostess's manner.	60
Twenty million dollars was the price of the Philippine Islands.	63
On January 1, 1863, Lincoln issued the Emancipation Proclamation.	65
In 1852 *Uncle Tom's Cabin* molded public opinion concerning slavery.	67
My collection has 250 books, 90 sheets of music, and 75 piano records.	70

3. Statistical Typing

Directions. Use the following paragraph for a series of 1-minute writings. Try to increase your stroking rate with each repeat writing.

	STROKES
The total expenditure of $129,085,670.65 for vocational education	66
which met the standards set in the Smith-Hughes and George-Barden	132
Acts included $26,622,938.12 from federal funds, $40,521,695.35 from state	207
funds, and $61,941,037.18 from local funds. These expenditures represent	281
an increase of $213,956.07 from federal funds, $10,082,760.22 from state	354
funds, and $3,657,582.78 from local funds.	396

LESSON 192

CONDITIONING PRACTICE 192

5 minutes

	STROKES
Andy saw Bix sail quietly into thick morning fog up the hazy Java Sea.	70
Their store sold 302 shirts, 75 belts, 196 handkerchiefs, and 84 ties.	70
No one realizes just how much good can be done until he finally tries.	70

PRODUCTION TYPING 192

35 minutes

Directions. Use the following paragraphs for four 5-minute writings. Set your machine for a 70-space line and double spacing; prepare one carbon for each writing. As you type correct all errors on both copies; uncorrected errors will receive a 10-word penalty. For each writing, compute your stroking rate, deducting 10 words for each uncorrected error. Find the average rate for all four writings.

Each paragraph has every letter of the alphabet and a syllable intensity of 1.35.

	STROKES	WORDS
The man who said "Only two things are certain—death and taxes"	64	13
forgot something. It is just as certain that you will never have time to	138	28
do all the things you need to do unless you establish the habit of using	211	42
your time fully. It always seems so futile to say this to students or to	285	57
beginning workers. Most young people seem to feel that they can beat	355	71
the game; but when the day of reckoning is upon them, they rush around	426	85
trying to do two things at once and succeeding superbly in doing neither	499	100
at all well. The last-minute rush that characterizes the worker who fails	574	115
to plan his work could be avoided if adequate practice in planning for	645	129
work were part of school training.	681	136

Directions. These sentences are in problem form. To type them in correct form, you must know the basic principles of technical English taught in the explanatory statements for the sentences preceding. Your teacher will tell you whether the sentences are to be dictated or whether they are to be typed from the copy. Type at a rate that will permit you to think of the correct form. If you are uncertain how to type a sentence, refer to the explanatory statements.

three hundred dollars a month is what he earns. alberts work is well done.
use february six 1952 as the date for the letter. joes weeks pay is forty dollars.
we use 20th century typewriting. they used one hundred twenty-nine letterheads.

PROBLEM TYPING 61   *20 minutes*

Directions. Use a full sheet of paper; a 60-space line; a 5-space paragraph indention; double spacing; a top margin of 2 inches; and type the heading in all capitals, centered horizontally. Triple-space after typing the heading. Encircle any errors. Then type the problem a second time with all errors erased and corrected. Note the time required to erase and correct an error. Are you paying too high a price for failure to develop control?

	STROKES	WORDS
SIMON BOLIVAR, THE GREAT LIBERATOR	35	7
~~Ask any~~ *Bolivar, the* Venezuelan ~~about the~~ Great Liberator, ~~and he will tell you~~	76	15
~~that Bolivar~~ was born in Caracas in 1783; ~~that~~ at 16, he was off to Spain	133	27
for education; ~~that~~ at 21, he stood in the crowd ~~which~~ *that* witnessed Na-	194	39
poleon's coronation in Paris and was overcome by the admiration which	264	53
Parisians expressed for their hero; ~~that~~ *in* Paris, young Bolivar met Baron	335	67
von Humboldt, but recently returned from his American explorings, who	405	81
told the Venezuelan that his native land was ripe for freedom and lacked	478	96
only a leader.	494	99
~~In 1810~~, Bolivar returned to his country, *in 1810.* For 13 years, ~~in defeat and~~	550	110
~~victory,~~ he led his armies through the lands now called Venezuela, Co-	610	122
lombia, Ecuador, Peru, and Bolivia, becoming general, president, pro-	678	136
tector, and Liberator. He wrote constitutions, *and* organized governments;	752	150
and *he* founded the Gran Colombia, which in 1830 became the independent	823	165
states of Ecuador, Colombia, and Venezuela.	868	174
~~It was in 1830, too, that Bolivar,~~ *Exile bound and* almost alone, ~~exile bound,~~ *Bolivar* died near	916	183
Cartagena *in 1830,* believing he had "ploughed in the sea."	974	195

SKILL MAINTENANCE 61

Directions. If time permits, take a number of 1-minute writings, using the sentence below. Additional 1-minute writings can be taken on the third sentence of the conditioning practice for this lesson.

	STROKES	WORDS
It saves time to take time to plan the typing before any work is done.	70	14

SECTION 32. Production Comparison

LESSON 191

CONDITIONING PRACTICE 191 *5 minutes*

Directions. Type each line twice. Double-space after the second typing of the line. Retype the lines as often as time permits. This will be the uniform assignment for typing the conditioning practices in all lessons in this section.

	STROKES
Dave quoted an excerpt from the Jasper Gazette about the Kyle wedding.	70
The hotel kept 14 rugs, 93 curtains, 652 sheets, and 780 pillow cases.	70
It is a fine thing to have a typing skill you can put to work for you.	70

SKILL RECONSTRUCTION 191 *35 minutes*

1. Sentences for Calling the Guide

Directions. Use the following lines for 1-minute writings with the teacher calling the guide in 15-, 12-, or 10-second intervals. *Type on the exploration level of practice.*

```
         1       2       3       4       5       6       7       8       9      10      11      12      13      14
There will be a sales meeting during the week.  All of us must attend.
All new products are to be displayed.  They can attract our customers.
We should learn useful sales methods.  Leaders may present some ideas.
Sales trainees begin their training early.  They are promoted quickly.
There are fine rewards for industrious men.  You should apply at once.
         1       2       3       4       5       6       7       8       9      10      11      12      13      14
```

2. Paragraphs for Calling the Guide

Directions. Use the following paragraphs for calling-the-guide writing. Your teacher may call the guide each 15, 12, or 10 seconds. Write each line on the call of the guide until you can type that line in the time allowed; then type the next line. Follow this procedure until you complete the paragraph. When you have written each paragraph under this plan, take additional writings but move from one line to the next with each call of the guide. *Type on the exploration level of practice.*

	STROKES	WORDS
Just as soon as you get high speed in typing from	50	10
straight copy, you should make plans at once for the	103	21
far more important job of learning how to use all that	158	32
speed in typing a large number of business problems. It	215	43
will be worth your time to work for skill in problem typing.	275	55
One of the things to keep in mind when you are asked to try	60	12
office typing is that the best work is done by those who stick	123	25
with a job until it is finished. They do not permit needless or	188	38
harmful interruptions; they make sure that no time is lost because	255	51
of poor work habits. Gain real skill through a wise use of your time.	325	65

LESSON 62

	STROKES
His visit to Mexico and Brazil was quietly planned by Jackson Fleming.	70
In the letter of the 13th of April, they enclosed a check for $15,620.	70
We can usually find the time we need to do those things we want to do.	70

RELATED LEARNING 62   *10 minutes*

Directions. Study the explanatory statements; then type each line twice. Double-space after the second typing of the line. Retype selected lines as time permits.

Line 1: When stating cents, use the figures without the decimal and spell "cents."
Line 2: Express measures (weights and dimensions) in figures.
Line 3: When two numbers immediately follow each other, it is generally better to spell out the smaller and express the larger in figures.
Line 4: A direct quotation is enclosed within quotation marks. The comma precedes the quotation mark.
Line 5: Note the way of typing fractions. Use the diagonal when typing "made" fractions.

	STROKES
The list showed an increase of 32 cents for all short items.	60
He used 5 gallons of red paint and 3 quarts of oil in the work.	63
He bought 26 one-cent stamps and 48 three-cent stamped envelopes.	65
"The best-laid schemes o' mice an' men gang aft agley," she quoted.	67
They should be uniform in typing all fractions, as, $\frac{1}{2}$, $\frac{1}{4}$, or 1/2, 1/4.	70

CORRECT IT AS YOU TYPE (OR DIRECT DICTATION)   *5 minutes*

we paid 26 and two thirds for the stock. "nothing is good or bad," he quoted.

i paid seventy-five cents for the paper. we need six gallons of oil.

we must buy eighteen three-cent stamps. the price is 25 3/4 or $26\frac{1}{4}$.

PROBLEM TYPING 62   *20 minutes*

Directions. This brief tabulated report gives the present area and the population of the three countries that were formerly the Gran Colombia founded by Simon Bolivar. Type the problem twice, each time on a half sheet of paper. Set the machine for double spacing. Set the margin and tabulator stops as directed for Technique Study 56, page 83. Leave six spaces between columns.

Center the three-line heading horizontally, starting the first line of the heading approximately 10 spaces from the top of the paper. Be sure to triple-space after typing the third line of the heading. Use the quotation marks for *ditto* (the same).

Area and Population
of the
Independent States of the Gran Colombia

Colombia	439,714 Sq. Mi.	11,259,730 Population
Ecuador	175,830 " "	3,467,399 "
Venezuela	352,143 " "	4,596,000 "

Directions. You are to type for 30 minutes. Type each **problem** once with a carbon. Proof-read each problem and correct all errors before removing **it from** the typewriter. Uncorrected errors will receive a 10-word penalty. If you complete the typing of the problems before time is called, retype as many as possible in the time remaining. At the end of the 30-minute period, compute your stroking rate per minute. *Type on the control level.*

PROBLEM 1

Directions. Use a full-size sheet of paper; double-space the body of the report.

						STROKES
POPULATION PER SQUARE MILE						27
						101
						175
State Groups	1900	1910	1920	1930	1940	212
						286
United States	25.6	30.9	35.5	41.2	44.2	330
New England	90.2	105.7	119.4	129.2	133.5	372
Middle Atlantic	154.5	193.2	222.6	261.3	274.0	418
East North Central	65.2	74.3	87.5	103.2	108.7	467
West North Central	20.3	22.8	24.6	26.0	26.5	516
South Atlantic	38.8	45.3	52.0	58.8	66.4	561
East South Central	42.0	46.8	49.5	54.8	59.7	610
West South Central	15.2	20.4	23.8	28.3	30.3	659
Mountain	1.9	3.1	3.9	4.3	4.8	698
Pacific	7.6	13.2	17.5	25.6	30.4	736
						810
						883

PROBLEM 2

Directions. Use a full-size sheet of paper; double-space the body of the report.

							STROKES
All caps → *Summary of Sales and Selling Costs*							35
							187
Ser	Salesman	Sales	Reports	Inter-views	Selling Cost	Per Cent	248
							324
1	Andrews	$43,313	167	849	#2,926.70	6.76	375
2	Cleaver	137,992	1,650	3,799	10,815.37	7.84	422
3	Dennis	80,049	820	1,829	8,264.31	10.32	468
4	Miller	49,732	821	1,840	6,610.01	13.29	514
5	Thomas	51,792	710	1,963	8,037.57	13.91	560
6	Horton	106,510	517	1,594	8,876.14	8.33	606
7	Banks	109,496	788	2,127	6,915.77	6.32	651
8	Morton	60,636	791	2,109	9,060.13	14.94	697
9	Mitchell	55,653	544	1,407	6,829.24	12.27	745
10	Underwood	154,979	1,107	2,402	15,057.29	9.72	794
							945

SKILL MAINTENANCE 62

Directions. If time permits, take a number of 1-minute writings, using the sentence below. Make the corrections indicated. The strokes and words shown are for the corrected copy.

	STROKES	WORDS
Plan ~~the~~ *your* work~~, and~~ work ~~y~~ *y*our plan; ~~for~~ *and* your typing skill *is sure* to grow.	70	14

LESSON 63

CONDITIONING PRACTICE 63   *5 minutes*

STROKES

Did William quickly reject the offer of five dozen more packing boxes?   70

Isn't Order #479-B to be shipped by September 26? (It comes to $500.)   70

He wrote, "Lose as if you like it; and win as if you were used to it."   70

RELATED LEARNING 63   *10 minutes*

Directions. Study the explanatory statements; then type each line twice. Double-space after the second typing of the line.

Line 1: After the name of a month, express the day in figures. Words in a series are separated by commas, and the comma is used before the conjunction.

Line 2: Use *d, st,* or *th* when the day of the month stands alone or when it precedes the month. In expressing even sums of money, do not use a decimal or ciphers.

Line 3: Express dimensions in figures, and spell *by* in full in ordinary business letters. (The symbol *x* is used for *by* in technical material.)

Line 4: Add *'s* to form the possessive of plural nouns not ending in *s*; if the plural ends in *s*, add *'* only.

Line 5: Add *'s* to form the singular possessive. Use Roman numerals to indicate a major division, such as Volume V, and figures to indicate a minor division, such as Section 5. (It is also correct to abbreviate Volume to Vol. and Section to Sec.)

STROKES

He wrote letters on March 3, 9, and 22; no reply came until August 14.   70

On the 15th of April, they bought furnishings that amounted to $1,720.   70

Their ten-page booklet, $4\frac{1}{2}$ by 7 inches, can be carried in your pocket.   70

The men's club met to discuss the boys' work that is to be undertaken.   70

I read Judge Parkinson's decision in Volume V, Section 5, pages 62-94.   70

CORRECT IT AS YOU TYPE (OR DIRECT DICTATION)   *5 minutes*

the childrens mother is ill. these girls reports are ready.

the goods were shipped on the tenth of may. they owe two hundred dollars.

the data are reported in volume 2. i read pages 129 and 290 of section 6.

PROBLEM 2—SKILL BUILDING IN TYPING TABULATED REPORTS

Directions. Take a series of 3-minute writings on the body of the report of Problem 1. At the end of each 3-minute writing, compute your typing rate. Try to improve your stroking rate with each timed writing.

SKILL MAINTENANCE 188 — 5 minutes

Directions. Use the following paragraph for 1-minute writings. *Type on the exploration level of practice.*

	STROKES	WORDS
You must work for freedom of finger movement. This is especially	66	13
necessary in the use of the keys in the lower (or first) row of the key-	137	27
board. Make the reach in the shortest and most direct manner. Avoid	207	41
twisting the elbow or moving the wrist in or out. Hit the center of the	280	56
key; then pull the finger upward and toward typing position. The right	352	70
way to strike the keys needs to be recalled from time to time through	422	84
some deliberate practice for improved stroking skill.	475	95

LESSON 189

CONDITIONING PRACTICE 189 — 5 minutes

	STROKES
Major Van Horne equipped Lowe with extra cargo of forty Army bazookas.	70
That baseball team bought 605 bats, 74 gloves, 192 shoes, and 83 caps.	70
Business is willing to pay for tasks that are done neatly and on time.	70

PROBLEM TYPING 189—SKILL BUILDING — 35 minutes

Directions. Make pencil notations on a piece of note paper of the problems listed below, and place the paper on the desk near your textbook so that you can refer to it as you complete the typing of each problem. You will be timed for 30 minutes. Correct all errors; uncorrected errors will receive a 10-word penalty. If you complete the typing of the problems before time is called, retype as many of them as possible. Compute your stroking rate at the end of the 30-minute period.

Problem 1, page 243—type once with a carbon copy.
Problem 1, page 244—type once with a carbon copy.
Problem 1, page 245—type once with a carbon copy.

LESSON 190

CONDITIONING PRACTICE 190 — 5 minutes

	STROKES
Jeff, vexed by tiresome quizzing of District Attorney Whick, appealed.	70
The dealers sold 107 used cars, 95 trucks, 234 radios, and 86 heaters.	70
It should not be difficult to learn how to adjust to office procedure.	70

Directions. Use a 60-space line, a 5-space paragraph indention, and double spacing. Type the heading in capital letters 2 inches from the top of the paper. Triple-space after typing the heading. Encircle each error. Type the problem again, but erase and correct each error, noting the time error correction takes. It pays to develop typing control as you can type several words in the time required to correct an error.

	STROKES	WORDS

MANUSCRIPT TYPING

	STROKES	WORDS
MANUSCRIPT TYPING	18	4
Type ⟨a⟩ manuscripts with double spacing. Quoted material of ⟨four or⟩ more ~~than~~	90	18
~~four~~ lines may be single spaced and indented. The omission of material	157	31
from the quoted matter, ⟨should be⟩ ~~is~~ indicated by an ellipsis—~~commonly~~ ⟨usually⟩ three	230	46
periods for the omission of a part of a sentence and four periods for the	304	61
omission of a whole sentence or the ⟨final⟩ ~~last~~ words of a sentence. In typing	378	76
the ellipsis, alternate the period and the space.	429	86
⟨Type the⟩ ~~The~~ superior figure for a footnote reference ~~should be typed~~ a half	486	98
space above the writing line, placed after the author's name in the text	559	112
or at the end of the ⟨quoted material:⟩ ~~quotation.~~ Type the figure to <u>follow</u> the punctuation	646	129
mark, if ~~any.~~ ⟨a punctuation mark is used.⟩	684	137
⟨never end a⟩ A page ~~should never end~~ with a hyphenated word. Do not have just	743	149
one line of a paragraph on a page. The bottom margin may be narrower	813	163
or wider to avoid, ⟨typing⟩ ~~carrying~~ the ⟨final⟩ ~~last~~ line of a paragraph, ⟨on⟩ ~~to~~ the ⟨succeeding⟩ ~~following~~	886	177
page.	893	179
The title of an article, ⟨should be⟩ ~~is~~ enclosed within quotation marks. ⟨Type the⟩ ~~The~~ title	976	195
of a book, ⟨a⟩ periodical, or ⟨a⟩ thesis ~~is typed~~ in all capital letters or under-	1044	209
scored. ⟨it, is you prefer,⟩ It is acceptable, but ⟨it is⟩ not the best practice, to quote the title of	1143	229
a book; ⟨it should be typed in all capital letters or underscored.⟩	1208	242

SKILL MAINTENANCE 63

Directions. If time permits, take a number of 1-minute writings, using the sentence below. Additional 1-minute writings can be taken on the third sentence of the conditioning practice.

	STROKES	WORDS
You can do all ~~of this~~ ⟨the⟩ work well if you ⟨will⟩ think right ~~and~~ ⟨as you⟩ typewrite.	70	14

LESSON 64

CONDITIONING PRACTICE 64   *5 minutes*

	STROKES
By zeal, pluck, and expert work Frederic is just moving quickly ahead.	70
The total of 9 and 6 and 31 and 40 and 82 and 95 and 63 and 50 is 376.	70
It is in our daily work that we make our future what we want it to be.	70

PROBLEM 2—SKILL BUILDING IN TYPING TABULATED REPORTS

Directions. Use the tabulated report in Problem 1 for a series of 1-minute writings. Your teacher will pace you at the end of each minute. Begin each writing with the first line of the body of the problem. At the end of the first minute when your teacher calls "Throw; Type," throw the carriage and start to type the first line of the body of the problem. At the end of the second, third, fourth, etc., minutes, the same procedure will be followed. Try to increase your stroking rate with each minute timing.

SKILL MAINTENANCE 187   *5 minutes*

Directions. Use the following paragraph for a series of 1-minute writings. *Type on the exploration level of practice.*

	STROKES	WORDS
Routine is an aid to success in learning to do things with ease and	68	14
sureness. Do the same thing in the same way day after day, and you will	141	28
set up the habit of exact control. A routine way of doing things does	212	42
not mean that you will work without interest and enthusiasm. Any work	283	57
that is done without joy will bog down sooner or later; for happiness in	356	71
work is the spark plug that transforms it.	398	80

LESSON 188

CONDITIONING PRACTICE 188   *5 minutes*

	STROKES
Philip and Ted reviewed a critique by Jack Graf on axioms and puzzles.	70
He packed 175 belts, 296 hats, 40 pistols, and 38 knives for the boys.	70
The latest styles will be shown at the fashion show held in the hotel.	70

PROBLEM TYPING 188—TABULATING BY THE BACKSPACE-CENTERING METHOD   *30 minutes*
PROBLEM 1—SKILL BUILDING IN TYPING TABULATED REPORTS

Directions. Center the following report vertically on a full-size sheet of paper. Double-space the body of the report. Use your judgment in spacing the primary and column headings and in assigning the number of spaces between columns. Proofread the typed copy before removing it from the typewriter.

	Number of Associations	Total Assets	Mortgage Loans	U. S. Gov't and Other Securities	STROKES
SAVINGS AND LOAN ASSOCIATIONS					30
TOTAL NUMBER AND SELECTED FINANCIAL ITEMS					72
					106
(Amounts in thousands of dollars)					180
					254
Selected Districts	Number of Associations	Total Assets	Mortgage Loans	U. S. Gov't and Other Securities	357
					431
United States	6,011	13,027,552	10,409,143	1,525,538	483
No. 1 Boston	336	1,179,162	962,989	135,675	535
No. 2 New York	734	1,664,381	1,286,867	238,197	589
No. 3 Pittsburgh	976	937,421	803,236	60,915	645
No. 4 Winston-Salem	871	1,625,436	1,417,595	95,234	704
No. 5 Cincinnati	776	2,145,343	1,555,504	376,574	760
No. 6 Indianapolis	306	744,995	548,437	111,931	818
No. 7 Chicago	737	1,318,905	1,066,089	144,094	871
					945
					1018

Directions. Study the explanatory statements; then type each line twice. Double-space after the second typing of the line.

Line 1: The titles of articles should be placed within quotation marks. When the quotation is a question, the question mark should precede the quotation mark.

Line 2: Type policy numbers without separating the hundreds from the thousands by a comma.

Line 3: Capitalize words that are personified. Type the quotation mark before the question mark if the material quoted is not a question.

Line 4: When the quotation mark is used with a comma or a period, the comma and the period are always typed before the quotation mark.

Line 5: When common possession is to be shown for two or more persons, use the apostrophe with the last name only. In typed material underscore (or type in capitals) the title of a book that is printed in italics.

STROKES

Frank Maxton's article, "Have You Had Your Daily Dozen?" is very fine. 70

Joe's Policy #84639 for $15,000 has been renewed for another 15 years. 70

Who did you say made profits of 42 per cent in '46 with "King Cotton"? 70

"Always do your best," Harry said, "and good will always come to you." 70

Has Mrs. Morrison read Wilson and Eyster's *Consumer Economic Problems?* 96

CORRECT IT AS YOU TYPE (OR DIRECT DICTATION)

5 minutes

he was known as the lone eagle. policy number 926410 is for one thousand dollars.

the article "do you earn?" is good. have you the article better typing

we use crabbe and salsgiver's book general business. he said, "i can type well

PROBLEM TYPING 64

20 minutes

Directions. Use a half sheet of paper and a 60-space line. Center the heading horizontally and center the problem vertically. Make one carbon copy.

STROKES

STRUCTURE OF AN OUTLINE

24

I. Numerals and letters are used to indicate divisions of 83
an outline. 96

  A. Main headings are usually marked by Roman numerals. 153
  B. Subdivisions under the main headings may be marked by 211
    1. Arabic numerals, or 234
    2. Small letters. 253

II. The spacing used within an outline is optional but should 316
be consistent throughout. 343

  A. A line space should be left before and after a main 399
    heading. 409
  B. After numbers or letters used to indicate divisions 465
    of an outline the spacing may be 498
    1. Two spaces after the period following a Roman 547
      numeral or a capital letter. 577
    2. One space after the period following an Arabic 627
      numeral or a small letter. 653

Directions. Use Problem 1 for a series of 3-minute writings for the purpose of increasing your stroking rate on tabulated reports. At the end of each writing, compute your stroking rate per minute.

SKILL MAINTENANCE 186 *5 minutes*

Directions. Use the following paragraph for a series of 1-minute writings. *Type on the exploration level of practice.*

	STROKES	WORDS
Make full use of the equipment of your typewriter. The machine has	68	14
parts to be used that will aid you to produce more work with more ease	139	28
and in less time than would otherwise be required. Take the tabulator	210	42
mechanism, for example. Instead of "thumbing it" to indent for a para-	280	56
graph or to a column, set a tabulator stop and use it.	334	67

LESSON 187

CONDITIONING PRACTICE 187 *5 minutes*

	STROKES
Jim and Lee were quite dazed by the extravagant ship I took to France.	70
The builders had 192 wrenches, 486 hammers, 50 pliers, and 73 chisels.	70
All offices will receive an order to increase the salaries of workers.	70

PROBLEM TYPING 187—TABULATING BY THE BACKSPACE-CENTERING METHOD *30 minutes*
PROBLEM 1—LEARNING THE NATURE OF THE PROBLEM

Directions. Center the following report on a full-size sheet of paper. Leave 2 spaces between the primary heading and the column headings and 2 spaces between the column headings and the body of the tabulation. Insert the ruled lines about midway in these spaces. Use double spacing throughout the body of the tabulation.

Leave 6 spaces between columns.

Proofread the typed copy before removing it from the typewriter. Then type the report a second time.

NOTE: To draw double lines, use either the ratchet release (No. 6) or the variable line spacer (No. 3). (The ratchet release is preferred when one desires to have the platen return to its original writing position.) Type a horizontal line. Release the platen and turn it forward (away from you) until the first line typed is even with the top of the alignment scale. Type the second horizontal line; then, return the platen to its original writing position.

RETAIL SALES BY BUSINESS GROUPS
IN
MILLIONS OF DOLLARS

Group	1937	1947	1949	1951	STROKES
					32
					35
					55
					128
					201
					227
					300
All Retail Stores	32,791	100,298	130,042	128,183	349
Motor Vehicle Dealers	3,863	7,995	17,530	21,085	402
Farm Implements	292	787	1,555	1,401	449
Building Material	1,105	4,137	6,801	6,020	498
Household Appliances	483	1,685	2,680	2,793	550
Women's Apparel	1,026	4,033	4,530	4,193	597
Men's Clothing	727	2,227	2,412	2,223	643
Drug Stores	1,233	3,520	3,687	3,005	686
Filling Stations	1,968	4,065	6,325	6,363	734
Shoes	511	1,459	1,537	1,478	771
Jewelry	235	1,343	1,264	1,100	810
					882

Directions. If time permits, take a number of 1-minute writings, using the sentence below. Additional 1-minute writings can be taken on the third sentence of the conditioning practice.

of us   *we   do*   STROKES WORDS

Most like to do the things that can ~~be done~~ with ease *and control.*   70   14

LESSON 65

CONDITIONING PRACTICE 65   *5 minutes*

STROKES

Jasper Dawson quickly began to save money for the next big cash prize.   70

The box measured 6 by 9 feet, and it weighed approximately 280 pounds.   70

It is well for all of us to do the very best work we can at all times.   70

RELATED LEARNING 65   *10 minutes*

Directions. Study the explanatory statements; then type each line twice. Double-space after the second typing of the line. Be certain that you understand the related knowledge taught in the explanatory statements.

Line 1: A quotation within a quotation is indicated by the single quotation mark (the apostrophe).
Line 2: The plural form of letters and of figures may be expressed with the apostrophe and *s*.
Line 3: In market quotations, the plural of figures is expressed by the addition of *s* without the apostrophe.
Line 4: Type distance in figures except when indicating a fraction of a mile; then use words.
Line 5: Use figures to state page numbers. Do not capitalize the word page unless it is the first word in the sentence. Use figures with a.m. or p.m. (also typed A.M. or P.M.) and separate the hour from the minutes by a colon.

NOTE: When time is followed by a phrase such as "in the morning" or "tonight," do not use a.m. or p.m.

STROKES

I heard him say, "I shall want to see the article, 'So Little to Do.'"   70

When Henry writes, I cannot read it for he makes his 2's like his z's.   70

United Funds 4s (Series B) are due in 1956 and are now selling at $85\frac{1}{4}$.   70

They drove 220 miles from Lynchburg, Virginia, to Annapolis, Maryland.   70

I must read pages 27-60 of GENERAL BUSINESS between 7:30 and 9:45 p.m.   70

CORRECT IT AS YOU TYPE (OR DIRECT DICTATION)   *5 minutes*

the town is twenty-eight miles from here. he said, "read the article, 'Typing Tips

how many A's did you earn? we sold Consolidated fours at sixty-seven and a half.

i shall walk a half mile more. study page ninety-five before ten thirty p.m.

SECTION 31. Tabulated Reports (Backspace-Centering Method)

LESSON 186

CONDITIONING PRACTICE 186 — *5 minutes*

Directions. Type each line twice. Double-space after the second typing of the line. Retype the lines as often as time permits. This will be the uniform assignment for all conditioning practices in this section.

	STROKES
Hal Roza was requested to pick five or six new judges by April or May.	70
Bob Mathews sent 46 necklaces, 193 clips, 520 pins, and 87 jade rings.	70
You cannot build good office skill on the wrong kind of typing habits.	70

PROBLEM TYPING 186—TABULATING BY THE BACKSPACE-CENTERING METHOD — *30 minutes*

Use this method as a rapid means of locating the margin and tabulator stops. Follow this procedure:

1. Determine the vertical placement in the usual way (See page 15).
2. Assign an even number of spaces between columns (4, 6, 8, or 10).
3. To set margin and tabulator stops:
   a. From the center of the page, backspace once for each two spaces in the longest item of each column. Backspace once for each two spaces between columns. Set the left margin stop.
   b. From the left margin, space forward once for each letter and space in the longest line in the first column and once for each space between column 1 and column 2; set the tabulator stop. Continue in this way until all stops have been set.
4. To determine the placement of columnar headings, first find the center of each column; then backspace once for each two spaces in the heading for each column.

Example: **Automobile Accessories $149,510 $163,200**

Step 2: Leave 6 spaces between columns.
   3: a. Left margin stop: 17 for pica-, 25 for elite-type machines.
      b. First tabulator stop: 45 for pica-, 53 for elite-type machines.
        Second tabulator stop: 59 for pica-, 67 for elite-type machines.

PROBLEM 1—LEARNING THE NATURE OF THE PROBLEM

Directions. Center the report vertically on a full-size sheet of paper. Use triple spacing after the heading and double spacing in the body of the tabulation. Leave 6 spaces between columns. Proofread the typed copy before removing it from the typewriter.

PATENTS ISSUED TO CITIZENS OF TEN STATES

State				STROKES
				41
				88
California	1,719	2,231	3,144	117
Connecticut	738	817	1,242	147
Delaware	213	235	297	174
Illinois	2,074	2,448	3,572	201
Massachusetts	1,046	1,336	1,841	233
Michigan	1,085	1,346	2,024	260
New Jersey	2,063	2,399	3,217	289
New York	3,690	4,664	6,313	316
Ohio	1,623	2,056	2,896	339
Pennsylvania	1,488	1,953	2,590	370
				416

PROBLEM I

Directions. Type the letter in the modified block form similar to Style Letter 3, page 71, except that you will add the personal return address and type your name 4 spaces below the complimentary close as is done in the personal letter of Lesson 27, page 43. Address an envelope. Place the typed letter under the flap of the envelope, address side up.

STROKES

2701 Woodmont Street	21
Richmond 6, Virginia	42
April 28, 195—	57

Lionel Investment Service 20 Ex-	88
change Place New York 18, New	118
York Gentlemen At a friend's home	152

STROKES

recently, I saw a copy of a booklet	188
published by you entitled *Problems*	231
of the Investor. I was told that I	282
can get a copy of this booklet by	316
writing to you. (P) You have had	346
long experience in advising inves-	380
tors. I have somewhat limited funds	416
to invest, but I would like to invest	454
in stocks or bonds that will yield the	493
maximum return with the maximum	525
security. (P) If there is a charge for	561
Problems of the Investor, bill me;	620
and I shall be glad to send you my	655
check promptly. Yours very truly	689
(Type your own name)	

PROBLEM 2. COMPOSITION AT THE TYPEWRITER

Directions. Write a letter to the Ritz-Claredge Hotel, Madison Avenue, New York 16, and ask that a medium-priced single room with bath be reserved for your occupancy for Wednesday and Thursday of the week following. (Be sure to give the exact dates for which you wish the room reserved.) In a second paragraph, say that you are motoring to New York and expect to arrive at the hotel between four and five o'clock.

In the original composition at the typewriter, do not erase errors or words to be changed. If it is necessary to change a word or more, X-out the material you want to omit and continue typing. If more than a word is to be crossed out, alternate the *x* and the *m*; thus xmxmxmxmxmxmxmxmx. You will find that it will be faster to use the first or second finger of each hand on the *x* and the *m* when crossing out a line or several words in this way.

Proofread your letter and make pencil corrections if any are needed; then insert a sheet of paper and type the letter with your own return address. Use the style of letter that you prefer. Make a carbon copy of the letter.

SKILL MAINTENANCE 65

Directions. If time permits, take a number of 1-minute writings, using the sentence below. Additional 1-minute writings can be taken on the third sentence of the conditioning practice for this lesson.

STROKES WORDS

You ~~can~~ *will* learn to write *a good* business letter if you will work *at it.*   70   14

LESSON 66

CONDITIONING PRACTICE 66   *5 minutes*

STROKES

Martin said the box was packed by Alan with five dozen jugs of liquid.	70
Albert Clayton sailed for Alaska on April 20. Elvin Clinton went too.	70
Not much work can be done by us if we do not know how we are to do it.	70

			STROKES
5	Brass Stop Valves	$ 5.75	698
3	2 in. Swing Check Valves	16.25	731
2	1 1/2 in. Gate Valves	11.15	761
1	3 5/8 x 5 1/4 Control Box	29.85	795
2	Horizontal Force Pumps	53.00	826
		————	836
	Total	$116.00	852

(P) As we knew you were in a great hurry for this material, we made the 920
substitutions without waiting to get your approval because we were sure 992
you would be pleased with the substituted items. If, however, you prefer 1066
to wait until we can get a supply of the items you originally ordered, we 1140
shall be glad to have you return the substitute material that has been 1211
shipped to you, and we shall send the other items as soon as possible. 1283
Very truly yours, OXFORD MANUFACTURING COMPANY 1330
W. A. Bowman, Sales Manager *(232)* 1357

PROBLEM 2

Directions. Type this letter according to the directions given for Problem 1, but allow 4 spaces between columns.

STROKES

Mr. Ralph J. McIlrath General Manager Roosevelt Hotel Indianapolis 83
7, Indiana Dear Mr. McIlrath: We have just completed a study of all 152
member hotels to determine what, if any, programs of expansion are now 223
under way. Each hotel contacted was asked to indicate in money value 294
an estimate of the total cost of the expansion program in progress at the 368
present time. The response to our request was gratifying, and some valu- 440
able data concerning our member hotels have been tabulated. I am list- 510
ing below the names of some of our leading hotels together with an esti- 581
mate of the total money value of their expansion programs: 641

				STROKES
Washington-Ritz	~~Macon,~~ *Rome,* Georgia	$ 750,000	425	683
Grey ~~Town~~ House	Denver, Colorado	~~900,000~~		721
City ~~Plaza~~ *Terrace*	Cleveland, Ohio	1,525,000		760
Gateway Towers	Pittsburgh, Pa.	2,500,000		801
The McGarvey	Orlando, Florida	~~2,550,000~~ 3,650		841
~~Weston~~ *Western* Mansions	St. ~~Louis, Mo.~~ *Paul, Minn.*	3,225,000		884

(P) I hope this letter will provide as interesting reading for you as the 954
report has for those of us who have been responsible for compiling the 1025
data. All data are being summarized in booklet form and will be available 1100
for distribution within the next 90 days. Very truly yours, U. S. HOTEL 1173
ASSOCIATION, INC. William T. Copes Executive Secretary *(193)* 1223

PROBLEM 3

Directions. Type the letter in Problem 2 twice. Send one letter to: **Mr. T. Burke Craver Manager** The Gallitin Hotel Fresno 6, California; and the other to: **Mr. John A. Eaton General Manager** The Continental Atlanta 7, Georgia. In both letters supply appropriate salutations.

Line 1: Space twice after the exclamation point when it is used at the end of a sentence.
Line 2: Space once after the exclamation point when it is used within a sentence.
Line 3: A request in the form of a question is usually punctuated with a period.
Line 4: The symbols ¢, @, and % may be used in typing statements and orders.
Line 5: Use figures to state exact age in years, months, and days. Use words to express approximate age.

STROKES

You must think! You must act! Then you will be a successful workman.   74

You must think! and act! if you desire to become a successful workman.   74

Will you please give them a full-size sheet of paper, 8½ by 11 inches.   70

The invoice of June 27 read: 450 pairs @ 39¢; 2% discount in 10 days.   70

Robert, Alfred, and Joe are exactly 16 years 3 months and 29 days old.   70

CORRECT IT AS YOU TYPE (OR DIRECT DICTATION)   *5 minutes*

i shall succeed! and so can you! will you please return order 3129.

order 65 lbs. of feed @ 95¢ a lb. the discount is 2 per cent in ten days.

jack is nearly 20 years old. the paper is eight and a half by 11 inches.

PROBLEM TYPING 66   *20 minutes*
PROBLEM I

Directions. Use a 60-space line and single spacing. After typing the first line of the first paragraph, reset the stop for the left margin so that the indented lines will be 5 spaces in from the left margin. Center the problem vertically and the heading horizontally.

	STROKES	WORDS
TO TYPE CHARACTERS NOT ON THE KEYBOARD	39	8
HORIZONTAL LINE. Strike the underscore key 10 times for an	99	20
inch of pica type or 12 times for an inch of elite type.	157	31
DOUBLE HORIZONTAL LINES. Push in the variable line spacer	216	43
(No. 3) and move the cylinder from you slightly; then	274	55
type the second line.	297	59
VERTICAL LINE. An acceptable vertical line can be made by	356	71
typing the colon, throwing the carriage, typing another	412	82
colon, throwing the carriage, and so on until the line	467	93
is the desired length. (If an unbroken vertical line	521	104
is desired, use a pencil or pen and ink.)	562	112

PROBLEM 2

Directions. Type a 2-inch line at the left margin. Move the carriage to approximately 50 or 55 and type a 2-inch line.

Remove the paper; reinsert it; operate the variable line spacer and roll the paper forward until the top of the aligning scale (No. 34) is slightly above the typed line. Type your name so that the letters are slightly above or on the first line. Move the carriage to the line at the right, gauge the line, and type your name properly aligned.

Study the relation of the letters to the line.

LESSON 184

CONDITIONING PRACTICE 184

5 minutes

STROKES

Of six quick judges, Mary, Walt, Vi, and Nan checked the puzzles best.	70
The garage distributed 483 chains, 72 wheels, 60 pumps, and 195 tires.	70
There will be a meeting of all new division managers early next month.	70

PROBLEM TYPING 184—SKILL BUILDING

35 minutes

Directions. Make pencil notations on a piece of note paper of the problems listed below, and place the paper on the desk near your textbook so that you can refer to it as you complete the typing of each problem. You will be timed for 30 minutes. Correct all errors; uncorrected errors will receive a 10-word penalty. If you complete the typing of the problems before time is called, retype as many of them as possible. Compute your stroking rate at the end of the 30-minute period.

Problem 1, page 238—type once with a carbon and an envelope.
Problem 1, page 239—type once with a carbon and an envelope.
Problem 1, page 240—type once with a carbon and an envelope.

LESSON 185

CONDITIONING PRACTICE 185

5 minutes

STROKES

John Gimbel vainly works wax on quiet, hazy days in the South Pacific.	70
The camp loaned 293 cots, 175 blankets, 80 pillows, and 46 mattresses.	70
All members of the group were interested in learning new filing rules.	70

PROBLEM TYPING 185—MEASUREMENT

35 minutes

Directions. You are to type for 30 minutes; at the end of the 30-minute writing, compute your stroking rate per minute. Type each problem once with a carbon. Proofread each problem and correct all errors before removing the problem from the typewriter. Uncorrected errors will receive a 10-word penalty. If you complete the typing of all problems before time is called, retype as many as possible in the time remaining. *Type on the control level.*

PROBLEM 1

Directions. Type in the modified block style with no indentions for paragraphs. Set your machine for a 60-space writing line. Use mixed punctuation and the current date. Allow 8 spaces between columns in the tabulation.

STROKES

Zenith Supply Company 4782 Highland Avenue Chicago 8, Illinois	80
Gentlemen: Your order of September 29 was shipped from our warehouse	150
today. We tried to fill the order just as you requested; but because of	223
current shortages in some of our stocks, it was necessary for us to make	296
several substitutions. The materials substituted were of the same quality	371
as those indicated in your order, but they were produced by one of our	442
other manufacturers. You will be interested to know that our regular	513
guarantee applies to these substituted items as well as to the ones regu-	585
larly carried in stock. The following list shows the changes made in your	660
order:	668

Then type two 2-inch lines as you did before; remove the paper; reinsert it; gauge the line; and type your name on the line at the left and the date on the line at the right.

PROBLEM 3

Directions. Draw a horizontal pencil line of approximately 6 inches without removing the paper from the typewriter. To do this, hold the point of the pencil against the paper and above the ribbon, resting firmly on the ribbon mechanism. Depress the left carriage release lever and move the carriage smoothly and rapidly the distance necessary.

Remove the paper; reinsert it; gauge the line; and type your name and the current date as you did for Problem 2.

SKILL MAINTENANCE 66

Directions. Take 1-minute writings as time permits.

	STROKES	WORDS
If you like to do *a* something, you will *almost surely* learn to do it *well*.	70	14

LESSON 67

CONDITIONING PRACTICE 67 *5 minutes*

	STROKES
Six dozen jugs of liquid cement will be moved to Paul Kearney's house.	70
Albert, Mary, and Jack will be in Atlantic City, New Jersey, in March.	70
We usually do well those things we like to do and know that we can do.	70

RELATED LEARNING 67 *10 minutes*

Line 1: Use figures to express dimensions. (Note the pica and elite spaces in a horizontal inch.)

Line 2: Enclose explanatory matter in parentheses when a comma would not be a sufficient mark of separation.

Line 3: The symbol # is used for No. when it precedes the figure. The symbol & (the ampersand) is correctly used in a firm name composed of personal names. When the symbol # follows a figure, it expresses pounds.

Line 4: Use Roman numerals to indicate a major division of a manuscript; use figures for minor sections; (Vol. and Sec. may be spelled in full); type page numbers in figures with the word *page* uncapitalized unless it is the first word of the sentence; and type in capitals (or underscore) the title of a book.

Line 5: Note the spelling of *principal* (chief) and *principle* (rule). Express the singular possessive by adding *'s*; express the plural possessive of a word ending in *s* by adding the apostrophe only.

	STROKES
The horizontal line of 6 inches has 60 pica spaces or 72 elite spaces.	70
Order #648 (File 291-B) will be shipped on April 30 to Harris & Myers.	70
The item on Bill #571 proves that Marks & Lang bought 2,940# of sugar.	70
They found the exact quotation in Vol. IX, Sec. 4, page 496, of TAXES.	70
The principal's talk to the girls' group dealt with principles of law.	70

LESSON 183

CONDITIONING PRACTICE 183   *5 minutes*

	STROKES
King County judges may quiz the wives or parents of Lexington Borough.	70
The baker made 157 muffins, 243 doughnuts, 80 pies, and 96 hard rolls.	70
All files will be moved to the new office before the end of the month.	70

PROBLEM TYPING 183—TYPING LETTERS WITH TABULATED REPORTS   *30 minutes*

PROBLEM 1—SKILL BUILDING IN TYPING LETTERS WITH TABULATED REPORTS

Directions. Type this letter in the modified block style with no indentions for paragraphs. Set your machine for a 60-space writing line. Use mixed punctuation and the current date; leave 8 spaces between columns. Proofread the typed copy before removing it from the typewriter; then type the letter a second time.

				STROKES
14 pcs.	2 x 4 x 10' Fir	$14.00		499
3 pcs.	2 x 4 x 14' Fir	6.00		529
2 sets	#8302 CYP Casing	2.80		560
35 pcs.	Drain Tile—4''	4.20		589
5 pcs.	3/8 x 4 x 6 Sheetrock	4.50		625
				633
		$51.50		641

	STROKES
The Colfax Lumber Company 4182	47
Brownsville Avenue Knoxville 4,	79
Tennessee Gentlemen: We have	109
just received your invoice No. 185673,	148
dated November 5, for materials or-	182
dered for the Bethel School project	218
on Lebanon Church Road. The ma-	249
terials were received November 3,	283
and the shipper's receipt was signed	320
at that time by A. L. Lucas. An ex-	355
amination of your invoice, however,	391
reveals an error in the total amount	428
of the bill. You list the following:	467

	STROKES
(P) The total shown on your invoice	673
is $51.50; actually, it should be only	712
$31.50. Your invoice, therefore, is in	752
error to the extent of $20. (P) I am	786
enclosing a check for $31.50 in full	823
payment of the invoice with the cor-	858
rected total. Please make the neces-	894
sary adjustments in your records to	930
show this account paid in full. Yours	969
very truly, HUNTER CONSTRUC-	996
TION COMPANY William A.	1020
Hunter Treasurer Enclosure *(194)*	1046

NOTE: As you do not have the check to be enclosed, attach a note to the letter to call attention to the needed enclosure.

PROBLEM 2—SKILL BUILDING IN TYPING LETTERS WITH TABULATED REPORTS

Directions. Use the letter in Problem 1 for a series of 3-minute writings. Begin typing with the tabulated report; write until your teacher calls "time." With each repeat timing, start at the beginning of the tabulated report.

SKILL MAINTENANCE 183   *5 minutes*

Directions. Use the following sentence for 1-minute writings; *type on the exploration level of practice.*

                       STROKES

All ~~men~~ *members* of our sales ~~crew~~ *staff* have been ~~asked~~ *invited* to ~~another~~ *special* sales meeting.   70

the page is eight and a half inches wide. this speakers talk is good.

order number 269 is for 500 pounds of coffee. read page twenty of volume eight.

he read the book, words have power. order number 473 (file 126) is ready.

PROBLEM TYPING 67   20 minutes

Directions. Use a 60-space line and single spacing. Triple-space between the main heading and the first division of the outline. Center the exercise vertically. Center the main heading horizontally, and type it in capitals. Begin Roman numeral "II" outside the left margin. The problem can be typed on either a full or a half sheet of paper.

		STROKES	WORDS
AMERICAN READINGS IN HISTORY		29	6
I. NATIONAL READJUSTMENT *(1865-1877)*		67	13
A. Diplomatic adjustments under Johnson		108	22
1. Purchase of Alaska		130	26
2. Settlement *of difficulties* with England		173	35
a. Sumner's statement *of American claims*		214	43
b. Treaty of Washington *(1871)*		245	49
B. Financial reorganization		274	55
add 1 line space 1. State of national finances *financial*		304	61
2. Opposition to revision of system		350	70
II. OPENING OF THE MODERN ERA *(1877-1898)*		393	79
A. Development of the West		421	84
1. Progress of settlement		447	89
2. Formation of *new* states		474	95
B. Transcontinental railroads		504	101

SKILL MAINTENANCE 67

Directions. Take 1-minute writings as time permits.

	STROKES	WORDS
as Use few motions when getting ready to *as you can use* type *do the typing*.	70	14

LESSON 68

CONDITIONING PRACTICE 68   *5 minutes*

	STROKES
Hazel Beggs works with fervor; Jim Knox typed quickly but with errors.	70
Max will be in Maine on June 30. Elvin sailed for Alaska on April 26.	70
You must learn to do all of the work without a sense of hurry or fear.	70

LESSON 182

CONDITIONING PRACTICE 182

5 minutes

STROKES

Juvenile zest for excitement whetted interest in parking by the quays.   70

An inventory showed 293 cards, 180 papers, 75 books, and 46 magazines.   70

This new office manual will be given to all workers for further study.   70

PROBLEM TYPING 182—TYPING LETTERS WITH TABULATED REPORTS   *30 minutes*

PROBLEM 1—SKILL BUILDING IN TYPING PROBLEMS WITH TABULATED REPORTS

Directions. Type this letter in the modified block style with no indentions for paragraphs. Set your machine for a 60-space writing line. Use mixed punctuation and the current date; allow 4 spaces between columns. Proofread the typed copy before removing it from the typewriter; then type the letter a second time.

STROKES

Mr. Earl W. Burns Purchasing Agent Burns Construction Company   62
1521 Washington Boulevard Chicago 12, Illinois Dear Mr. Burns: In   129
your letter of the 12th, you ask whether or not we can make immediate   199
shipment of selected materials in specified quantities and the cost of the   274
shipment. Because of material shortages, we are not able to quote prices   348
on all items requested, but we can supply the following items at the prices   424
indicated: 436

~~425~~ 250 ft.	2-wire A~~r~~mored ^Entrance Cable	$~~175.50~~ 50.00	483
1 ea.	35-amp. Wells Time~~r~~ Switch 25	8.95	524
150 ft.	Underground Cable, #14	43.50	562
~~35~~ 60 ft.	Asbestos Heating ~~Wire~~ Cable	8.95	600
3 ea.	6-circuit Fuseless Switch	~~69.85~~ 89.85	642
			650
	Total	$~~365.65~~ 201.25	666

(P) The prices listed will apply for a 60-day period only. After 60 days,   747
they will no longer be in effect. To avail yourself of this offer, therefore,   826
you must notify us of your acceptance promptly. (P) May we have the   891
pleasure of hearing from you soon. Very truly yours, MILLAR ELEC-   956
TRICAL SUPPLIES COMPANY William Millar Sales Manager *(149)*   1008

PROBLEM 2—SKILL BUILDING IN TYPING PROBLEMS WITH TABULATED REPORTS

Directions. Use the letter in Problem 1 for this writing. Take a series of 1-minute writings on the tabulated part of the letter only. At the end of the first minute when the teacher calls "Throw. Type," return the carriage and start with the first line of the tabulated report again. Follow the same procedure for the second and third minutes. Try to increase your stroking rate with each timing.

SKILL MAINTENANCE 182   *5 minutes*

Directions. Use the following sentences for 1-minute timed writings; *type on the exploration level of practice.*

STROKES

Through travel one can gain a real knowledge of how other people live.   70

Those who wish to be well informed should read good books quite often.   70

Line 1: Explanatory expressions are set off by commas. In the sentence, *Ohio* is considered explanatory for Toledo and *1950* explanatory for April 29.

Line 2: Words in apposition and words of direct address are set off by commas.

Line 3: When two or more adjectives modify a noun, separate them by commas if they bear the same relation to the noun. (A comma is not used between listed adjectives when the adjectives contribute to one complete thought.)

Line 4: Words in a series are separated by commas, and the comma is used before the conjunction.

Line 5: When two unrelated groups of figures come together, separate them by a comma.

	STROKES
Joe moved to Toledo, Ohio, on April 29, 1950, and I saw him on May 30.	70
Mr. Andrews, the teacher, is ill. Will you, Mr. Lewis, teach for him?	70
The young, inexperienced workers have much to learn about office work.	70
A typist must have speed, control, and a command of technical English.	70
In 1949, 263 clerks were working here; in 1950, 629; and in 1951, 857.	70

CORRECT IT AS YOU TYPE (OR DIRECT DICTATION)   *5 minutes*

claude left dallas texas on the 26th. my friend jack long is ill.

you must type with ease speed and control. in 1951 296 men left.

the older experienced workers earn more. i was in waco texas a year.

PROBLEM TYPING 68   *20 minutes*

Directions. Write a letter to an acquaintance, asking him to recommend you for part-time store or office work. The letter may be addressed to someone engaged in business or to one of your teachers or to any other person who knows you well enough to be able and willing to recommend you.

Ask that the recommendation be sent to Mr. James Y. Neasmith, Employment Manager, Harrison-Bidwell Company, of your town or a nearby city.

Type your name in the signature position, four spaces below the complimentary close. Use the style of letter you prefer.

NOTE: Never type *Mr.* in the signature line; and never sign a letter with the title *Mr.* An unmarried woman may type the title *Miss* before her typed signature. If the typed signature is omitted, the title *Miss* may be written in parentheses before the penwritten signature.

Make pencil corrections, if needed; then retype the letter and address an envelope.

SKILL MAINTENANCE 68

Directions. Take 1-minute writings as time permits.

	STROKES	WORDS
Know when your own work is right and when it needs correction.	70	14

LESSON 69

CONDITIONING PRACTICE 69   *5 minutes*

	STROKES
Frank Beckwith was just spending the day quietly in Vera Cruz, Mexico.	70
Janice met Martha in Panama on March 29. Al Black will speak in Erie.	70
Do the same kind of work in the same way day after day to get control.	70

SECTION 30. Letters with Tabulated Reports

LESSON 181

CONDITIONING PRACTICE 181   *5 minutes*

Directions. Type each line twice. Double-space after the second typing of the line. Retype the lines as often as time permits. This will be the uniform assignment for all conditioning practices in this section.

	STROKES
Fred and Jim quivered weakly at six big prizes won in March and April.	70
There were 265 Fords, 140 Pontiacs, 87 Mercurys, and 93 Dodges parked.	70
There will be increases in all sales prices because of mounting costs.	70

PROBLEM TYPING 181—TYPING LETTERS WITH TABULATED REPORTS   *30 minutes*

PROBLEM 1—LEARNING THE NATURE OF THE PROBLEM

Directions. Type the following letter in a modified block style with no indentions for paragraphs similar to Style Letter 5, page 154. Set your machine for a 60-space writing line. Use mixed punctuation and the current date. Tabulate the list in the second paragraph in three columns with four spaces between columns. Proofread the typed copy before removing it from the typewriter.

	STROKES
Mr. Ralph H. McKenzie Build-	43
ers Supply Company 1492 Center	74
Avenue Springfield 9, Massachu-	104
setts Dear Mr. McKenzie: We	132
have contracted with the home own-	165
ers listed below to build their homes	203
during this next spring and sum-	234
mer. The types of homes to be built	271
are indicated by the specifications	307
numbers shown for each owner; and	341
the locations of the building sites	377
are also given. It is our plan to be-	414
gin construction of these five homes	451

	STROKES
not later than April 15. All of them,	490
by the way, will be within the city	526
limits.	535
Ralph C. Appleton, 6325, 4970	563
Brandon Avenue Paul M. Green-	591
wood, 3006, 8157 Maple Avenue Wil-	622
liam Patterson, 8203, 2065 Center	654
Avenue Harold Emsworth, 5935,	682
1623 Walnut Street Frank L. Leo-	713
pold, 1002, 1251 Eastern Drive.	744
(P) Will you examine the specifica-	774
tions for each home listed and	805
submit to us, at your earliest con-	839
venience, an estimate of the cost of	876
materials you can supply. Your esti-	912
mate should be completely itemized	947
and should be figured in terms of an-	983
ticipated prices of materials. Yours	1021
very truly, COMBS HOMEBUILD-	1048
ERS, INC. L. I. Combs, Jr., Presi-	1082
dent *(181)*	1086

PROBLEM 2—SKILL BUILDING IN TYPING LETTERS WITH TABULATED REPORTS

Directions. Type the letter in Problem 1 twice, but change the names of the addressees. Send the first letter to: **Mr. James A. Enterkin, Electrical Supplies Company, 2805 Western Avenue, Worcester 5, Massachusetts;** and send the second one to: **Mr. William B. Trice, Dilworth Lumber Company, 1569 Commonwealth Boulevard, Brockton 5, Massachusetts.** Supply an appropriate salutation for each letter. Proofread each letter before removing it from the typewriter.

SKILL MAINTENANCE 181   *5 minutes*

Directions. Use the following sentence for 1-minute timed writings; *type on the exploration level of practice.*

	STROKES
A good writer will make positive that his work is done very well.	70

Line 1: When two or more words have the force of a single modifier before a noun, they are hyphened.

Line 2: Compounds are hyphened when otherwise a vowel would be confusingly doubled in combination. Exceptions: *cooperate* and *coordinate* and their derivatives are often written as solid forms because of their great frequency and familiarity.

Line 3: The possessive of titles, firm names, initials, abbreviations, and the like, may be formed by adding apostrophe and *s*. An apostrophe followed by *d* is used to form the past and past participle of arbitrarily coined verbs.

Line 4: The apostrophe is often omitted in titles and geographic names. No apostrophe is used in the possessive pronouns *his, hers, its, ours, yours, theirs*. The omission of a letter from a word is indicated by an apostrophe; as, it's (for *it is*).

Line 5: The apostrophe with an added *s* is used with each of two or more possessives joined by a coordinate conjunction, when referring to separate possessions, and with only the last possessive when referring to joint ownership.

	STROKES
Your up-to-date setup calls for up-to-the-minute information each day.	70
The co-owners of the business cooperate well and coordinate all plans.	70
Mr. C. D. King, Jr.'s, expense account was O. K.'d by President Smith.	70
The Farmers Bank is certain of its report. It's to be published soon.	70
Tom's and Frank's books, Park and Hill's PUNCTUATION, were inadequate.	70

CORRECT IT AS YOU TYPE (OR DIRECT DICTATION)   *5 minutes*

go uptown to get the up to date file. its a very good file, i know.

the coowner of the house may reenter it. yours is a good book.

sue and marys duet was lovely. jacks and freds papers were typed.

PROBLEM TYPING 69   *20 minutes*

PROBLEM I

Directions. Use a half sheet of paper. Type the tabulated report with double spacing and a top margin of 1½ inches. Determine the correct machine adjustments for typing the columns by the steps given with Technique Study 56, page 83. Center the heading horizontally and leave two spaces between it and the first line of the report.

Comparative Cost of Promotion for Three Years				STROKES
				46
Newspaper Advertising	$12,385.40	$10,460.50	$13,575.95	104
Circulars	8,492.50	9,856.00	10,265.75	144
Samples	10,260.75	11,092.50	12,450.00	182
Direct Mail	3,295.50	6,480.31	7,506.25	224
Miscellaneous Costs	495.00	736.50	815.20	274
				311
Total	$34,929.15	$38,625.81	$44,613.15	357

PROBLEM 2

Directions. This is a 5-minute timed writing of Problem 1, above. If you complete the typing of the problem before time is called, insert a new sheet of paper and continue typing until time is called.

SKILL MAINTENANCE 69

Directions. Take 1-minute writings as time permits.

	STROKES	WORDS
Train yourself right now to think through each problem as you meet it.	70	14

LESSON 180

STROKES

Mickey, June, Ed, and Gil have fixed tables for two pop quiz problems.   70

Our grocer sold 180 pears, 239 oranges, 75 bananas, and 64 grapefruit.   70

The new building will be completed before the end of the current year.   70

SPEED EMPHASIS 180—MEASUREMENT — *15 minutes*

Directions. Use the following paragraph for two 5-minute writings. Your teacher will collect the better of the two writings. *Type on the control level.*

This paragraph has every letter of the alphabet and a syllable intensity of 1.35.

	STROKES	WORDS
A time record of workers will reveal some interesting facts about the	70	14
quantity of work that is done by different workers in the same length of	143	29
time. In many large offices, typists are paid on the basis of the number	217	43
of lines typed. This is fair for those workers who have well-defined jobs	292	58
that do not call for taking time out to meet unexpected problems. In sales	368	74
work, men are frequently "clocked" and their record of sales is checked	440	88
against their average time spent in making calls. It is fair to the worker	516	103
to receive pay on the basis of his ability to produce; and more and more	589	118
this is becoming the basis for determining salaries. "Clock" yourself in	663	133
your own work just to see what you would earn with your ability to type;	736	147
then organize for improvement so that you need have no fear if you are	807	161
paid on the basis of the work you can do.	848	170

PROBLEM TYPING 180—MEASUREMENT — *20 minutes*

Directions. You are to type for 15 minutes. Proofread each problem and correct all errors before removing it from the typewriter. (Uncorrected errors will receive a 10-word penalty.) If you finish before time is called, retype as much as possible in the time remaining. At the end of the 15-minute period, compute your stroking rate per minute. *Type on the control level.*

LETTER. Send a letter to: **raymond b morley traffic co-ordinator dyersburg, tennessee.** Type form paragraphs 7 and 8, page 233. Close the letter with the following paragraph:

	STROKES
The loss on shipments from your station has been unusually high dur-	67
ing the present season. We suggest that in all future shipments you be	139
sure to bulkhead each section of the stop-off car with steel strap anchored	215
to the wall stanchions. We hope this will tend to reduce the loss caused	289
from bruises suffered when crates are moved unnecessarily. *(60)*	347

POSTAL CARD. Type a postal card using form paragraphs 5 and 6. Use the return address and signature of *Transportation Association, Inc.,* as shown in Illustration 63.

LESSON 70

STROKES

Both of them realized I was extremely prejudiced against quick revolt.   70

The warehouse is at 64 East 59th Street; the store, at 28 Park Avenue.   70

There is work for you to do. Your job is to learn to do it with ease.   70

RELATED LEARNING 70 — 10 minutes

Line 1: Capitalize a direct question within a sentence even though it is not quoted.

Line 2: Capitalize names of definite geographical divisions, but not points of the compass used to denote direction only.

Line 3: An exclamation point is used after an ejaculation, and after any phrase or sentence of wish, command, irony, or the like to indicate forceful utterance or strong feeling.

Line 4: A hyphen is used as the equivalent of *to and including* between extreme dates or numbers. Use a dash (made with two hyphens without space before or after) to mark an abrupt suspension of the sense, an unexpected turn of the thought, or a sudden change in the construction.

Line 5: Before "of" in phrases indicating residence, position, or title, a comma is ordinarily used. Use the colon to separate the hour and minutes in stating time. Type a.m. or A.M.—either is correct.

STROKES

It is said the eighteenth century asked of any action, Is it decorous?   70

The Middle West is an area for expansion; but I am going farther west.   70

The art of conversation is lost! What a monologist he has come to be!   74

In the decade 1941-1950, I wrote many books—but you may know of them.   70

Mr. Murray, of New Orleans, will speak at 9:30 a.m. on Monday, May 29.   70

CORRECT IT AS YOU TYPE (OR DIRECT DICTATION) — 5 minutes

the question is, how well can you type? i liked her southern cooking.

you must think! mr. harmon of portland will arrive at 9:45 tonight.

you must read pages 29-164. know what you are to do—then do it well!

ACTION TYPING 70 — 20 minutes

Directions. Pay attention to the meaning of what you type. If the sentence you type tells you to do something, complete the typing of the sentence and then do what you are told to do. For example, assume that in the typing you find this sentence: Your name should be typed in all capital letters and centered horizontally. AFTER you have typed that sentence, space up and type your name centered horizontally in all capital letters; then continue to type the paragraph Use a 70-space line and a 5-space paragraph indention. Use double spacing.

1   Think as you type. Type over the first word of the preceding sen-

tence to make it appear in bold type. To type well, think as you type.

Underscore each word of the preceding sentence. Type your name

centered two spaces below this line, using all capitals.

	STROKES	WORDS
Type it right the first time. What is the use of hurrying through	67	13
work without organizing your effort so you can be certain that what	140	28
you do is acceptable? Businessmen do not like to pay twice for the work	213	43
that is done. The cost of running an office is high enough even when	283	57
competent workers do their work so that they infrequently, if ever, have	356	71
to do it over. A lot of the trouble in the classroom stems from the lack	430	86
of interest of the students coupled with a lack of understanding of just	503	101
what is expected. The idea seems to be that classroom work doesn't count	576	115
—but it does count. It is on the basis of the daily class work that the	650	130
habits and skills are developed that make for success or failure.	716	143

PROBLEM TYPING 179—TYPING POSTAL CARDS   *25 minutes*

Postal cards are used frequently to send routine acknowledgments, announcements of meetings, or other impersonal messages. The spacing used is determined by the length of the message. The style of address on the front of the card is the same as that used on an envelope.

Government postal cards measure 5½ by 3¼ inches. After allowing for margins, about 50 horizontal pica spaces (60 horizontal elite spaces) and 18 vertical lines are left for use.

The return address and the current date should be typed in the upper right-hand corner on the message side of the card. Omit from this side of the card the address of the person or the company to whom you are writing. The salutation and the complimentary close may be omitted if it is necessary to save these lines for the message itself. Use single spacing on postal cards except when the message is very short. Double-space between paragraphs.

PROBLEM 1—LEARNING THE NATURE OF THE PROBLEM

Directions. Type a postal card similar to that in Illustration 63. Use form paragraphs 1 and 6; and for the return address use **1429 Webster Street, Trenton 10, New Jersey.** Use the current date. Proofread the card before removing it from the typewriter; then type it a second time.

PROBLEM 2—SKILL BUILDING IN TYPING POSTAL CARDS

Directions. Type two postal cards using form paragraph 7. On the reverse side of the typed message, address the cards to the following: Rankin Transportation Company 319 Rebecca Street Baltimore 10, Maryland; and Joyce Trucking Lines, Inc. 1572 Woodward Avenue Wilmington 7, Delaware.

```
                              1429 Webster Street
                              Trenton 10, New Jersey
                              January 25, 195-

 Gentlemen:

     Perishable Protective Tariff No. 10 covers
 rules and regulations governing the handling of
 perishable freight.

     Make front of load flush by trimming or fill-
 ing in the spaces.  Brace with steel strapping.
 Be sure to use wood corner posts or light bulkhead-
 ing to protect packages from steel strap.

          Very truly yours,

          TRANSPORTATION ASSOCIATION, INC.
```

Illustration 63 — Postal Card Message

2   In composing the first draft at the typewriter, it is not necessary to erase and correct each error. Instead, it is recommended that you X-out a word or a line that is to be omitted. Use the x and the m keys to X-out material, and control the keys with the first fingers. The first sentence is to be crossed out; do so. Type the next sentence on one line without changing the margin stops and have it begin 3 spaces outside the left margin. It is the duty of a typist to check each typed page and to correct all the errors.

SKILL MAINTENANCE 70

Directions. Take 1-minute writings as time permits.

	STROKES	WORDS
The right kind of typing practice will surely bring real typing skill.	70	14

SECTION 11. Typing for Control
LESSON 71

CONDITIONING PRACTICE 71   *5 minutes*

	STROKES
A lazy stenographer will be quite vexed if much poor work is rejected.	70
Invoice No. 712936 for $213.51 is subject to a 2% discount in 10 days.	70
Let's take stock of what we have, what we are, and what we want to be.	70

TYPING FOR CONTROL 71   *15 minutes*

Directions. Use a 70-space line; a 5-space paragraph indention; and double spacing. Type each paragraph once without error or three times if you make an error in the typing.

Each of the following paragraphs has every letter of the alphabet.

		STROKES	
		PARA.	TOTAL
1	Accuracy is needed by all workers. An artist portrays accuracy in	67	
	line and angle. A singer has accuracy in tone quality. Business, too, de-	141	
	mands accuracy, exactness. All those who enter business must realize	211	
	that work inaccurately done is half done, and half-done work is never	281	
	adjudged acceptable.	301	
2	Books are my joy and hobby. There are excellent books for every	65	366
	mood—books for lazy days and books for bright or balmy days. I like to	138	439
	browse in a quiet library, away from the babble and the problems of busi-	210	511
	ness. I like to borrow books, lend books, and buy books. Yes, books are	284	585
	my joy and hobby.	301	602

LESSON 178

CONDITIONING PRACTICE 178

5 minutes

STROKES

Tex Hays was quickly judged brave by all zestful Hoosier Speedway men.   70

Some farmers had ordered 40 pails, 396 jars, 27 urns, and 185 baskets.   70

Once you begin to move your fingers rapidly, your typing will improve.   70

SPEED EMPHASIS 178

10 minutes

Directions. Select paragraphs from Speed Emphasis 176, page 232. Take three 3-minute writings from these paragraphs, writing with a 70-space line rather than the ones shown. *Type on the exploration level of practice.*

PROBLEM TYPING 178—SKILL BUILDING IN TYPING FORM PARAGRAPHS   *25 minutes*
PROBLEM 1—SKILL BUILDING IN TYPING LETTERS FROM FORM PARAGRAPHS

STROKES

Directions. An agent has inquired where he can find the rules under which loss and damage expense is apportioned. Write this agent: **clark e harrison louisville & nashville railroad company franklin, tennessee.** Type form paragraphs 4, 1, and 2, and add the following statement as a closing paragraph:

If we can be of further help to you   36
in getting started in your new work,   73
do not hesitate to write us. *(22)*   101

Proofread the letter before removing it from the typewriter; then type it a second time.

PROBLEM 2—SKILL BUILDING IN TYPING LETTERS FROM FORM PARAGRAPHS

STROKES

Directions. Send a letter to: **m k westerfield claim agent santa fe railroad company jasper, missouri.**

Type form paragraphs 1, 4, and 8 and close with the paragraph at the right.

You can help to reduce the great   33
loss caused by improper handling of   69
perishable freight if you will check   106
all freight shipments and clearly   140
identify those that are perishable,   176
whether by cold, heat, or deteriora-   211
tion. *(35)*   216

LESSON 179

CONDITIONING PRACTICE 179

5 minutes

STROKES

Zita and Paul have made queer wax cakes for buyers in July and August.   70

The bookstore had 295 books, 340 pads, 68 ink erasers, and 17 manuals.   70

There are several bonds that must be sold before our quota is reached.   70

SPEED EMPHASIS 179

10 minutes

Directions. Use the paragraph at the top of page 236 for three 3-minute writings; *type on the exploration level of practice.*

Directions. 1. Type for 1 minute with the guide for the line ending called each 20 seconds (unless your teacher directs otherwise). Then type for 2 minutes with the guide for the line ending called. Start at the beginning of the paragraph for each writing. *Type on the control level of practice.* Type each paragraph in this way.

2. Select an appropriate goal to type a 1-, a 2-, and a 3-minute writing. Start at the beginning of the first paragraph and continue into the second paragraph if you complete the typing of the first paragraph before time is called. Use a 70-space line.

3. If time permits, type for 5 minutes. Use a 70-space line.

	STROKES	
	PARA.	TOTAL
There are many ways to build typing skill and not	50	
just one way that is right for all. Each of us must	103	
find the right way to type so that maximum growth will	158	
come in the quickest time and with the least effort. It	215	
is up to us to practice in such a way that each will realize	276	
his finest skill in the least time. This is the work to be done.	341	
If you want to reach out into new speed areas, exert	53	394
yourself to use more rapid stroking when you type for a	109	450
short period of time. You will know when you are pushing	167	508
yourself too much. Just as long as you type with ease, the	227	568
pattern of typing is right for you. When you realize there is	290	631
more tension than is good for your typing, that will be a cue for	356	697
a quick change in the purpose as well as in the procedure of practice.	426	767

LESSON 72

CONDITIONING PRACTICE 72   *5 minutes*

	STROKES
Dr. Robertson's office hours will be 12:30 to 4:30 after September 30.	70
Zeal, pluck, vim, and a wish to excel quickly brought joy to Frederic.	70
Now is the time to be very sure that all of the work habits are right.	70

TYPING FOR CONTROL 72   *15 minutes*

Directions. Use a 70-space line; a 5-space paragraph indention; and double spacing. Type each paragraph once without error or three times if you make an error in the typing.

Each of the following paragraphs has every letter of the alphabet.

		STROKES	
		PARA.	TOTAL
1	If the typewriter is kept clean and oiled, it should not require much	70	
	further attention. All extra oil should be wiped off. Remove dust with	143	
	a long-handled brush. The care of the machine is just as much a part of	216	
	your responsibility as the care of your desk. Realize this and form the	289	
	habit now of taking good care of your typewriter. It will pay to do this.	363	

PROBLEM 2—SKILL BUILDING IN TYPING FORM PARAGRAPHS

Directions. Use the numbered form paragraphs you have just typed for a series of 1-minute writings. For each timing, select a different paragraph. *Type on the exploration level of practice.*

LESSON 177

CONDITIONING PRACTICE 177

5 minutes

STROKES

Monty and Dick relaxed by fishing just five weeks in quiet Printz Bay. 70

Our clerks handled 582 stamps, 693 cards, 10 packages, and 74 folders. 70

It is a good idea to learn all about the problems of office procedure. 70

SPEED EMPHASIS 177

10 minutes

Directions. From the paragraphs in Speed Emphasis 176, page 232, select materials for a series of 1-minute writings with your teacher calling the guide each 15 seconds. *Type on the exploration level of practice.*

PROBLEM TYPING 177—TYPING LETTERS FROM FORM PARAGRAPHS

25 minutes

General Directions. Type each letter made up of the form paragraphs in block style with open punctuation. All lines should start at the left margin except the date and file number lines, which will end approximately at the right margin. See Illustration 61.

Use the current date and provide an appropriate salutation and complimentary close for each letter.

March 30, 19--

File No. 260-1

Illustration 61 — **One Placement of the File Number**

On the first letter, type File No. 260-1 a double space below the date (Illustration 61), on the second letter, No. 260-2, and so on, consecutively identifying each letter by the number following the hyphen. At the end of each period make a notation of the file number of the last letter typed.

The letters will be mailed without a pen signature. Type the company name in capitals, and use 17 as the dictator's identifying figure for the reference line. Type your own initials in small letters to complete the reference notation. (Illustration 62)

Yours very truly

TRANSPORTATION ASSOCIATION, INC.

17:ms

Illustration 62 — **Closing Lines Showing a Typewritten Company Name and the Use of a Number to Identify the Dictator**

PROBLEM 1—LEARNING THE NATURE OF THE PROBLEM

Directions. Send a letter to: samuel h porter freight claim officer 59 e burns street chicago 26, illinois. Use: **File No. 260-1.** Type form paragraphs 3, 7, and 5. Proofread the typed copy before removing it from the typewriter; then retype the letter the second time.

PROBLEM 2—SKILL BUILDING IN TYPING LETTERS FROM FORM PARAGRAPHS

Directions. Send a letter to: **clyde a gaylord traffic manager united trucking lines sharon tennessee.** Use form paragraphs 2, 5, and 6.

	STROKES	
	PARA.	TOTAL

2   Mental quickness is an attribute that will always help when one is an- | 69 | 432
swering questions or solving a problem. Queer questions very often re- | 139 | 502
quire quickness of thought for the answer. For example, to draw designs | 212 | 575
in applique was a queer quiz question to test the quality of reasoning; yet | 288 | 651
it was so used just recently in a test to determine upper level students. | 361 | 724

3   Purpose is prized by all thoughtful persons. Promotion is certain for | 71 | 795
that person who exhibits persuasive personality and who keeps his ob- | 139 | 863
jective plainly in mind. Probably no part is of more importance in pro- | 210 | 934
moting success than quietly but pleasantly pushing persistently on | 277 | 1001
through purposeful work. | 301 | 1025

SKILL BUILDING 72

20 minutes

Directions. Use a 70-space line and single spacing.

The figures above and below the following sentences indicate the number of 5-stroke words. You are to select a goal that you believe you can reach in 15 seconds. If your 15-second goal is 7, you are trying to write at the rate of 28 words a minute; if it is 14, 56 words a minute.

Take a 1-minute writing on the first line, trying to reach your goal 4 times in the minute. Start each 15-second writing at the beginning of the line. You will be paced by the 15-second call of the guide.

Use each of the other lines in the same way; but, if you can, increase your goal as you move from one line to another. Your teacher may also instruct you to select goals for other time intervals, such as 12 or 20 seconds, and to type with the guide called for those times.

```
        1      2      3      4      5      6      7      8      9     10     11     12     13     14
Know what you are to do.  Plan the work well.  Use the plans you make.
If you make an error, pause; and begin to type without hurry or worry.
Think the words.  Hit the key and turn loose of it.  Just keep typing.
Type with ease.  Hold the arms still.  Let your fingers do their work.
There is magic in believing.  Think as you type.  Manage your fingers.
        1      2      3      4      5      6      7      8      9     10     11     12     13     14
```

LESSON 73

CONDITIONING PRACTICE 73

5 minutes

STROKES

A dozen lawyers object to the remarkable question of the grave expert. | 70
Bart Barbour is bright, but Robert Webster brought home better grades. | 70
There is work for you to do. Your job is to learn to do it with ease. | 70

TYPING FOR CONTROL 73

15 minutes

Directions. Type each sentence without error or type each sentence three times if you make an error in the typing.

Drill for

STROKES

a   A frank statement was made by the man from Alaska about Alaskan needs. | 70
b   Bart Barbour read the beautiful lines from Robert Burns's best poetry. | 70
c   Can such a characteristic as conceit check the achievement of success? | 70
d   Donald said he hoped he had developed a good device for handling feed. | 70
e   Every earnest endeavor helps me to achieve the best results in a test. | 70

For answers to frequently recurring questions or for some general sales letters, form paragraphs can be combined to make acceptable letters.

In this section, you are employed by the *Transportation Association, Inc.* One of your assignments is the typing of letters made up of form paragraphs. For the convenience of the dictator, the paragraphs are numbered.

PROBLEM I—LEARNING THE NATURE OF THE PROBLEM

Directions. Type the numbered paragraphs given below. Center the heading FORM PARA-GRAPHS approximately 1½ inches from the top of the page. Use a 60-space line and single spacing; double-space between paragraphs. Proofread the typed copy before removing it from the typewriter.

FORM PARAGRAPHS

1

	STROKES
Perishable Protective Tariff No. 10	36
covers rules and regulations govern-	71
ing the handling of perishable	102
freight. *(15)*	110

2

National Perishable Freight Com-	31
mittee Circular No. 20-A contains	65
the code of rules for handling perish-	102
able freight. *(17)*	115

3

It is now time to rethink your pro-	34
gram. How can needs and remedies	68
be more effectively presented and	102
applied? Is every department keyed	138
up and ready to get the jump on	170
claim causes? Does the "man in	202
charge" realize that repetition is	237
reputation, that repeated bad-order	273
deliveries make a reputation for un-	308
reliable service? *(54)*	325

4

Freight Claim Rule 60, of the	30
Freight Claim Division, covers the	65
rules under which loss and damage	99
expense is apportioned among the	132
carriers who are parties to the haul	169
whenever there is a failure in trans-	205
portation resulting in loss and dam-	240
age to perishable freight. *(44)*	266

5

Suggest to the shipper that all cases	38
should be marked with arrows on all	74

	STROKES
four vertical sides pointing to top.	112
Load right side up. *(24)*	131

6

Make front of load flush by trim-	32
ming or filling in the spaces. Brace	70
with steel strapping. Be sure to use	108
wood corner posts or light bulkhead-	143
ing to protect packages from steel	178
strap. *(32)*	184

7

Perishable freight represents a large	38
traffic, and the loss and damage ex-	73
pense in connection with its trans-	107
portation is much heavier than need	143
be. The great variety of different	179
articles in this group, the many dif-	215
ferent localities that produce these	252
articles, the variety of climates	286
through which they move, and the	319
great distances they are hauled	351
make it necessary to accord this	384
traffic specialized handling service	421
under close supervision. *(68)*	445

8

Rule 1 in Circular 20-A contains a	35
list and definition of perishable	69
freight. It is not all inclusive, but it	111
does list 124 items. From this list it	151
is easy to determine the unlisted	185
items that may belong in the cate-	218
gory of perishable freight subject to	256
deterioration or decay, and also the	293
items that may be protected by re-	326
frigeration, icing, ventilation, or	362
against cold. *(68)*	375

f	Frequently officials refuse to inform the unfortunate of their defeat.	70
g	George Gregory greatly exaggerated the meaning of the Governor's talk.	70
h	Harry Johnson, the British author, emphasized good writing techniques.	70
i	I will not risk intervention by having this evidence seized in a raid.	70
j	Judge Johnston was prejudiced in his judgment of your just objectives.	70
k	Knowledge taken from books makes you seek to know more and shirk less.	70
l	Let all citizens realize fully the actual value of the public schools.	70
m	Most of the members of their summer community come from Massachusetts.	70

TIMED WRITING 73   *15 minutes*

Directions. Take a 10-minute writing on the paragraphs of Timed Writing 60, page 87. *Type on the control level of practice.* The purpose of this writing is not to measure your typing speed but to measure your typing stamina. If you wish to compare your 10-minute writing with the scores made on the 5-minute writings, do so; but expect a slight decrease in the cwpm because of the longer period of writing. If you complete the paragraphs before time is called, start at the beginning of the first paragraph and type until time is called.

SKILL MAINTENANCE 73   *5 minutes*

Directions. Take a series of 1-minute writings on the following sentences.

STROKES

Check to see if you are wasting time in getting ready to do your work.	70
It is a law of the mind that each of us will reap just what each sows.	70

LESSON 74

CONDITIONING PRACTICE 74   *5 minutes*
STROKES

That big, jovial chemist quickly analyzed the mixture of brown powder.	70
Your short-term policy has a pay-as-you-go clause that Mr. Long likes.	70
Good work habits come through the right kind of daily typing practice.	70

GUIDED WRITING 74   *20 minutes*

Directions. 1. Take several 1-minute writings with the 20-second call of the guide for the line endings unless you are otherwise instructed. Type the copy line for line. *Type on the control level of practice.*

2. Use the paragraphs for 2-, 3-, and 5-minute writings. Your teacher will tell you whether these writings will be with the call of the guide. If the guide is called, type the copy line for line; if the guide is not called, use a 70-space line.

		STROKES PARA.	TOTAL
45-space lines.	When you erase a carbon copy, the eraser will	46	
	get dirty. Keep an emory stick in the desk	90	
	so the eraser can be cleaned as it is needed.	135	
50-space lines.	To type on a page that is bound at the top, insert	51	186
	a piece of paper and put the bound page back of the	103	238
	top edge of the paper; roll all pages backward.	150	285

SECTION 29. Form Paragraphs and Postal Cards

LESSON 176

CONDITIONING PRACTICE 176 — *5 minutes*

Directions. Type each sentence twice. Retype the sentences as often as time permits. This will be the uniform assignment for all conditioning practices in this section.

	STROKES
Jacks and Webb got Aztec relics in quantity from the Peru excavations.	70
He will print 85 blotters, 173 cards, 29 leaflets, and 406 newspapers.	70
We shall hear a reading of these great books from this hall next week.	70

SPEED EMPHASIS 176 — *10 minutes*

1. Sentences for Calling the Guide

Directions. Use the following sentences for 1-minute writings with the teacher calling the guide each 10 seconds. *Type on the exploration level of practice.*

```
    1    2    3    4    5    6    7    8    9    10   11   12   13   14
All new orders will be processed this week.  They will be billed soon.
His letter requested additional information.  We will mail it at once.
The lease on their premises will expire soon.  It will not be renewed.
    1    2    3    4    5    6    7    8    9    10   11   12   13   14
```

2. Paragraphs for Calling the Guide

Directions. Use the paragraphs for 1-minute writings with the teacher calling the guide each 15 seconds. *Type on the exploration level of practice.*

	STROKES	
	PARA.	TOTAL
50-space line.		
One who can proofread quickly and properly can be	50	
sure that his skill will be sought by those firms	100	
having a great deal of pride in the efficiency of	150	
their workers. Try to improve your own abilities.	200	
55-space line.		
There are some things to check while getting ready for	55	255
work in a business office. One should be most certain	110	310
that his personal traits are developed; he should also	165	365
be sure that his basic office skills are ready for use.	220	420
60-space line.		
Men in business tell us that people lose their jobs because	60	480
they have never learned how to get along well with others.	120	540
History, too, often tells us that world strife is caused by	180	600
the same type of human weakness. Try to know others better.	240	660
65-space line.		
It is a fine thing to be able to type your personal and business	65	725
letters in both appealing and forceful style. When you have had	130	790
a chance to employ your fine writing skill, you will be quick to	195	855
notice what a worth-while investment of time and energy you made.	260	920
70-space line.		
One who seeks employment in a modern business must know how to finish	70	990
his duties exactly on time. No boss will stand for a worker who does	140	1060
not complete his work in the time allowed. Each person must learn to	210	1130
budget his time in order to keep all jobs moving at the accepted rate.	280	1200

	STROKES	
	PARA.	TOTAL

55-space lines.   If the machine does not have a page gage, stick a piece   56 341
of gummed paper near the end of the carbon sheet as a   110 395
signal that the typing is close to the end of the page.   165 450

60-space lines.   When two keys clash and stick, operate the shift key before   60 510
you reach to pull the keys down. With some machines, this   119 569
will release the stuck keys and will keep your fingers clean.   180 630

65-space lines.   Clip off the four ends of the carbon paper. You can then remove   65 695
all carbon sheets from a pack without removing each page one at   129 759
a time. Hold the edge of the pack of papers and pull the carbons.   195 825

70-space lines.   When you type office reports, you may need to type a word or a set of   70 895
figures in red without having a two-color ribbon. You can do this by   140 965
typing with a piece of red carbon put between the ribbon and the paper.   211 1036

TYPING FOR CONTROL 74   *15 minutes*

Directions. Type each sentence without error or type each sentence three times if you make an error in the typing.

Drill for   STROKES

n   Ninety men in the conquered countries have been negotiating for peace.   70
o   Overcome your errors in stroking by avoiding the use of wrong methods.   70
p   Popular newspapers plan to oppose appeals to the public by propaganda.   70
q   Quick responses to a quiz question quite frequently require quick wit.   70
r   Real progress toward freedom for workers will carry the world forward.   70
s   System in offices, it is said, is as necessary as sales organizations.   70
t   That talk was right and thorough; yet that plan is too time consuming.   70
u   Unfailing truthfulness cannot hurt us; such a virtue will surely help.   70
v   Very few ever strive to advance who do not eventually achieve success.   70
w   "Wisdom will be worth while if we can win it—and we can win," I said.   70
x   Exciting experiences at Oxford were excelled by the experts at Exeter.   70
y   You are always ready to play your part loyally for every worthy cause.   70
z   Both zeal and zest should ever be utilized, harmonized, and idealized.   70

LESSON 75

CONDITIONING PRACTICE 75   *5 minutes*

STROKES

The puzzled judge soon became quite vexed at your wonderful knowledge.   70
Our six-page booklet, 4 1/3 by 7 inches, will not fit into this space.   70
Let us each day try to learn to do better whatever work we have to do.   70

Problem 1. Type the purchase order in a form similar to that used in Illustration 58, page 226.

Order No.　AB 69119　The Wallingford Manufacturing Company　47
1592 South Brackenridge Boulevard Kansas City 15, Kansas　104
Date　November 19, 195—　Ship via　Imperial Trucking Lines, Inc.　152

Requisition	Quantity	Description	Price	
				191
				230
XT 17172	1	R. H. Impeller, 9 1/2″ Finish #4	130.68	282
XT 17172	2	Impeller Guide E. Rings	22.62	325
OS 06014	55	CH-26 Gates, Model #915612	40.15	371
OS 06014	90 ft.	1 1/4″ H. D. Gates Hose	54.90	418
RM 97523	6	#532529 Pull Rods	66.00	455
BR 68391	18	#45-1901-1A Ret Rings	6.30	496
BR 72054	18	#45-1759-1A Plugs	22.50	533
				539
			343.15	545

Problem 2. Type the following bill of lading for the items listed in a form similar to that used in Illustration 59, page 227.

Shipper's No.　201684　Company　Baltimore and Ohio Railroad　From　35
Household Manufacturers, Inc.　At　Evansville, Indiana　November 20,　98
195—　Consigned to　The Shelby Electrical Supply Company　Destination　140
Baltimore 3,　State of　Maryland　Route　Your Line　Car Initial　BMV　176
Car No.　069573　182

Packages	Description	Weight	
			210
			238
2	12.5 cu. ft. Home Freezers	800#	273
3	9.0 cu. ft. Refrigerators	632#	308
5	41 x 24 x 36 Electric Stoves	1605#	345
2	46 in. Electric Washers	438#	377
1	26 in. Nutype Electric Ironer	186#	415

Shipper　Household Manufacturers, Inc.　Permanent address of shipper　445
5091 Sixth Avenue, Evansville 12, Indiana　486

Problem 3. Type the freight bill for the Wilshire Transportation Company in a form similar to that used in Illustration 60, page 229.

To　Universal Maintenance & Repair Co.　4109 West Thomas Boulevard　62
Kalamazoo 9, Michigan　Date　11/20/5—　Shipper　United Distributors, Inc.　119
2102 Brownsville Avenue　Columbus 10, Ohio　161

No. Pieces	Description	Weight	Rate	Collect	
					204
					247
18 drums	S. A. E. Compounded Motor Oil	8100	.87	70.47	302
10 drums	High Pressure Chassis Gun Grease	1200	.85	10.20	360
14 drums	Heavy Duty Transmission Grease	1680	.85	14.45	417
15 cases	12 one-gal. cans Enamel, mixed	2160	.78	17.16	473
24 cases	12 one-gal. cans Red Roof Paint	4608	.78	36.66	530
20 cases	12 one-gal. cans House Paint	3600	.78	28.08	583
8 cases	12 one-gal. cans Trim Varnish	960	.78	7.80	638
					644
				184.82	650
	3% Federal Tax			5.54	671
					677
				190.36	683

Directions. Set the machine for a 70-space line and double spacing. Use the material for three 5-minute writings. Determine the cwpm. *Type on the control level.*

	STROKES	WORDS
When you are to type on the control level, drop back in speed five	67	13
words or so below your skill-building rate—a drop back of at least ten	139	28
words below your forced speed. This is the way to practice when you	208	42
are learning to type new forms and when you are working to build skill	279	56
in typing office materials. This is the level for building skill in action	355	71
typing—in typing material other than paragraphs. This level of typing	427	85
is good when errors are to be counted against you or when all errors can	500	100
be corrected.	515	103
When typing on the control level, you should type at least five words	585	117
slower than the skill-building level, about ten words below the forced	656	131
speed on one-minute writings. This is the level of typing to use when	727	145
the work is to be handed in for record. Marks are usually given on the	799	160
basis of your control level typing. It is not expected that your rate will	875	175
be your highest, but it is expected that you will produce work at a usable	950	190
rate and with a high degree of accuracy. Each level of typing is impor-	1021	204
tant, but the control level is the one that will pay the real dividends	1093	219
when you work in an office. You should build the highest speed you can	1165	233
build in the time you have for practice, but more important than speed is	1239	248
the control that is a part of your typing mastery. Practice in the right	1313	263
way and with the right purpose for high basic skill, and your production	1386	277
on the control level will be good.	1420	284

SKILL BUILDING 75   *15 minutes*

Directions. Use the following lines for 1-minute writings with the 15-second call of the guide in the same way as you used Skill Building 72, page 104.

```
      1     2     3     4     5     6     7     8     9    10    11    12    13    14
You can type well now.  Believe in yourself.  There is magic in faith.

Hit the keys lightly and release them quickly.  Hold the elbows still.

Center the typing action in the fingers.  Each of us can do more work.

Try to grow in skill each day.  Think of how you can do the work well.
      1     2     3     4     5     6     7     8     9    10    11    12    13    14
```

Directions. Use the following paragraph for three 1-minute writings. Between timings, identify the awkward or difficult words and type each in a three-word group—including the word preceding and the word immediately following. *Type on the exploration level of practice.*

This paragraph has every letter of the alphabet.

	STROKES	WORDS
An office is a busy place. It usually lacks the quiet orderliness of	70	14
the classroom; yet the worker must produce at maximum speed. To do this,	144	29
he must organize his work habits with just as much care as he organizes	216	43
his work materials. Much of the work may be of a routine nature, but	286	57
daily problems vary; and the unexpected situations that arise call for	357	71
the ability to think quickly, decide accurately, and work efficiently.	427	85

LESSON 174

CONDITIONING PRACTICE 174   *5 minutes*

	STROKES
Judge Combs viewed six of the quorum as lacking zest in April and May.	70
Lorraine sold 207 handkerchiefs, 185 ties, 34 belts, and 96 new shoes.	70
Even when you get little pay for what you do, apply your best efforts.	70

PROBLEM TYPING 174—SKILL BUILDING   *35 minutes*

Directions. Make pencil notations on a piece of note paper of the problems listed below, and place the paper on the desk near your textbook so that you can refer to it as you complete the typing of each problem. You will be timed for 30 minutes. Correct all errors; uncorrected errors will receive a 10-word penalty. If you complete the typing of the problems before time is called, retype as many of them as possible. Compute your stroking rate at the end of the 30-minute writing.

Problem 2, page 226—type once with a carbon copy.
Problem 2, page 228—type once with a carbon copy.
Problem 2, page 229—type once with a carbon copy.

LESSON 175

CONDITIONING PRACTICE 175   *5 minutes*

	STROKES
Jinx, Pam, and Guy have seen Antigua wrecked often by sizeable quakes.	70
Our inventory showed 350 pipes, 97 jackets, 162 slippers, and 84 bags.	70
The margin release control is one on which you should spend much time.	70

PROBLEM TYPING 175—MEASUREMENT   *35 minutes*

Directions. You are to type for 30 minutes. Type each problem once with a carbon. Proofread each problem and correct all errors before removing it from the typewriter. (Uncorrected errors will receive a 10-word penalty.) If you complete the typing of all problems before time is called, retype as many as possible. At the end of the 30-minute period, compute your stroking rate per minute. *Type on the control level.*

PART 2

PERSONAL AND OFFICE TYPING PROBLEMS

INSTRUCTIONAL BLOCK 6

RECONSTRUCTION OF BASIC SKILLS

SECTION 12. Technique Improvement

Machine Checkup and Adjustments. Use the following directions for each lesson in this section for the machine checkup and adjustments. These directions will not be repeated in the remaining lessons of this section.

1. Each day check the placement of the paper guide, the **paper-bail** rolls, and the paper bail. Set the ribbon lever for typing on the upper portion of the ribbon.

2. Unless you are otherwise directed, use a 70-space line, double spacing, and a 5-space paragraph indention for all paragraphs, and single spacing for all other copy.

LESSON 76

CONDITIONING PRACTICE 76   *5 minutes*

Directions. Type each line twice. Double-space after the second typing of a line. As time permits, practice any line that may have caused you trouble. Type at a well-controlled pace.

	STROKES
Maxine was puzzled by the lack of interest in the five good quay jobs.	70
His life insurance was under Group Policy Nos. OL 75423 and MCI 18960.	70
The eight girls kept the auditor and the chairman busy with a problem.	70

TECHNIQUE STUDY 76   *10 minutes*
WORD-RECOGNITION LEVEL OF TYPING RESPONSE

Directions. Type each line three times. Think and type each word as a unit. To help you type on the word-recognition level, pronounce each word (silently) just before typing it.

Technique Emphasis. Keep the fingers well curved and close to the keys; hit each key with a quick, snap stroke and release it quickly.

	STROKES
if it is to do so go of or us he an am if it is to do so go of or us he	71
and the sir may men due tie rig big fir did for via rid aid fog but bus	71
Due to the fog the men may tie the rig to a big fir and go via the bus.	71

STROKE LEVEL OF TYPING RESPONSE

Directions. Type each line three times. Type each word at a well-controlled pace. Think and type each word letter by letter, using a quick, snap stroke.

Technique Emphasis. Hit each key with uniform stroking power. Let the fingers do the work. Hold the hands and arms quiet.

	STROKES
tag you far joy bad hop get nip vex mop eat ill dab kin cab ink cad oil	71
was lip saw pin wax ply add pip zax him few pop art lop rag pun bet hum	71
I saw that he was vexed by my puns about the wax jobs on the oily cabs.	71

Freight bills are a type of invoice issued by transportation companies for hauling charges. In Illustration 60 the rate given is the rate per 100 pounds. In calculating the amount to be charged for each item, any fraction of 100 pounds is counted as an even 100 pounds. For example, 2490 pounds is charged for as 2500 pounds.

PROBLEM 1—LEARNING THE NATURE OF THE PROBLEM

Directions. Type the freight bill as shown in Illustration 60. Determine the tabulator adjustments before you begin to type. Proofread the typed copy before removing it from the typewriter; then type the freight bill a second time.

STROKES

WILSHIRE TRANSPORTATION CO. INTRASTATE CARRIERS - P. U. C. 79012

HOME OFFICE: 6915 EMPIRE BOULEVARD, CLEVELAND 6, OHIO

To The Wilson Iron & Forge Co.   Date November 15, 195-
2096 South Michigan Avenue
Chicago 11, Illinois   Shipper   Wadsworth Manufacturing Co.
1007 East Marshall Avenue
Youngstown 12, Ohio

46
73
122
148
168

No. Pieces	Description of Articles to be Transported and Marks	Weight	Rate	Prepaid	Collect	
2 bxs.	Pipe Fittings, Iron and Steel	2490	.57		14.25	225
86 drums	" " " " "	9250	.75		69.75	280
218 pcs.	Seamless Tubing	21975	.68		149.60	322
10 kegs	FF-N-191 2 1/2" Steel Nails	1080	.55		6.05	376
4 drums	Carbon Tetrachloride	2800	.63		17.64	424
5 ctns.	Chrome Plated Cabinet Hardware	325	.50		2.00	472
15 ctns.	3 1/4" Ball Bearing Casters	1300	.55		7.15	533
					266.44	540
						547
	3% Federal Tax				7.99	569
					274.43	575
						581

Received the above described property in good order.

ORIGINAL FREIGHT BILL   Consignee_____ Date_____

Illustration 60 — Freight Bill

PROBLEM 2—SKILL BUILDING IN TYPING A FREIGHT BILL

Directions. Type this freight bill in a form similar to that in Problem 1. Proofread the typed copy before removing it from the typewriter; then type the freight bill a second time.

STROKES

To **The Whitehall Construction Company 4106 North Aberdeen Boulevard** 65
Grand Rapids 13, Michigan Date 11/15/5— Shipper The Levinson Tool 118
and Die Works Main at Hollingwood Avenue Dayton 7, Ohio 174

No. Pieces	Description	Weight	Rate	Collect	
					217
					260
25 ctns.	Adjustable Tap, Die Sets	1200	.56	6.72	310
15 bxs.	GGG-T-581 Screwplate Sets	1890	.61	11.59	360
10 bxs.	Reinforced Roller Tool Cabinets	710	.75	6.00	416
55 bxs.	90-piece Mechanics' Tool Sets	7150	.70	50.40	471
40 bxs.	115-piece Mechanics' Tool Sets	8880	.70	62.30	526
					533
				137.01	540
	3% Federal Tax			4.11	561
					568
				141.12	575

Directions. 1. Type several 1-minute writings on the following paragraph *at the exploration level of practice.* (Refer to page 48 for a discussion of levels of practice.) Type for speed. As you try to reach a new speed rate, you may make more typing errors than usual. Keep the carriage moving, stay relaxed, and type without a sense of hurry to reach a new speed level.

2. Type for 2 minutes *at the exploration level of practice.* Try to maintain the speed rate you set on the 1-minute writings. Your teacher will guide your writing by calling each half-minute interval.

3. Type one or two 3-minute writings *at the exploration level of practice.* Select an appropriate speed rate for yourself and attempt to maintain this rate for the 3-minute writing. Your teacher will guide your writing by calling each half-minute interval.

This paragraph has all letters of the alphabet and a syllable intensity of 1.30

	STROKES
In order to type with proper techniques and a quick, snap stroke, you	70
must recognize the need for keeping the fingers curved and close to the	142
keys. The hands and arms should be held in a quiet, relaxed position and	216
all reaches should be made with the action in the fingers. The keys should	292
be struck with the tips of the fingers and released quickly. The fingers	366
should be held in an upright position to avoid glancing strokes which	436
often cause clashing and locking of the keys. As you type this paragraph,	511
try to hit the keys quickly and release them just as quickly, and keep the	586
carriage moving for best results.	619

SKILL-BUILDING PROCEDURES 76   *10 minutes*

Directions. In the time that remains, type as many lines of the preceding paragraph as you can. Type each line three times as follows: (1) Type the line at an easy pace and maintain a continuous stroking rate; (2) Keep the fingers close to the keys, use a quick, snap stroke, and type the line at a slightly faster pace; and, (3) Try to type at your top speed without breaks or pauses in the line. If any words in the line cause you to slow up or pause, type such words several times.

LESSON 77

CONDITIONING PRACTICE 77   *5 minutes*

Directions. Type each line twice. As time permits, practice any line that may have caused you trouble. Type at a well-controlled pace.

	STROKES
We had to spell kumquat, justify, bovine, xebec, and fright in a quiz.	70
The fisherman caught 84 albacore, 3,215 barracuda, and 7,690 mackerel.	70
They lent the ancient ornament to their neighbor by the big city dock.	70

PROBLEM 2—SKILL BUILDING IN TYPING A BILL OF LADING

Directions. Type this bill of lading in a form similar to that in Problem 1. Proofread the typed copy before removing it from the typewriter; then type the bill of lading a second time.

STROKES

Shipper's No. **196704**   Company **New York Central Railroad**   At **Syracuse,** 43
New York   From **The National Heating Company, Inc. November 18, 195—** 105
Consigned to **The Woodward Furnace Company**   Destination **Boston 9,** 144
State of **Massachusetts**   Route **Your Line**   Car Initial **RMV**   Car No. **689024** 179

Packages	Description	Weight	
			207
			235
4	24 x 40 x 32 Gas Furnace	170#	268
1	26 x 32 x 38 Furnace Blower	145#	304
8	Welded Steel Furnace	1080#	333
5	Cast Iron Fittings	165#	360
1	No. 2 Oil-Fired Boiler	235#	391
1	Conversion Oil Burner	125#	421

Shipper **The National Heating Company, Inc.**   Permanent address of 456
shipper **1259 Borden Avenue, Syracuse 6, New York** 496

SKILL MAINTENANCE 172
5 minutes

Directions. Use the following paragraph for a series of 1-minute writings. Between timings, identify the awkward or difficult words and type each in a three-word group—including the word preceding and the word immediately following. *Type on the exploration level of practice.*

This paragraph has every letter of the alphabet.

	STROKES	WORDS
You need expert skill in manipulating your typewriter to do office	67	13
work. When you must type on ruled lines or when you must align your	136	27
copy to match other material, you must be just as precise in manipulat-	206	41
ing the typewriter as you are accurate in typing the figures and words.	279	56
Utilize the mechanism of the machine to the fullest and make the adjust-	350	70
ments quickly. Every second saved adds to your opportunity to increase	422	84
your production—and thus to increase your earning power.	479	96

LESSON 173

CONDITIONING PRACTICE 173
5 minutes

STROKES

Jim Lebamof expects veterans to get the weekly quiz on American Drama.	70
I stored 285 books, 74 games, 396 magazines, and 10 pieces of luggage.	70
Not much work can be done by anyone who does not feel sure of himself.	70

Word-Recognition Level of Typing Response. Type each line three times. Think and type each word as a unit. To help you type on the word-recognition level of response, pronounce each word (silently) just before typing it.

Technique Emphasis. Keep the fingers well curved and close to the keys; hit each key with a quick, snap stroke and release it quickly.

STROKES

they lend paid them when flap work firm with form hand pair land girl   69

their right signs audit shake right angle sight field spend chair visit   71

They may pay the firm for the work when they sign the right audit form.   71

Stroke Level of Typing Response. Type each line three times. Type each word at a well-controlled pace. Think and type each word letter by letter, using a quick, snap stroke.

STROKES

dear pull were lump data look test jump gate hook best link rate only   69

union draft imply aware pupil staff nylon weave plump great jumpy react   71

We were not aware that you would get the best rates on the union tests.   71

GUIDED WRITING 77   *15 minutes*

Directions. Type several timed writings on the following paragraph. *Type at the exploration level of practice.* Use the same practice procedures as given for Guided Writing 76, page 109. Your teacher will guide your writing by calling each half-minute interval.

This paragraph has all letters of the alphabet and a syllable intensity of 1.30

STROKES

"Hug the keys" with your finger tips. This is a good suggestion if   68

you are to become a rapid and accurate typist. The reach for a key should   143

be quick and continuous with no pause of the finger when the key is struck.   220

It is a good idea to imagine that the keys are red hot. You must release   294

them quickly when they are struck. Just tense the finger briefly in order   369

to get the right amount of power behind each stroke, then immediately   439

relax the finger when it is not in use. If you keep your fingers stiff and   515

tense, you will tire quickly and your speed will decrease. Good typists   588

recognize this fact. Keep your fingers curved, relaxed, and close to the   662

keys to increase your speed.   690

SKILL-BUILDING PROCEDURES 77   *10 minutes*

Directions. Practice typing as many lines of the preceding paragraph as is possible. Type each line three times as outlined in Skill-Building Procedures 76, page 109.

Directions. Use Skill Maintenance 168, page 224, for a series of three 1-minute writings. Between timings, identify the awkward or difficult words and type each in a three-word group— including the word preceding it and the word following it. *Type on the exploration level of practice.*

LESSON 172

CONDITIONING PRACTICE 172   *5 minutes*

STROKES

Max Joyce backed his quota of five groups over Danish and Welsh zones.   70

Their druggist stocked 82 salves, 970 pills, 54 tonics, and 613 drugs.   70

A poor worker is too expensive for a business to place on its payroll.   70

PROBLEM TYPING 172—TYPING BILLS OF LADING   *30 minutes*

Three copies of a bill of lading are prepared: the *original* is mailed to the buyer; the *shipping order* is retained by the transportation company; and the *memorandum* is retained by the seller.

PROBLEM I—LEARNING THE NATURE OF THE PROBLEM

Directions. Type the bill of lading shown in Illustration 59. Gauge the line of writing so the typewritten material will rest slightly above the printed lines. Avoid having the lines run through the typed words. Proofread the typed copy before removing it from the typewriter; then type the bill of lading a second time.

STROKES

		STROKES
(Uniform Domestic Straight Bill of Lading, adopted by Carriers in Official, Southern, Western and Illinois Classification territories, March 15, 1922, as amended August 1, 1930.)		
UNIFORM STRAIGHT BILL OF LADING--ORIGINAL--NOT NEGOTIABLE Shipper's No. 189765		7
Southern Railway **Company** Agent's No.		24
RECEIVED, subject to the classifications and tariffs in effect on the date of the issue of this Bill of Lading,		
at High Point, North Carolina FROM The United Furniture Company October 26, 195-		53 / 97
Consigned to The McCausland Furniture Company		130
Destination Cleveland 12, State of Ohio County of		149
Route Your line		159
Delivering Carrier Car Initial TXY Car No. 146028		170

No. Packages	Description of Articles, Special Marks and Exceptions	*WEIGHT (Subject to Correction)	Class or Rate	Check Column		STROKES
1	42 x 30 Extension Table	130#			Subject to Section 7 of conditions, if this shipment is to be delivered to the consignee without recourse on the consignor, the consignor shall sign the following statement:	201
1	60 x 21 Credenza Buffet	195#			The carrier shall not make delivery of this shipment without payment of freight and all other lawful charges.	233
4	37 in. Regular Side Chairs	80#			(Signature of Consignor)	267
2	38½ in. Large Arm Chairs	50#			If charges are to be prepaid, write or stamp here, "To be Prepaid."	299
1	42 x 17 x 71 China Cabinet	195#			Received $ to apply in prepayment of the charges on the property described hereon.	333
1	34 x 18 x 34 Matched Server	85#			Agent or Cashier	368

*If the shipment moves between two ports by a carrier by water, the law requires that the bill of lading shall state whether it is "carrier's or shipper's weight." Note—Where the rate is dependent upon value, shippers are required to state specifically in writing the agreed or declared value of the property. The agreed or declared value of the property is hereby specifically stated by the shipper to be not exceeding _____ per _____

Per (The signature here acknowledges only the amount prepaid.)

Charges Advanced: $ _____   397

The United Furniture Company ___ *Shipper* _____ *Agent, Per* ____   444

Permanent post-office address of shipper 1436 Burbank Avenue, High Point, North Carolina

Illustration 59 — Bill of Lading

LESSON 78

CONDITIONING PRACTICE 78

Directions. Type each line twice. As time permits, select for repetitive practice the sentence or sentences on which you made errors.

STROKES

Van's amazing ability on the saxophone quickly changed their few jeers. 71

Back order these items: 10 doz. pens @ 75¢; 1 gross pencils @ 85¢ doz. 71

R. J. Asham, T. O. Black, A. E. Byrd, and Mary King made A's in typing. 71

He may sign the usual form by proxy if they make an audit of the firms. 71

TECHNIQUE STUDY 78

10 minutes

COMBINATION LEVEL OF TYPING RESPONSE

Directions. Type each line three times. Some of the words in this drill will have to be typed on the stroke level of response as they are written entirely by either the right or the left hand. Other words should be typed on the word level. Try to type the phrases and sentences on a combination level of word, letter, and syllable response.

Technique Emphasis. Hit all keys with uniform stroking power. Keep the carriage moving, and work for a smooth, fluent rhythm.

STROKES

case, the case, of the case, address, the address, at the address, the 70

data, the data, and the data, union, the union, with the union data to 70

card, on the card, statement, the statement, gave the statement to the 70

They gave the statement to the union at the address shown on the card. 70

Send a statement of the case with the union data to them as requested. 70

They requested the union to have the data on the case referred to him. 70

GUIDED WRITING 78

15 minutes

Directions. 1. Type several 1-minute writings of the following paragraph *at the control level of practice.* The purpose of this level of practice is to improve your accuracy. To do this, reduce your speed approximately 10 words a minute below your speed rate at the exploration level. Your teacher will guide your writing by calling each half-minute interval. Keep your eyes on the copy, maintain good techniques, and concentrate on the material to be typed to improve your accuracy.

2. Type for *2 minutes at the control level.* Your teacher will guide your writing by calling each half-minute interval. Try to maintain a uniform pace each half minute.

3. Type one or two 3-minute writings *at the control level.* Your teacher will guide your writing by calling each half-minute interval. As a tentative goal, try to type with not more than three errors. At the end of the writing, proofread your paper carefully and encircle each error. Determine your cwpm.

SECTION 28. Shipping Papers

LESSON 171

CONDITIONING PRACTICE 171
5 minutes

Directions. Type each line twice. Retype the lines as often as time permits. This will be the uniform assignment for typing the conditioning practice in each lesson of this section.

	STROKES
Zeta Pi may relax its fine views on quotas to help get Bea and Jackie.	70
I shall issue 502 slacks, 78 knives, 64 guns, and 139 leather jackets.	70
When a job is once begun, it should not be left until it is well done.	70

PROBLEM TYPING 171—PROBLEM I—LEARNING THE NATURE OF THE PROBLEM
30 minutes

Directions. Type the purchase order shown below. Set tabulator stops so that you can indent to the columns quickly and accurately. Proofread; then retype the problem.

STROKES

PURCHASE ORDER

KECK CONSTRUCTION COMPANY

6902 Lincoln Boulevard   OMAHA 8, NEBRASKA

MARK ORDER No. ON INVOICE
AND ON ALL PACKAGES

Order No. JK 10921 — 9

The Weston Supply Company — *Date* November 27, *195-* — 51
1897 Fairview Avenue — 72
St. Louis 16, Missouri — 95

Ship via National Trucking Lines — 119

REQUISITION	QUANTITY	DESCRIPTION	PRICE	
WA 26704	1,000	3/4 x 48" Roof Bolts	532.70	163
WA 26704	1,000	OB #21889 Shell & Plug	280.00	209
WA 26704	1,000	6 x 6 x 3/8" Plates	281.50	252
ON 14165	179	B 1477-A Journal Bearings	1124.76	301
MT 17134	20	1 1/2" Galv. Pipe Cap Mall	10.50	351
MT 17135	15	1 1/2" M. I. Galv. GH Union Pipe	42.75	414
				422
			2272.21	429

Illustration 58 — Purchase Order

PROBLEM 2—SKILL BUILDING IN TYPING A PURCHASE ORDER

Directions. Type the purchase order in the form used in Problem 1. Proofread the typed copy before removing it from the typewriter; then type the order a second time.

STROKES

Order No. AB 69017 The Morrison Manufacturing Company 8905 Auburndale — 60
Avenue Kansas City 12, Missouri Date November 28, 195— Ship Via — 110
United Trucking Lines, Inc. — 138

Requisition	Quantity	Description	Price	
				177
BB 03502	2	Sauter Time Switches, type ZWN 40 II	266.00	216 / 275
CA 13049	1	Cameron Condensate Return Unit	1,271.00	328
PG 17067	300 lb.	1/4" Airco #90 Elect.	12.10	376
SO 99782	2	C. S. 8" Sheaves, Pattern #15427	104.00	431
DF 38416	4	#343523 Dome Reflector Units	8.00	482
				490
			1,661.10	498

This paragraph has all letters of the alphabet and a syllable intensity of 1.30

	STROKES
Rhythm is an important factor of typing skill. You must type with	67
rhythm if you are to reach high levels of speed and accuracy. Some words	141
must be typed at a fairly slow rate because they are typed entirely with	214
the fingers of one hand. There are other words that can be typed at a	285
high rate of speed because they are typed with alternate fingers of both	358
hands. All typing is composed of one-hand and balanced-hand stroking	428
patterns which when properly typed should result in a smooth, flowing	498
rhythm. As you type, just try to keep the carriage moving evenly and	568
avoid pauses. Do this by staying relaxed, by keeping your eyes on the	639
copy, and by striking the keys quickly. You will soon be typing with	709
rhythm and you will be amazed at your progress.	756

SKILL-BUILDING PROCEDURES 78
10 minutes

Directions. Type three times each word on which you made errors in the 3-minute timed writing. After typing the word on which you made the error, type it in a three-word group—include the word preceding the error and the word following the error. In the time that remains, practice typing as many lines of the paragraph as is possible. Repeat each line until you can type it without error at your best rate of speed.

LESSON 79

CONDITIONING PRACTICE 79
5 minutes

Directions. Type each line twice. As time permits, select for repetitive practice the sentence or sentences on which you made errors.

	STROKES
Jovial Jack Bogaz squirmed into a tuxedo and went to the formal party.	70
Type the following fractions and mixed numbers: $\frac{1}{2}$, $\frac{1}{4}$, $5\frac{1}{4}$, $7\frac{1}{2}$, and $2\frac{1}{4}$.	70
They wish to go to the city with the chairman for the profit due them.	70

TECHNIQUE STUDY 79
10 minutes

Directions. 1. Type each sentence for one minute on either the 20-second, 15-second, or 10-second guide as directed by your teacher. If you complete the sentence before the guide is called, throw the carriage and continue typing but pace your typing a little more slowly. If you have not completed the sentence when the guide is called, increase your speed of stroking slightly. When the first sentence has been typed as directed, proceed to the second sentence and continue until the list is finished.

2. If your teacher directs you to type the sentences without the call of the guide, type each sentence five times.

Directions. You are to type for 30 minutes. Type each problem once with a carbon. Proof-read each problem and correct all errors before removing it from the typewriter. (Uncorrected errors will receive a 10-word penalty.) If you complete the typing of all problems before time is called, retype as many as possible. At the end of the 30-minute period, compute your stroking rate per minute. *Type on the control level.*

PROBLEM 1—UNRULED INVOICE

Directions. Type the invoice in a form similar to that used in Illustration 55, page 221.

STROKES

Sold to **The Rapid Transit Company** **8156 Ardmore Boulevard**				50
Minneapolis 6, Minnesota Terms **Net 30 days** Date **November 1, 195—**				104
Our No. **RJ 91569** Cust. Order No. **61580** Shipped Via **Freight Prepaid**				135

Quantity	Description	Unit Price	Amount	
				174
				213
50 ft.	1 5/8 Radiator Hose	.73 ft.	36.50	257
25	7 x 7/8 16A Sanding Discs	.53 ea.	13.25	303
20 gal.	21-B Brake Fluid	4.95 gal.	99.00	346
8 C	A-548 Spark Plug Nuts	2.00 C	16.00	388
15 sets	MS-18013 Manifold Gaskets	.40 set	6.00	439
3 M	1/2 x 1 1/4 S. A. E. Cap Screws	37.50 M	112.50	491
35 gal.	DQE 8001 Black Enamel Paint	6.08 gal.	212.80	545
				551
			496.05	557

PROBLEM 2—RULED INVOICE

Directions. Type the invoice in a form similar to that used in Illustration 56, page 222.

STROKES

Sold to **The Fergerson Luggage Company** **2104 West Avondale Avenue**				56
Knoxville 7, Tennessee Date **November 1, 195—** No. **58278**				102
Terms **Net 30 days** Shipped Via **Norfolk and Western**				144

Quantity	Description	Price	Amount	
				178
				212
14	Catalog Cases	20.70	289.80	245
12	Ladies' Patent Purses—Style C	4.45	53.40	295
8	Ladies' Patent Belts—Style C	1.80	14.40	344
2	Dressing Sets—Standard	22.50	45.00	387
10	Dressing Sets—De Luxe	27.90	279.00	429
2	Wear-Rite Special Wardrobe Trunks	172.80	345.60	482
6	Evans Billfolds	8.10	48.60	517
				525
			1,075.80	533

PROBLEM 3—CREDIT MEMORANDUM

Directions. Type the credit memorandum in a form similar to that used in Illustration 57, page 223.

STROKES

No. **30853** **November 23, 195—** **Philadelphia Transportation Company**				59
1495 West Brighton Avenue Philadelphia 7, Pennsylvania				114

Quantity	Description	Price	Amount	
				148
				182
10 sets	RE-18-24H Ignition Points	.87 set	8.70	232
30 rolls	3/4 x 66 Electrical Tape	1.50 roll	45.00	283
15	FP-1039 Water Pumps	5.43 ea.	81.45	321
				327
			135.15	333

Technique Emphasis. Throw the carriage quickly at the end of the line, keep your eyes on the copy, and start the new line without a pause.

	Strokes	Words 20"	Words 15"	Words 10"
You can learn to do what you want to do.	40	24	32	48
I should type some words on the word level.	43	26	34	52
I did the work with the action in my fingers.	45	27	36	54
Relax the hands and let the fingers do the work.	48	29	38	58
The way he worked had much to do with what he did.	50	30	40	60

GUIDED WRITING 79 · *15 minutes*

Directions. Type several timed writings of the following paragraph. *Type at the control level of practice.* Use the same practice procedure as given for Guided Writing 78, page 111. Your teacher will guide your writing by calling each half-minute interval.

This paragraph has all letters of the alphabet and a syllable intensity of 1.30

STROKES

You have often been told to throw the carriage quickly at the end of ... 69

a line. To throw the carriage quickly, keep the elbow fairly close to the ... 144

side of your body, extend the forearm and hand only far enough out to ... 214

reach the carriage-return lever. Be sure to reach out with the hand and ... 287

pivot it at the wrist. Catch the carriage-return lever between the first ... 361

and second joints of the index finger. Keep the rest of the fingers in ... 433

line with the index finger to get added power. Then throw the carriage ... 505

with a quick snap or flick of your wrist. Do not follow the carriage ... 575

across, but quickly bring your hand back to typing position so that you ... 647

can start the new line without pause or break. A quick carriage return ... 719

will help you realize your typing speed. ... 759

SKILL-BUILDING PROCEDURES 79 · *5 minutes*

Directions. In the time that remains, follow the practice procedures outlined in Skill-Building Procedures 78, page 112, for the 3-minute timed writing you typed for this lesson.

PROBLEM 2—SKILL BUILDING IN TYPING A CREDIT MEMORANDUM

Directions. Type the memorandum in a form similar to that used in Problem 1. Proofread. Then type the memorandum a second time.

STROKES

No. 274 May 25, 195— Island Transportation Company 1203 Newport Avenue 71
Norfolk 5, Virginia 91

Quantity	Description	Price	Amount	
				124
				158
5 gal.	DQE 70019 Red Enamel Paint	7.56	37.80	205
2 C	L. S. H. Tire Cross Chains	19.41	38.82	249
25 ft.	5/16 Copper Tubing	.24	6.00	292
				298
			82.62	303

SKILL MAINTENANCE 168
5 minutes

Directions. Use the paragraph for three 1-minute writings. *Type on the exploration level of practice.* Between timings, identify the difficult words and type each in a three-word group— including the word preceding it and the word following it.

	STROKES	WORDS
Much of the work in an office has to be done under pressure. True,	68	14
the employer may not stand with watch in hand to time your production;	139	28
but the mail must go out, and frequently an extra rush of important mail	212	42
will come just near the end of the day. It is at such a time that every	285	57
worker will realize the benefit of good work habits and the stamina that	358	72
comes from having learned to work without waste effort.	413	83

LESSON 169

CONDITIONING PRACTICE 169
5 minutes

	STROKES
Dr. Wayvel exposed hazards of quack medicine to King Junction jobbers.	70
The club exchanged 87 uniforms, 314 bats, 92 shoes, and 605 baseballs.	70
One hard thing to learn is that we must wait for growth to take place.	70

PROBLEM TYPING 169 — SKILL BUILDING
35 minutes

Directions. Make pencil notations on a piece of note paper of the problems listed below, and place the paper on the desk near your textbook so that you can refer to it as you complete the typing of each problem. You will be timed for 30 minutes. Correct all errors; uncorrected errors will receive a 10-word penalty. If you complete the typing of the problems before time is called, retype as many of them as possible. Compute your stroking rate.

Problem 2, page 221—type once with a carbon copy.
Problem 2, page 222—type once with a carbon copy.
Problem 2, page 224—type once with a carbon copy.

LESSON 170

CONDITIONING PRACTICE 170
5 minutes

	STROKES
Mike Weaver signed excitedly dozens of copies of his novel, QUIET JOB.	70
His picnic basket holds 68 knives, 405 forks, 93 cups, and 172 spoons.	70
The office is a place to work and not a place to have social meetings.	70

LESSON 80

CONDITIONING PRACTICE 80 *5 minutes*

Directions. Type each line twice. As time permits, select for repetitive practice the sentence or sentences on which you made errors.

STROKES

A quick tax was levied on the fez to help defray a club judgment cost.   70

The #346 item will cost Donovan & Company $921.78 (less 10% for cash).   70

She may go with them down the lane to the shale rocks by the big lake.   70

TECHNIQUE STUDY 80 *10 minutes*

Space-Bar Control. Learn to space quickly between words so that the carriage can be kept moving. Keep the thumb close to the space bar. Strike and release the space bar quickly after the last letter of each word and start the new word without a pause.

Directions. Type each sentence five times, or more, as time permits. Try to improve your control of the space bar.

STROKES

If he is to do the work for them as it must be done, he will need aid.   70

Ten men may be needed to clean the storage bin for the new grain crop.   70

They will soon try to rush several men to help you with all such work.   70

GUIDED WRITING 80 *15 minutes*

Directions. 1. Type a 3-minute timed writing *at the control level.* As your goal, try to type without error, or with not more than one or two. Determine your cwpm.

2. Type several 1-minute writings *at the skill-building level of practice.* Try to type at a rate which will be approximately five words higher than the rate you made on the 3-minute writing. Then, if you can, gradually increase this rate on each minute writing. When you begin to lose control and make errors, you will have pushed your rate high enough for the present. Your teacher will guide your writing by calling each half-minute interval.

3. Type a 3-minute timed writing *at the skill-building level of practice.* Try to maintain a rate that will be approximately five words a minute higher than the rate you made on the 3-minute timed writing at the control level. Your teacher will guide your writing by calling each half-minute interval. Determine your cwpm.

This paragraph has all letters of the alphabet and a syllable intensity of 1.30

STROKES

If a book had to be used for frequent reference, you would not think   69

of keeping it on a bookshelf across the room from your desk. You would   141

keep it on your desk for efficient work. We all make many waste motions   214

if we do not plan our work. The elimination of waste motions in typewrit-   287

ing will result in an amazing increase in speed. The waste time can be   359

turned into typing time. The additional typing time means an increase in   433

	STROKES	WORDS
How much can you do in a given time? You have worked under the	64	13
plan of timing your production. This experience should give you the	133	27
judgment needed to know with some exactness the quantity of work you	202	40
can do in a given time. Do not minimize the importance of learning to	273	55
estimate the work you are able to do.	310	62

LESSON 168

CONDITIONING PRACTICE 168   *5 minutes*

	STROKES
Jackson quietly explained to the Navy why he zigzagged in Farmers Bay.	70
Today Earl sold 62 suspenders, 185 ties, 704 belts, and 93 dark suits.	70
It pays to form the habit of checking each page of work as it is done.	70

PROBLEM TYPING 168—TYPING CREDIT MEMORANDA   *30 minutes*

A credit memorandum is a business form issued by a seller to show credit given to a buyer. It contains detailed information concerning a return of merchandise, an overcharge on an invoice, or an allowance for goods received by the purchaser in a damaged condition. The form used for credit memoranda and the number of carbon copies required will differ among companies.

PROBLEM 1—LEARNING THE NATURE OF THE PROBLEM

Directions. Type the credit memorandum. Proofread; then type the memorandum a second time.

STROKES

CREDIT MEMORANDUM

HARRINGTON COMPANY

OAKLAND

	STROKES
No. 54 April 21, 195-	18
Martin Paint Company	39
224 North Main Street	61
Springfield, Ohio	79

WE CREDIT YOUR ACCOUNT AS FOLLOWS:

QUANTITY	DESCRIPTION	PRICE	AMOUNT	STROKES
5	100-lb. "Pure-Mix" White Lead	19.50	97.50	124
2	1-gal. Lead Chromate	3.00	6.00	161
2	5-gal. Pure Wood Turpentine	3.70	7.40	211
			110.90	218
				224

Illustration 57 — Credit Memorandum

	STROKES
speed. For instance, a quick carriage return saves time if you start the	507
new line without a pause. The keys can be struck quickly only if the	577
fingers are kept close to the keys. Typists may make waste motions in	648
the use of the space bar. It is impossible to space quickly between words	723
if the thumb is held too far above the space bar. If you want to be an	795
expert typist, think about ways to improve your typing techniques. Then,	869
just put your improved techniques to work.	911

SKILL-BUILDING PROCEDURES 80 *10 minutes*

Directions. In the time that remains, practice typing as many lines of the preceding paragraph as is possible. Repeat each line until you can type it without error at your best rate of speed.

LESSON 81

CONDITIONING PRACTICE 81 *5 minutes*

Directions. Type each line twice. As time permits, select for repetitive practice the sentence or sentences on which you made errors.

	STROKES
The commander quizzed J. G. Koplyn about the use of five new sextants.	70
Send order #1280-YL ($4,936.70 less 15%) for $4\frac{1}{4}$ C&B Oak via C&NW R. R.	70
She shot eight ducks by the lake and kept six of them for the auditor.	70

TECHNIQUE STUDY 81 *10 minutes*

Carriage Return and Tabulator-Key Control. Throw the carriage quickly at the end of the line and bring the hand back to typing position instantly so that the new line can be started without a break or pause.

Directions. Clear all tabulator stops. Set a tabulator stop at 60 for an elite- or at 50 for a pica-type machine. Start the first sentence at this point. Then, start each new sentence at the same point by using the tabulator key or bar.

Type the drill three or more times as time permits. *Type at the exploration level of practice.*

		STROKES
	Maintain good position	23
at the typewriter.	Keep the fingers well	65
curved and close to the keys.	Be sure to keep the	116
hands and arms quiet.	Keep the stroking action	164
in your fingers.	Strike the keys with a	205
quick, snap stroke.	Avoid pushing the keys	249
as the reaches are made.	Type with continuity and	300
keep the carriage moving.	Try to keep your eyes	349
on the copy.	Throw the carriage quickly	390
at the end of the line.	Start the new line	434
without a pause.	Shift for all capital	474
letters without loss of time.		503

CONDITIONING PRACTICE 167 *5 minutes*

He toured Mexico equipped with dozens of Spanish-English travel books. 70
They ordered 512 sweaters, 403 caps, 86 mittens, and 97 new overcoats. 70
It is always easy to gain high speed when correct techniques are used. 70

PROBLEM TYPING 167—TYPING INVOICES WITH RULED COLUMNS *30 minutes*
PROBLEM I—LEARNING THE NATURE OF THE PROBLEM

Directions. Type the appropriate information under the headings within the ruled columns. Set tabulator stops so the typing will not touch the vertical or horizontal lines. Proofread; then type the invoice a second time.

STROKES

HARRINGTON COMPANY
OAKLAND

Sold to Martin Paint Company   **Date** April 14, 195-   36
224 North Main Street   58
Springfield, Ohio   **No.** 949   80

Terms 1/30,n/60   **Shipped Via** Western Trucking   107

QUANTITY	DESCRIPTION	PRICE	AMOUNT	
25	100-lb. "Pure-Mix" White Lead	19.50	487.50	156
20	5-gal. Pure Linseed Oil	12.25	245.00	200
10	5-gal. Pure Wood Turpentine	3.70	37.00	248
12	1-gal. Lead Chromate	3.00	36.00	289
25	5-gal. "Econo" Utility House Paint, White	9.15	228.75	351
10	5-gal. "Econo" Utility House Paint, Ivory	9.15	91.50	413
10	5-gal. "Econo" Utility House Paint, Yellow	9.15	91.50	484
			1,217.25	493
				501

Illustration 56 — Invoice with Ruled Columns

PROBLEM 2—SKILL BUILDING IN TYPING AN INVOICE

Directions. Type the invoice. Proofread; then type it a second time.

STROKES

Sold to **The Lucas-Demler Pump Company   1856 McMillan Avenue**   51
Cincinnati 2, Ohio   Date   **November 1, 195—**   No.   **58277**   93
Terms   **2/10,n/30**   Shipped Via   **Baltimore and Ohio**   122

Quantity		Description	Price	Amount	
					156
					190
96	CP169	Factory-type Water Pumps	5.80	556.80	240
48	CP138	Factory-type Water Pumps	6.83	327.84	290
54	CP158	Factory-type Water Pumps	7.06	381.24	340
10	CP162	Factory-type Water Pumps	10.00	100.00	390
48	WS1296	Water Pump Shafts	2.67	128.16	433
					441
				1,494.04	449

SKILL MAINTENANCE 167 *5 minutes*

Directions. Use the paragraph for a series of three 1-minute writings. *Type on the exploration level of practice.* Between timings, identify the awkward or difficult words and type each in a three-word group—including the preceding word and the word immediately following.

Directions. 1. Type several 15-second writings on the first sentence. Pause briefly after each writing to relax your hands and arms and relieve tension.

Start at an easy pace and gradually work up to your best rate. It is suggested that you start at approximately 30 words per minute (about 8 words each 15 seconds). Increase this rate by 1 word for each 15-second writing until you are typing at your top speed.

Follow the same procedure for the second and third sentences. Try to equal your top speed on the first sentence.

2. Type a 1-minute writing on each of the sentences. Compare the rates you make on each sentence. You should make your best rate on the first sentence as the sentences become progressively more difficult.

The figures above and below the sentences indicate the number of 5-stroke words up to that point.

```
     1        2        3        4        5        6        7        8        9       10       11       12       13       14
The eight girls kept the auditor and the chairman busy with a problem.

If the date of the statement is correct, then I may sign the contract.

We were not aware that you would get the best rate on the union tests.
     1        2        3        4        5        6        7        8        9       10       11       12       13       14
```

Directions. Type a 5-minute timed writing on the paragraph given for Guided Writing 76, page 109. *Type at the exploration level of practice.* Determine your cwpm.

Directions. Type the following material from your teacher's dictation. Think the word and type the word as a unit.

if it is, if it is, if it is, and the, and the, and the, and if the

pay pay pay, for for for, men men men, work work work, them them them

Pay them. Pay the men. Pay the men for it. Pay the men for the work.

LESSON 82

Directions. Type each line twice. As time permits, select for repetitive practice the sentence or sentences on which you made errors. Underscore the italicized words in the second line.

STROKES

Six women in the valley heard piercing squawks of dozens of blue jays.   70

Did Frederic read *Office Methods, Systems, and Procedures* by Herrmann?   109

Pay the man for the form and ask the auditor to make the usual checks.   70

AUTOMOTIVE SUPPLY COMPANY

1027 State Street   **Akron 3, Ohio**

		STROKES
Sold to Island Transportation Company 1203 Newport Avenue Norfolk 5, Virginia	**Date** November 1, 195-	47
	Our No. RJ 91567	67
	Cust. Order No. 61578	96
Terms Net 30 days	**Shipped Via** Freight Collect	102

QUANTITY	DESCRIPTION	UNIT PRICE	AMOUNT	STROKES
5 C	L. S. H. Tire Cross Chains	19.41 C	97.05	178
8 C	1/2 x 1 1/4 S. A. E. Cap Screws	3.75 C	30.00	231
10 M	3/8 x 1 1/2 U. S. S. Cap Screws	29.50 M	295.00	284
65 lb.	Acid Core Solder	1.22 lb.	79.30	325
24	JC Oil Filter Cartridges	1.04 ea.	24.96	371
20 gal.	DQE 70019 Red Enamel Paint	7.56 gal.	151.20	425
125 ft.	5/16 Copper Tubing	.24 ft.	30.00	475
			707.51	482
				488

Illustration 55 — Invoice Without Columnar Rulings

PROBLEM 2—SKILL BUILDING IN TYPING AN INVOICE

Directions. Type the invoice in a form similar to that used for Problem **1**. Proofread the typed copy before removing it from the typewriter; then type the invoice a second time.

	STROKES
Sold to **Philadelphia Transportation Company** 1495 West Brighton Avenue	62
Philadelphia 7, Pennsylvania Terms **Net 30 days** Date **November 1, 195——**	120
Our No. **RJ 91568** Cust. Order No. **61579** Shipped Via **Freight Collect**	151

Quantity	Description	Unit Price	Amount	STROKES
				190
				229
25 sets	RE-18-24H Ignition Points	.87 set	21.75	281
40 pints	DAL 41072 Lacquer Paint	1.35 pint	54.00	333
100 rolls	3/4 x 66 Electrical Tape	1.50 roll	150.00	386
15	FP-1039 Water Pumps	5.43 ea.	81.45	427
20	Cylinder Head Gaskets	1.10 ea.	22.00	470
50 pr.	DL-9 Wiper Blades	.90 pr.	45.00	513
5 M	1/4 x 1/2 U. S. S. Cap Screws	20.00 M	100.00	564
				570
			474.20	576

SKILL MAINTENANCE 166   *5 minutes*

Directions. Use the following paragraph for a series of three 1-minute writings. *Type on the exploration level of practice.* Between timings, identify the awkward or difficult words and type each in a three-word group—including the word preceding and the word following.

This paragraph has every letter of the alphabet.

	STROKES	WORDS
In business, the worker often has to use his own judgment—and the	67	13
decisions that are made are frequently very important. Problems present	140	28
themselves rapidly, and the ability to use good judgment in meeting	208	42
unexpected problems will save you a good many agonizing hours of won-	276	55
dering if you have done the right or the wrong thing.	329	66

Improving the Stroking Action of the Third and Fourth Fingers. The following drill emphasizes the use of the two outside fingers on each hand. Its purpose is to help you improve your stroking of the keys controlled by these fingers. As you type the drill, try to keep the stroking action in the fingers. Make the fingers do the work and keep the wrists and arms quiet and relaxed. Try to strike each key with a quick, getaway stroke and use uniform power behind each stroke.

Directions. Type each line three times. Start at an easy, well-controlled rate and gradually increase your stroking rate with each repetition. If time permits, retype selected lines.

	STROKES
quad quip quiz lap load lope aqua away axle opal ooze olio zeal zigzags	71
zealous quasi quill quezal loll loop look azole awhile asleep opus pool	71
opaque zany zipper zoology quadruple question quixotic loppy loquat lap	71
appall apples allows opinion opposite option zeppelin zwieback zodiacal	71

PACE WRITING 82 *10 minutes*

Directions. 1. Type several 15-second writings on each of the following sentences. Follow the same practice procedures given for Pace Writing 81, page 116.

2. Type a 1-minute writing on each of the sentences. Compare the rates you make on each sentence.

```
        1     2     3     4     5     6     7     8     9    10    11    12    13    14
They wish to go to the city with the chairman for the profit due them.

They gave the statement to the union at the address shown on the card.

We received 182 chairs, 30 typewriters, and 75 desks on Order No. 649.
        1     2     3     4     5     6     7     8     9    10    11    12    13    14
```

TIMED WRITING 82 *8 minutes*

Directions. Type a 5-minute timed writing on the paragraph given for Guided Writing 77, page 110. *Type at the exploration level of practice.* Determine your cwpm.

DIRECT DICTATION 82 *7 minutes*

Directions. Type the following material from your teacher's dictation. Think the word and type the word as a unit.

to do, to do, to do the work for, and if it is the, and if it is the

sign sign sign, form form form, audit audit audit, right right right

Sign the form. Sign the right form. Sign the audit form for them.

SECTION 27. Invoices and Credit Memoranda

LESSON 166

Directions. Type each line twice. Double-space after the second typing of the line. Retype the lines as often as time permits. This will be the uniform assignment for all conditioning practices in this section.

                                                          STROKES

Joseph and Norval just caught six prize salmon off rock at Brown Quay.   70

In this order they wanted 148 keys, 209 locks, 73 doors, and 65 files.   70

Make the fingers move quickly, but hold the hands and arms motionless.   70

PROBLEM TYPING 166—TYPING INVOICES   *30 minutes*

Before typing an invoice, study the columnar headings as they indicate the position for the different types of information.

In typing tabulated work, make full use of the special tabulator attachments on your typewriter. For a column of numbers, set a tabulator stop for the indention that occurs most often. You can then space forward or backward if necessary. For example, if you have a column made up largely of numbers representing hundreds, set a stop for the hundreds point. Then if you have a number representing thousands, backspace once from the tabulator stop. If you have a number representing tens, space forward once. This procedure will effect a saving in time that will increase your production.

WINDOW ENVELOPES

Window envelopes have transparent or cut-out openings in the lower center through which the address typed on a letter, a statement, or an invoice can be seen. Such envelopes may be used for invoices, monthly statements, or regular correspondence.

In the folding of correspondence for the window envelope, the important thing is to keep in mind that the complete address must show through the window in the envelope. Fold a full-page invoice or letter from the top down fully two thirds the length of the paper; then fold back the required distance to make the address come to the correct position. Only two folds are usually necessary for a paper that is to be inserted into a window envelope. Fold a half sheet through the center, keeping the typewritten side on the outside. Insert the paper into the envelope with the address toward the front.

Illustration 54 — Window Envelope

PROBLEM I—LEARNING THE NATURE OF THE PROBLEM

Directions. Type the invoice shown in Illustration 55. Determine the tabulator adjustments before you begin to type. The columnar headings indicate where the various items should be typed. Proofread the typed copy before removing it from the typewriter; then type the invoice a second time.

LESSON 83

CONDITIONING PRACTICE 83 *5 minutes*

Directions. Type each line twice. As time permits, select for repetitive practice the sentence or sentences on which you made errors.

	STROKES
The explorer quickly adjusted the beams as the freezing wave hit them.	70
Special catalog items were indicated by the *; as, 5B*, 6C*, 7A*, 8D*.	70
The plane made stops at Chicago, Detroit, Cleveland, and Philadelphia.	70
They may make the soap with the coal flame and spend their own profit.	70

TECHNIQUE STUDY 83 *10 minutes*

Improving the Stroking Action of the Third and Fourth Fingers. Try to strike each key with a quick, getaway stroke and use uniform power behind each stroke.

Directions. Type each line three times. Start at an easy, well-controlled rate and gradually increase your stroking rate with each repetition. If time permits, retype selected lines.

	STROKES
was wax woo pox plow plop saw sow spa xenia xylan xylene wall wasp wow	70
pulp pawn plea six soap slap xenon xylol xylem pique powwow plump slow	70
swap squaw coaxial wool wallow wallop policy plaque people squad sappy	70
swoop oxbow wahoo wampum wallpaper plexus plural platoon squall sloops	70

PACE WRITING 83 *10 minutes*

Directions. 1. Type several 15-second writings on each of the following sentences. Follow the same practice procedures given for Pace Writing 81, page 116.

2. Type a 1-minute writing on each of the sentences. Compare the rates you make on each sentence.

```
       1     2      3      4      5     6      7     8      9     10     11      12     13     14
She may go with them to the town by the lake to do work for the widow.

You will deliver the statement and the contract to them for signature.

Mr. Mayne, of the First National Bank and Trust Company, is in Europe.
       1     2      3      4      5     6      7     8      9     10     11      12     13     14
```

TIMED WRITING 83 *8 minutes*

Directions. Type a 5-minute timed writing on the paragraph given for Guided Writing 78, page 112. *Type at the control level.* Determine the cwpm.

DIRECT DICTATION 83 *7 minutes*

Directions. Type the following material from your teacher's dictation. Type with continuity and rhythm.

and if it is, and if it is right, and if it is the right form to sign

to the address, all the letters, if the statement, sign the statement

Address it. Address the letter. Address all letters and statements.

LESSON 165

CONDITIONING PRACTICE 165

5 minutes

STROKES

Victor required Alex to manage dozens of New York export jobs for him. 70

She will review 310 plays, 964 biographies, 57 novels, and 82 stories. 70

There are times when one should try to do work that he might not like. 70

PROBLEM TYPING 165—MEASUREMENT

35 minutes

Directions. You are to type for 30 minutes. Type each problem once with a carbon. Proofread each problem before removing it from the typewriter and correct all errors. (Uncorrected errors will receive a 10-word penalty.) If you complete the typing of all problems before time is called, retype as many as possible. At the end of the 30-minute period, compute your stroking rate per minute. *Type on the control level.*

PROBLEM 1

STROKES

NIGHT LETTER. (Charge to	
Leeman Manufacturing Company)	31
Boston, Massachusetts, Current Date	70
Harrison Transportation Company	102
1856 Bennett Boulevard Baltimore,	136
Maryland Will have five cars of in-	170
terior sheeting ready for shipment	205
September 7. Can you handle trans-	239
portation to Providence and Bos-	270
ton? Wire reply together with rates.	309
Leeman Manufacturing Company	338
5782 Hartshorn Avenue MPS:rh	366

PROBLEM 2

STROKES

TELEFAX MESSAGE. BLZ DL	7
P D Camden, New Jersey Current	40
Date Consolidated Steel Company	72
Parkland Building Philadelphia,	104
Pennsylvania (P) What is the status	136
Order No. 76926? When may we	166
expect delivery? Construction must	202
be stopped unless received by	232
November 25. Webster Construction	267
Company CRB:mh	281

(Remember that errors on Telefax messages are properly corrected with the diagonal.)

PROBLEM 3

STROKES

INTEROFFICE LETTER

To: Walker T. Roper, President	32
Date: (Current)	55
From: Oscar M. Barber, Regional	88
Office Manager	103
File: H-Pont. 149-3	124
Subject: A. G. Hartzig, Insurance,	160
Pontiac Sedan	174

Mr. A. G. Hartzig, Regional En-	204
gineer of the Lennox Steel Com-	234
pany, has requested an explanation	269
of the charge made for Public Lia-	302
bility and Property Damage Insur-	334
ance on his Pontiac sedan for the	368
period July 19 to February 18. (P)	400
As you know, Mr. Hartzig was trans-	434
ferred from Detroit, Michigan. He	469
reports that he garages his car out-	504
side of the city limits and uses his	541
car mostly in outlying points. (P)	573
If an error has not been made, why	608
does the difference in cost between	644
Seattle and Detroit amount to	674
$14.02? dbn	686

PROBLEM 4

STROKES

FULL-RATE TELEGRAM.	
(Charge to Sanitary Distributors,	25
Inc.) Jackson, Mississippi, Current	68
Date Keystone Carton Company 3186	97
Lansing Avenue Norfolk, Virginia	130
Add 10,000 cartons, Stock No. 815602,	168
to Invoice No. 18794 dated October	203
2. Rush shipment at once. Sanitary	240
Distributors, Inc. TJD:blc	266

LESSON 84

CONDITIONING PRACTICE 84 — 5 minutes

Directions. Type each line twice. As time permits, select for repetitive practice the sentence or sentences on which you made errors.

STROKES

B. V. Mark recognized the quaint, jagged flowers with spurred calyxes. 70

Type the following fractions: 3/4, 2/5, 1/2, 7/8, 3/8, 7/12, and 1/4. 70

They will suspend the penalty for the fiducial payment when they wish. 70

TECHNIQUE STUDY 84 — 10 minutes

Long, Consecutive Reaches with the Same Finger. The purpose of this drill will be to help you improve your stroking when the same finger is required to strike a key on the upper bank of keys and then move immediately to the lower bank, or vice versa, for the next stroke. Try to make direct, quick reaches with the finger and hold the hands and arms in a quiet, relaxed position.

Directions. Type each line twice. Work for quick, smooth stroking action as you type the line. If time permits, retype selected lines.

STROKES

ce cease center celery cession certain century ceilings censurer ceremony 70

ec echo eczema eclair ecstacy eclipse economy economic eclectic eccentric 70

br brow bribe bring break brand brief bright bronze breach breeze bracket 70

un undue under united unable unfurl uneven unjust unique unless uncertain 70

mu must much music mural mumps mummy mumble murmur muscle mutual multiple 70

PACE WRITING 84 — 15 minutes

Directions. Type several short guided writings on the following sentences. Each sentence calls for a slight increase in your typing rate.

1. Type the first sentence on the call of the 20-second guide. This will be at a rate of 30 words a minute. Try to type at exactly this pace. Relax briefly; then type the second sentence on the call of the 20-second guide. Increase your pace just slightly to type at the rate of 33 words a minute. Next, type the third sentence on the call of the 20-second guide. Again, increase your stroking pace just slightly to type at the rate of 36 words a minute.

2. Follow the same procedure and type each of the sentences again on the call of the 15-second, the 12-second, and the 10-second guide. As the time is decreased, you may not be able to type the entire sentence in the time allowed; however, try to increase your pace so that you can type as much of it as possible.

3. Type each of the sentences for 1 minute on the call of either the 20-, 15-, 12-, or 10-second guide as directed by your teacher.

	Strokes	Words 20″	Words 15″	Words 12″	Words 10″
It is their wish to do all the work for him today.	50	30	40	50	60
They may do the work for him if he will sign six forms.	55	33	44	55	66
The chairman paid for the eight chairs and signed the forms.	60	36	48	60	72

TIMED WRITING 84 — 10 minutes

Directions. Type a 5-minute timed writing on the paragraph given for Guided Writing 79, page 113. *Type at the control level of practice.* Determine the cwpm. As time permits, retype each line on which you made an error until you can type it with ease.

to see the personal contacts our men 237
get when they deliver duplicates of 273
letters to which no response has 306
been made. Our men have been in- 338
structed to follow up the contact 371
with an offer of personal help in de- 407

termining the adequacy of insurance 443
based on an inventory of household 478
furnishings and personal effects. (P) 512
I shall inform you within two or 545
three weeks of the outcome of this 580
new sales personal-contact plan. cr 616

PROBLEM 2—SKILL BUILDING IN TYPING INTEROFFICE MEMORANDA

Directions. Type the following interoffice memorandum, using the current date. In typing this problem, strive to improve your skill in handling this specialized form.

STROKES

To: Leslie I. Combs 21
Date: (Current) 38
From: Robert R. Rankin 62
File: OE 39-1-306 81
Subject: Office Equipment Status 135

It has been reported that much 166
of the office equipment in use in your 205

department is in need of major re- 238
pair. Within the next ten days, 271
therefore, will you compile a list of 309
all machines that are not in good 343
condition. Also will you list sepa- 378
rately any machines that are in good 415
condition but that should be replaced 453
by more efficient models. (P) If you 487
anticipate changes in office furni- 521
ture, will you please list the changes 560
you plan to make. gvh 582

PROBLEM 3—SKILL BUILDING

Directions. Retype Problem 2 with the following change: **To: John H. McManus**

SKILL MAINTENANCE 163   *5 minutes*

Directions. Use the following sentence for one-minute timed writings. *Type on the exploration level of practice.*

STROKES

One of the ̣*best* ̣finest ways to ̣build up *increase* your vocabulary is to ̣always ̣read *use* good books. 70

LESSON 164

CONDITIONING PRACTICE 164   *5 minutes*

STROKES

Toby quenched the blaze just before Max brought the Park View firemen. 70

This toy shop has 805 trucks, 192 scooters, 63 derricks, and 74 games. 70

The real test of typing skill is measured by the growth you have made. 70

PROBLEM TYPING 164—SKILL BUILDING   *35 minutes*

Directions. Make pencil notations on a piece of note paper of the problems listed and place the paper on the desk near your textbook so that you can refer to it as you complete the typing of each problem. You will be timed for 30 minutes. Correct all errors; uncorrected errors will receive a 10-word penalty. If you complete the typing of the prob-

lems before time is called, retype as many of them as possible. At the end of the writing, compute your stroking rate per minute.

Page 215, Problem 2, once with 1 carbon.
Page 216, Problem 2, once with 1 carbon.
Page 217, Problem 1, once with 1 carbon.
Page 218, Problem 2, once with 1 carbon.

LESSON 85

Directions. Type each line twice. As time permits, select for repetitive practice the sentence or sentences on which you made errors.

	STROKES
By his frequent adjustments, the amazing executive kept our good will.	70
This rug (12′ x 13′6″) was $147.90, but it is now on sale for $118.50.	70
They paid for the gowns with the money she received for her handiwork.	70

TECHNIQUE STUDY 85   *10 minutes*

Reading the Copy. The following paragraph has the words marked in groups. Use normal spacing as you type the copy, and try to read and type as a group the words given between the vertical lines. In order to do this, you will need to keep your eyes on the copy and think the words as they are typed. This will require a high degree of concentration, but it will help you increase your stroking rate.

Directions. Type the following paragraph three or more times as time allows. Try to read the copy as directed. *Type at the exploration level of practice.*

	STROKES	WORDS
In order | to become | a skilled typist, | you must | learn to keep |	60	12
your eyes | on the copy | from which | you are typing. | In addition, |	123	25
you must | think and type | many words | and word groups | as wholes |	184	37
in order | to gain speed. | Try to read | this copy | in word groups |	246	49
as you | type it.	261	52

PACE WRITING 85   *10 minutes*

Directions. Type several 1-minute guided writings on the paragraph given for Guided Writing 80, page 114. Start typing at an easy, well-controlled pace. The purpose of this drill will be to type each minute writing without error. Your teacher will guide you in your writing by calling each 15-second interval.

It is suggested that you type the first minute writing at the rate of 20 words a minute (5 words each quarter minute). When you can type at this rate without error, increase your rate by about 10 words a minute until you can type 30 words a minute without error. Continue increasing your rate when you type without error on a minute writing until you reach the highest level of writing at which it is possible for you to type with good control.

TIMED WRITING 85   *8 minutes*

Directions. Type a 5-minute timed writing on the paragraph given for Guided Writing 80, page 114. *Type at the skill-building level of practice.* Determine the cwpm.

DIRECT DICTATION 85   *7 minutes*

	STROKES	WORDS
In typing | business letters | or any other type | of problem work, | you	66	13
must | remember to type | with good form. | In addition, | all the work | should	138	28
be | carefully planned | and organized. | These are | some of the factors | that	210	42
will help you | get higher rates | when typing | from problem copy.	271	54

	STROKES		STROKES
Marshfield Supply Company Plaza	48	pound delivered—is 15 cents higher	511
Building Indianapolis 7, Indiana	81	than the price quoted us on a similar	549
Gentlemen: We have just received	115	compound by one of your competi-	580
your message which reads as fol-	146	tors. If you are to increase your	615
lows: (P) "Can ship 5000 pounds Ex-	176	price on 491, we shall in the future	652
celsior Compound 491 at $2.95 per	210	have to use a substitute for this ma-	688
pound delivered. Quotation good	243	terial or make a substantial increase	726
until 15th when price increase be-	276	in the prices of all our manufactured	764
comes effective. Quantity Order 492	313	articles. (P) Please notify us imme-	796
can be shipped immediately $3.15	346	diately if you can ship 7000 pounds	832
per pound." (P) We are unable to	375	of Compound 491 within ten days.	866
use Compound 492, as the price you	410	Yours very truly, Rowland-Logan	898
quote is prohibitive. (P) The price	443	Manufacturers, Inc. James C. Rich-	931
quoted on Compound 491—$2.95 a	475	ards, General Manager JCR:lc *(160)*	959

SKILL MAINTENANCE 162   *5 minutes*

Directions. Use the following sentence for one-minute timed writings. *Type on the exploration level of practice.*

STROKES

He is a~~n~~ *wise man* ~~intelligent person~~ who tries to develop a variety of *personal* ~~good~~ interests.   70

LESSON 163

CONDITIONING PRACTICE 163   *5 minutes*

STROKES

Mr. Given fixed brick walks joining the quiet zones at Mercy Hospital.	70
The jeweler ordered 94 rings, 85 glasses, 320 pens, and 167 necklaces.	70
There is little gained by seeking success without some good hard work.	70

PROBLEM TYPING 163—TYPING INTEROFFICE MEMORANDA   *30 minutes*

Many companies use specially prepared forms for correspondence within their organizations. When such a form is used, the typist must type appropriate information opposite the headings. Titles (Mr., Mrs., Dr., etc.), the salutation, and the complimentary close are usually omitted. Reference initials are included; and when enclosures are sent, the enclosure notation appears below the reference initials.

PROBLEM I—LEARNING THE NATURE OF THE PROBLEM

Directions. Type the following interoffice memorandum. Study carefully Illustration 53 to become acquainted with the way in which the copy is to be arranged. Proofread the typed copy before removing it from the machine. Then type it a second time.

STROKES

To: Walker T. Roper, President	32
Date: September 18, 195—	58
From: M. W. Morrowfield	83
File: ML 21-A-138	102
Subject: Personal-Contact Plan	134
We are trying out a new plan	163
with a sampling of Mailing List 21-A	200

INTEROFFICE CORRESPONDENCE

T. D. BENSON COMPANY

To: Walker T. Roper, President   Date: September 18, 195-

From: M. W. Morrowfield   File: ML 21-A-138

Subject: Personal-Contact Plan

    We are trying out a new plan with a sampling of Mailing List 21-A to see the personal contacts our men get when they deliver duplicates of letters to which no response has been made. Our men have been instructed to follow up the contact with an offer of personal help in determining the adequacy of insurance based on an inventory of household furnishings and personal effects.

    I shall inform you within two or three weeks of the outcome of this new sales personal-contact plan.

cr

Illustration 53 — Interoffice Memorandum

THE BUSINESS LETTER

PLACEMENT OF THE LETTER

Generally speaking, short letters should have wider margins and be typed farther down the page than long letters. At first, you will find the use of a placement table, such as is given here, helpful in the placement of letters. After writing several letters, however, you should be able to estimate the length of a letter and to decide upon its placement without the help of a table.

Certain points must be kept in mind in using the following placement table. These points are:

1. When plain paper is used as a substitute for a letterhead, type the date on the 12th line from the top of the page.

2. Check the placement of the paper guide so that the horizontal centering of the letter will be accurate.

3. Letters having unusual features, such as tabulated material, long quotations, or an unusual number of lines in the address or the close, may necessitate modifications in the adjustments called for in the placement table.

| CLASSIFICATION OF LETTER | WORDS IN BODY OF LETTER | LENGTH OF LINE | | SPACES BETWEEN DATE AND ADDRESS |
		PICA SPACES	ELITE SPACES	
Short	Fewer than 100	50	50	8-12
Average	100-200	50	60	4-8
Long	200-300	60	70	3-6
Two-page	More than 300	60	70	3-6

Very short letters of fewer than 75 words may be typed with double spacing in the body of the letter and with a 50-space line, or with single spacing and a 40-space line.

If elite type is used, a long letter of from 300 to 375 words may be typed on one page unless the letter has some unusual features, such as a long tabulated list.

If the letter is too long for one page, at least four lines of the body of the letter should be carried to the second page. The first line of a paragraph should not be typed by itself at the bottom of a page nor the last line of a paragraph typed by itself at the top of a page.

SECTION 13. Business Letter Problems

GENERAL DIRECTIONS

Bonus Typing. If time permits when you have completed the problems for each lesson, practice typing each line of the conditioning practice until you can type the line without error at your best rate of speed. Label all such work *Bonus Typing.*

Machine Checkup and Adjustments. Make the following machine checkup for each lesson, and practice the control of the nonkeyboard operative parts:

1. Each day check the placement of the paper guide, the paper-bail rolls, and the paper bail. Set the ribbon lever for typing on the upper portion of the ribbon. Practice the carriage-return throw and the control of the shift keys. Make the reach to the tabulator bar or key two or three times and to the backspace key and the margin-release key.

2. Set the machine for a 70-space line and single spacing. The machine adjustments for typing the problems are indicated in the directions for the problems.

As the message is transmitted from the carbon copy, erasing is not permitted. To make corrections, a letter that is to be omitted is crossed out by striking over it with a diagonal.

Each company using Telefax is assigned an identifying code consisting of a series of "call letters." These letters must be typed on all messages; they are used for processing and accounting purposes. Special letters are used, too, for designating the class of service de-

sired: DL, for Day Letter; NL, for Night Letter. If no designation appears, messages are sent as full-rate telegrams and charged accordingly.

When a message is to be sent collect, type the abbreviation COL after the letters indicating the service desired. If the message to be sent is to be paid, type the abbreviation PD.

At the bottom of the telegram, preferably in the lower left corner, write numbers, codes, etc., appearing in the body of the message for confirmation purposes. Study Illustration 52 to learn the arrangement of a Telefax message.

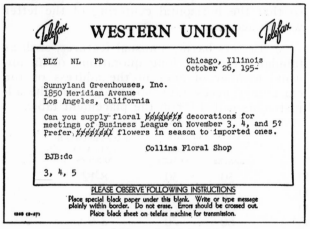

Illustration 52 — A Telefax Message

PROBLEM 1—LEARNING THE NATURE OF THE PROBLEM

Directions. Type the following Telefax message, using Illustration 52 as a model. Type the message correctly, if possible. If you make errors, cross them out by striking over them with the diagonal in the manner shown in the illustration.

The letters *BLZ* appearing in the upper left corner of the Telefax message are the "call letters" used by the company sending the message. Use these call letters for all Telefax problems.

				STROKES
BLZ NL PD	Chicago, Illinois	Current Date		44
Sunnyland Greenhouses, Inc. 1850 Meridian Avenue Los Angeles, California				110
Can you supply floral decorations for meetings of Business League				183
on November 3, 4, and 5? Prefer flowers in season to imported ones.				253
Collins Floral Shop BJB:dc 3, 4, 5				287

PROBLEM 2—SKILL BUILDING IN TYPING A TELEFAX MESSAGE

Directions. Type the following Telefax message as a prepaid day letter. The word set in italics in the message is an error. Type the word; backspace; then delete the word by striking the diagonal. Strive to improve your skill in making corrections and in typing the complete message.

			STROKES
BLZ DL PD	Chicago, Illinois	Current Date	44
Universal Plastics Company 5829 Eighth Avenue Madison, Wisconsin			109
Shipped by air *Monday* today flowers for Annual Banquet. Corsages and			191
centerpiece of roses to be furnished by our local store.			249
Collins Floral Shop RJB:dc			275

PROBLEM 3—SKILL BUILDING IN TYPING A LETTER

Directions. Type the letter once with a carbon. Use the current date, mixed punctuation, and the modified block form with no indentions for paragraphs. The quoted message

should be typed in block form and indented five spaces from the left and right margins of the letter. *When a quotation is typed in this form, quotation marks are not used.*

LESSON 86

Directions. Type each line twice; double-space after each group of two lines. As time permits, select for repetitive practice the sentence or sentences on which you made errors. This will be the uniform assignment for typing the conditioning practices in all lessons in this section.

	STROKES
Steven was intrigued by the quizzical expression on Judge Mark's face.	70
On August 29 or 30, 1957, he will return to his home at 486 Elm Drive.	70
It is a good plan to do your very best on each typing job that you do.	70

WORD DIVISION

You have been following the rule that when you are typing a line and hear the bell ring, you should complete the word you are typing and throw the carriage. This method is satisfactory for much typing, but it does not give as even a right margin as is often desired for business letters.

In order to obtain a fairly even right margin, a long word containing two or more syllables may be divided between syllables. The division must be indicated by a hyphen at the end of the first line. At this time you should become familiar with the rules for word division given in Word-Division Study 86.

WORD-DIVISION STUDY 86   *10 minutes*

Directions. Use a half sheet of paper. Type with a 60-space line. Center the copy vertically and center the heading horizontally.

	STROKES	WORDS
RULES FOR WORD DIVISION	24	5
1. Divide a word only between syllables; therefore never	82	16
divide a word of only one syllable.	119	24
2. Do not separate from the remainder of the word:	172	34
a. A one-letter syllable at the beginning of a word.	227	45
b. A one- or two-letter syllable at the end of a word.	284	57
c. A syllable that does not contain a vowel.	331	66
3. If possible, put enough of the word to be divided on the	392	78
first line to suggest what the complete word will be.	447	89
4. Avoid the division of words at the end of two or more	505	101
successive lines, or the final word on a page, or the	559	112
word at the end of the last complete line of a paragraph.	618	124
5. Avoid dividing hyphened words and compounds, such as	675	135
self-explanatory, except at the hyphen.	716	143
6. Avoid dividing a surname and separating titles, initials,	778	156
and degrees from a surname.	805	161

WESTERN UNION

Illustration 51 — A Telegram

Morrowfield Construction Co.

Birmingham, Alabama, December 23, 195-

Rankin Builders Supply Company
8156 East End Avenue
Chattanooga, Tennessee

Wire best quotation five thousand bags Hygrade Cement. State
delivery date. Can you ship to Point Breeze siding?

Morrowfield Construction Company
1018 Forward Avenue·

CRB:mh

PROBLEM 2—SKILL BUILDING IN TYPING A TELEGRAM

Directions. In typing the problem given below, strive to improve the pattern of hand motion used in assembling the forms for typing and speed up the actual typing of the telegram. Type the night letter in triplicate. Charge it to the Morrowfield Construction Company.

PROBLEM 3—SKILL BUILDING

Directions. Type Problem 2 as directed except that you will change the class of service desired to a day letter.

	STROKES
Birmingham, Alabama, (Current Date) Universal Distributors, Inc.	101
2975 Penn Avenue Detroit, Michigan Present inventories of household	169
appliances extremely low. Shipment of quarterly orders not yet received.	244
Please advise disposition of requisitions 71985 and 71986, dated July 12.	319
Imperative that some stock be received this week. Indicate at once your	392
shipping plans. Morrowfield Construction Company 1018 Forward Ave-	458
nue CRB:mh	468

SKILL MAINTENANCE 161 — 5 minutes

Directions. Use the paragraph for a series of 1-minute writings. *Type on the exploration level of practice.* Between timings, identify awkward or difficult words and type each in a three-word group—including the word preceding and the word immediately following.

This paragraph has every letter of the alphabet.

	STROKES	WORDS
Try the plan of typing with exactness and with quick stroking at the	69	14
same time. You may find that, if you pay attention to what you are doing,	144	29
you will not only type with more interest and enjoyment but with even	214	43
more speed and accuracy. Emphasize ease in typing, and keep the	279	56
carriage moving at an even pace.	306	61

LESSON 162

CONDITIONING PRACTICE 162 — 5 minutes

	STROKES
Quinn will go back in April or July for extremely hazardous Navy duty.	70
Our tug hauled 72 stoves, 309 office chairs, 561 lamps, and 84 radios.	70
There are many values to be gained through building sound work habits.	70

PROBLEM TYPING 162—TYPING TELEFAX MESSAGES — 30 minutes

If a business receives and sends numerous telegraphic messages, Western Union will supply the business with a device known as a Telefax that may be used in transmitting and receiving messages. When Telefax is used, the message is typed on the form illustrated on the following page.

Telefax messages are typed on special forms provided for this purpose. The second copy, which is carbon coated, is used in the Telefax machine to transmit the message. The first copy is retained for the files of the business. Other carbon copies may be made with the use of carbon paper if they are desired.

PROBLEM TYPING 86

Although you may not be able to type business letters, or other problem-type work, at as high a rate of speed as you can type from straight copy, it is very important that you use good techniques of typewriting in all your work. Keep your eyes on the copy from which you are typing; strike the keys with quick, finger action; try to maintain a continuous stroking rate; and, use every machine part in a quick, precise manner.

PROBLEM 1

Directions. Type Style Letter 4 as it is shown on page 124, but use the current date and use your initials as the reference initials.

From the placement table on page 121 you will find that this letter of 149 words requires a line of 50 pica spaces or 60 elite spaces with 4 to 8 line spaces between the date and the address.

This letter is typed in the modified block style with the date line blocked under the address on the letterhead, with indented paragraphs, and with the closing lines all beginning 5 spaces to the left of the center of the letter. The dictator's name and title are typed 4 spaces below the company name in the closing lines. Mixed punctuation is used.

Type the letter on the exploration level of practice and do not correct any errors you may make.

PROBLEM 2

Directions. 1. Proofread carefully the letter you typed as Problem 1. Indicate by making pencil corrections any changes that need to be made in your letter copy.

2. Retype the letter using your copy of the style letter with your penciled corrections as the copy from which you type. Make the corrections you have indicated in your letter as you retype it. *Type at the control level of practice.*

LESSON 87

CONDITIONING PRACTICE 87

STROKES

Marv picked up six crowbars and quickly began razing the front joists.   70

The numbers for the Royal typewriters are KMG—306287 and KMM—507149.   70

It is by our daily work that we make our future what we want it to be.   70

WORD-DIVISION STUDY 87

Directions. Use a half sheet of paper. The problem has three columns. The first column gives the undivided word; the second column shows the syllables of each word as found in a standard dictionary; and the third column shows the division for those words that may be divided at the end of a line.

Use a half sheet of paper and type with a 60-space line. Set the first tabulator stop 23 spaces from the left margin; set the second tabulator stop 24 spaces from the first stop. Type across the page, depressing the tabulator bar or key to indent to the second and third columns. Remember to align the 0 in 10 under 9.

1. confessed	1. con-fessed	1. con-fessed
2. pony	2. po-ny	2. pony
3. about	3. a-bout	3. about
4. teacher	4. teach-er	4. teacher
5. shouldn't	5. should-n't	5. shouldn't
6. didn't	6. did-n't	6. didn't
7. rolling	7. roll-ing	7. roll-ing
8. getting	8. get-ting	8. get-ting
9. transcend	9. tran-scend	9. tran-scend
10. transport	10. trans-port	10. trans-port

INSTRUCTIONAL BLOCK 15

OFFICE FORMS

If the printed forms for typing the problems of this instructional block are not available, do not type the material that would ordinarily be printed; but arrange the typewritten material in the same manner as that in which the insertions would be typed on the printed forms.

SECTION 26. Telegrams and Interoffice Memoranda

LESSON 161

CONDITIONING PRACTICE 161
5 minutes

Directions. Type each line twice. Double-space after the second typing of the line. Retype the lines as often as time permits. Increase your stroking rate with each repetition. This will be the uniform assignment for typing the conditioning practice in all lessons in this section.

STROKES

Jacob with Elvin fixed a sizable young quail for the Kappa Delta game.	70
Frank Owens stored 67 hammers, 340 picks, 182 shovels, and 95 trowels.	70
It is what we think and what we do that makes us the men we truly are.	70

PROBLEM TYPING 161—TYPING TELEGRAMS
30 minutes

When typing a telegram on a telegraph blank, type an "X" in the space provided to indicate the kind of service desired. When the telegram is to be charged to the company by which you are employed, type the company name in the space headed "Charge to the account of." Type the city, state, and date on one line at the right of the form a double space below the printed heading. Begin the address one double space below the date. Type the address with single spacing, but type short messages with double spacing. The title "Mr." before a name in a telegraphic address will not be transmitted and should therefore not be used; but the title "Miss" or "Mrs." will be transmitted and should be used.

Type the sender's address on the line below the name of the sender if the address is to be transmitted.

If the telegram is signed with a company name, type the dictator's and transcriber's initials in the lower left corner of the telegraph blank. These initials are not transmitted by the telegraph company, but they are desirable for reference.

Several copies of a telegram are usually made. The *original copy* is sent to the telegraph office for transmittal. The *file copy* is filed in its proper location. The billing copy is used for checking the monthly bill. A *confirmation copy* may be sent to the addressee to confirm a message.

Arrange the copy on the telegram as shown in Illustration 51, page 215. The length of line to be used will depend upon the length of the message to be typed.

PROBLEM 1—LEARNING THE NATURE OF THE PROBLEM

Directions. For the Morrowfield Construction Company, 1018 Forward Avenue, type the following full-rate telegram in triplicate. Use Illustration 51 as a model. Charge the telegram to the Morrowfield Construction Company. Type the word "File" on the third copy.

Proofread the typed copy before removing it from the typewriter; then type the telegram a second time. *Type this copy on the skill-building level.*

STROKES

Birmingham, Alabama, (Current Date) Rankin Builders Supply Com-	98
pany 8156 East End Avenue Chattanooga, Tennessee Wire best quota-	162
tion five thousand bags Hygrade Cement. State delivery date. Can you	233
ship to Point Breeze siding? Morrowfield Construction Company 1018	301
Forward Avenue CRB:mh	322

Letterhead.

Better Letters, Inc.

520 Broadway
New York 3, New York

STROKES WORDS

Date Line. June 26, 195-   14   3

Address.

Mr. Warren Brown   31   6
Ellsworth & Brown Company   57   11
978 Michigan Avenue   77   15
Chicago 4, Illinois   97   19

Salutation. Dear Mr. Brown: 114   23

    First impressions are important impressions!   162   32
The reader will judge a letter first of all by its 213   43
form. For this reason, you have a strike against   263   53
you in getting your message across to the reader if 315   63
the letter is not attractively placed on the page   365   73
and neatly typed.   384   77

    We are sending you and Mr. Parish, the head of 431   86
Body of Letter. your Stenographic Bureau, copies of our illustrated 483   97
booklet showing letter styles. This booklet offers 535 107
various suggestions for achieving a well-balanced   585 117
and harmonious letter arrangement.   621 124

    Now, let us assume that your letter is set up   667 133
in good form. The next test of a business letter   717 143
is its content. Does it bring the desired action   767 153
from the reader? This is where our correspondence 818 164
consultants are ready to help you get better letter- 870 174
writing results.   888 178

    Your signature on the enclosed card will bring 935 187
you complete information about our letter-writing   985 197
program for your company.   1012 202

Complimentary Close. Very truly yours,   1030 206

Company Name. BETTER LETTERS, INC.   1051 210

James Newman

Typewritten Signature and Official Title. James Newman, President   1075 215

Reference Initials. bk   1078 216

Enclosure Notation. Enclosure   1088 218

(Words in body of letter, 149)

Style Letter 4 — Modified Block Letter with Mixed Punctuation

LESSON 160

STROKES

Bill and Jeff won five May prizes by exceeding the April goal quickly.   70

Ray has planted 35 roses, 68 irises, 197 jonquils, and 402 sweet peas.   70

Get out of the rut before you lose the power to do things worth while.   70

PROBLEM TYPING 160   *10 minutes*

Directions. Type the following problem on word division on a half sheet of paper. Follow the directions outlined for Problem Typing 159, page 212.

1. recurrence
2. elapsed
3. progression
4. sectional
5. correctly
6. indicated
7. paragraph
8. temporarily
9. official
10. conditions

SUSTAINED WRITINGS   *25 minutes*

Directions. Take 5-minute writings on the following copy; your teacher will NOT pace you. *Type at your control rate.* At the end of the lesson, your teacher will collect the two writings with the fewest number of errors.

	STROKES	WORDS
No one is free from the effects of business. All of us talk in terms	70	14
of business. The farmer wants to know how conditions are. When the	139	28
office clerk, the teacher, the salesman, or the banker meets others, one	212	42
of the first questions asked is, "How is business?" Just what is meant	284	57
by this? A businessman considers that his own business is bad when his	356	71
sales are slow and his profits are low; he believes that it is good when	429	86
his sales are many and his profits are high. Even though he may know	499	100
the state of his own affairs, he does not realize how business conditions	573	115
are in general until he knows conditions in many businesses of a similar	646	129
nature and those in a wide variety of businesses, such as, for example,	718	144
the steel, the lumber, and the mining industries.	767	153
By the time the average person is grown, he frequently hears the term	837	167
"business cycle." Just what is meant by this term? The business cycle	909	182
is computed from the business pointers that show the ups and the downs	980	196
of business. As a rule, the cycle extends over a period of from three to	1054	211
nine years and shows alternate times of prosperity and depression. Most	1127	225
of us realize that changes occur, but we do not know why the changes	1196	239
come. We know that when there are good times most men have work,	1262	252
wages and prices are high, and business makes profits.	1316	263

PROBLEM 1

Directions. Use the current date, mixed punctuation, and type the letter in the modified block form with indented paragraphs. The figure in parentheses at the end of the letter indicates the number of words in the body of the letter. Use this figure and refer to the placement table on page 121 to determine the length of line for the letter as well as the number of spaces to leave between the date line and the address. The (P) indicates the start of a new paragraph.

In the address, the official title is to be placed on the second line and separated from the name of the company by a comma.

(To the strokes for the first line of the letter, 16 strokes have been added to provide for an average date.)

	STROKES		STROKES
Mr. E. G. Farnwell Manager, Plas-	48	many years, and they have stood the	467
tics Company 2938 South Broadway	81	"use" test. In other words, our let-	503
Chicago 23, Illinois Dear Mr. Farn-	115	ters have brought better sales, fewer	541
well: "It pays to be friendly" is a	152	adjustments, and higher returns for	577
motto that letter writers could well	189	many companies. (P) We should	604
adopt. Some of the things that make	226	like to help you get better letter-	639
for friendliness in a letter are these:	267	writing results. Your signature on	675
the "You" attitude, courtesy, sin-	300	the enclosed card will bring you	708
cerity, enthusiasm, and naturalness	336	complete information in the next	741
of expression. (P) BETTER LET-	362	mail. Very truly yours, BETTER	773
TERS, INC., has been applying	392	LETTERS, INC. James Newman,	801
these principles of letter writing for	431	President Enclosure *(101)*	820

PROBLEM 2

Directions. Use the same directions as given for Problem 1.

	STROKES		STROKES
Mr. Elwood P. Fitzpatrick Secretary,	53	line of the address. It is good prac-	402
Pax Company 4739 Telegraph Road	85	tice to place the title on the shorter	441
San Francisco 5, California Dear	118	of the two lines in order to give bet-	478
Mr. Fitzpatrick: We are pleased to	154	ter balance. (P) We are always	506
answer your letter regarding the	187	happy to answer inquiries regarding	542
placement of official titles when used	226	letter-writing procedures. Please feel	582
with personal names. (P) The place-	257	free to call on us when you have	615
ment of the official title with a per-	294	other problems. Very truly yours,	650
sonal name is optional; it may be	328	BETTER LETTERS, INC. M. H.	677
placed on either the first or second	365	Craddock, Consultant *(88)*	697

LESSON 88

CONDITIONING PRACTICE 88   *5 minutes*

	STROKES
The great man was frequently vexed by the quizzical joker from Prague.	70
He bought the #39572 die for $84.60, taking an 11% discount of $10.46.	70
Do all the work in the right way and you will find it very easy to do.	70

LESSON 159

STROKES

Loren Waltz was a varsity quarterback for the Dixie Paige junior team.   70

He may destroy 873 cantaloupes, 15 bananas, 40 pears, and 269 oranges.   70

Hold your right thumb curved above the space bar ready for the stroke.   70

PROBLEM TYPING 159   *10 minutes*

Directions. Use a half sheet of paper. Type this problem on word division as a 2-column tabulated report. In the first column type each number and word given below. In the second column type each word, indicating by a hyphen the best place to divide the word. Assume that the bell rang for the end of the line as you were typing the first letter of the word. If the word should not be divided, type it solid.

If a word is divided at a one-letter syllable, that syllable is ordinarily typed on the first line rather than on the second. For example: *sepa-rate*; not *sep-arate*.

1. instructions	5. expression	8. thought
2. separate	6. transcription	9. nationally
3. enough	7. approximately	10. correspondence
4. occurring		

SELECTED-GOAL WRITING 159   *25 minutes*

Directions. Use the following paragraph for control-writing practice; follow the steps already outlined. In this lesson, extend your goal in Step 5 to 4-minute writings. Your teacher will call, "One," "Two," "Three," and "Time" for the 1-, 2-, 3-, and 4-minute goals.

This paragraph has every letter of the alphabet and a syllable intensity of 1.35.

STROKES

In school, students tend to rate themselves on the basis of how many   69

words a minute they can type under forced effort. In an office, employers   144

tend to rate workers on the basis of how much they can do plus the kind   216

of persons they are. Expert copying speed is just a means to an end, and   290

the end is the skill to transfer this speed to the typing of business   360

forms, such as letters, invoices, and reports. Production is what counts   434

when it comes to the measurement of your work; and your character traits   507

enter into the extent of your fitness for quick promotion. Do not minimize   583

output, of course; but do not overlook the importance of a poised and bal-   656

anced personality. What you are as a person will count almost as much   727

as how much work you turn out as a typist.   769

Directions. Assume that you are typing and that the bell rings for the end of the line as you are typing the first letter of each of the words given below. You are to show where you would divide the word. Number each word, space twice, and type the word with the hyphen at the place you consider most desirable for the division. If a word cannot be divided, type it solid.

1. business
2. alone
3. very
4. learned
5. stressing
6. commercial
7. possession
8. reference
9. registration
10. self-control
11. through
12. difficulty
13. scaffolding
14. Bob Adams
15. deliberation
16. alphabet
17. thirty-four
18. bought
19. elite
20. doesn't

PROBLEM TYPING 88   *25 minutes*

PROBLEM I

Directions. Use the current date, mixed punctuation, and type the letter in the modified block style with indented paragraphs. In the closing lines, type the long official title on the line below the typewritten signature.

This letter includes the attention line, which is typed on the second line below the last line of the address. In the block and modified block styles, it begins at the left margin as is shown in the illustration. In the indented form, which will be illustrated later, the line may be either centered or begun at the paragraph point.

```
Modern Office Equipment Co.
382-388 Eighth Street
Detroit 12, Michigan

Attention Mr. Ralph Briggs

Gentlemen:

        Please send us a catalog of your office furniture.
We are especially interested in comparing the prices
```

Illustration 37 — Address with an Attention Line

	STROKES
Modern Office Equipment Co. 382-	48
388 Eighth Street Detroit 12, Mich-	82
igan Attention Mr. Ralph Briggs	114
Gentlemen: Please send us a cata-	147
log of your office furniture. We are	185
especially interested in comparing	220
the prices you quote for office divans,	260
chairs, desks, filing cabinets, etc.,	298
with prices quoted by other manu-	330
facturers for the same equipment.	365
(P) We usually buy office equipment	397
from Hull & Jenkins, of Lansing. As	434
they do not carry in stock any of	468
your office equipment or furniture,	504

	STROKES
we are writing directly to you, even	541
though we understand that you usu-	574
ally sell through agencies only. If	611
you wish us to send our inquiry to a	648
sales agency, let us know to whom	682
the letter should be addressed. (P)	715
May we have this information	744
promptly. Yours very truly, Jona-	777
than M. Hodge Director of Pur-	806
chases *(107)*	812

PROBLEM 2

Directions. Use the current date, mixed punctuation, and type the letter in the modified block form with indented paragraphs. Type the official title on a separate line in the address. Center the subject line a double space below the salutation in the form shown in the following illustration.

```
Dear Mr. Hodge:

            Subject:  Low Desk Prices

        We thank you for your order for office divan
No. 82140 and the two matching chairs.  The ship-
ment should reach you early next week.
```

Illustration 38 — One Placement of the Subject Line

	STROKES
Mr. Jonathan M. Hodge Director of	50
Purchases Great Lakes Insurance	82
Co. Kalamazoo 3, Michigan Dear	114
Mr. Hodge: Subject: Low Desk	145
Prices We thank you for your order	180
for office divan No. 82140 and the	215
two matching chairs. The shipment	250
should reach you early next week.	285
(P) We invite quality and price com-	316

LESSON 158

CONDITIONING PRACTICE 158

5 minutes

STROKES

Jack, Sam, Paul, and Wes had a very long tax quiz before the last day. 70

Bob stocked 385 gaskets, 92 wrenches, 60 pliers, and 147 hoist levers. 70

It is a mark of immaturity to waste time in noisy and useless actions. 70

CORRECT IT AS YOU TYPE 158

10 minutes

Directions. Type the sentences correctly; then verify them with your teacher. If time permits, retype the sentences.

Line 1: If several numbers are used in a sentence, type all numbers in figures.

Line 2: When two numbers immediately follow each other, it is better to spell out the smaller and to express the larger in figures.

Line 3: Spell out names of small-numbered avenues and streets. State house numbers in figures except the number *One*.

Line 4: Use figures to express page numbers.

Line 5: Policy numbers may be typed without a comma separating hundreds and thousands; they may also be typed with spaces to indicate divisions.

STROKES

That new camp needs six tennis courts, thirty rackets, and one hundred one tennis balls. 70

Elvin bought 275 3-cent stamps and 195 2-cent stamped envelopes. 70

They moved their office from 1 Lexington Avenue to 270 5th Avenue. 70

Margaret Rogers should have studied pages one to eleven instead of twelve to twenty. 70

The Veterans Administration policy issued to Jim Wise was V (*space*) 328 (*space*) 75 (*space*) 92. 70

SELECTED-GOAL WRITING 158

25 minutes

Directions. Use the following paragraph for control-writing practice; follow the steps outlined for Selected-Goal Writing 156, page 209. For Step 5, increase the length of your writings to 3 minutes. Your teacher will call "One," "Two," and "Time" for the 1-, 2-, and 3-minute goals.

This paragraph has every letter of the alphabet and a syllable intensity of 1.35.

STROKES

There are many things to be overcome if the work of each day is to be 70

done in such a manner that there will be a feeling of satisfaction when it 145

is viewed at the close of the day. In typing, just for example, we can 217

make a long list of problems that must be solved if we wish to achieve our 292

best skill. One of the first problems to be faced is that of self-mastery. 369

Control of oneself must always precede control of machine, of conditions, 443

or of office problems. We must control ourselves so that we can produce 516

on an increasing quantity and accuracy scale. Great typists know this 587

fact. They realize that self-mastery wins contests. 639

parison of our desks with those sold 353
by any other manufacturer. On page 389
31 of our catalog we show a picture 425
of a desk 32 inches wide by 60 inches 463
long by 30 inches high. This desk 498
is made from quarter-sawed white 531
oak and can be furnished in light 565
golden oak, mahogany, walnut, or 598
fumed oak finish. We know of no 631

other manufacturer who sells the 664
same quality of desk at the price we 701
quote—$64.20 f.o.b. factory. (P) The 736
demand for this desk has exceeded 770
our expectations. We know you 800
will be pleased with it. Very truly 838
yours, MODERN OFFICE EQUIP- 864
MENT CO. Ralph Briggs, Manager 894
(135)

LESSON 89

CONDITIONING PRACTICE 89 — *5 minutes*

STROKES

Six big juicy steaks sizzled in a pan as five workmen left the quarry. 70
The inventory includes 56 pamphlets, 1,827 books, and 3,490 magazines. 70
If you organize and plan your work, your efficiency will be increased. 70

WORD-DIVISION STUDY 89 — *10 minutes*

Directions. Assume that you are typing and that the bell rings for the end of the line as you are typing the third letter of each of the words given below. You are to show where you would divide the word. Number each word, space twice, and type the word with the hyphen at the place you consider most desirable for the division. If a word cannot be divided, type it solid.

1. demobilization
2. thought
3. architecture
4. consequence
5. proprietorship
6. Clark Evans
7. accommodation
8. indebtedness
9. plumber
10. oversimplification
11. semi-intelligent
12. knocked
13. humanitarian
14. fictitious
15. constitutional
16. self-supporting
17. submitting
18. reservoir
19. subordination
20. pertaining

PROBLEM TYPING 89 — *25 minutes*

PROBLEM I

Directions. Type the letter in the modified block form with indented paragraphs. Use the current date and open punctuation (see page 43 for a discussion of open punctuation). Type the date so that it ends approximately even with the right margin. Type the official title on the first line in the address. The dictator's name and official title are to be typed on the same line, 4 spaces below the Council name.

STROKES

Mr. E. T. Hegeman, President 45
Radio-Television Corporation 2739 79
East Elmhurst Avenue Philadelphia 113
10, Pennsylvania Dear Mr. Hege- 143
man At a recent meeting of the 174
Council on Visual Education, we saw 210
"Education Begins at Home," spon- 242
sored by your company. We wish 274
to commend you for making this pro- 308
gram available to the many televi- 341
sion owners. (P) The thought oc- 369
curred to us that television has great 408
possibilities for our schools. If we 446

could be sure of receiving such fine- 483
quality programs, we should like to 519
start a campaign to introduce tele- 553
vision into the many schools of the 589
nation. (P) Would it be possible to 622
have one of your representatives 655
speak to us at our next meeting on 690
the possibility of such a plan? May 727
we hear from you in order that we 761
may set a definite date. Very truly 798
yours COUNCIL ON VISUAL 822
EDUCATION M. P. Smith, Secre- 850
tary *(114)* 854

LESSON 157

CONDITIONING PRACTICE 157   5 minutes

STROKES

Inspector Ray Bowen quizzed vaguely the excited jet flier from Kansas.   70

Our baker prepared 715 rolls, 93 cakes, 80 pies, and 462 small loaves.   70

Have equal power behind all of your strokes to make the typing neater.   70

CORRECT IT AS YOU TYPE 157   10 minutes

Directions. Type the sentences correctly; then verify the results with your teacher. Retype the sentences if time permits.

Lines 1 and 2: Express distance in figures unless it is a fraction of a mile.
Line 3: Add an apostrophe and *s* to form the singular possessive when the noun does not end in *s*.
Line 4: When a proper name of one syllable ends in *s,* add an apostrophe and *s* to show possession.
Line 5: When common possession is to be shown for two or more persons, use the apostrophe and *s* with the last name only.

STROKES

Earl traveled twelve thousand, five hundred miles by air during his recent
European vacation.   70

All the races in this current season will be run on a ½-mile track.   70

Bobs new fleet of trucks was used for moving the high-priority goods.   70

Burns new Tudor sedan was parked in the rear of that storage garage.   70

The latest high-speed camera was shown in Dye and Overmans catalogue.   70

SELECTED-GOAL WRITING 157   25 minutes

Directions. Use the following paragraph for control-writing practice. Follow the steps outlined in Selected-Goal Writing 156; but in Steps 4 and 5, set goals and type for 2 minutes instead of 1½ minutes. In these 2-minute writings your teacher will guide you by calling "Half," "One," "Half," and "Time."

This paragraph has every letter of the alphabet and a syllable intensity of 1.35.

STROKES

Teachers say that it is not easy to encourage students to analyze and   70

improve their technique to the point where they will always be able to   141

type with control. It is possible that most students do not know just how 216

to analyze their typing habits. Surely, all of us have the desire to do   289

our best work on all occasions. There is that quality in each of us which 364

makes us want to excel in whatever we do. It should not be too difficult, 439

then, to interest each student in building his skill through the use of   511

right techniques.   528

PROBLEM 2

Directions. Type the letter in the modified block form with indented paragraphs. Use the current date and open punctuation. Type the official title in the closing lines on the line below the typewritten signature.

STROKES

Mrs. Adele H. Martin 2946 Rampart Road Lexington 15, Kentucky	45
part Road Lexington 15, Kentucky	78
Dear Mrs. Martin We do not handle	112
the Royal radio about which you in-	146
quired in your letter of the 10th. We	185
have other excellent radios, how-	217
ever, any one of which will give you	254
fine service. (P) For use in your	285

STROKES

guest room, we suggest one of the	319
table models of the Superior Radio	354
Company. Descriptions of the differ-	390
ent models are enclosed. (P) If you	423
wish, we shall be glad to place a	457
radio in your home for a week's trial.	497
This trial use of the radio will not	534
obligate you in any way. It is our	570
way of advertising these radios. A	606
telephone call to EDgewood 5-4308	640
will bring a radio to your home with-	676
in the hour. Yours very truly Alvin	713
B. Stoddard Manager Enclosure	742
(116)	

LESSON 90

CONDITIONING PRACTICE 90   *5 minutes*

STROKES

Virgil met Jack and went for the bumpy squash next to the azalea case.	70
He bought 80 pencils @ 6¢ each; 23 erasers @ 9¢ each; 1 punch @ $4.75.	70
Make a sincere effort every day to improve your own typewriting skill.	70

PRODUCTION TYPING 90   *35 minutes*

You are to be timed for 25 minutes on typing the letter problems given below. This will help you build sustained production skill. Arrange your materials so that you can work with a minimum of waste motion.

Time Schedule

Making notation of directions and preparation (setting margins, arranging papers, etc.) .... 5 minutes

Timed production of letters .... 25 minutes
Proofreading and determining
cwpm. .... 5 minutes

Directions. Make pencil notations of the following directions for the timed production of letters. Keep the notations where you can read them easily.

Type each of the letters on a separate sheet of paper.

   a. Type Problem 1, Lesson 86, page 123.
   b. Type Problem 1, Lesson 87, page 125.
   c. Type Problems 1 and 2, Lesson 88, page 126.
   d. Type Problems 1 and 2, Lesson 89, pages 127 and 128.

If you complete typing the letter problems before time is called, start over. Type all letters in the modified block form with indented paragraphs. Use the current date and mixed punctuation. *Type at the skill-building level of practice.* Do not erase or correct any errors you make in typing the letters unless otherwise directed by your teacher.

When time is called, proofread each letter carefully and determine your cwpm. To the total strokes given for each letter, add the number of strokes used for the reference initials.

SECTION 25. Control Building
LESSON 156
CONDITIONING PRACTICE 156

5 minutes

Directions. Type each sentence three times, or more if time permits. Start writing slowly and increase your stroking rate gradually with each repetitive typing. This will be the uniform assignment for typing the conditioning practice for all lessons in this section.

	STROKES
Amy Swietzer drove Jack and Paul to the big quiz show for mixed teams.	70
The report showed 407 new parts, 615 tires, 29 locks, and 83 car keys.	70
When you think you are doing a great job, just know you can do better.	70

CORRECT IT AS YOU TYPE 156

10 minutes

Directions. Type the sentences correctly; then verify them with your teacher. Retype the sentences if time permits.

Lines 1 and 2: Capitalize names of the days of the week and months of the year; after the name of a month, express the day in figures.

Line 3: When expressing a date within a sentence, set off the year with commas.

Lines 4 and 5: When the day of the month precedes the name of the month or when the day of the month stands alone, use a figure for the day and follow it with *th, st,* or *d.*

	STROKES
The meeting will be held on wednesday february twenty-two at eleven o'clock.	70
The business convention will be held in Detroit on march eight nine and ten.	70
In the Bikini Atoll on june thirty nineteen forty-six the fourth atomic bomb exploded.	70
On the fifteenth of may they will attend the annual horse show for fillies.	70
The discounts may be taken by paying all invoices in full by the sixteenth.	70

SELECTED-GOAL WRITING 156

25 minutes

Directions. 1. Type the paragraph without being timed.

2. With a small check mark indicate half-minute and minute goals that are five words a minute under your best rate.

3. Take repeated 1-minute writings with your teacher calling "Half" and "Time" so that you may know whether you are reaching your goals. Between writings, practice any words or groups of words that have given you difficulty. If you reach your goal with not more than one error, set slightly higher goals.

4. Set half-minute goals for a 1½-minute writing.

5. Continue the paced writings until you can reach your goals for 1½ minutes with not more than one error.

This paragraph has every letter of the alphabet and a syllable intensity of 1.35.

	STROKES
If you want to take your work earnestly while you are in training for	70
business, mix with people who now work in an office. Ask about the ad-	140
justments that they had to make as a beginner. You may be amazed to	209
learn of the little things that workers meet that upset them. Adjustments	284
of beginners often must be made with no help. You can never quite fore-	355
see all adjustments.	375

SECTION 14. Form Letters

General Directions. 1. Make the usual machine checkup and adjustments at the beginning of each lesson.

2. Unless you are instructed to the contrary, erase and correct neatly any errors made in typing the problems for these lessons.

3. If time permits when you have completed the problems for each lesson, practice typing the material given for the Production Comparison Typing in each lesson. *Type at the exploration level of practice.* Label all such work *Bonus Typing.*

LESSON 91

CONDITIONING PRACTICE 91   *5 minutes*

Directions. Type each line twice; double-space after each group of two lines. As time permits, select for repetitive practice the sentence or sentences on which you made errors. This will be the uniform assignment for typing the conditioning practice in all lessons in this section.

	STROKES
The proud man quickly won five prizes in the high jumping exhibitions.	70
The purchase price is $14,675.89 plus 3% sales tax and 20% excise tax.	70
When he went for the stock, the men remained with her by the big bank.	70

PRODUCTION COMPARISON TYPING 91   *10 minutes*
(Straight Copy)

Directions. Type a 5-minute timed writing. Use a 70-space line, a 5-space paragraph indention, and double spacing. *Type at the control level.* Determine the cwpm. Keep a record of your rate per minute so that you can compare this rate with your rates on other types of material given as the Production Comparison Typing in the next three lessons.

This paragraph has all letters of the alphabet and a syllable intensity of 1.30.

	STROKES	WORDS
Business letters are the personal representatives of the business by	69	14
which they are mailed. They tell the sales story, record the complaint,	142	28
bargain over price, and close the business transaction. They do more, too;	218	44
they show the standards of the office from which they come and give an in-	291	58
dex to the kind of work the typist does. If the letters are well arranged	366	73
and well typed, they may be just about the finest kind of representative	439	88
a business can have. If the letters are not well placed on the page and	512	102
are not typed with care, they may fail in their mission and cause the loss	587	117
of quite large sums of money to the company. The message is the im-	654	131
portant part of the letter, of course; it must be clear, concise, and com-	727	145
plete. The thought must be organized and well stated. This is the work	800	160
of the writer, but the typist can help make the letter effective by typing	875	175
it with due care for form.	901	180

Directions. Type the sentences correctly; then verify them with your teacher. Retype the sentences if time permits.

Line 1: Market quotations are expressed in figures; in market quotations the plural of figures is expressed by the addition of *s* without the apostrophe.
Line 2: Titles of books may be underscored or typed in all capitals.
Line 3: Titles of articles are enclosed in quotation marks.
Line 4: For the dash, use two hyphens without a space before or after. It is also permissible to use one hyphen with a space before and after.
Line 5: Results of balloting should be expressed in figures.

STROKES

All regular members of the board bought General Electric fives at thirty-one
    and three-eighths.   70

Jane's boss has just finished writing his book, industrial management.   70

Mr. Combs wrote an article, reducing office costs, for our magazine.   70

All parents—and most businessmen—were interested in the Senior Play.   70

The county tellers counted one hundred seventy-five against and ninety-three
    in favor of the measure.   70

LESSON 155

CONDITIONING PRACTICE 155   *5 minutes*

STROKES

Jim Vale, wizard of the keyboard, played exquisitely at Carnegie Hall.   70

He sold 75 batteries, 693 chains, 40 hub caps, and 128 ignition locks.   70

One should not forget the rights of others when he identifies his own.   70

SELECTED-GOAL WRITING 155   *25 minutes*

Directions. Use the paragraph at the top of page 207 for this practice. Take five 1-minute writings; between writings, practice the words that cause breaks in your stroking continuity. Follow the procedures outlined in Selected-Goal Writing 154.

CORRECT IT AS YOU TYPE 155   *10 minutes*

Directions. Type the sentences correctly; then verify them with your teacher. Retype the sentences if time permits.

Line 1: Use figures to express invoice terms.
Line 2: Spell out numbers at the beginning of a sentence.
Lines 3 and 4: Use figures for house numbers except for number *One*.
Line 5: When two numbers immediately follow each other, spell out the smaller.

STROKES

The discount terms of four per cent, ten days, will apply on all June credit sales.   70

one hundred thirty-three members were present for the monthly meeting.   70

Mr. Marly lives at thirteen thirty-three elizabeth boulevard wilkinsburg
    pennsylvania   70

Mr. James T. Thompson visits at one grand avenue detroit 5 michigan.   70

Barbara bought thirty-five six-cent stamps and twenty-four three-cent stamped
    envelopes.   **70**

This lesson and the next three lessons will deal with a series of form letters as might be used by a bank. In typing the letter problems for these lessons, you should work for an increased stroking rate as you become familiar with the letter forms used. Be sure to organize your work and work with a pattern of efficient motions.

PROBLEM I

Directions. Use the current date. Use the modified block form with no indentions for paragraphs similar to Style Letter 3, page 71. In the closing lines, the dictator's name and title are to be typed on the same line.

current date   no indention

	STROKES		STROKES
Mr. A. C. Edgeworth Pacific Na-	46	No. 29743 for $5,000. We shall ap-	409
tional Bank 4836 West Ranier	75	preciate your extending the services	446
Boulevard Seattle 19, Washington	108	of your bank to him. We are confi-	480
Dear Mr. Edgeworth The bearer	138	dent you will find this new business	517
of this letter, Mr. Stephen Quincy,	174	relationship pleasant. (P) Attached	550
is entering business in your city.	210	to this letter is an identification card	591
Since he will be located in your	243	showing a specimen signature of	623
vicinity, we have referred him to	277	Mr. Quincy. Very truly yours CITI-	657
you. (P) Mr. Quincy has been a	305	ZENS BANK OF CHICAGO L. D.	684
valued depositor of ours for several	342	Pierce, Vice President Enclosure	716
years and has with him our Draft	375	*(94)*	

PROBLEM 2

Directions. Type the letter given in Problem 1, making the following changes:

1. Address letter to: Mr. E. T. Erliner
   Florida State Bank
   1437 West Sixth Street
   St. Augustine, Florida

2. Supply an appropriate salutation

3. Bearer of the letter: Mr. John Bernard

4. Draft No. 32714

5. Amount of Draft: $4,500

LESSON 92

CONDITIONING PRACTICE 92   *5 minutes*

STROKES

Lee quizzed Max about the jackknife he won pitching rings by the vale.   70

He thought $24.36 too much for a 150# bag of sugar and offered $18.79.   70

J. B. Lane may visit Chicago, New York, Boston, New Haven, and Albany.   70

PRODUCTION COMPARISON TYPING 92   *10 minutes*
(Statistical Copy)

Directions. Type a 5-minute timed writing on the following copy containing numerous figures and symbols. Use a 70-space line, a 5-space paragraph indention, and double spacing. *Type at the control level.* Determine the cwpm. Compare this rate with the rate you made on the straight-copy material given in Lesson 91.

Directions. Use the following paragraph for 1-minute paced writings. Follow the procedures used in the preceding lesson for adjusting goals and determining practice routines.

STROKES

Each boy and girl should remember that this is an age of competition;   70

each of us must compete, at some time or other, with himself, his friends,   145

his associates. To be successful in competition, we must have the type of   220

preparation that can be relied upon in times of pressure. The things we   293

do each day decide whether or not we will win or lose to our competitors.   368

Be certain that each day counts.   400

CORRECT IT AS YOU TYPE 153   *10 minutes*

Directions. Type the sentences correctly; then verify them with your teacher. Retype the sentences if time permits.

Lines 1, 2, and 3: Weights, dimensions, and measures are expressed in figures.
Lines 4 and 5: State exact age in figures; use words to state approximate age.

STROKES

Wilbert shipped a box of classical records weighing nine pounds seven ounces.   70

The size of that antique bronze table top was twenty-four and five-eighths by
    eighteen and three-fourths inches.   70

The janitor used eight gallons of gasoline and three quarts of oil on the job.   70

Ann West listed her age on the blank as sixteen years four months and ten days.   70

Most of the men on the hockey team were about 21 years of age.   70

LESSON 154

CONDITIONING PRACTICE 154   *5 minutes*

Herb Quill fixed seven large razing jacks for wiry Jim Thompson's use.   70

They used 80 planes, 65 tanks, 417 mortars, and 239 large field units.   70

One can realize great gain by selecting and developing a unique hobby.   70

SELECTED-GOAL WRITING 154   *25 minutes*

Directions. Use the paragraph at the top of page 206 for this practice. Take five 1-minute writings; between writings, practice words that may be speed traps for your fingers. Type the word identified as difficult with the word before and the word immediately after it.

Identify your best 1-minute writing. Add 2 words to your cwpm on this best writing and take additional 1-minute writings with the call of the half-minute guide.

When you can type for one minute at your new rate with a feeling of ease, increase your minute goal by 2 more words and take additional writings.

	STROKES	WORDS
At the beginning of a sentence, numbers are spelled no matter how	66	13
large or how small they are. Measures are expressed in figures; as, 60	138	28
pecks, 5 quarts, and 8 grams. Dimensions are typed in figures, too; as,	211	42
4 by 6 feet. Sums of money, whether dollars or cents, should be typed in	285	57
figures; as, Todd earned $12 last week, but James earned only 90 cents.	358	72
The decimal and ciphers are not needed when typing even sums of money	426	85
but are required when expressing uneven sums; as, $37 was earned by	495	99
Anne and $38.29 was earned by Dale.	530	106

PROBLEM TYPING 92   *25 minutes*

PROBLEM 1

Directions. Use the current date, mixed punctuation, and the modified block form with no indentions for paragraphs. Because this is a friendly type of letter, note that *Sincerely yours* is used as the complimentary close.

	STROKES		STROKES
Mr. Edward F. Robertson 3129 East	50	and service possible. (P) We should	461
Sentinel Avenue Chicago 8, Illinois	86	like to call your attention to our per-	499
Dear Mr. Robertson: We welcome	118	sonal loan service, savings account	535
you as a depositor of our bank and	153	plan, safe-deposit boxes, and invest-	571
take this opportunity to thank you	188	ment financing service to which you,	608
for your account. (P) Just as you	219	as a depositor, are entitled. (P) Your	644
take pride in helping your family	253	interest in Citizens Bank is appre-	678
and friends, so do we pride ourselves	291	ciated, and we welcome further op-	711
on giving every member of our bank-	325	portunities to serve you. Sincerely	748
ing family friendly, courteous serv-	360	yours, CITIZENS BANK OF CHI-	775
ice. It is the aim of each of our	395	CAGO L. D. Pierce, Vice President	808
employees to give you every help	428	*(108)*	

PROBLEM 2

Directions. Type the letter given in Problem 1, making the following changes:

2. Supply an appropriate salutation.

1. Address letter to: Mr. R. T. Peyton
                713 Edgewater Road
                Chicago 14, Illinois

LESSON 93

CONDITIONING PRACTICE 93   *5 minutes*

	STROKES
Quiet Muscovy ducks from Brazil were judged by the experts as winners.	70
The address is 2361 Hanford Way, Denver 5; the telephone, AShby 49807.	70
Paul King reviewed the article, "Dave Duncan and His Fighting Camera."	70
Are you trying to type on the upper row by reaching with your fingers?	70

Men and women who have been successful in life tell us that it is im- 68

portant for young people to develop a pleasant, appealing voice. They 139

tell us that the way we say things is almost as important as what we say. 214

They remind us of the fact that others tend to remember us in terms of 285

pleasing personal qualities rather than in terms of academic factors. Try 360

to speak in pleasant tones at all times. 400

CORRECT IT AS YOU TYPE 152
10 minutes

Directions. Type the sentences correctly; then verify them with your teacher. Retype the sentences if time permits.

Lines 1 and 2: With a.m. and p.m. use figures; use words with o'clock.
Lines 3 and 4: Express dollars and cents in figures; write *cents* as a word.
Line 5: Use figures to express percentage.

STROKES

At ten am and four pm Wednesday, there will be two committee meetings. 70

The afternoon train from Kansas City will arrive here at four oclock. 70

Don Collins requested a number of good season football tickets at thirty-five 70
dollars.

Nancy and James paid ninety cents for their tickets to the school benefit. 70

The company estimated that about six per cent of the books were damaged. 70

LESSON 153

CONDITIONING PRACTICE 153
5 minutes
STROKES

Mel told Vera of six huge quartz deposits being worked in Jade County. 70

Janet prepared 279 letters, 483 cards, 65 film strips, and 10 posters. 70

When you love your work and do it well, you have the key to happiness. 70

CALLING THE GUIDE 153
10 minutes

Directions. Take 1-minute writings with the guide called every 15 seconds. Follow the practice procedures used in Calling the Guide 151, page 204.

All invoices were typed today. They will be dropped in the late mail.

The auditors will check the totals. A complete summary will be filed.

Special credit terms may be given. Many prefer getting cash payments.

Directions. Type the following rough-draft, making all corrections indicated.

In correcting manuscript, the use of a few simple proofreaders' marks is a convenience. The proofreaders' marks that are used in this rough draft are shown at the right.

After you have typed the complete paragraph, take a 5-minute timed writing from the original copy. Make all corrections. Determine the cwpm. Compare this rate with the rate you made on the straight-copy material given in Lesson 91. Were you able to type at at least two thirds of your straight-copy rate?

∧ Insert   ∪ or ↶ Transpose

ℑ Delete   ⊂ Close up

¶ Begin paragraph

This paragraph has a syllable intensity of 1.30.

	STROKES
When the typist works from Rough-draft copy, he must divide	60
his attention among many tasks. Some of them are these: using	124
good typing techniques, reading the copy carefully, and looking	184
ahead to see what changes are called for in the copy, It is a	302
good trick to take a quick look at the copy as a whole see to what	369
kind of change may be called for in the typing. Then, if the	432
typist is well-acquainted with the symbols used in proof reading	496
and those used in rough-draft work and is skilful in the use of	561
his machine, he should have no trouble turning out finished work	626
at a fast rate. *and, lastly, making those changes in the right places.*	641

PROBLEM TYPING 93

20 minutes

PROBLEM I

Directions. Use the current date, mixed punctuation, and type the following form letter covering *Overdrafts on a Checking Account.* Use the modified block form with no indentions for paragraphs.

	STROKES
Mrs. Fred H. Martin 613 North Hill-	50
side Drive Chicago 28, Illinois Dear	87
Mrs. Martin: When we opened an	119
account for you, we emphasized the	154
necessity of maintaining an account	190
balance at least equal to the total of	229
all checks written. (P) Today it was	263
necessary for us to return another of	301
your checks because you had insuffi-	336
cient funds on deposit to cover it.	373
This procedure involves attention	407

	STROKES
and expense over and above that	439
necessary for a normally operating	474
account. (P) We urge you to adjust	506
immediately your present checking	540
account procedure; otherwise, it	573
will be necessary for us to close	607
your account with us. Very truly	641
yours, CITIZENS BANK OF CHI-	668
CAGO L. D. Pierce, Vice President	701
(88)	

CORRECT IT AS YOU TYPE 151

Directions. Type each sentence in correct form; each place at which a correction is to be made is indicated by an asterisk. When you finish, check the results with your teacher. If time permits, retype the sentences.

Line 1: The comma and period are typed before the quotation marks.
Line 2: Type the question mark before the quotation marks if the quoted matter is a question.
Line 3: Type the quotation mark before the question mark when the entire sentence is a question and the quoted part is not a question.
Line 4: Type the quotation mark before the semicolon.
Line 5: A quotation within a quotation is indicated by a single quotation mark.

	STROKES
"Always work carefully* he said, "and you can get the answer easily*	70
Mr. King asked, "Who did you say paid the invoice for the last month*	70
Did he write, "All the orders shipped have the stipulated priorities*	70
Your present stroking goal is "speed;* next, it will be for "control*	70
Burke said, "Be sure to read this article, 'Harnessing Atomic Power*	70

LESSON 152

CONDITIONING PRACTICE 152

	STROKES
Jane and Sue were asked by five Chi Omegas to quiz pledges at a mixer.	70
The boys used 67 maps, 490 pencils, 185 graphs, and 23 drawing boards.	70
The world will make room for a man who says he knows he can make good.	70

CALLING THE GUIDE 152

Directions. Take 1-minute writings with the guide called every 15 seconds. Follow the practice procedures used in Lesson 151.

```
     1      2      3      4      5      6      7      8      9     10     11     12     13     14
It is an easy thing to increase speed.  I shall always try to improve.

The little things count.  I shall be certain that they aid my writing.

My typing skill is growing.  I can now use it in school or on the job.
     1      2      3      4      5      6      7      8      9     10     11     12     13     14
```

SELECTED-GOAL WRITING 152

Directions. For this practice, use the rate you used in the sentence writings. Place two check marks* in the paragraph: one, at your half-minute goal; the other, at your minute goal. Your teacher will pace you by calling "Half" at the end of 30 seconds and "Time" at the end of one minute. Try to reach the check marks as the teacher calls "Half" and "Time."

When you are able to write at your new rate with a feeling of ease, add 5 strokes (one word) to your half-minute rate and 10 strokes (two words) to your minute rate.

Continue to increase your goal by five-stroke intervals. Between timings, practice selected sections.

---

* If you are instructed not to mark your book, mentally note the half-minute and minute goals.

PROBLEM 2

Directions. 1. Type the letter given in Problem 1, but use the address given at the right.

2. Supply an appropriate salutation.

Miss Mildred Watkins
3144 South Maryland Street
Chicago 67, Illinois

ADDRESSING THE ENVELOPE

Use long envelopes for letters of more than one page and for letters with enclosures. For all others, use short envelopes.

Spacing. Three-line addresses for envelopes should be typed with double spacing, even though the letter is single-spaced. When four or more lines are used for the envelope address, single-space the address. Always use at least three lines for an envelope address. If no street address is given, type the name of the city and that of the state on separate lines. The city and state names should be separated by a comma when they are typed on the same line. Never use *City* in the place of the city's correct name.

The Attention Line. The attention phrase may be typed on the line immediately follow-

ing the company name, or it may be placed in the lower left corner of the envelope.

In care of, or the special symbol *c/o*, should be typed in either of the positions indicated for the attention phrase. If space permits, it is better to spell out *In care of* instead of using the symbol *c/o*. Never use the sign %.

Placement of the Address. When using a large envelope, 4⅛ by 9½ inches, type the first line of the address at approximately the vertical center and 5 spaces to the left of the horizontal center.

Addresses for short envelopes, and folding a letter and inserting it into a short envelope, are illustrated on pages 66 and 72. Addresses for long envelopes are illustrated below.

STUDEBAKER PUBLISHING CO.
742 Wayne Avenue
MUNCIE, INDIANA

The Office Equipment Co.
Attention Mr. E. R. Locke
286-290 Sixth Street
Flint 13, Michigan

The address on the envelope shown below is double-spaced as it contains three lines only.

The Office Equipment Co.
286-290 Sixth Street
Flint 13, Michigan

Attention Mr. E. R. Locke

Illustration 39
Styles of Addresses for a Large Envelope

FOLDING AND INSERTING A LETTER INTO A LONG ENVELOPE

Step 1: Fold slightly less than one third of the letterhead up toward the top.

Step 2: Fold down the top part of the letterhead.

Step 3: Insert the creased edge of the letter into the envelope with the letterhead toward the front.

OFFICE TYPING PROBLEMS

INSTRUCTIONAL BLOCK 14

THE IMPROVEMENT OF TYPING POWER

General Directions. Unless specifically directed to do otherwise, use a 70-space line and single spacing for all drill work; use a 70-space line, a 5-space paragraph indention, and double spacing for all timed writings.

SECTION 24. Speed Emphasis

LESSON 151

CONDITIONING PRACTICE 151   *5 minutes*

Directions. Type each sentence three times, or more if time permits. Start writing slowly and increase your stroking rate gradually with each repetitive typing. This will be the uniform assignment for typing the conditioning practice for all lessons in this section.

	STROKES
Betty Porter and Jo Sands will quilt thick, heavy rugs of mixed sizes.	70
Rose ordered 284 records, 96 needles, 175 folders, and 30 player lids.	70
You should try to keep your fingers moving quickly and without pauses.	70

GOAL SELECTION 151   *15 minutes*

Directions. Type each paragraph without being timed. Then use each paragraph for a series of 1-minute writings. Compute your cwpm for each writing. Use the highest stroking rate as the base rate for the calling-the-guide sentences that follow.

	STROKES	WORDS
There is a time in the life of each typist when he feels like striving	71	14
for new and higher levels of writing. It is in his desire to improve that	146	29
he gains his greatest momentum; the greater his desire, the greater his	218	44
chances for achieving his goals.	252	50
One of the best ways to start a program for improving stroking skill	69	14
is to forget about the speeds at which you are trying to write. If you	141	28
will think only of the ease with which you can already stroke, you will	213	43
be amazed at your unexpected results.	250	50

CALLING THE GUIDE 151   *10 minutes*

Directions. Set a goal for a 15-second writing that is 2 words more than the number of words you wrote in 15 seconds in the paragraph typing. Type for 1 minute attempting to reach your goal each 15 seconds as your teacher calls the guide. When you can type at this rate for 1 minute with a feeling of ease, increase your goal as directed by your teacher.

   1   2   3   4   5   6   7   8   9   10   11   12   13   14

The order will be checked soon. It should be shipped within two days.
We shall verify your address. Our fee clerk will arrange to bill you.
There will be a small charge for packing. It should be paid promptly.

   1   2   3   4   5   6   7   8   9   10   11   12   13   14

LESSON 94

STROKES

Jerome quickly realized that six lively polliwogs would soon be frogs.   70
Order No. 8475 for 36 chairs ($9.75 ea.) will be shipped May 19 or 20.   70
The Future Business Leaders of America will meet in New York or Maine.   70
The chairman spent the profit for the eight forms of the big rhapsody.   70

PRODUCTION COMPARISON TYPING 94
(Letter Copy)
10 minutes

Directions. Type a 5-minute timed writing on Problem Typing 93, Problem 1, page 132. Before beginning to type, set tabulator stops for the date line and the closing lines so that you can move quickly to the proper position for these lines.

If you finish the letter before time is called, start over on another sheet of paper.

Determine the cwpm. Compare this rate with the rate you made on the straight-copy material given in Lesson 91.

PROBLEM TYPING 94
25 minutes

PROBLEM 1

STROKES

Directions. Use the current date, mixed punctuation, and the modified block form with no indentions for paragraphs. Make a carbon copy and address an envelope.

The four loan services given in the third paragraph are to be centered (longest line only, start other lines at this point) and listed in a column. Single-space the list of services, but leave a double space both before and after the list.

When two or more items are enclosed in a letter, the enclosure notation may include the word *Enclosures* and the figure indicating the number of enclosures. This is the method used in the following illustration.

~~~~~~~~~~~~~~~~~~~~~~~~~~~~~~~~~~~~~~

We shall be pleased to assist you with any of your
future banking or loan service problems.

                   Sincerely yours,

                   CITIZENS BANK OF CHICAGO

                   L. D. Pierce, Vice President

eds

Enclosures 2

~~~~~~~~~~~~~~~~~~~~~~~~~~~~~~~~~~~~~~

Illustration 40 — Closing Lines with
the Enclosure Notation

STROKES

Mr. L. W. Johnston 615 West Wash-   48
ington Street Chicago 18, Illinois   83
Dear Mr. Johnston: We enclose   114

---

your Personal Note No. Z-349-207   147
which has been paid in full. (P) It   180
is a pleasure to enclose, also, a "Citi-   219
zens Plan" Credit Card in recogni-   252
tion of your prompt payment record   287
with us. This card will be helpful   322
to you in discussing future loan   355
needs here or at any of our branch   390
banks. (P) Here are a few of the   420
"Citizens Plan" loan services in   453
which you might be interested: 485

     Loans on automobiles   506
     Property improvement loans   533
     Investment loans   550
     Auto repair loans   568

(P) We shall be pleased to assist   598
you with any of your future banking   634
or loan service problems. Sincerely   671
yours, CITIZENS BANK OF CHI-   698
CAGO L. D. Pierce, Vice President   732
Enclosures 2 *(104)*   744

PROBLEM 2

Directions. Type the letter given in Problem 1, making the following changes:

1. Address
   letter to: Mr. R. S. McDonald
              2371 South Kingsley Street
              Chicago 45, Illinois

2. Supply an appropriate salutation

3. Personal Note No. X-684-900

LESSON 150

          STROKES

Six picturesque sloops took a frenzied crowd via the big mooring jetty.   71

Davis & Lewis sent their $758.69 check for 20 #41 radios, deducting 3%.   71

The Cape of Good Hope is the southern tip of the Union of South Africa.   71

The proficient secretary paid the busy clerks for the eight handy pens.   71

PROBLEM TYPING 150   *35 minutes*

Directions. Type the following problems with any style of letter and form of punctuation that you prefer. Capitalize and punctuate correctly the opening and closing lines of each letter. Paragraph signs are not indicated in the copy. Study each letter carefully and divide it into appropriate paragraphs. (Each letter should have three or more paragraphs.)

If a letter refers to an enclosure, add the appropriate notation to the closing lines.

Make a carbon copy and address an envelope for each letter.

In the third letter the dictator's name is not given, but the initials are given for use in the reference notation.

PROBLEM 1

treadwear tire company automotive building cleveland 4 ohio attention mr j b harmon gentlemen We had so many complaints from our customers about your Treadwear tires not wearing well that it seemed advisable to put in a stock of some other kind of tire. This is the reason we have not ordered any of your tires for several months. We are returning to you by express a tire that a customer asked us to replace. This tire was used for approximately 5,000 miles. You will see that the tread is worn smooth. Even the pyramid-shaped blocks of rubber on the side walls are worn through. Five thousand miles does not represent enough use to cause the wear that this tire shows. We can return to you two or three other used tires from this same shipment if you wish us to do so. yours very truly charles h mcconnell manager *(131)*

PROBLEM 2

treadwear tire company automotive building cleveland 4 ohio attention mr j b harmon gentlemen subject defective tires As you requested in your recent letter, we are glad to give you the details regarding the last shipment of Treadwear tires we bought from you. Eight of the tires are unsatisfactory. We have replaced three of them with new tires of another kind. Five tires are therefore still in use. The complaint has been made by the users of these tires that the tread is worn so smooth that the tire does not have even normal nonskid protection. If you will make a satisfactory adjustment for these defective tires, we shall be glad to consider carrying Treadwear tires in stock again. yours very truly charles h mcconnell manager *(102)*

PROBLEM 3

the office equipment co 286-290 sixth street flint 13 michigan attention mr e r locke gentlemen Your catalog No. 56 came this morning. The filing cabinet we want is similar to No. 03865, shown on page 34 of your catalog. Is the price of $42.75 given on the supplementary sheet f.o.b. your factory? Also, in what colors can the cabinet be furnished? We are also in need of additional office supplies that are not listed in your catalog. These are given on the enclosed sheet. Please let us have your quotation on these items promptly. Although our office needs are not large just at this time, we shall be needing tables and other office equipment from time to time. When you again open an agency in Indianapolis, please let us know. very truly yours director of purchases fbh *(128)*

LESSON 95

STROKES

Jack amazed the audience by his expert knowledge of the unique violin.	70
The 1952 Edition contained 380 charts, 275 drawings, and 1,469 tables.	70
Dr. James Kerr, President of the International Society, is in Chicago.	70
Sign the cards and then be sure to attach the bank statements to them.	70

TECHNIQUE STUDY 95   *5 minutes*

Control of the Hyphen and Shift-Lock Keys. The purpose of this drill is to improve your control of the hyphen and shift-lock keys. Make the reaches as called for with a minimum of waste time and motion.

Directions. Type each line four times, or more if time permits.

STROKES

up-to-date, son-in-law, well-to-do, first-class, happy-go-lucky, up-bow	71
HONESTY, SINCERITY, and INITIATIVE are important attributes of SUCCESS.	71

PRODUCTION TYPING 95   *30 minutes*

You are to be timed for 20 minutes on typing the letter problems given below. Work with ease and stay relaxed so that you can build a high sustained letter-production rate. Arrange your materials properly and work with a minimum of waste time and motion.

Time Schedule

Making notations of directions and preparation (setting margins, arranging papers, etc.) . . . . 5 minutes	Timed production of letters . . . . . . .20 minutes Proofreading and determining cwpm. . . . . 5 minutes

Directions. Make pencil notations of the following directions for the timed production of letters. Keep the notations where you can read them easily.

Type each of the letters on a separate sheet of paper.

1. Type Problem 1, Lesson 91, page 130.
2. Type Problem 1, Lesson 92, page 131.
3. Type Problem 1, Lesson 93, page 132.
4. Type Problem 1, Lesson 94, page 134.

Type all letters in the modified block form with no indention for paragraphs. Use the current date and mixed punctuation. Do not erase or correct any errors you make in typing the letters unless otherwise directed by your teacher. *Type at the skill-building level of practice.* If you complete typing the letter problems before time is called, start over.

When time is called, proofread each letter carefully and determine your cwpm.

LESSON 96

STROKES

Zuma is just 26 miles from Bogota, and your drive should pass quickly.	70
In 1950, we had 78 office chairs, 34 office desks, and 26 work tables.	70
The Pacific Express Line trucks between Los Angeles and San Francisco.	70
Ask the office manager to refer you to the correct file of statements.	70

June 2, 195–   13   3

Mr. T. C. Wright   30   10
1259 North Sixth Street   54   11
New York 5, New York   75   15

Dear Mr. Wright: 93   19

One of our salesmen, Mr. H. T. Harmsworth, has sent   145   29
us a first order from you. We thank you for this   195   39
order, and we hope that our business relations will   247   49
be satisfactory.   265   53

We should like very much to grant you credit, but we   318   64
have a disturbing report on your credit rating which   371   74
states that some firms are doing business with you   422   84
for cash only. We know that credit reports are some- 474   95
times in error; so we wish you would let us have the   527   105
name of your local bank and other firms with whom you 581   116
have had credit. We can then ask them for a complete 635   127
report on your credit standing.   668   134

As soon as we establish a favorable rating for you,   720   144
we can make shipments to you on open account. Until   773   155
we can do this, may we ship your order on cash terms   826   165
to avoid delay?   843   169

Very truly yours,   861   172

E. H. Brown, Credit Manager   889   178

EHB:LC   895   179

GUIDED WRITING FOR CONTROL 149   *17 minutes*

Directions. 1. Take several 1-minute writings on the material in the Straight-Copy Timed Writing 146, page 197. Type at the best rate at which you can type with control. Your accuracy goal will be to type with not more than 1 error in each minute writing. Your teacher will guide your writing by calling each quarter-minute interval.

After you have met your goal, you are to type a 3-minute timed writing in which you will try to maintain your 1-minute rate. As an accuracy goal, try to type with not more than 3 errors. Your teacher will guide your writing by calling each half-minute interval.

2. Follow the same procedure as outlined above for the letter copy on this page. As a tentative goal, try to type at a rate which is approximately 75 per cent of your straight-copy rate. Maintain the same degree of accuracy.

Directions. Type a 5-minute timed writing on the material given for Production Comparison Typing 91, page 129. *Type at the skill-building level of practice.* Determine your cwpm. Keep a record of the rate you make so that you can compare it with your rates on other types of material.

PROBLEM TYPING 96 *25 minutes*

This lesson and the next three lessons will deal with a series of credit and collection letters. Be sure that you work for an increased stroking rate as you become familiar with the letter forms used. Plan and organize your work so that you can type with a pattern of efficient motions.

PROBLEM I

Directions. Use the current date, open punctuation, and type the following letter in the block form similar to Style Letter 2, page 65. In the closing lines, type the official title on the line below the dictator's name. Make a carbon copy and address an envelope.

	STROKES
Mrs. Ralph G. Hess 2938 East Col-	48
fax Avenue Denver 10, Colorado	79
Dear Mrs. Hess Thank you for re-	110
questing credit at our store. It is a	149
pleasure to tell you that a charge	184
account has been opened in your	216
name. We hope you will make fre-	248
quent use of the privilege it offers.	287
(P) Arrangements have been made	315
to grant you credit amounting to	348
$100. If you wish to make purchases	385
of a larger amount, we shall be glad	422
to discuss your requirements with	456
you. (P) An identification plate for	490
your convenience in making credit	524

	STROKES
purchases is enclosed. In addition,	561
we are enclosing a booklet which ex-	596
plains in detail the privileges to	631
which you are now entitled. (P)	660
High-quality merchandise and cour-	693
teous service have been our standard	730
for many years. We look forward to	766
counting you among our satisfied	799
customers. Very truly yours Wil-	831
liam Bradley Credit Manager En-	861
closures 2 *(124)*	871

PROBLEM 2

Directions. Type the letter given in Problem 1, making the following changes:

1. Address letter to: Mrs. Robert M. Miller
3146 Madison Avenue
Denver 13, Colorado

2. Supply an appropriate salutation

3. Amount of credit: $150

LESSON 97

CONDITIONING PRACTICE 97 *5 minutes*

	STROKES
Fill the big jug quickly with five or six pints of Zimmer's Grape Ade.	70
The 546 copies, priced at $3.78 each, may be shipped on June 19 or 20.	70
The Karr School offers classes in Italian, French, Polish, and German.	70
The expert accountant will be here today to answer your tax questions.	70

PRODUCTION COMPARISON TYPING 97 *10 minutes*

Directions. Type a 5-minute timed writing on the material given for Production Comparison Typing 92, page 131. Use a 70-space line, a 5-space paragraph indention, and double spacing. *Type at the skill-building level of practice.* Determine the cwpm. Compare this rate with your straight-copy typing rate.

			STROKES	WORDS
JUSTIN & HARDING			17	3
Outstanding Accounts			38	8
Walter C. Adams	958 West Second Street	$516.30	87	17
Floyd N. Carver	564 East Main Street	30.25	130	26
Ralph M. Edwards	4967 Longshore Drive	17.57	174	35
Katharine Holmes	16 West Eighth Street	28.13	219	44
Edmund K. Justus	3946 Pennsylvania Avenue	113.95	269	54
Frances Lovelace	2147 Elmwood Drive	74.50	311	62
Martha Nelson	6148 South Arizona Avenue	29.82	357	71
Raymond Osborn	1003 Ohio Avenue	16.49	395	79
Anthony Peterson	1295 Delaware Place	470.50	440	88
Meredith O. Pierce	1748 Columbia Boulevard	8.23	489	98
Margaret Sparks	4780 North Broadway	62.17	531	106
Keith L. Stewart	901 Santa Fe Drive	89.20	573	115
Stanley W. Tobias	1593 North Boulevard	23.49	618	124
Theodora Townsend	2147 Curtis Road	6.93	659	132
Marvin C. Williams	4157 West Wedgeworth Street	415.12	713	143

TECHNIQUE STUDY 148 *As time permits*

Directions. As time permits in this lesson, type the sentences emphasizing one-hand words given in the Calling-the-Guide Drills on page 143. Type each sentence three times. Keep the carriage moving and hit each key with uniform stroking power.

LESSON 149

CONDITIONING PRACTICE 149 *5 minutes*

	STROKES
Six jet fighters buzzed a mapped city and quickly veered off westward.	70
She paid for them with Silver Certificate No. B4618502F, Series 1937D.	70
The clansmen got into the dory by the shale rock and circled the lake.	70

STRAIGHT-COPY TIMED WRITING 149 *8 minutes*

Directions. Take a 5-minute timed writing. Use the Straight-Copy Timed Writing given in Lesson 146, page 197, for this writing. Determine the cwpm.

LETTER-COPY TIMED WRITING 149 *10 minutes*

Directions. Take a 5-minute timed writing on the letter copy on page 202. Type the letter in the modified block style with no indentions for paragraphs. Use a 50-space line, mixed punctuation, and leave 8 spaces between the date and the address. Type the date line so that it ends at the right margin. (Set a tabulator stop for the date line.) Use single spacing for the body of the letter with double spacing between paragraphs. Determine the cwpm. Compare your letter-copy rate with your straight-copy rate.

PROBLEM 1

Directions. Use the current date, open punctuation, and type the following collection letter in the block form similar to Style Letter 2, page 65. In the closing lines, type the official title on the line below the dictator's name. Make a carbon copy and address an envelope.

STROKES

Mrs. O. A. Howell 2074 West 35th	49
Street Denver 16, Colorado Dear	81
Mrs. Howell The statement which	113
was recently mailed to you indicated	150
a balance of $25.78 due on your ac-	184
count. (P) When accounts run past	215
the due date, we find that most of	250
our customers appreciate receiving	285
a brief reminder. (P) If you haven't	319
already made payment, won't you	351
please attach your check to this let-	387
ter and return it to us. (P) We	416
sincerely appreciate your continued	452
patronage. Very truly yours Wil-	484
liam Bradley Credit Manager (67)	511

PROBLEM 2

Directions. Type the letter given in **Problem** 1, making the following changes:

1. Address
   letter to: Mr. H. L. Thomas
   126 West Lowder Road
   Denver 6, Colorado

2. Supply an appropriate salutation

3. Balance of account: $34.25

PROBLEM 3

Directions. Type the letter given in Problem 1, making the following changes:

1. Address letter to: Dr. E. M. McKinley
   408 Medical Building
   5293 Broadway Circle
   Denver 3, Colorado

2. Supply an appropriate salutation

3. Balance of account: $62.98

LESSON 98

CONDITIONING PRACTICE 98

5 minutes

STROKES

The quiet king came forth to extend prizes to very bewildered jesters.	70
We will ship your order, #35790, for 126 boxes and 48 cartons Tuesday.	70
The Cashier, Mr. Ted King, will return from Fargo on Sunday or Monday.	70
The man addressed his remarks to the group of boys seated in the rear.	70

PRODUCTION COMPARISON TYPING 98

10 minutes

Directions. Type a 5-minute timed writing on the material given for Production Comparison Typing 93, page 132. Use a 70-space line, a 5-space paragraph indention, and double spacing. *Type at the skill-building level of practice.* Determine the cwpm. Compare this rate with your straight-copy typing rate.

PROBLEM TYPING 98

25 minutes

PROBLEM 1

Directions. Use the current date, open punctuation, and type the following collection letter in the block form. In the closing lines, type the official title on the line below the dictator's name. Make a carbon copy and address an envelope.

STROKES

Mrs. Walter J. Peterson 560 Colo-	48
rado Parkway Denver 5, Colorado	80

STROKES

Dear Mrs. Peterson Have you ever	113
reminded someone to do something,	147
only to find, upon checking, that the	185
task was still undone? If so, you	220
were probably a bit disappointed.	255
(P) We were disappointed, too,	282
when we found that you did not re-	315
spond to our monthly statement or	349
to our letter reminding you that	382
your account of $72.38 was still un-	417

Directions. 1. Take several 1-minute writings on the material in the Straight-Copy Timed Writing 146, page 197. In each writing, select a rate at which you will try to type. Your accuracy goal will be to type with not more than 1 error in each minute writing. As you meet your goal, increase your stroking rate slightly for the additional 1-minute writings. Your teacher will guide your writing by calling each quarter-minute interval.

After you have met your goal, you are to type a 3-minute timed writing in which you will try to maintain your 1-minute rate. As an accuracy goal, try to type with not more than 3 errors. Type without a sense of hurry to increase your accuracy. Keep your fingers close to the keys and the carriage moving. Your teacher will guide your writing by calling each half-minute interval.

2. Follow the same procedure as outlined above for the statistical-copy on page 199. As a tentative goal, try to type at a rate which is approximately 75 per cent of your straight-copy rate. Maintain the same degree of accuracy.

TECHNIQUE STUDY 147 *As time permits*

Directions. As time permits in this lesson, type the balanced-hand sentences given in the Calling-the-Guide Drills on page 143. Type each sentence three times. Try to type most of the words at the word level of response. Keep the carriage moving.

LESSON 148

CONDITIONING PRACTICE 148 *5 minutes*

STROKES

A mad boxer shot a quick, gloved jab to the jaw of his dizzy opponent.   70
The new pool (15′ wide x 60′ long x 7½′ deep) will cost but $3,248.90.   70
The Bill of Rights is a part of the Constitution of the United States.   70
If they pick the eight fowls for the widow, she will pay them in cash.   70

STRAIGHT-COPY TIMED WRITING 148 *8 minutes*

Directions. Take a 5-minute timed writing. Use the Straight-Copy Timed Writing 146, page 197. Determine the cwpm.

TABULATION TIMED WRITING 148 *10 minutes*

Directions. Take a 5-minute timed writing on the tabulation material at the top of the following page. For pica type, set your left margin at 8 and tabulator stops at 34 and 71; for elite type, set your left margin at 17 and tabulator stops at 43 and 80. Move the right margin stop to the end of the scale. In the amount column, the tabulator stop is set for the most frequently recurring amount (the *tens* column). Use double spacing for the data.

Determine the cwpm. Compare your tabulation rate with your straight-copy rate.

GUIDED WRITING FOR CONTROL 148 *15 minutes*

Directions. 1. Take several 1-minute writings on the copy for Straight-Copy Timed Writing 146, page 197. Your goal should be errorless writing or not more than one error in each minute.

Type a 3-minute timed writing in which you will try to maintain your 1-minute rate with not more than one error a minute.

2. Follow the same procedure as outlined for the tabulation copy on page 201. As a tentative goal, try to type at a rate which is 25 to 40 per cent of your straight-copy rate. Maintain the same degree of accuracy.

paid. (P) Our liberal credit terms 449
are possible only if our customers 484
continue to make their payments 516
promptly. (P) Won't you please 544
send us your check now while this 578
reminder is fresh in your mind. Very 616
truly yours William Bradley Credit 651
Manager *(94)* 658

PROBLEM 2

Directions. Type the letter given in Problem 1, making the following changes:

1. Address letter to: Mr. R. G. Bell
   3116 Logan Street
   Denver 15, Colorado

2. Supply an appropriate salutation

3. Balance of account: $84.59

LESSON 99

CONDITIONING PRACTICE 99

5 minutes

STROKES

Lizzy quickly pulled down five extra pints of her good strawberry jam. 70
The house located at 23968 Richmond Street sold for $14,750 last year. 70
I am very glad that you will be able to be with us for a week or more. 70

PRODUCTION COMPARISON TYPING 99

10 minutes

Directions. Take a 5-minute timed writing on Problem Typing 98, Problem 1, page 137. If you finish the letter before time is called, start over on another sheet of paper. Determine the cwpm. Compare this rate with your straight-copy typing rate.

PROBLEM TYPING 99

25 minutes

PROBLEM 1

Directions. Use the current date, open punctuation, and the block form. Because this letter contains a short tabulated report which will affect its placement on the page, use a 60-space line and leave approximately 6 spaces between the date and the address. Tabulate the report in two columns indented 15 spaces from the left margin with 12 spaces between columns.

STROKES

Mr. Henry W. Beecher 385 North 47
Grant Street Denver 4, Colorado 79
Dear Mr. Beecher Our record of 110
your account shows the following 143
unpaid charges: 160

		STROKES
January 15	$13.47	179
February 3	9.03	196
February 14	28.56	214
		222
	$51.06	230

(P) When a "prompt pay" account 258
suddenly appears on the delinquent 293
list, we begin to wonder what can be 330
the cause. Since our previous re- 363
minders have not brought the usual 398
prompt reply, can it be that adverse 435

circumstances have prevented pay- 467
ment? (P) If you cannot make full 498
payment at this time, please see us 534
at once so that we may assist you in 571
working out some plan of settlement 607
suitable to your particular needs. 643
(P) It is our desire to serve you in 676
any way we can, and we should like 711
to help you restore your account to 747
a condition which will enable you to 784
enjoy the convenience it affords. 819
(P) Won't you please give this mat- 849
ter your prompt attention. Very 882
truly yours William Bradley Credit 917
Manager *(149)* 924

PROBLEM 2

Directions. Type the letter given in Problem 1, making the following changes:

1. Address letter to: Mrs. W. C. McLaughlin, 4312 Tenth Street, N. E., Denver 26, Colorado.

2. Supply an appropriate salutation

3. Unpaid charges: January 21 $18.26
   January 29   9.54
   February 8   37.63
   $65.43

After you have met your goal, you are to type a 3-minute timed writing in which you will try to maintain your 1-minute rate. As an accuracy goal, try to type with not more than 3 errors. Your teacher will guide your writing by calling each half-minute interval.

2. Follow the same procedure as outlined above for the rough-draft copy on page 198. As a tentative goal, try to type at a rate which is at least 50 per cent of your straight-copy rate. Maintain the same degree of accuracy.

TECHNIQUE STUDY 146   *As time permits*

Directions. As time permits in this lesson, type the Technique Study—Reading the Copy, page 141, as many times as possible. Type at a well-controlled rate and work for continuity of writing.

LESSON 147

CONDITIONING PRACTICE 147   *5 minutes*

	STROKES
Six skaters jumped grotesquely in a veritable frenzy of wacky rhythms.	70
He sold Reo Record Nos. 47-3115-B, 86-2725-A, 92-0413-C, and 64-80151.	70
Mount Robson is a big Rocky Mountain peak in British Columbia, Canada.	70
The eight men handled the historical ornament with the utmost caution.	70

STRAIGHT-COPY TIMED WRITING 147   *8 minutes*

Directions. Take a 5-minute timed writing. Use the Straight-Copy Timed Writing 146, page 197, for this writing. Determine the cwpm.

STATISTICAL-COPY TIMED WRITING 147   *10 minutes*

Directions. Take a 5-minute timed writing of the following statistical-copy material. Determine the cwpm. Compare your rate on this material with your rate on the straight-copy material. Proofread your material carefully for any errors you may have made.

STROKES

Due to the payment of the special bonus, business activity in the — 66

Great Lakes region quickly zoomed upward during the month of June, — 133

continuing the upward trend of the past four months. — 187

The First State Bank's index in June stood at 327.5 of the "average" — 256

as compared with 298 in May, a jump of 9.9%. The bank said it was one — 327

of the sharpest rises ever to occur in any one month during the 25-year — 399

span covered by the index, which was up 36% over June of last year. — 468

Department store sales showed one of June's greatest gains, up 37% — 535

over May with a jump of 48% over June of last year. — 588

Employment figures showed an increase of 4.2% for June over May and — 656

a gain over June of last year of 10.7%. — 695

LESSON 100

STROKES

Frances Marx was puzzled to have her quick plan rejected by the group.   70

Your order of October 29 was shipped to 8057 Second Street, Dayton 46.   70

North Valley Union High School will hold a Commercial Day on Thursday.   70

If they give him a key to the office, he might finish the work for us.   70

TECHNIQUE STUDY 100   *5 minutes*

Carriage Throw. As you type the following sentences, throw the carriage quickly at the end of the sentence, return the hand immediately to typing position, and start the new line without a pause. Hold your eyes on the copy and use just the right amount of power for the carriage throw.

Directions. Type each sentence for one minute at either the 20-, 15-, 12-, or 10-second call of the guide as directed by your teacher. Work for an improved carriage return.

	Strokes	Words 20″	Words 15″	Words 12″	Words 10″
The men may do the work and fix the big bus today.	50	30	40	50	60
Bob paid them for the chairs and then signed the forms.	55	33	44	55	66
They plan to spend some time visiting with them in the city.	60	36	48	60	72

PRODUCTION TYPING 100   *30 minutes*

You are to be timed for 20 minutes on typing the letter problems given below. Work with ease and stay relaxed so that you can build a high sustained letter-production rate. Arrange your materials properly, use good typing techniques, and work with a minimum of waste time and motion.

Time Schedule

Noting directions and preparation (setting margins, arranging papers, etc.) .... 5 minutes

Timed production of letters .... 20 minutes
Proofreading and determining cwpm. .... 5 minutes

Directions. Make pencil notations of the following directions for the timed production of letters. Keep the notations where you can read them easily.

Type each of the letters on a separate sheet of paper.

1. Type Problem 1, Lesson 96, page 136.
2. Type Problem 1, Lesson 97, page 137.
3. Type Problem 1, Lesson 98, page 137.
4. Type Problem 1, Lesson 99, page 138.

Type all letters in the block form. Use the current date and open punctuation. Do not erase or correct any errors you make in typing the letters unless otherwise directed by your teacher. *Type at the skill-building level of practice.*

When time is called, proofread each letter carefully and determine your cwpm.

Directions. Take a 5-minute timed writing on the following rough-draft copy. Before starting to type the copy, read it through and note the corrections indicated. Determine the cwpm. Compare your rough-draft copy rate with your straight-copy rate.

Proofreaders' marks used in this rough draft but not illustrated on page 132 are:

$\#$ Add space $]$ Move over $\equiv$ Capitalize

	STROKES	WORDS
all caps → Proofreading *triple space*	13	3
no matter ~~Regardless of~~ how perfectly a person "thinks" he types,	64	13
or how good his ~~judgment~~ placement of copy may be, there is	115	23
real need always a ~~place~~ for proofreading, ~~in the typing process. For,~~ *all typed work.*	168	34
In spite of the typist's *skill* ~~ability~~, errors of *one kind or another* ~~various kinds~~	230	46
creep in.	241	48
The ~~logical~~ steps in proofreading a *typed* ~~typewritten~~ letter	282	56
are these:	294	59
1. Check the ~~general~~ form of the letter: Does it	337	67
follow a uniform style? Is it well balanced?	384	77
Is it neat?	397	79
2. Check the *proper* correctness [the of] address: Is it	446	89
the ~~correct~~ address for the person to whom you	492	98
are writing? Are the street name and numbers	538	108
correct?	548	110
needs to 3. Check the *exactness* ~~accuracy~~ of the content: Does it say	601	120
~~want~~ ~~should~~ be said? Are all ~~the~~ amounts and	645	129
other figures correct?	669	134
4. Check the sentence structure and the use of	717	143
words: Does the letter make good sense? Is	762	152
it punctuated correctly and does it make for easy	812	162
reading? Are the words used and spelled	853	171
correctly?	865	173
have been When this process has been completed and all errors, corrected,	938	188
then it is safe to submit the let~~t~~er *to be signed* ~~for signature~~ and *mailed.* ~~mailing.~~	999	200

GUIDED WRITING FOR CONTROL 146   *15 minutes*

Directions. 1. Take several 1-minute writings on the material in the Straight-Copy Timed Writing 146, page 197. In each writing, select a rate at which you will try to type. Your accuracy goal will be to type with not more than 1 error in each minute writing. As you meet your goal, increase your stroking rate slightly for the additional 1-minute writings. Your teacher may direct you to set quarter-minute goals and may guide your writing by calling each quarter-minute interval.

INSTRUCTIONAL BLOCK 8

IMPROVEMENT OF TYPING POWER

SECTION 15. Technique Improvement

LESSONS 101 TO 105

Machine Checkup and Adjustments. 1. Make the usual machine checkup and adjustments at the beginning of each lesson. Practice briefly the carriage-return throw and the control of the shift keys. Make the reach to the tabulator bar or key two or three times.

2. Use a 70-space line and single spacing, unless otherwise directed. Double-space between unrelated single-spaced groups of lines. For the timed writings, use a 70-space line, a 5-space paragraph indention, and double spacing.

DAILY OUTLINE FOR LESSONS 101 TO 105

Conditioning Practice . . . . 5 minutes

Technique Study—Response Levels (Lessons 101, 103, and 105) . . . . . 10 minutes

Technique Study—Reading the Copy (Lessons 102 and 104) . . . . 10 minutes

Timed Writing (Lessons 101, 103, and 105) . . . . 15 minutes

Guided Writing (Lessons 102 and 104) . . . . 15 minutes

Calling-the-Guide Drills (Lessons 101, 103, and 105) . . . . 10 minutes

Speed and Accuracy Building (Lessons 102 and 104) . . . . 10 minutes

CONDITIONING PRACTICE—LESSONS 101 TO 105   *5 minutes*

Directions. In each lesson in this section, type each line of the conditioning practice twice. As time permits, select for repetitive practice the sentence or sentences on which you made errors.

STROKES

Paul was very keen in quoting from the job chart on the quiz next day.   70

The test for April 8 will cover pages 64-75, 98-130, 152-239, and 403.   70

Phil left the train at Reno, Nevada, but Joe went on to Dallas, Texas.   70

To type rapidly, hold your arms quiet and let the fingers do the work.   70

TECHNIQUE STUDY—RESPONSE LEVELS—LESSONS 101, 103, AND 105   *10 minutes*

Directions. In Lessons 101, 103, and 105, type the phrases given below three times, or more if time permits. *Type at the exploration level of practice.*

Each phrase is arranged in a vertical-horizontal pattern to enable you to read a group of words at a glance. Concentrate on the copy, think the words, and type the phrases as regular lines of copy. A line of your typing will then appear as follows:

`if the case for the date he may read the due date and it was to the`

The first two words in each phrase under (1) are balanced-hand words which you can type at the word-recognition level of response. The last word in each phrase is a one-hand word which

SECTION 23. Production-Comparison Typing

LESSON 146

CONDITIONING PRACTICE 146   *5 minutes*

Directions. Type each line twice. As time permits, select for repetitive practice the sentence or sentences in which you made errors. This will be the uniform plan for typing the conditioning practices in all lessons in this section.

	STROKES
The capable man jerked a big arrow from his quiver and shot a lazy fox.	71
He bought a book with 2,967 illustrations, 450 tables, and 38 pictures.	71
Kitty Hawk, North Carolina, is the site of the Wright Brothers' flight.	71
He lay by the rocks on the shore and watched the ships come in to dock.	71

STRAIGHT-COPY TIMED WRITING 146   *8 minutes*

Directions. Take a 5-minute timed writing. Determine the cwpm. Type with ease and with good control. Keep the carriage moving steadily and smoothly. Keep your hands relaxed and the stroking action in the fingers.

This timed writing has a syllable intensity of 1.30.

	STROKES
By this time you should be quite skilled in handling your machine.	68
You can type with reasonable speed and a fair degree of accuracy; you	138
know how to set up and type many office-type problems; and you have	206
learned to use the parts of the machine to make your typing simpler.	276
Even though you have developed skill in these phases of typing, there	346
is still a wide range of difference between your performance and that of	419
the expert typist. His many hours of well-planned practice give him quite	494
an "edge" over you; but you, too, can make rapid strides toward perfec-	564
tion if you are willing to spend the time in pursuit of such a goal.	634
Start, first of all, with a critical appraisal of the way you plan your	706
work, set up your problems, and do the actual typing of a job. Then, with	781
such an appraisal as a basis for practice, begin a campaign against waste	855
time and waste motions in all of your typing work. If you have the	923
right goals in mind and a set of wholesome attitudes, you will be amazed	996
at the speed with which you reach expert performance.	1051

you may have to type at the stroke level of response. As you type the phrases, combine the two levels of response into a fluent rhythmic pattern.

The first word in each phrase under (2) calls for the stroke level of response; the second and third words can be typed at the word-recognition level of response. Again, combine the two levels of response into a fluent rhythmic pattern.

(1)

if the case	for the date	he may read	the due date	and it was	to the fact
of the opinion	they may cease	and the average	and they gave	owns the deed	for the debt

(2)

agree with them	saw them go	draft of the	at the end	was it due	look for the
regard for their	only their work	referred them to	join with them	agreed to pay	extra pay for

TECHNIQUE STUDY—READING THE COPY—LESSONS 102 AND 104 *10 minutes*

Directions. In Lessons 102 and 104, type the following paragraph material as many times as possible in the time allowed. The material given below is arranged in a special form to give you practice in reading your copy in word groups, and to help you learn to type with continuity. The words are arranged in a vertical-horizontal pattern to enable you to read a group of words at a glance. Type the material in regular paragraph style.

At first you may find it a little difficult to type from material arranged in this manner, but with a little practice it will not be difficult. Concentrate on the copy and try to keep the carriage moving. *Type at the exploration level of practice.*

The words	in this drill	are arranged	in this manner	to help you	read your copy	in word groups
for better	typing results.	Fix your attention	on each	word group	as you type	this drill.	When you
type from	regular copy,	try to read	your copy	in word groups.	This will	help you	increase your
typing speed.	In much	of the copy	that you	will be asked	to type,	the words	may be grouped
into patterns	that can	be read	in much	the same way	as the	word groups	you are typing	right now.

GUIDED WRITING—LESSONS 102 AND 104 *15 minutes*

Directions. In Lessons 102 and 104, type a 1-minute timed writing on the paragraphs given for the Timed Writing, page 142. *Type at the exploration level of practice* and try to force yourself into a new speed area.

Divide your 1-minute rate by 2 to identify your half-minute rate. Set goals for each half minute up to 3 minutes and, unless you are instructed to the contrary, indicate them by small,

lowing: (P) "Compilation revealed 871 differentiated duties. The median number of duties performed by the individual secretary was about 130. Three fourths of the secretaries, however, performed fewer than 210 duties each." (P) As interesting as the list of duties is, I find a study of the table showing the vocational traits of secretaries even more helpful. I enclose a copy of Table 4, which shows the trait and its rank. Perhaps you can make some use of this information until you obtain a copy of the book. (P) Let me know if there is anything more that I can do to help you or your teachers in the curriculum revision that you are now making. Yours very truly William Bradford Murray Associate Professor of Education Enclosure *(191)*

552 586 621 656 696 730 763 801 837 873 908 945 978 1014 1045 1082 1117 1154 1187 1218 1247

PROBLEM 12

Directions. Type the following copy in tabulated form, using four columns. The first and third columns will contain the names of the traits; the second and fourth columns, the numbers representing the frequency ranking. You will find an uneven number of traits given; therefore, place the extra trait and its corresponding ranking in the first two columns.

Plan the entire problem with pencil and paper, then tabulate all four columns on the first line, the second line, etc. When you have finished, you will read down the first two columns, then the last two columns; and the rankings, 1 to 47, will be in proper sequence.

Center the copy vertically and leave 4 spaces between the first and second columns, 10 spaces between the second and third columns, and 4 spaces between the third and fourth columns. Use single spacing with a triple space between the main heading and the secondary heading and a double space between the secondary heading and the columns. Type the main heading in capitals. Do not type the punctuation marks.

VOCATIONAL TRAITS OF SECRETARIES

Frequency Ranking

Accuracy, 1; Responsibleness, 2; Dependability, 3; Intelligence, 3; Courtesy, 5; Initiative, 5; Judgment, 5; Tact, 8; Personal Pleasantness, 9; Personal Appearance, 9; Interest in Work, 11; Speed, 11; Reticence, 13; Adaptability, 14; Businesslikeness, 14; Neatness, 14; Memory, 17; Good Breeding, 18; Poise, 19; Self-confidence, 19; Graciousness, 21; Honesty, 21; Health, 23; Industriousness, 24; Executive Ability, 25; Loyalty, 25; Pleasant Voice, 25; Orderliness, 28; Grooming, 28; Alertness, 30; Drive, 30; Ambition, 32; Curiosity, 32; Forcefulness, 32; Foresight, 32; Thoughtfulness, 32; Thoroughness, 37; Willingness, 37; Modesty (Not Conceit), 39; Originality, 39; Patience, 41; Resourcefulness, 41; Self-control, 43; Versatility, 43; Fairness, 45; Self-respect, 45; Sense of Humor, 47

BONUS TYPING
As time permits

Directions. If you have any extra time after completing all of the problems, type the paragraphs used for the timed writing in this section. Repeat each paragraph several times. With each repetition, try to improve your speed and control until you can type the paragraph at your best rate of speed with a high degree of accuracy.

easily erased check marks. Type a 2-minute timed writing. Attempt to reach your goal each half minute. You will be guided in your writing by the call "Half," "One," "Half," "Two."

Type a 3-minute writing in the same way.

After you have typed for 3 minutes maintaining your half-minute rate, increase the half-minute rate by 5 strokes and take additional timed writings. Continue to increase your goals as much as you can during these two lessons.

TIMED WRITING—LESSONS 101, 103, AND 105   *15 minutes*

Directions. In Lessons 101, 103, and 105, type a 10-minute timed writing on the following paragraphs. *Type at the skill-building level of practice.* Determine your cwpm.

Each paragraph has every letter of the alphabet and a syllable intensity of 1.30.

	STROKES	
	PARA.	TOTAL
Businessmen and women have a keen interest in the work that stu-	63	
dents and teachers are doing in the classrooms of our schools, for they	135	
realize that out of the schools will come the men and women who will be	207	
the next leaders in business. Leadership is not now the exclusive privi-	279	
lege of men. There is quite a large number of women who lead the parade,	353	
so to speak, of those who achieve the great and worth-while in business.	427	
There is just as much chance for success now as there has ever been,	496	
but the world of business requires more of its workers now than it did	567	
formerly.	578	
As I talk with businessmen and women, I often ask them to tell me	66	644
just what I shall say to young men and women who are now enrolled in	135	713
business education courses. For the most part, I get the same suggestion	208	786
—in different words, of course, but the same in thought. They say busi-	280	858
ness requires workers who can work without constant supervision, who	349	927
can prove their own work and know that it is right or wrong. They say,	421	999
too, that employers expect students, while yet in school, to learn to work	496	1074
up to capacity, to form the habit of holding themselves to their best work	571	1149
at all times. There is no place in business for the lazy man or woman.	642	1220

at the time I originally opened the 448
account with you will be sufficient. 489
If additional references will be nec- 522
essary before the change is made, 556
please let me know. Very truly 588
yours, (Mrs. W. C. Bayne) Enclos- 620
ure (85) 623

PROBLEM 10

Directions. Type the following letter in the modified block form with 5-space paragraph indentions. Use open punctuation. As Mr. Munson's official title is long, it should be typed on a line by itself. Make two carbon copies of this letter.

The notation appearing below the following letter is to be typed on the two carbon copies only. After you have typed the letter, remove it from the typewriter; lay the original letterhead and the top carbon sheet aside; insert the carbon copies of the letter and one carbon sheet into the machine. Type the notation with single spacing and a 5-space indention below the reference initials. Do not type the word "Notation." The notation will appear on the two carbon copies only; the top carbon copy will be retained for the files and the all-carbon copy will be sent to Mr. Hughes.

Mr. C. A. Munson Superintendent of 51
Shipments Pittsburgh Coke Com- 80
pany Pittsburgh 3, Pennsylvania 112
Dear Sir We have your letter with 146
regard to the handling of PCC Cars 181
875 and 1202, the last report on 214
which indicated that the cars were 249
empty at New Castle on February 9 283
and 10, respectively. (P) We find 314
that Car 875 was moved from New 346
Castle to McKees Rocks on Feb- 375
ruary 13. From this point it was 409
moved to Dickerson Run on Feb- 438
ruary 14 and was delivered to the 472
Pennsylvania Railroad at Summit 504
Transfer on February 16. (P) Car 534
1202 was moved from New Castle to 568
New Castle Junction on February 600
12; from New Castle Junction to 632
McKees Rocks on February 13; and 665

from this point to Dickerson Run on 701
February 14. It was delivered to the 739
Pennsylvania Railroad at Summit 771
Transfer on February 16. (P) You 801
will note that these cars were de- 834
layed slightly at New Castle and at 870
Dickerson Run. The cause for the 904
delay is being investigated. We 937
shall let you hear from us further 972
in connection with this matter as 1006
soon as we have completed the in- 1038
vestigation. Yours very truly J. L. 1075
O'Toole Supt., Freight Transporta- 1108
tion (178) 1113

Notation 1122

Mr. Hughes: Will you please inves- 1156
tigate the delay of these cars at New 1194
Castle and Dickerson Run and let 1227
me know the reason for the delay. 1262
At the same time see that it is thor- 1298
oughly understood by all concerned 1333
at these points that the PCC cars 1367
must be given prompt movement in 1400
the future. J. L. O'Toole 1426

PROBLEM 11

Directions. Type the letter in the block form. Type the third paragraph, which is a quotation, in the block form with a 5-space indention at the left and the right. Use open punctuation. This problem is an incoming letter that is not to be typed on a letterhead. Type the word C O P Y at the top of the page as you did in Problem 2, page 191.

Dr. Earl O. Beatty Principal, Long 51
Academy Omaha 6, Nebraska Dear 82
Dr. Beatty The Charters and Whit- 114
ley study, *Analysis of Secretarial* 149
Duties and Traits, is perhaps the 183
best source of secretarial traits that 222
you can find. This book is published 260
by The Williams & Wilkins Com- 289
pany, Mount Royal and Guilford 320
Avenues, Baltimore, Maryland. (P) 351
I have before me a summary of this 386
study. The summary is published 419
by the National Junior Personnel 452
Service, Inc., at 70 Fifth Avenue, 487
New York. From it I quote the fol- 521

Directions. In Lessons 101, 103, and 105, type several 1-minute writings on the following sentences for calling the guide. Be guided in your writing by the call of the 15-, 12-, or 10-second guide as directed by your teacher. Progress from one sentence to the next when you have succeeded in writing a sentence the required number of times in one minute.

Group 1: The sentences in this group call for the word-recognition level of response. You should be able to make your best rate of speed on these sentences. Think the words as you type.

Group 2: The sentences in this group call for the stroke level of response, although you will be able to type a few of the words at the word-recognition level. Work for equalized power behind each stroke as you type these sentences. Keep the carriage moving.

Group 3: The sentences in this group call for the combination-level of response. Work for a smooth, fluent rhythm as you type these sentences.

(I) Balanced-Hand Sentences

	Strokes	Words 15″	Words 12″	Words 10″
(1) It is their turn to do work for us.	35	28	35	42
(2) He kept the big bicycle he got for them.	40	32	40	48
(3) The giant robot can handle the digit problem.	45	36	45	54
(4) He may work with them if they sign the usual form.	50	40	50	60
(5) They may spend the day by the lake in the ancient city.	55	44	55	66
(6) She kept the ornaments but spent the profit for the bicycle.	60	48	60	72

(2) Sentences Emphasizing One-Hand Words

	Strokes	Words 15″	Words 12″	Words 10″
(7) You were assessed the minimum rate.	35	28	35	42
(8) You are regarded by him as a monopolist.	40	32	40	48
(9) We referred him to you as the only addressee.	45	36	45	54
(10) His humility was great as we segregated the brave.	50	40	50	60
(11) The best pupil read the wage data from the trade paper.	55	44	55	66
(12) You will be awarded the maximum fee if you accept the order.	60	48	60	72

(3) Sentences Combining One-Hand and Balanced-Hand Sequences

	Strokes	Words 15″	Words 12″	Words 10″
(13) Call them if the contract is ready.	35	28	35	42
(14) We sent the statement with the contract.	40	32	40	48
(15) You will be delighted with the wage increase.	45	36	45	54
(16) It is certain that he will sign the two contracts.	50	40	50	60
(17) In my opinion the statements are contrary to the facts.	55	44	55	66
(18) These gazettes will last a long time if you treat them well.	60	48	60	72

of April 28. They offer the follow- 321
ing as substitutions (See *Brewer's* 364
Catalog No. 86-72B): (P) For Stock 414
Item #3, they offer their #72 which 450
is similar to #3, as specified, except 489
that the dimensions are 45 x 24¼ 522
inches instead of 45 x 24½ inches. 558
They offer this substitute item in 593
dozen sheet lots @ 75¢ each sheet, 628
less a special 15% discount in gross 665
lots. (P) For Stock Item #6, they 696
offer their new Stock Item #8X* (#6 732
discontinued). This new improved 766
item lists @ $5 in lots of 100 as com- 803
pared with $5.25 for Item #6. (P) 834
For Stock Item #7, they offer an- 866
other new Stock Item #9X* (made 898
completely of plastic). This mate- 932
rial is quoted in gross lots @ 15¢ 967
each; less-than-gross lots, 17½¢ 1000
each. (P) The discount and terms 1030
of payment remain the same: 5/10, 1065
2/30, N/60. (P) Let me know if 1093
these substitutions are satisfactory 1130
to your office so that the Purchase 1166
Order may be written. 1187

PROBLEM 8

Directions. Use the modified block form
with no indentions for paragraphs. Use open
punctuation. Those paragraphs beginning
"Quantity," "Price," and "Terms" are to be
typed in inverted style, indented 5 spaces on
the left and the right, with the headings in
capital letters. Type the dictator's name in the
position for the reference initials.

```
In answer to your recent letter making inquiry as to the
best price we can quote on 300 pairs of hinges, we quote
you as follows:

QUANTITY:   300 pairs hinges, like sample #714,
            flat back, 3" joint, left leaf 1½",
            right leaf 1¼".

PRICE:      Net price of $50 for the lot.

TERMS:      C. O. D.

We shall be glad to receive this initial order from you.
Immediate shipment of the 300 pairs of hinges can be made.
```

Illustration 50 — Inverted Paragraphs with
Subjects Typed in Capitals

De Luxe Furniture Company 2354 47
Euclid Avenue Cleveland 14, Ohio 79
Attention Purchasing Agent Gen- 109
tlemen In answer to your recent let- 144

ter making inquiry as to the best 178
price we can quote on 300 pairs of 213
hinges, we quote you as follows: 247
(P) QUANTITY: 300 pairs hinges, 276
like sample #714, flat back, 3" joint, 315
left leaf 1½", right leaf 1¼". (P) 347
PRICE: Net price of $50 for the lot. 386
(P) TERMS: C. O. D. (P) We shall 411
be glad to receive this initial order 449
from you. Immediate shipment of 482
the 300 pairs of hinges can be made. 520
(P) We do not believe that you can 551
duplicate this quotation elsewhere. 588
We have these hinges in stock and 622
are willing to quote you an attrac- 656
tive price in order to dispose of them 695
promptly. Very truly yours (L. C. 729
Walleck) Manager, Sales Depart- 758
ment *(125)* 762

PROBLEM 9

Directions. Type the following letter in the
indented form with 5-space paragraph indentions. As a letterhead is not used, the heading
contains the complete address of the writer.
Use close punctuation. Type the street number
and name on the twelfth line from the top of
the sheet.

The signature "Mrs. W. C. Bayne" should
be typed in parentheses 4 single spaces below
the complimentary close. The spaces between
the complimentary close and the typed signature are left for the penwritten signature "Bess
R. Bayne." This letter illustrates the correct
method for a married woman to use in signing
a business letter.

Observe that a personal name representing
a corporation requires the use of the salutation *Gentlemen.*

1164 Ridgeway Avenue, Plainfield, 50
New Jersey. John Wanamaker, 79
Ninth Street, New York 8, N. Y. 111
Gentlemen: I am enclosing an ap- 143
plication card for a change in my 176
charge account. This account should 213
be changed from the name of Bess 246
R. Thomas to Mrs. W. C. Bayne. 278
(P) As I am not opening a new ac- 306
count but merely changing the name 341
in which the account is to be used, 377
I assume that the references given 412

Directions. In Lessons 102 and 104, type 1-minute writings on the following paragraphs. Start with the first paragraph and repeat the paragraph until you can type it in one minute without error. Then, progress to the next paragraph. The first paragraph calls for a rate of 30 words per minute.

Stay relaxed, concentrate on the **material to be typed,** and type without a sense of hurry to improve your accuracy.

		STROKES	WORDS
30-word paragraph.	A typist's position at the machine is of great importance. He must	68	14
	sit erect, squarely in front of the machine. Such a position will reduce	142	28
	tension.	150	30
35-word paragraph.	The body of the typist should be held in an upright position. It	66	13
	should be erect, but relaxed. The comfort of the typist should be	133	27
	kept in mind when we talk of good position.	176	35
40-word paragraph.	Typists often sit too close to their machines or too far from them.	69	14
	Either of these positions will throw the hands and arms out of posi-	136	27
	tion and create tension. Your teacher will show you how to sit.	200	40
45-word paragraph.	The elbows must be held close to the sides of the body, and the	64	13
	arms should rise from the elbow at a thirty-degree angle. When the	132	26
	arms are out of position, free movement of the fingers is hindered	199	40
	and undue motion creeps in.	226	45
50-word paragraph.	All of us make some mistakes as we type. The number of errors	63	13
	will vary in inverse ratio to the amount of thought we give to what	131	26
	we are doing and how we are doing it. You must train your mind to	198	40
	avoid distractions and to concentrate upon your work.	251	50
55-word paragraph.	Another factor that adds to the number of errors we make and	61	12
	keeps us from reaching high speeds is the habit of taking the eyes	128	26
	off the copy to see what is being typed. If you read the copy care-	195	39
	fully, the fingers will make the correct strokes and you will get good	266	53
	results.	274	55
60-word paragraph.	You should make it a point to get the most out of your typewriter.	68	14
	Make it work for you rather than against you. You should get great	136	27
	pleasure out of the success you experience from day to day. You will	206	41
	see this growth best if you will plot the results of your timed writ-	274	55
	ings on a progress chart.	299	60

Agent Gentlemen: Our sales man- 144
ager has just handed me a message 178
straight from the shoulder. Here it 215
is: (P) The American Engineering 245
Society should have a copy of our 279
new pamphlet, *Visible Purchase* 325
Control. The sales record card of 366
this society shows that, although 400
Fidex visible card records are now 435
being used in other departments, 468
one of the most important depart- 500
ments, the purchasing department, 534
has been overlooked. (P) *Visible* 571
Purchase Control, which is the 618
pamphlet our sales manager wants 651
you to read, has been carefully pre- 686
pared and explains in an interesting, 724
concise way the methods that sim- 756
plify and multiply the usefulness of 793
the vital records that are so essential 833
to the success of a progressive pur- 868
chasing department. (P) If you 896
want a copy of this pamphlet, just 931
make a note of the fact on the lower 968
margin of this letter and return the 1005
letter to us. The rest will be up to 1043
us. We will do our part without obli- 1081
gating you in any way. Yours very 1116
truly, (C. A. Neeley, Jr.) Manager, 1152
Systems Department. (P) Since the 1182
Society has found our Fidex visible 1218
card records so useful in other de- 1252
partments, you may wish to check 1285
with the managers of some of the 1318
other departments about their suc- 1351
cess with Fidex. *(193)* 1367

PROBLEM 6

Directions. Type the letter in the modified block form. Use mixed punctuation. No indention is to be made for the paragraphs, and the attention line is to be started even with the left margin. Use a 50-space line for the letter and leave 7 spaces between the date and the address.

Tabulate the list of salesmen and the amounts of annual premiums in two columns. Leave 6 spaces between columns.

STROKES

Automobile Insurance Company 3927 50
North Michigan Avenue Chicago 4, 83
Illinois Attention Mr. John H. Shel- 118

don Gentlemen: Below is the list 152
of annual premiums for each of the 187
five salesmen in our region: 217

Logan R. Kirkwood $ 8,250.00 247
Philip A. Condon 10,965.75 274
Edward T. O'Malley 12,345.50 303
Raymond C. Connelly 15,084.30 333
Lawrence G. Triplett 17,940.85 364

(P) The total of $64,586.40 repre- 393
sents an increase of 12 per cent over 431
our premium income for last year. 466
Sincerely yours, Karl G. Bragg, 498
Branch Manager *(100)* 512

PROBLEM 7

Directions. Type as an Interoffice Communication the following material, which provides for a review of all the symbols on the typewriter. The material is to be typed on a full sheet of paper. If a printed form is not available, the heading, INTEROFFICE COMMUNICATION, is to be centered 2 inches from the top edge of the paper. Type your initials for reference at the left margin, a triple space below the last line of the memorandum.

Adjust your marginal stops so that you will have left and right margins of approximately $1\frac{1}{2}$ inches. Indent each paragraph 10 spaces. Study Illustration 49 and note the arrangement of the opening lines as well as the spacing between parts.

INTEROFFICE COMMUNICATION
(triple space)

Date: May 5, 195-
From: Allan Jones, Specification's Clerk
To: R. W. King, Purchasing Agent
           (double space)
Subject: Brewer & Company Quotation
           (triple space)

Brewer & Company are unable to quote on Stock Items #3, #6, and #7 as requested in the "bid sheet" sent to them with

Illustration 49 — Heading for an Interoffice Communication

STROKES

Date: May 5, 195— From: Allan 49
Jones, Specification's Clerk To: R. 86
W. King, Purchasing Agent Sub- 115
ject: Brewer & Company Quotation 150
(P) Brewer & Company are unable 178
to quote on Stock Items #3, #6, and 214
#7 as requested in the "bid sheet" 249
sent to them with Mr. Brown's letter 286

INSTRUCTIONAL BLOCK 9

PROBLEMS IN TABULATING

As soon as you begin using the greater part of your period for typing business papers such as tabulated reports, you will find some loss in straight-copy skill unless you do the needed daily practice for skill maintenance. The lessons of this instructional block provide for the minimum of drill and straight-copy work. Whenever you complete the assigned work and have some time left, use the time for drill or straight-copy typing. Label all such work *Bonus Typing*.

SECTION 16. Tabulating: Judgment Placement

LESSON 106

CONDITIONING PRACTICE 106   *5 minutes*

Directions. Type each line of the conditioning practice twice. As time permits, select for repetitive practice the sentence or sentences on which you made errors. This will be the uniform assignment for typing the conditioning practices in all lessons in this section.

	STROKES
With amazing dexterity, the jovial squaws plucked the big white fowls.	70
Please ship Order No. 750 for 36 typewriters, 49 desks, and 128 lamps.	70
Jack Brown and Don Hutson will visit Chicago, New York, and St. Louis.	70
Typing with a sense of hurry will often cause you to make many errors.	70

TABULATION SPEED-UP 106   *10 minutes*

Directions. 1. Set the stop for the left margin at 7 for a pica- or at 16 for an elite-type machine; move the stop for the right margin to the end of the line. The first column will be typed at the left margin. Clear the tabulator rack. You will set the machine so as to have 6 spaces between columns; therefore, set the tabulator stops as directed below:

	PICA	ELITE
First tabulator stop	16	25
Second tabulator stop	25	34
Third tabulator stop	34	43
Fourth tabulator stop	43	52
Fifth tabulator stop	53	62
Sixth tabulator stop	63	72
Seventh tabulator stop	73	82

2. Use double spacing and type two 3-minute timed writings. If you finish the drill before time is called, start at the beginning and repeat as much of the drill as possible. Determine the cwpm for each writing. Type the first writing at the *control level of practice*; type the second writing at the *skill-building level of practice*.

Technique Emphasis: Hold the tabulator bar or key down until the carriage has stopped its movement. As all typing will be done on the third and fourth banks of keys, keep the fingers well curved so that the reaches may be made easily and quickly. Let the fingers do the work and keep the hands and arms quiet.

								STROKES
try	546	you	697	ripe	4803	tour	5974	36
top	590	yet	635	rope	4903	were	2343	72
rot	495	rut	475	wire	2843	wipe	2803	108
tow	592	tie	583	your	6974	type	5603	143

correctly. Our office is located in 734
the Grant Building and not in the 768
Oliver Building. Yours very truly, 804
WRIGHT SIGN AND POSTER 827
COMPANY Jasper L. Wright, Pres- 857
ident Enclosure *(117)* 872

PROBLEM 3—ENCLOSURE FOR PROBLEM 2

Directions. Center this copy vertically and horizontally on a full sheet of paper. Use double spacing with a triple space after the heading. Type the heading in capitals. Center each line from the same number on the scale.

WRIGHT SIGNS

Wright Signs at the Right Prices

Signs for Every Purpose

Silk Screen Displays

Picture Painting

Outdoor Signs

Card Signs

WRIGHT SIGN AND POSTER CO.

Grant Building

Telephone ATlantic 4838

PROBLEM 4

Directions. Use the modified block form, 10-space paragraph indentions, and close punctuation. Make one carbon copy. As the company name is long, type the official title in the address on the first line and separate it from the personal name by a comma. Begin the subject at the paragraph point. Type the dictator's name in the position for the reference initials. Address an envelope.

STROKES

Mr. Jasper L. Wright, President, 49
Wright Sign and Poster Company, 81
Grant Building, Pittsburgh 7, Penn- 115
sylvania. Dear Sir: SUBJECT: 147
Directory Advertisement (P) Thank 178
you for the copy for your directory 214
advertisement. We are glad to in- 247
crease your space to a half column. 284
(P) The second line of the copy you 316

sent will not fit the space exactly. 354
The column is 2½ inches wide. Un- 387
less the line is set in small type, we 426
shall have to crowd the copy some- 459
what to get it on one line. Would 494
you agree to have the line read as 529
follows? 539

Wright Signs—Right Prices 567

(P) With this change the line will 598
look good and can be set in the same 635
type as the other lines in the copy. 673
(P) If you have some other sugges- 702
tion that we can use in setting up 737
this advertisement, write us. Yours 774
very truly, (F. M. Johnson) Man- 803
ager *(119)* 807

PROBLEM 5

Directions. Type the letter in the modified block form with no indentions for paragraphs. Center the attention line (See Illustration 48). Type the second paragraph, which is quoted material, in block form indented 5 spaces from the right and left margins. Use mixed punctuation. Type the dictator's initials and name in the position for the reference initials.

The final paragraph is a postscript that is to be started on the second line below the reference initials. It need not be preceded by the letters *P. S.* that are sometimes added to indicate a postscript.

```
American Engineering Society
3856 Marchand Street
Milwaukee 10, Wisconsin

                Attention Purchasing Agent

Gentlemen:

Our sales manager has just handed me a message straight from
the shoulder.  Here it is:

        The American Engineering Society should have a copy
        of our new pamphlet, Visible Purchase Control.  The
        sales record card of this society shows that, although
        Fidex visible card records are now being used in other
        departments, one of the most important departments,
        the purchasing department, has been overlooked.

Visible Purchase Control, which is the pamphlet our sales mana-
ger wants you to read, has been carefully prepared and explains
in an interesting, concise way the methods that simplify and
```

Illustration 48 — Modified Block Form with a Centered Attention Line and an Indented Quotation

STROKES

American Engineering Society 3856 50
Marchand Street Milwaukee 10, 80
Wisconsin Attention Purchasing 113

TABULATING

Analyze carefully the facts and figures to be tabulated before you determine the placement of the general headings and the headings of the columns. The width of each column and the general layout of the whole must then be determined. All this should first be worked out *with pencil and paper*.

In the arrangement of words or phrases in tabulated form, the left margin of the column should be kept straight. In the tabulating of figures, the right margin of the column should be kept straight unless decimals are being used, in which case the decimal points must be kept in a vertical column.

TABULATING STEPS

On most typewriters, six single line spaces make a vertical inch. Pica type has 10 spaces to the horizontal inch; elite type has 12 spaces to the horizontal inch. Paper 8½ x 11 inches has 66 writing lines of 85-pica or 102-elite spaces.

1. **Determine the vertical placement:**

   a. Count the lines required to type the material; include extra lines needed between the main and the secondary or columnar headings. Note also if the material is to be single or double spaced.

   b. Subtract this number from 66, the number of available lines on 8½ x 11 inch paper. If the remainder is an odd number, subtract 1 from it so that it will be a number evenly divisible by 2.

   c. Divide by 2. This result is the number of lines you must leave at the top of the paper before you type the main heading.

2. **Determine the horizontal placement of the columns:**

   a. Count the number of spaces that will be used in typing the longest line in each column.

   b. Decide upon the number of spaces to be left between columns for best appearance of the tabulated copy.

   c. Add the number of spaces required to type the longest line of each column to the total number of spaces to be left

between columns. Subtract this sum from 85 for pica type or from 102 for elite type.

   d. Divide this number by 2. This is the space to be left for the margins. If an extra space remains, add it to the left margin.

3. **Set the stop for the left margin and the tabulator stops for the columns:**

   a. Set the stop for the left margin at the point determined by Step 2-d.

   b. Add to this number the number of spaces to be used in typing the longest line of the first column and the number of spaces to be left between the first and second columns. Set the first tabulator stop at the point that corresponds to this sum.

   c. To the number representing the tabulator stop for the second column, add the number of spaces to be used in typing the longest line in the second column and the number of spaces to be left between the second and third columns. Set the second tabulator stop at the point that corresponds to this sum.
   Continue in this way until the tabulator stops for all columns in the problem have been set.

   d. It will not be necessary to set the stop for the right margin. It may be moved to the end of the scale.

4. **Type the headings:**

   a. Space down to allow for the top margin determined in Step 1-c.

   b. Center the main heading. (Rules for horizontal centering are given on page 57.)

   c. Center the secondary heading or headings, if any.

5. **Type the columns:**

   a. Space down to allow the number of spaces desired between the main or the secondary heading and the body of the tabulation.

   b. Start the columns at the points at which the stop for the left margin and the tabulator stops were set in Step 3.

PROBLEM I

Directions. Type the letter with two carbon copies. Use close punctuation, 10-space paragraph indentions, and the following special modifications:

1. Place the date to end at the right margin.

2. Type the address with all lines blocked at the left margin.

3. Use the initials and the name of the dictator in the reference notation. See Illustration 45 for the arrangement of the closing lines.

```
          We certainly wish for you all success in
your new business venture.

                    Yours very truly,


                              Manager


FMJohnson/abs

Copy to Mr. Wexford, Service Engineer
```

Illustration 45 — Closing Lines with Special Variations

	STROKES
Mr. Kenneth L. MacArthur, 2979	47
Brighton Road, Bellevue, Pennsyl-	79
vania. Dear Mr. MacArthur: We	111
appreciate the request for telephone	148
service contained in your recent let-	184
ter. (P) Before we can say definitely	219
that we can furnish the service at	254
your new place of business, it will be	293
necessary for us to investigate all	329
the facilities available. Our Bellevue	369
lines are used practically full time.	407
(P) The survey of available facilities	442
will be completed in a day or two.	478
If any class of service is available,	516
we shall immediately send you an	549
application card. (P) We certainly	581
wish for you all success in your new	618
business venture. Yours very truly,	655
(F. M. Johnson) Manager Copy to	685
Mr. Wexford, Service Engineer *(89)*	714

PROBLEM 2

Directions. Use the modified block form with no indentions for paragraphs and mixed punctuation. The attention and the subject lines are to be blocked, and the word *Subject* is to be made prominent by being typed in capitals.

```
The Bell Telephone Company
Seventh Avenue
Pittsburgh 16, Pennsylvania

Attention Mr. F. M. Johnson

Gentlemen:

SUBJECT:  Copy for Directory Advertisement

We want to increase our advertising space in the
next issue of your directory.  This directory is
one of our most effective advertising mediums.
```

Illustration 46 — **Placement of the Blocked Attention and Subject Lines. Note that the Word *Subject* Is Made Prominent by Being Typed in Capitals.**

This problem is an incoming letter. It is therefore not to be typed on the letterhead. Indicate that you are typing a copy, not an original letter, by typing the word C O P Y (with a space after each letter) centered about $1\frac{1}{2}$ inches from the top of the paper. Note how this heading is shown in Illustration 47.

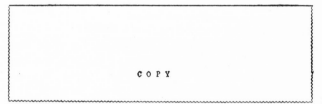

```
                    C O P Y
```

Illustration 47 — The Copy Notation for the Copy of an Incoming Letter

	STROKES
The Bell Telephone Company Sev-	46
enth Avenue Pittsburgh 16, Pennsyl-	80
vania Attention Mr. F. M. Johnson	114
Gentlemen: SUBJECT: Copy for	145
Directory Advertisement (P) We	173
want to increase our advertising	206
space in the next issue of your direc-	243
tory. This directory is one of our	279
most effective advertising mediums.	316
(P) In the next issue of the direc-	346
tory, we want to use a half column.	383
According to our contract, a column	419
is $2\frac{1}{2}$ by $10\frac{1}{4}$ inches. We believe	452
that the copy we enclose is spaced	487
properly for a half column. If you	523
find that changes must be made in	557
our copy, however, submit proof for	593
our approval. (P) Let us remind you	626
that in the current printing of the	662
directory our address was listed in-	697

PROBLEM 1

Directions. Type the problem in two columns as shown. Center the problem vertically on a half sheet of paper. (There are 33 writing lines on a half sheet of paper that is $8\frac{1}{2}$ x $5\frac{1}{2}$ inches in size.)

In solving the problem, first determine the vertical placement and then determine the horizontal placement as outlined in the *Tabulating Steps.*

In determining the vertical placement, allow for a triple space after the main heading (to be counted as two blank lines). Double-space the lines of the columns (each double space to be counted as one blank line).

In determining the horizontal placement of the columns, leave 20 spaces between columns. When typing the data, backspace once for the dollar symbol with the first amount in the second column. *Note:* The longest line in the first column contains 14 spaces; the longest line in the second column contains 9 spaces not including the dollar symbol which is to be used with the first amount only.

COMPARISON OF JULY SALES BY DEPARTMENTS		STROKES
		40
Clothing	$26,132.56	61
Cosmetics	2,374.50	81
Dry Goods	1,981.70	101
Furniture	42,728.65	121
Jewelry	7,090.26	139
Sporting Goods	10,567.19	163

PROBLEM 2

Directions. Center this problem vertically on a half sheet of paper. Leave 10 spaces between columns.

NAMES AND NUMBERS OF NEW EMPLOYEES		STROKES
		35
Barker, Norma A.	9392	57
Carpenter, James F.	498	82
Goode, Mary Ann	2485	103
Mansfield, Ernest R.	793	129
Steelman, Harriet	3064	152
Winters, Robert J.	577	175

PROBLEM 3

Directions. 1. If time permits, proofread carefully the table you typed for Problem 2. Indicate by making pencil corrections any changes that need to be made in your copy.

2. Retype the table using your copy with penciled corrections, if any, as the copy from which you type. Make the corrections you have indicated as you retype the copy. Type with good techniques; hold your eyes on the copy; use each machine part properly; and try to type the table in less time than was needed for typing it as Problem 2.

SECTION 22. Special Problems in Office Procedure

Directions. In each lesson in this section, type each line of the conditioning practice twice. As time permits, select for repetitive practice the sentence or sentences in which you made errors.

	STROKES
A crazy driver quickly jumped the curb to stop the getaway of six men.	70
She bought Royal radio No. 16743 and matching record player No. 28950.	70
H. V. McGil, President of McGil & Company, just returned from England.	70
They may go today if they work with vigor on the big fiducial problem.	70

Directions. Take a 10-minute timed writing in Lessons 141 and 144. Determine the cwpm.

Each paragraph has every letter of the alphabet and a syllable intensity of 1.30.

	STROKES PARA.	TOTAL
Letters tell the story of what is to be sold, and they handle the	66	
details of credit and collection. If they are poor, the effect will show	140	
in the volume of business. There are many kinds of letters and each may	213	
have a slant all its own. Letters of power, though, have some things in	286	
common. Look at a sales letter, for instance. The first requisite of a	359	
good sales letter is that it be worded to persuade, just as the letter that	435	
refuses credit must be tactfully worded to hold good will. You can't	505	
refuse credit bluntly and still hope to get the cash order. Besides, a	577	
poor risk now may be "in the money" next month or next year. Most	644	
businessmen realize that it pays to build good will for their company	714	
through the right kind of letters.	748	
Every letter is a sales letter even though it is written about credit,	71	819
the collection of an account, or an adjustment on a shipment. The cus-	141	889
tomer should always be sold on the company with which he is dealing.	211	959
This is frequently done best through the letters that deal with the many	284	1032
phases of business transactions. If a letter has the "you attitude" and	357	1105
is couched in clear, tactful, and friendly language, it is a true sales	429	1177
letter no matter with what subject it deals. Writers of good letters are	503	1251
made and not born; they learn through study and practice. The writer	573	1321
of a good letter must know the facts about which he is writing; next, he	646	1394
must take time to think through the ideas he wants to express; and	713	1461
he must be sure to say what he wants to say in a way that will give	781	1529
the desired effect. You can learn something of how to write good	855	1603
letters if you study with zeal those that you are to type in these lessons.	922	1670

LESSON 107

CONDITIONING PRACTICE 107

5 *minutes*

STROKES

A jovial man in this plaza fixed Will's bicycle during a quick squall.   70
These contributions of $389, $156.74, $12.74, and $4.50 total $562.98.   70
The Official Court Reporter of the Supreme Court is Raymond L. Bryant.   70
Let your fingers do their work by keeping your wrists and hands quiet.   70

TABULATION SPEED-UP 107

10 *minutes*

Directions. Type two 3-minute timed writings on the material given as Tabulation Speed-Up 106, page 145. Follow the same directions but work for an increase in your stroking rate.

PROBLEM TYPING 107

25 *minutes*

PROBLEM 1

Directions. Type the problem in two columns as shown. Center the problem vertically on a half sheet of paper. Triple-space between the main heading and the secondary heading. Double-space between the secondary heading and the columnar headings and between the columnar headings and the first line of the columns. Single-space the lines of the columns. In determining the horizontal placement of the columns, leave 20 spaces between columns. The columnar headings are to be centered over the longest line in each column.

To determine the horizontal placement of each columnar heading:

1. First, determine and set the stops for the columns as outlined in the *Tabulating Steps.*

2. Second, from each stop, space forward to the center of the longest line in the column.

At this point, backspace once for each 2 spaces in the columnar heading. For example, the longest line in the first column has 14 spaces. At the point where you have set the stop for the left margin for this column, space forward 7 spaces; then backspace once for each 2 spaces in the columnar heading.

> NOTE: As the columnar heading is longer than the longest line in the column, it will be necessary to use the margin release when backspacing in order to move the carriage beyond the marginal stop.

Type the columnar heading in its proper position. Next, move the carriage to the tabulator stop set for the second column. Space forward 4 spaces (longest line has 9 spaces—disregard the extra space) and then backspace to center the columnar heading for the second column.

		STROKES
UNIVERSAL DEPARTMENT STORE		27
August Comparison of Sales, 195—		60
Name of Department	Amount of Sales	130
Clothing	$56,283.21	151
Dry Goods	7,469.23	171
Furniture	98,892.00	191
Jewelry	6,789.45	209
Millinery	3,526.75	229
Notions	1,479.40	247
Pottery	5,148.25	265
Shoe	11,500.00	280
Sporting Goods	33,678.90	305
Stationery	679.36	325

LESSON 138

STROKES

Exquisite rings were quickly made by the jovial friends on the piazza.   70

Check #3149 will pay the premiums on Policies #5869, #2057, and #7395.   70

Mauna Loa is a huge volcano in Hawaii National Park, Hawaiian Islands.   70

Lay the rocks end to end by the ivy bed and put the clay between them.   70

PROBLEM TYPING 138   *35 minutes*

PROBLEM 1

Directions. Type the letter in the indented style with close punctuation. Use the current date. Make a carbon copy of the letter and address an envelope for it.

STROKES

	STROKES
Mr. Theodore Van Buren, 4723 Sun-	48
set Boulevard, Los Angeles 38,	79
California. Dear Mr. Van Buren:	113
Subject: SUPERIOR TELEVI-	138
SION We have just published a new	172
pamphlet which no dealer should	204
miss reading. Its title is SUPERIOR	241
TELEVISION, and it contains care-	273
ful descriptions of a large number of	311
SUPERIOR television sets that are	345
available to dealers at wholesale	379
prices. (P) Over a period of years,	412
we have developed what we con-	441
sider to be the ultimate in television	480
style and performance. We should	514
like you to make our sets available	550
to your own customers. We know	582
that both you and your customers	615
would be pleased. (P) Just sign	644
your name on the enclosed postal	677
card, drop it in the mail, and a copy	715
of this new pamphlet will be yours.	752
Very truly yours, HOLLYWOOD	780
TELEVISION COMPANY A. J.	805
Fisk, Manager Enclosure (107)	828

PROBLEM 2

Directions. Type the letter with a carbon copy. Use the indented style, close punctuation, and the current date. Capitalize and punctuate the entire letter correctly. Add an appropriate salutation and complimentary close. Address an envelope.

STROKES

	STROKES
mr bradley o jefferson 4983 beech-	52
wood drive springfield 10 illinois	91
subject better hotel accommodations	147
when you go to a first-class hotel	182
you have a right to expect first-class	221
accommodations at a reasonable cost.	259
you want good food a comfortable	293
and attractive sleeping room cour-	327
teous service luxurious lounge and	364
all the other facilities of a hotel that	405
caters to a first-class clientele. you	445
get all this—and more—when you	478
become the guest of THE LAKE-	506
SHORE chicago's famed hotel situ-	539
ated on chicago's famous lake front.	577
(P) on your next trip to chicago	606
make our hotel your home. bring the	643
family too. the enclosed rate card	690
lists the type of accommodations we	726
have at the reasonable prices quoted.	765
note too that as our guest you will	803
have the use of our library and your	840
children will have the use of our	874
playroom. (P) a request by card let-	907
ter telephone or telegram will re-	942
serve suitable accommodations for	976
you. i shall look forward to seeing	1013
you soon. roger m davidson man-	1064
ager enclosure (151)	1078

PROBLEM 2

Directions. Retype the table given as Problem 1, making the following changes:

1. Leave 10 spaces between columns.

2. Heading for first column: *Department;* heading for second column: *Sales*

Make the machine adjustments called for as quickly as possible. Maintain good techniques and work for an increased stroking rate as you type the table.

LESSON 108

CONDITIONING PRACTICE 108 — 5 minutes

STROKES

An amazing and exciting cove rescue was made quickly by the fast jeep.	70
The shipment included 132 divans, 156 lamps, 48 desks, and 790 chairs.	70
The Audit Report of Continental, Ltd., was prepared by Bryant & Keats.	70
Concentration and relaxation will help you conquer your typing errors.	70

TABULATION SPEED-UP 108 — 10 minutes

Directions. Set the stops as you had them set for Problem 1, page 148. Then type two 3-minute timed writings on this problem. If you finish the tabulation before time is called, start again at the beginning of the columns.

Determine the cwpm for each writing. Type the first writing *at the control level of practice.* Type the second writing *at the skill-building level of practice.*

25 minutes

PROBLEM TYPING 108

PROBLEM 1

Directions. Type the problem in three columns as shown. Center the problem vertically on a full sheet of paper. Double-space the data in the columns. Use the correct spacing after the main heading, the secondary heading, and the columnar headings. Use 6 spaces between columns. Divide the remaining spaces between the left and right margins.

STROKES

Northwestern Supply Company			28
Comparison of Monthly Sales Figures			64
Month	1951	1952	96
January	$150,362	$155,750	124
February	234,896	240,298	149
March	98,467	134,648	171
April	173,905	157,832	193
May	267,094	276,230	213
June	319,810	346,118	234
July	76,578	84,230	255
August	95,100	110,459	278
September	176,226	187,956	304
October	349,578	385,750	328
November	364,290	375,640	353
December	186,439	190,478	377

LESSON 137

STROKES

The gig limped back to the jetty rendezvous with six quick men-of-war.   70

He rented the 15-unit apartment building at 3479 Pier Road for $2,680.   70

The huge Roosevelt Dam across the Salt River is near Phoenix, Arizona.   70

With your eyes on the copy, throw the carriage and start the new line.   70

PROBLEM TYPING 137   *35 minutes*
PROBLEM 1

Directions. Type the letter in the indented style with close punctuation. Use the current date. Capitalize and punctuate correctly the address, the subject line, and the closing lines. Add an appropriate salutation and complimentary close. Address an envelope for the letter.

STROKES

mr robert w simpson manager mar-	51
tin-mccullough manufacturers inc	87
wheeling 4 west virginia subject or-	127
der no 8754 We appreciate the order	164
you recently gave our salesman,	196
Walter Lockner. The order is being	232
prepared for immediate shipment.	266
(P) We lack the facts concerning	295
your business that may enable us to	331
set up adequate terms for your ac-	364
count. We therefore shall appreciate	402

STROKES

your sending us a current financial	438
statement and such other informa-	470
tion as we need to determine just	504
what your requirements may be and	538
how we can best regulate our credit	574
terms to meet your needs. (P) So	604
that there will be no delay in your	640
receiving the merchandise you have	675
ordered, we suggest that you author-	710
ize us to send a sight draft with bill	749
of lading attached. In the mean-	781
time, we shall review the statements	818
you send us to determine the most	852
satisfactory credit terms for you.	888
(P) Thank you again for your order.	921
We hope you will authorize us to	954
ship it immediately as suggested.	989
e r west sales manager *(146)*	1014

PROBLEM 2

Directions. Study the following paragraphs on erasing errors on carbon copies; then type the copy in manuscript form. Make a carbon copy. Erase and correct all errors.

ERASING ERRORS ON CARBON COPIES

To erase errors on carbon copies follow these steps: (1) Turn the cylinder forward a few spaces to provide working room; (2) Move the carriage to the extreme right or left so that the eraser crumbs will not fall into the machine; (3) Lift or move the paper bail out of the way; and, (4) Pull the papers in the machine forward so that you can erase the last carbon copy first.

It is good practice to use a soft eraser for erasing on carbon copies. When the error has been erased on the last carbon copy, blow the eraser crumbs from between the sheets with a quick puff of air, and then place a card (3 by 5 inches, or slightly larger) between the carbon sheet and the last carbon copy to protect the copy from carbon smudges as the next carbon copy is erased. Flip the next carbon copy into position for erasing and erase the error. Blow the crumbs from between the sheets and bring the protective card forward to this position. Erase all other carbon copies in a similar manner. Then, erase the original sheet with the usual hard eraser. Be sure to remove the protective card before typing the correction.

PROBLEM 2

Directions. Type the table given as Problem 1, making the following changes:

1. Single-space the data in the columns.

2. Use your judgment in deciding the number of spaces to leave between columns, but do not use the 6 spaces that you used in Problem 1.

Make the machine adjustments called for with a minimum of waste time. Try to type the table in less time than was needed for typing it in Problem 1. Maintain good techniques by keeping your eyes on the copy, your fingers well curved, and your wrists and arms quiet. Be alert, think as you type, and use each machine part in a quick, precise manner.

LESSON 109

CONDITIONING PRACTICE 109   *5 minutes*

	STROKES
Six big flaming rocket ships zoomed over the picturesque wooden jetty.	70
The zoo ordered 785 birds, 4 bears, 2 wolves, 9 lions, and 163 snakes.	70
Henry may edit the Annual Report of the Office Management Association.	70
Keep your mind on the work to be done, and the progress will be rapid.	70

TABULATION SPEED-UP 109   *10 minutes*

Directions. Set the tabulator stops as you had them set for Problem 1, page 149. Then type two 3-minute writings.

Proceed as you did in Tabulation Speed-Up 108, but work for an increase in your stroking rate.

PROBLEM TYPING 109   *25 minutes*

Directions. 1. Type the tabulated report on a half sheet of paper. Use triple spacing after the main heading and double spacing for the rest of the report.

2. After completing the tabulation, insert a new sheet of paper into the machine and use this problem for a 5-minute timed writing. Determine your cwpm. Contrast your rate with the rate made on the 5-minute timed writing on straight copy.

LIBERTY COLLEGE
BOND HOLDINGS AND INCOME FROM BONDS

Name	Book Value	Actual Value	Income	STROKES
				16
				52
				88
Abbott & Company	$ 4,962.25	$ 5,250.00	$ 200.00	137
Boonesville Ind. School Dist.	500.00	500.00	22.50	193
Tweed Products, Inc.	3,890.00	3,480.00	220.00	240
McKnight, Bourne & Co.	200.00	200.00		282
Homestate Gas & Fuel	2,805.00	2,700.00	120.00	329
Glasgow Lodge (1st Series)	12,591.50	7,554.90	679.58	382
Community Bakeries	3,840.00		200.00	419
Farm Products, Inc.	500.00		15.00	457
Davidson Sales	4,500.00			482
				521
	$33,788.75	$19,684.90	$1,457.08	559

WARD & BERKSTROM

Correspondence Consultants

NEW YORK 5, NEW YORK

January 14, 195-.

STROKES WORDS
19   4

←First Tabulator Stop
←Second Tabulator Stop

Mr. Wallace H. Walker,
   1438 South Delaware Place,
      Roanoke, Virginia.

	STROKES	WORDS
	42	8
	69	14
	89	18

Dear Mr. Walker: 107   21

This letter is written in the indented letter style with   164   33
close punctuation. It differs in these respects from other   224   45
letter styles: 240   48

1. In the address, the second line is indented   288   58
   5 spaces from the left margin; the third line,   335   67
   10 spaces from the left margin.   368   74

2. The attention line, when used, is either cen-   416   83
   tered or begun at the paragraph point.   456   91

3. The subject line, when used, is centered.   503   101

4. The paragraphs are indented 5 or 10 spaces.   552   110

5. In the closing lines, the first line begins   600   120
   5 spaces to the left of center; the second   643   129
   line, at center; and the third line, 5 spaces   689   138
   to the right of center.   714   143

The vertical spacing of the letter will follow the same   770   154
general rules of placement as the other letter styles you   828   166
have used.   840   168

Very truly yours,   858   172

WARD & BERKSTROM   875   175

A. G. Berkstrom

A. G. Berkstrom, Manager   900   180

  906   181

Third Tabulator Stop 5 spaces to left of center →
Fourth Tabulator Stop →
Fifth Tabulator Stop →

AGB:LC

In this letter a period is used at the end of the date line; a comma, after each line of the address except the last; a period, after the last line of the address; a colon, after the salutation; and a comma, after the complimentary close. This form of punctuation is known as *close punctuation.*

(Words in body of letter, 131)

Style Letter 6 — Single-Spaced Indented Letter with Close Punctuation

LESSON 110

CONDITIONING PRACTICE 110

5 minutes

STROKES

The maze box puzzle was quickly solved by the good students from Fiji.	70
These fishing boxes (9½″ x 8¼″ x 14½″) with 6/0 reels sell for $23.75.	70
Alaska Cypress Folding Patio Chairs will be sold by Lane & Kingley Co.	70
The goal is to type the form and handle the elements with proficiency.	70

TABULATION SPEED-UP 110

10 minutes

Directions. Set the tabulator stops as you had them set for Problem Typing 109, page 150. Then type two 3-minute writings on this problem. If you finish the tabulation before time is called, start again at the beginning of the columns.

Determine the cwpm for each writing. Type the first writing *at the control level of practice.* Type the second writing *at the skill-building level of practice.*

PROBLEM TYPING 110

25 minutes

PROBLEM 1

Directions. Type the following unarranged problem on a half sheet of paper. The data are to be arranged in an attractive 4-column table. Double-space the data in the columns.

Main Heading: **MARINE EXCHANGE REPORT OF VESSELS IN PORT**
Secondary Heading: Monday, January 31, 195—
Column Headings: Vessel   Berth   Operator   Destination
Vessel, Coastal Nomad; Berth 51; Operator, Grace Line; Destination, San Francisco
Vessel, Cotton State; Berth B-3; Operator, State Marine Lines; Destination, New Orleans
Vessel, Hawaiian Rancher; Berth 159; Operator, Matson Navigation Co.; Destination, Los Angeles
Vessel, Hulda Maersk (Dan.); Berth 179; Operator, Maersk Line; Destination, New York
Vessel, Poza Rica (Mex.); Berth 107; Operator, Mexican Lines; Destination, Galveston
Vessel, Tosca (Swed.); Berth 178; Operator, Fred Olson Line; Destination, Antwerp

PROBLEM 2

Directions. Type the following unarranged problem on a half sheet of paper. The data are to be arranged in an attractive 4-column table. Double-space the data in the columns.

Main Heading: **HANCOCK COMPANY**
Column Headings: City   Dealer   Location   Telephone
In the city of Sidney the dealer, Collins & Hall, Inc., is located at 23 Water Street. Telephone 6-2780.
In the city of Middleton the dealer, Middleton Appliance Service, is located at 276 Fourth Street. Telephone 5-5850.
In the city of Brownville the dealer, Johnson Electric Co., is located at 25 Mohawk Place. Telephone 7-3003.
In the city of Newton the dealer, Andrews and Maxwell, Inc., is located at 990 Central Avenue. Telephone 3-6357.
In the city of Monroeton the dealer, Walter's TV Shop, is located at 88 Pine Street. Telephone 4-4932.

Sec. 16, Lesson 110

[151]

PROBLEMS IN OFFICE PROCEDURE

SECTION 21. Business Letter Variations

LESSON 136

CONDITIONING PRACTICE 136   *5 minutes*

Directions. Type each line twice, or more if time permits. This will be the uniform assignment for typing the conditioning practices in all lessons in this section.

	STROKES
Helicopters buzz over the unique skyway and free the next jag of mail.	70
Send 15 rolls of #620 films and a #3 filter for Best Pix Camera #47890.	70
The Riviera is a tourist resort along the Mediterranean Sea in Europe.	70
They kept the sprig of ivy they found when they crossed the rye field.	70

PROBLEM TYPING 136   *35 minutes*

PROBLEM I

Directions. Type Style Letter 6 as it is shown on page 187, but use the current date and use your initials as the reference initials.

Use a 60-space line, single spacing, and close punctuation. Leave 6 spaces between the date and the address. Indent the enumerated items 5 spaces from the left and right margins. Set tabulator stops for the indented lines and use the tabulator bar or key to move quickly to those points.

Note the following characteristics of the style letter:

1. The date is centered under the printed letterhead.

2. The company name in the signature is typed in capital letters.

3. The dictator's name and official title are typed on the fourth line below the company name.

4. The reference initials are typed flush with the left margin, 2 spaces below the closing lines. The dictator's initials followed by the typist's initials are used in the reference initials line. If the dictator's name is typed in the signature, it is not necessary, although it is permissible, to include his initials in the reference line as is done in this letter.

PROBLEM 2

Directions. Use close punctuation, the current date, and the indented form similar to Style Letter 6, page 187. Study Illustration 44 and note the placement of the attention line. The attention phrase does not affect the form of the salutation; the letter is addressed to the company and therefore takes a salutation appropriate for a company.

```
Ellsworth & West Company,
     459 Market Street,
          Oakland 3, California.

          Attention Mr. J. D. West
```

Illustration 44 — Indented Address with Attention Line Centered

	STROKES
Ellsworth & West Company, 459	46
Market Street, Oakland 3, California.	85
Attention Mr. J. D. West Gentle-	116
men: This letter is just a reminder	153
that the payment of your account is	189
overdue. We know how easily such	223
things are overlooked and, therefore,	261
take this means of bringing the mat-	296
ter to your attention. (P) We know	328
you will realize that prompt collec-	363
tion of our accounts is required if we	402
are to meet our own bills on time.	438
(P) May we expect a check from you	469
soon. Very truly yours, HARDY &	502
HAMILTON J. F. Hardy, Collec-	530
tions *(65)*	535

PROBLEM 3

Directions. Type the following unarranged problem on a half sheet of paper. The data are to be arranged in an attractive 4-column table. Double-space the data in the columns.

Main Heading: G. W. Mead Corporation

2680 Westwood Avenue

Capital City, Iowa

Secondary Heading: Price List for 1953

Column Headings: <u>Number</u>   <u>Fabric</u>   <u>Colors</u>   <u>Price*</u>

Number 7; Fabric, Silk Shantung; Colors, Blue, Yellow, Lavender; Price*, $17.25

Number 19; Fabric, Orlon; Colors, Green, Navy, Brown; Price*, $16.75

Number 23; Fabric, Rayon Bengaline; Colors, Red, Green, Blue; Price*, $12.50

Number 4; Fabric, Cotton Poplin; Colors, Black, Grey, Purple; Price*, $15.00

Number 54; Fabric, Rayon Suiting; Colors, Green, Blue, Pink; Price*, $14.50

* Gown only; detachable white snap-on collar, 50¢ extra.

LESSON 111

CONDITIONING PRACTICE 111
5 minutes

STROKES

Just strive for maximum progress by quickly organizing the daily work.	70
The bonds of United, Inc., (Series 64032) will mature January 8, 1957.	70
R. H. Dalton of Aubrey, Moore & Wallace Company is visiting in Newark.	70
Be sure to send the letter with these statements to their new address.	70

TABULATION SPEED-UP 111
10 minutes

Directions. Set the tabulator stops as you had them set for Problem Typing 109, page 150. Then type two 3-minute writings on this problem. If you finish the tabulation before time is called, start again at the beginning of the columns.

Determine the cwpm for each writing. Type the first writing at the *control level of practice.* Type the second writing at the *skill-building level of practice.*

PRODUCTION TYPING 111
25 minutes

You are to be timed for 15 minutes on typing the tabulation problems listed on the following page. The time is to include your preparation (determining placement of each problem, setting margins and tabulator stops, etc.) for each problem. Plan the arrangement of each problem quickly so that most of your time will be spent in typing. As you type the problems, maintain good techniques by keeping your eyes on the copy, your fingers well curved, and your wrists and arms quiet. Think as you type and use each machine part in a quick, precise manner.

LESSON 134

CONDITIONING PRACTICE 134

5 minutes

STROKES

With the expert advice of Judge Jackson, I may be able to do the quiz.   70

Is the total charge on Order No. 2378, dated June 10, $45.69 or $4.56?   70

Cape Horn on the lower tip of South America is below Tierra del Fuego.   70

They may visit their friend in the city in order to see the ball game.   70

Skill Maintenance 134. Use each sentence of Conditioning Practice 134 for two 1-minute timed writings. *Type at the control level.*   *12 minutes*

Timed Writing 134. Take a 10-minute timed writing. Use the paragraphs of Timed Writing 131, page 182. Determine your cwpm.   *15 minutes*

Typing for Control 134. In the time that remains, type as many lines of the paragraphs given for Timed Writing 131, page 182, as possible. Your goal is to be errorless writing. Use the following practice procedures: *8 minutes*

(1) Type a line at a slow, easy rate.

(2) Type the line a second time at a slightly increased stroking rate.

(3) Type the line a third time at a rate which is approximately equal to your best stroking rate.

LESSON 135

CONDITIONING PRACTICE 135

5 minutes

STROKES

Fix your mind on the vexing quiz and work the jig problems called for.   70

Today he typed 45 letters, 10 reports, 369 orders, and 278 statements.   70

John Brown made his famous raid at Harpers Ferry before the Civil War.   70

The touching rhapsody of the child prodigy filled us with enchantment.   70

Skill Maintenance 135. Use each sentence of Conditioning Practice 135 for two 1-minute timed writings. Type for control.   *12 minutes*

Progression Typing 135. Use the paragraphs of Progression Typing 133 for errorless typing, according to the instructions given on page 184.   *15 minutes*

Typing for Control 135. Type several 1-minute timed writings on the paragraphs of Timed Writing 131, page 182. Try to type at a rate which is approximately 10 words a minute faster than the best rate you have made on the 10-minute writings on this material. Your goal is to be errorless writing.   *8 minutes*

Reading and making notes of
    directions .... 5 minutes
Timed tabulation production ......15 minutes
Proofreading and determining
    cwpm .... 5 minutes

Directions. Make pencil notations of the following directions for the timed production of tabulation problems. Keep the notations where you can read them easily.

1. Type Problem 1, Lesson 106, page 147.

2. Type Problem 1, Lesson 107, page 148.

3. Type Problem 1, Lesson 108, page 149.

Type each problem according to the directions given for the problem. If you complete the tabulation problems before time is called, start over.

When time is called, proofread each problem carefully and determine your cwpm. Compare your rate with your straight-copy rate. Were you able to type the tabulation problems at approximately 25 to 40 per cent of your straight-copy rate?

LESSON 112

CONDITIONING PRACTICE 112

5 minutes

STROKES

The quaint boat from Jackson capsized by the great wall of Saxon Cove. 70

He sent $234.98 for the camera and $16.75 for the case (plus 20% tax). 70

Order the Damp Proof Red Primer from Barnes & Delaney, New York, N. Y. 70

He may use eight or more of the unusual forms in order to do the work. 70

TIMED WRITING 112

10 minutes

Directions. Type a 5-minute timed writing on the straight-copy material given on page 142. Use a 70-space line, a 5-space paragraph indention, and double spacing. Determine the cwpm.

PROBLEM TYPING 112

25 minutes

PROBLEM 1

Directions. Type Style Letter 5, page 154. Use a 5-inch line, the modified block form with no indentions for paragraphs, and mixed punctuation. For pica-type machines leave 4 single spaces between the date and the address; for elite-type machines leave 6 single spaces. Tabulate the report; leave a double space before and after the tabulation.

To determine the horizontal placement of the report, subtract the total number of spaces in the longest lines of both columns and the number of spaces between columns (leave 5 spaces between columns) from the number of spaces in the letter line. Divide the difference by 2. The result represents the number of spaces to be used in the left and right indentions.

Horizontal Placement of the Report

	PICA TYPE	ELITE TYPE
Total spaces available	50	60
Spaces required:		
By longest line of first column 26		
By longest line of second column .. 9		
By spaces between columns 5	40	40
Total spaces to be used for left and right indentions	10	20
Spaces to be indented on the left and the right	5	10

	PICA TYPE	ELITE TYPE
Stop for left margin	17	20
Tabulator stop for first column ....17+ 5=22		20+10=30
Tabulator stop for second column ....22+26+ 5=53		30+26+ 5=61

LESSON 133

CONDITIONING PRACTICE 133

5 minutes
STROKES

The kind queen received extra jewels from a dozen brave young pirates.   70

I had to rent the 5-room house at 37 East 169th Street at $85 a month.   70

Circle Tour No. 102 includes New York, Miami, Havana, and Mexico City.   70

The auditor will mail a new contract to them by the end of this month.   70

Skill Maintenance 133. Use each sentence of Conditioning Practice 133 for two   *12 minutes*
1-minute writings. *Type at the control level.*

PROGRESSION TYPING 133   15 minutes

Directions. Type for a half minute without error. Type for a minute without error. Continue to add a half minute to each errorless writing until you can type for 5 minutes without error. Start at the beginning of the paragraph with each writing. You need not check your speed in these writings. Your goal is errorless typing.

Each paragraph has every letter of the alphabet.

	STROKES	WORDS
I walked into a typewriting classroom the other day, and the teacher	69	14
was, as she expressed it, in the midst of "laying them out." I looked on	143	29
the floor to see how many had already been "laid out"; but they were very	217	43
much alive—too much so, for I felt that those pupils were getting a keen	291	58
sense of joy out of seeing the teacher wrought up. What was the matter?	365	73
You can guess without much trouble. The teacher had been trying, quite	437	87
without success, to get the pupils to check their own errors. I must admit	513	103
that the papers I saw seemed to have been marked by pupils who had	580	116
little zeal for correct work.	609	122
That was not good sportsmanship, nor was it good policy on the part	677	135
of those pupils. They thought they could "get by" without marking all	748	150
their own errors. They believed that the teacher would be too busy or	819	164
too tired to check their work. They just did not stop to realize that they	895	179
were acquiring a habit of work that would cripple them when they got	964	193
into business. Had I mentioned that fact to them, they would have an-	1033	207
swered that in business they would not expect to "get by." They would	1104	221
thus forget that habits fasten themselves on us through the repetition of	1178	236
thought and of act. Each day we spin the web of our lives, good or evil,	1252	250
never to be undone.	1271	254

TYPING FOR CONTROL 133   8 minutes

Directions. In the time that remains, type as much of the paragraphs given for Timed Writing 131, page 182, as possible. Your goal is to be errorless writing; therefore, each time you make an error you are to throw your carriage and start again at the beginning of the first paragraph.

Webster Associates

SPECIALISTS IN BUSINESS PROMOTION

2111 *State Street* • *Chicago 23, Illinois*

November 18, 195-

	STROKES	WORDS
	18	4

	STROKES	WORDS
Mr. Harold Blair, President	46	9
Blair-Stevenson Company	70	14
2800 Wabash Avenue	89	18
Evanston, Illinois	108	22
Dear Mr. Blair:	125	25
In June a form letter that we prepared was mailed	175	35
by one of our clients. As you frequently use such	226	45
letters, you will be interested in the following	275	55
data reported to us by our client:	311	62
Number of letters mailed 114,000	345	69
Number of replies received 38,000	381	76
Percentage of replies 33%	413	83
Business obtained $140,000	440	88
Campaign cost $7,250	463	93
Percentage of sales cost 5%	498	100
The spectacular success of this campaign emphasizes	550	110
the value of our service in planning and writing	599	120
letters for our clients. Within a few days,	644	129
Mr. Roger Whiting of our office will call on you.	695	139
You will find it profitable to give him the oppor-	744	149
tunity to tell you more about our service.	788	158
Very truly yours,	806	161
WEBSTER ASSOCIATES	825	165
Charles A. Cochrane	845	169
rul	852	170

(Words in body of letter, 130)

Style Letter 5 — Modified Block Letter Containing a Tabulated Report

	STROKES	
	PARA.	TOTAL

You can learn to solve problems just by going about the task in an   67   1165
orderly manner. First, make a summary of the main parts of the problem.   141   1239
Next, find or acquire the skills that are needed to solve the problem.   213   1311
It is foolish to try to solve a problem that requires skills that you do   286   1384
not have and cannot learn soon enough for the work that must be done.   357   1455
Finally, be willing to give the time and effort needed for doing the work.   433   1531
If you realize the importance of these points, the result will be a fine   506   1604
achievement for you.   528   1626

Judgment, courtesy, and tact are some of the qualities that bring suc-   69   1695
cess in all kinds of work. Office workers should realize that good sense   143   1769
is just as important as skill when it comes to doing the work that they   215   1841
must do. Quick, sound judgment comes with experience as a result of the   288   1914
growth gained through solving problems rather than through evading   355   1981
them. Regard for others sums up what is meant when such words as   421   2047
"courtesy" and "tact" are used. Do not be content just with skill. True   495   2121
values are to be found in the qualities that will help you to use your   566   2192
skill.   572   2198

SPEED SPURTS 131   *8 minutes*

Directions. In the time that remains, type several 1-minute timed writings on the paragraphs given for Timed Writing 131. *Type at the exploration level of practice.* As a tentative goal, try to type at a rate which is approximately 10 to 15 words a minute faster than your 10-minute rate. Gain speed by typing with good techniques, by typing without a sense of hurry, and by reading your copy properly.

LESSON 132

CONDITIONING PRACTICE 132   *5 minutes*

STROKES

Xavier quickly raced the motor when the fleeting jet planes buzzed by.   70

He paid $362.48 in 1915 for two (7' x 10') oriental rugs for his home.   70

The Ganges flows many miles from the Himalayas into the Bay of Bengal.   70

They expect to make the audit of the offices at the end of this month.   70

Skill Maintenance 132. Use each sentence of Conditioning Practice 132 for two   *12 minutes*
1-minute timed writings. *Type at the exploration level.*

Timed Writing 132. Take a 10-minute timed writing. Use the paragraphs of Timed   *15 minutes*
Writing 131. Determine your cwpm.

Speed Spurts 132. Type several 1-minute timed writings on the paragraphs given   *8 minutes*
for Timed Writing 131. Try to type at a rate which is approximately 10 to 15 words a
minute faster than your 10-minute rate.

PROBLEM 2

Directions. 1. Proofread carefully the letter you typed as Problem 1. Indicate by making pencil corrections any changes that need to be made in your letter copy.

2. Retype the letter using your copy of the style letter with your penciled corrections, if any, as the copy from which you type. Try to increase your stroking rate as you retype the letter.

LESSON 113

CONDITIONING PRACTICE 113

STROKES

Six good men worked with zeal and a quick pace to do this job by five. 70

A 100% hardwood 3-shelf bookcase (38″ x 23″ x 7 3/4″) sells for $6.95. 70

Peace, Taffeta, Fashion, Nocturne, and Forty-Niner are names of roses. 70

Both of them will help the city auditor with the work that is pending. 70

TIMED WRITING 113   *10 minutes*

Directions. Type Style Letter 5, page 154, for 5 minutes. Make all machine adjustments before you start to type. If you complete the typing of the letter before time is called, use the back of the sheet (or insert another page) and start to type the letter a second time. Determine the cwpm.

PROBLEM TYPING 113   *25 minutes*

Directions. 1. Type the letter in the modified block form without paragraph indentions. Use Style Letter 5, page 154, for your model. Use open punctuation.

2. As this is a 2-page letter, use a 60-space line for pica type or a 70-space line for elite type, with about 5 line spaces between the date and the address.

3. Tabulate the list following the first paragraph. Use 10 spaces between columns and equal side margins.

4. Indent the numbered paragraphs 5 spaces from the left and the right margins of the letter.

5. Illustration 41 shows two satisfactory forms for the heading of the second page of a letter. Unless you are instructed to the contrary, use the form shown at the left, beginning about 9 spaces from the top of the page. Leave 3 or 4 spaces between the heading and the first line of the body of the letter.

(To assist you in planning this letter, the body of the letter is arranged by paragraphs.)

Miss Margaret T. Wallace
Page 2
November 12, 19--

It is important that oil be used sparingly and knowingly when it is used at all. A drop of oil should be put on each rod or rail. After this is done, move the carriage back and forth to distribute the oil; then wipe off the excess. If this is done once a week, there will be little trouble with sluggish carriage movement.

Miss Margaret T. Wallace   2   November 12, 19--

It is important that oil be used sparingly and knowingly when it is used at all. A drop of oil should be put on each rod or rail. After this is done, move the carriage back and forth to distribute the oil; then wipe off the excess. If this is done once a week, there will be little trouble with sluggish carriage movement.

Dirt should be kept from the type-bar basket. If the students

Illustration 41 — Two Forms of the Heading of the Second Page of a Letter

Either form may be typed 9 to 12 spaces from the top of the page. Three or 4 spaces are used between the heading and the first line of the paragraph.

INSTRUCTIONAL BLOCK 12

IMPROVEMENT OF TYPING POWER

SECTION 20. Speed and Control Emphasis

LESSON 131

CONDITIONING PRACTICE 131   *5 minutes*

Directions. Type each line twice, or more if time permits. This will be the uniform assignment for typing the conditioning practices in all lessons in this section.

STROKES

The dazzling onyx jewel from Cavite is quaint but will keep its style.   70

Will you enter machine Nos. 11-93045 and 11-87236 on the repair cards.   70

Important conferences were held at Dumbarton Oaks during World War II.   70

If they are to go with us to the big city, we shall be there at eight.   70

Skill Maintenance 131. Use each line of Conditioning Practice 131 for two 1-minute writings. *Type at the exploration level.*   *12 minutes*

TIMED WRITING 131   *15 minutes*

Directions. Take a 10-minute timed writing. Determine your cwpm.

Each paragraph has every letter of the alphabet and a syllable intensity of 1.30.

	STROKES	
	PARA.	TOTAL

	PARA.	TOTAL
Just a few finger gymnastics when you start your practice will free	68	
the muscles of stiffness and thus help you get a quicker key stroke than	141	
you can get with tense muscles. You should relax the hands and arms,	211	
too. Relaxed muscles and a good measure of confidence will give you the	284	
poise that will make for power in typewriting. You must organize your	355	
whole effort and train yourself in good typing habits if you want to pro-	427	
gress at a rapid rate in the time allowed.	471	
Begin now to train yourself to think through each problem that you	67	538
do. You will have few puzzled moments if you will take extreme care to	139	610
understand each problem before you start typing it. The knack of follow-	211	682
ing directions must not be overlooked. If you type well, think straight,	285	756
and work hard, you will win. There is no element of chance when the right	360	831
technique is joined with the right attitude. Success is certain! Now	433	904
is the time for you to make sure that your work habits are right. Read	505	976
for errors every piece of work that you do. The time to correct the error	580	1051
is before you release the work for signature.	627	1098

Miss Margaret T. Wallace Central High School Elizabethtown, Kentucky Dear Miss Wallace

The typewriters listed below were cleaned, oiled, repaired, and placed in good working condition on Tuesday and Wednesday of last week:

Smith-Corona	1-A1702931
Smith-Corona	1-A1679647
Royal	2564209
Royal	2805718
Underwood	4903910
Underwood	4903972
Underwood	4906218

You asked me to list the steps in cleaning the typewriter. I am glad to do this. It has been my experience that most typewriters are more damaged by dirt than from any other cause. Here are some things the students should *know* and *do* in order to keep the typewriters clean and in good working condition:

1. Dust the surface of the typewriter and underneath it each day.

2. Clean the type each day with a stiff brush. Brush the type to and from you—not from left to right. If the type is brushed at the beginning of the period and at the end of the period, it will not be necessary to use a cleaning fluid. If a cleaning fluid is used, cover the keyboard with a sheet of paper held in position behind the top row of keys.

3. Move the margin stops to the ends of the carriage scale. Move the carriage to the left as far as it will go. Use an oiled cloth to clean the rods as far as you can reach them. Move the carriage to the right as far as it will go. Clean the rods on the other side of the machine.

It is important that oil be used sparingly and knowingly when it is used at all. A drop of oil should be put on each rod or rail. After this is done, move the carriage back and forth to distribute the oil; then wipe off the excess. If this is done once a week, there will be little trouble with sluggish carriage movement.

Dirt should be kept from the type-bar basket. If the students are forced to use the correct procedures for erasing, there will be little, if any, erasure dirt that will fall into the basket to slow down the type-bar action. Clean the type bars each week. To do this, gently depress all the keys to raise the bars; then brush under the bars with a stiff brush. Try to get the accumulated and sometimes gummed dirt from the "action end" of the bars—the point where the bar moves upward when the key is struck. Drop the type bars gently back into the basket after they have been brushed. Caution the students to move the type bars with care—never bend them or disturb their alignment. Incidentally, this is a needed caution when keys clash. In pulling the keys down, students sometimes force the keys and bend them—and then they wonder why it is that the type bars won't respond to their stroke with the right movement.

The right care of your typewriters will pay dividends to your students in increased operating ease and skill. There will be fewer annoying interruptions to your class work if the machines are kept in good condition.

I hope that this letter will enable you to convince your students that their typewriter is a partner in their adventure in learning to type, and the typewriter-partner should be kept in top working condition.

Yours very truly (Robert C. Kramer)* Branch Manager *(593)*

---

* The name of the dictator is given in parentheses so you can have the information for typing the reference initials. Do not type the name when it is enclosed in parentheses.

Directions. In Lessons 129 and 130 only, type a 5-minute timed writing on the material given as Timed Writing 119, page 168. Determine the cwpm.

PROBLEM TYPING—LESSONS 128 TO 130   *20 or 25 minutes*

Directions. Assume that you have been elected temporary chairman of a group of business students who are interested in forming a local club of the Future Business Leaders of America. You face several problems in getting ready to preside at the meeting that will be held to organize your chapter.

Compose your letters on the typewriter; your teacher will check them; and you may have to rewrite one or two of them. You can best compose your letter at the typewriter if you first think through the letter you plan to write and jot down a few brief notes on what you want to cover in the letter.

PROBLEM 1

You want to be well informed as to the purpose of the organization and the obligations of membership. Type a letter to Mr. Hollis P. Guy, Executive Secretary, United Business Education Association, 1201 Sixteenth St., N. W., Washington 6, D. C., and ask for complete information about the organization. Tell Mr. Guy of your personal interest in this work and something of the general student interest in such an organization.

PROBLEM 2

You have heard from Mr. Guy, who has sent you information and materials concerning the Future Business Leaders of America. Write a notice to the business students in your school telling them (1) that you have the necessary information and materials for organizing a chapter; (2) that you are calling a meeting on October 15 during the regular school club period; and (3) that you are attaching the agenda for the meeting so that they can go over the items thoughtfully and be prepared to discuss the points as they are brought up at the meeting.

PROBLEM 3

Type a tentative agenda for your organization meeting. (Agenda: Memoranda of things to be done, as items of business or discussion to be brought up at a meeting; hence, a program consisting of such items.)

AGENDA FOR ORGANIZATION MEETING
OF
FUTURE BUSINESS LEADERS OF AMERICA

1. Election of Temporary Secretary.

2. Purposes of Future Business Leaders of America.

3. Eligibility Requirements.
   a. Must be taking subject in Business Department.
   b. Must have a good attendance.
   c. Must have an ambition to work in the field of store or office occupations or to become a proprietor of a store or an office.
   d. Must have a favorable attitude toward the school and its functions.

4. Organization Plans.
   a. Charter.
      (1) Cost.
      (2) Significance.
   b. Steps in organizing chapter.
      (1) Submit list of charter members to the state sponsoring body.
      (2) Submit name of school sponsor and student officers.
      (3) Submit a proposed project or projects that the chapter will undertake.

5. Some Possible Chapter Projects.
   a. Community study to determine job possibilities for graduates.
   b. Follow-up study of graduates of the school.
   c. Organization of a speakers' bureau of business students who can appear before school assemblies, luncheon clubs, and business groups to speak on school activities and problems.
   d. Planning with local radio stations for broadcasts.

MANUSCRIPT TYPING

SECTION 17. Special Problems

LESSON 114

CONDITIONING PRACTICE 114   *5 minutes*

Directions. Type each line twice, or more if time permits. This will be the uniform assignment for typing the conditioning practices in all lessons in this section.

	STROKES
Six flying fish whizzed quickly over my jigs as a big tuna approached.	70
The 6.70 x 15, 4-ply tires (natural rubber) may cost more than $23.89.	70
The Pittsburgh Pirates will play the Brooklyn Dodgers at Forbes Field.	70
The right techniques coupled with the right attitudes aid your typing.	70

RELATED LEARNING 114—CAPITALIZATION GUIDES   *10 minutes*

Directions. Study the explanatory statements; then type each line one or more times as time permits.

Line 1: Capitalize the first word of every sentence and the first word of every complete direct quotation.
Line 2: Do not capitalize fragments of quotations.
Line 3: Do not capitalize a quotation resumed within a sentence. A period or a comma precedes the ending quotation mark.
Line 4: Capitalize the first word after a colon if that word begins a complete sentence.
Line 5: In business letters, capitalize the first and last words, all titles, and all proper names used in the salutation.

	STROKES
She said, "There is no substitute for hard work in attaining success."	70
Among other things, he stressed the importance of "a sense of values."	70
"I'll toot your horn," she said impatiently, "while you start my car."	70
These are the directions: Use a 5-space indention and double spacing.	70
The salutation "My dear Sir" is more formal than "Dear Mr. Johnstone."	70

CORRECT IT AS YOU TYPE (OR DIRECT DICTATION)   *5 minutes*

Directions. These sentences are in problem form. To type them in correct form, you must know the basic principles of technical English given in the explanatory statements for the preceding sentences. Your teacher will tell you whether the sentences are to be dictated or whether they are to be typed from the copy. Type at a rate that will permit you to think of the correct form. If you are uncertain how to type a sentence, refer to the explanatory statements.

she replied, "when you play, play hard; and when you work, work hard."

i re-emphasized the importance of "product knowledge" to all salesmen.

follow this rule: use dear mr stewart for the less formal opening.

Directions. The heading requires two or three lines. Decide which words you will write on a line; then center each line. Type the problem in two columns with 32 pica or 39 elite spaces in each column. Use a 3-space paragraph indention and single spacing. Type the work copy with the diagonal to show the needed variable spacing for each line. After you have prepared the work copy, retype the material, making the line endings uniform.

ROBOTYPER WRITES LETTERS THREE TIMES AS FAST AS AVERAGE STENOGRAPHER

Here's how the Robotyper works: As a stenographer types a letter, holes are punched in a roll that looks like that used on player pianos. The roll is put in the robot. Through compressed air, the holes in the roll are made to pull the proper type bars on the typewriter.

If the office wants to "personalize" the letters, the robot can be stopped while the stenographer types in a name, a price quotation, or other material.

The robot can type nearly three times as fast as the average stenographer; and one operator can supervise four machines, thus accomplishing the work of twelve stenographers.

LESSONS 128 TO 130

CONDITIONING PRACTICE—LESSONS 128 TO 130   *5 minutes*

Directions. In each lesson type each line twice, or more if time permits.

	STROKES
We quickly razed six massive buildings as five jittery people watched.	70
He ordered 72 pencils, 36 pens, 49 erasers, and 185 cardboard folders.	70
Mrs. T. James O'Malley gave a report on life in San Juan, Puerto Rico.	70
He will meet them at the end of the lane when the clock strikes eight.	70

RELATED LEARNING 128—NUMBER GUIDES   *10 minutes*

Directions. Type the following related learnings for Lesson 128 only. Study the explanatory statements; type each line one or more times as time permits.

Lines 1 and 2: In business letters, the per cent sign (%) is preferred usage when preceded by definite figures. With approximations and in most formal writing, *per cent* (spelled out) is preferred.

Line 3: Numbers preceded by nouns are usually expressed in figures.

Lines 4 and 5: Spell out names of small-numbered avenues and streets. State house numbers in figures except for house number *One*.

	STROKES
This interest rate of $4\frac{1}{2}\%$ will be changed to $6\frac{1}{4}\%$ on your future loans.	70
Approximately 50 per cent of the students have completed all the work.	70
We found the exact quotation in Volume VIII, Section 4, pages 210-213.	70
They moved their office from One Lexington Avenue to 270 Fifth Avenue.	70
The factory is at 18 First Street; the store, at 164 West 59th Street.	70

CORRECT IT AS YOU TYPE (OR DIRECT DICTATION)   *5 minutes*

all orders will be subject to a trade discount of 20 per cent, 10%, and 5 percent

the assignment covers Chapters nine and 10, Volume II, pages 985-1024

you may send your check to 147 6th street or to 859 West twenty-sixth avenue

20 *minutes*

PROBLEM I

Directions. Type the following problem on a full sheet of paper. Use double spacing. Leave a top margin of approximately 2 inches and have 1-inch side margins. Center the heading and type it in all capital letters. Leave a triple space after the heading.

	STROKES	WORDS
MANUSCRIPT TYPING	18	4

Manuscripts or reports are usually double spaced and typed on paper — 86 — 17
which is 8½ by 11 inches in size. The first line of each paragraph may be — 161 — 32
indented either 5 or 10 spaces from the left margin. Quoted material of — 234 — 47
more than 4 lines is usually single spaced and indented on the left and — 306 — 61
the right. — 318 — 64

As a general rule, 1-inch top, bottom, and side margins are allowed on — 389 — 78
all pages except the first, which has a top margin of approximately 2 — 459 — 92
inches. If the manuscript is to be bound, a margin of 1½ inches must be — 532 — 106
left on the side that is to receive the binding. This is usually the left side, — 613 — 123
although manuscripts are sometimes bound at the top. — 667 — 133

Each page except the first is numbered. The number may be typed in — 735 — 147
the upper right corner approximately even with the right margin and — 803 — 161
one-half inch from the top of the page. It is also correct to number each — 878 — 176
page in the center. If the manuscript is to be bound at the top, the page — 953 — 191
number is typed in the center, approximately one-half inch from the bot- — 1024 — 205
tom edge of the page. — 1045 — 209

PROBLEM 2

Directions. Study the instructions for manuscript typing given in Problem 1. Then type the following copy as a manuscript.

	STROKES	WORDS
THE USEFULNESS OF THE SQUEAK	29	6

The squeak has come into its own. It is used to tell real pearls and — 99 — 20
diamonds from counterfeits. Touch them with a piece of dry ice, and the — 172 — 34
real article will give a squeak that the imitations can't imitate. — 240 — 48

Scientists say the mechanism of the squeak is simple. Solid carbon — 308 — 62
dioxide, when heated, passes directly from the solid to the gaseous state, — 383 — 77
skipping the liquid state. When a pointed piece of the dry ice is pre- — 453 — 91
sented to a conductor of heat, such as a metal plate, heat is conducted — 525 — 105
by the plate to the ice and turns some of the latter to gas. A powerful — 598 — 120
stream of gas issues from the point, as from a nozzle, and pushes away — 669 — 134
part of the plate immediately in front of it. As soon as this happens, the — 745 — 149
passage of heat to the dry ice stops, the gas stream stops, and the plate — 819 — 164
because of its elasticity returns to contact. The whole thing is repeated — 894 — 179
over and over from a thousand to four thousand times a second. The — 962 — 192
plate is thus set into vibration, emitting high-pitched notes from two to — 1036 — 207
four octaves above middle C. If a piece of glass or other nonconductors — 1109 — 222
of heat are touched with dry ice, no sound is emitted. Yes, the squeak — 1181 — 236
has come into its own. — 1203 — 241

LESSON 127

Seven puzzling words completed the extra job of a busy, quick student.   70

A special "J&B" rug (8'10" x 12') sells for $346.79 less 15% discount.   70

Refer the papers to Miss Sally Barclay, Secretary to McCrae & Company.   70

It is easier to make the figure-key reaches if the fingers are curved.   70

RELATED LEARNING 127—NUMBER GUIDES   *10 minutes*

Directions. Study the explanatory statements; type each line one or more times as time permits.

Line 1: As a general rule, numbers under ten are spelled out; and, numbers above ten are written in figures. If several numbers both under and over ten are used in a sentence, however, all the numbers should be typed in figures or spelled out in order to be consistent in the expression of numbers.

Line 2: If a number begins a sentence, it should be spelled out.

Line 3: As a general rule, spell out the shorter of two numbers forming one item.

Lines 4 and 5: Isolated fractions in a sentence are usually spelled out, but a series of fractions is written in figures. Note: Use the diagonal for "made" fractions.

                                                    STROKES

He ordered 72 books on English, 8 on mathematics, and 36 on geography.   70

One hundred applications for the job are on file. Ten men were hired.   70

Order No. 1350 called for ten 50-gallon drums and 350 ten-gallon cans.   70

He has completed two thirds of the problems that were assigned to him.   70

Divide the circles into the following parts: 1/8, 3/8, 2/5, and 1/10.   70

CORRECT IT AS YOU TYPE (OR DIRECT DICTATION)   *5 minutes*

order no 236 for 40 business law books and five case books was received

80 persons filed applications but only one third of them got jobs

he bought two fifty foot lengths of cable and fifteen one foot pieces of rope

PROBLEM TYPING 127   *20 minutes*

Typing Columnar Headings. The columnar headings for a school paper are usually separated from the context by two line spaces. The headings may be centered as follows:

1. Measure by spacing on the typewriter, or with a ruler, the center of the column.

2. Note the number on the scale that indicates the center.

3. From the center point on the scale, backspace one half the number of strokes in the heading. For example, "Columnar Headings" has 17 type spaces; so you would backspace 8 spaces (disregard the extra space in an uneven number). At this point begin typing the heading.

PROBLEM 1

Directions. You are to center the columnar headings at the right over a maximum writing line of 32 pica or 39 elite spaces used in preparing the dummy form for the school paper.

NIMBLE FINGERS TALK

THE STARS TYPE

FATAL COMMA

SMILES, CHUCKLES, AND LAUGHS

PROBLEM 3

Directions. The problem has three columns. The first column gives the undivided word; the second column shows the syllables of each word as found in a standard dictionary; and the third column gives the only correct form of the word when it appears at the end of a line. You will observe that some of the words listed cannot be divided.

Center the problem vertically on a half sheet of paper. Double-space the data. Leave six spaces between columns. Set stops for the columns and type across the page.

1. controlled	1. con-trolled	1. con-trolled
2. knowledge	2. knowl-edge	2. knowl-edge
3. around	3. a-round	3. around
4. against	4. a-gainst	4. against
5. ready	5. read-y	5. ready
6. greatly	6. great-ly	6. greatly
7. wouldn't	7. would-n't	7. wouldn't
8. guessing	8. guess-ing	8. guess-ing
9. quitting	9. quit-ting	9. quit-ting

LESSON 115

CONDITIONING PRACTICE 115 — 5 minutes

STROKES

This quick quiz will cover exceedingly important factors of job skill.	70
Order #6890 for 2 gross of buttons totals $3.72 (24 doz. @ 15½¢ each).	70
Mt. McKinley in the Alaska Range is the highest peak in North America.	70
Keep the right thumb close to the space bar in order to space quickly.	70

RELATED LEARNING 115—CAPITALIZATION GUIDES — 10 minutes

Directions. Study the explanatory statements; then type each line one or more times.

Line 1: Capitalize only the first word of the complimentary close of a business letter.
Line 2: In business letters, all titles appearing in the address should be capitalized.
Line 3: If a title follows the name of the dictator in the closing lines of a business letter, it must be capitalized.
Lines 4 and 5: When an official title immediately precedes a name, it should be capitalized. When a title occurs elsewhere in the sentence, it may be written without the capital unless it is a title of high distinction or it is used to refer to a specific person.

STROKES

He uses either "Very truly yours" or "Sincerely yours" as the closing.	70
The letter from Mr. Drake was addressed to Mr. John Howard, President.	70
Type the dictator's name and title as follows: Daniel Drake, Manager.	70
On Tuesday, President Fairbanks of the Ottawa Company will address us.	70
Edward Smith is the president of the club. The Governor will be here.	70

CORRECT IT AS YOU TYPE (OR DIRECT DICTATION) — 5 minutes

"sincerely yours" and "d k saunders manager" are the closing lines.
the governor will be welcomed by president wilson of general steel co.
cal mercer is the president of the club, and jack wagner is the secretary.

PROBLEM 1

Squeezing Letters. In the rush of work, it is often advisable to "squeeze" an omitted letter in a half space and thus save erasing the entire word or retyping the page.

When a letter has been omitted from the beginning or the end of a word and if your typewriter has the half-space mechanism, move the carriage to the last space before the omission; depress and hold down the space bar as you type the omitted letter. If your typewriter does not have the half-space mechanism, move the carriage to the space following the omission; depress the backspace key halfway and hold it in that position as you type the omitted letter.

Directions. Type the following sentence just as it is shown; then move the carriage to the correct position for adding the letter *t* in the word *that*. The letter *t* will occupy half of the space between the words.

```
He claimed that he knew all about tha kind of work.
```

The corrected sentence should look like this:

```
He claimed that he knew all about that kind of work.
```

Type the following sentence as it is shown; then move the carriage to the correct position for adding the "(" before the word "number."

```
The underscore is the shift of 6 and the # number) is the shift of 3.
```

The corrected sentence should look like this:

```
The underscore is the shift of 6 and the # (number) is the shift of 3.
```

PROBLEM 2

Variable Spacing. School papers are often duplicated on a mimeograph, a kind of printing machine with which you may be somewhat familiar. Stencils (wax sheets) are typed with the ribbon lever disengaged. The stencil is placed on the mimeograph, and copies of the material are printed. Your teacher will show you the stencil; later in your work you will use the mimeograph.

The stencil for a school paper is usually typed in two columns. In order to give the page the appearance of a printed page, the right margin of each column is even, except for the last line of each paragraph. In order to obtain an even right margin, extra spaces are added between words to fill out short lines, and half spaces are used between words to squeeze the words on long lines.

Directions. Type the following copy with a 32-space line for pica type, or with a 39-space line for elite type, a 3-space paragraph indention, and single spacing. Indicate with the diagonal the number of spaces that must be taken care of in order to have the lines end at the proper point. The copy, as it appears when typed with pica type, is shown below.

```
When you hike, bike, or tour/
by car, take your camera along./
New scenes and new faces will///
greet you wherever you go, and//
snapshots will permanently record
them.
```

The first four lines call for juggling the spaces to get the desired line length. The fifth line has one extra space. Distribute the spaces so that in your opinion they will be the least noticeable. Squeeze any word in the fifth line to adjust the words to the line length.

One student typed the paragraph as follows

```
When you  hike, bike, or tour
by car, take your camera  along.
New scenes  and  new faces  will
greet you  wherever  you go, and
snapshots will permanently record
them.
```

PROBLEM I

Directions. Use a 60-space line and single spacing. Center the copy vertically on a half sheet; and center the heading horizontally. Triple-space between the heading and the first sentence.

	STROKES WORDS

THINGS TO AVOID IN DIVIDING WORDS   34   7

1. Avoid diving [*id*] a word of five [*or six*] letters. (A word of one   100   20
   syllable or a word of four letters must never be   149   30
   divided.)   160   32

2. Avoid separating a two-letter sylable [*l*] at the begin-   215   43
   ning of a word from the remiander [*i*] of the word.   263   53

3. Avoid dividing a surname and separating titles, ini-   318   64
   tials, or degrees from a surnae. [*m*]   353   71

4. Avoid dividing figures or abbreviations.   399   80

5. Avoid dividing hyphaned [*e*] words and compounds, such as   456   91
   <u>self-explanatory</u> and <u>cross-examination</u>, except at the   543   109
   hyphen.   550   110

PROBLEM 2

Directions. The problem has three columns, the third of which is incomplete. The first column gives the undivided word and the second column shows the syllables of each word as found in a standard dictionary. You are to complete the third column by typing the word with the hyphen to indicate the correct division of the word at the end of the line. If the word cannot be divided at the end of the line, type it without the hyphen. If you are uncertain as to how to divide the word, refer to the rules for word division given on page 122.

Center the problem vertically on a half sheet of paper. Single-space the data and use your judgment in determining the number of spaces to leave between columns. Be sure to align the numbers correctly.

1. also	1. al-so	1.
2. today	2. to-day	2.
3. already	3. al-read-y	3.
4. C. O. D.	4. C. O. D.	4.
5. self-sufficient	5. self-suf-fi-cient	5.
6. stopped	6. stopped	6.
7. didn't	7. did-n't	7.
8. simplify	8. sim-pli-fy	8.
9. pressure	9. pres-sure	9.
10. willing	10. will-ing	10.
11. stopping	11. stop-ping	11.
12. democracy	12. de-moc-ra-cy	12.

bers announcing the demonstration. Type the announcement as shown below on a postal card or on a sheet of paper 5½ by 3¼ inches. (Change the date to make it correspond with Thursday in the first week of next month.) Center the problem vertically, and center each line horizontally. Double-space the lines of the announcement.

As each card is finished, type the address on the reverse side. The partial address list is given at the right. Use the name of your city and state for each address. Type the city and state on the same line and separate them by a comma; as *Nashville 6, Tennessee*, or *Berea, Kentucky*.

Macon High School Commercial Club

announces

A SPECIAL TYPEWRITING DEMONSTRATION

by

J. DUDLEY O'BRIEN

2:00 p.m., Thursday, December 3

Room 145

Partial Address List

Mr. Patrick LeRoy
3026 Welburn Street

Miss Natalie Hamilton
1419 Park Street

Mr. J. Rex Minton
152 Sixth Street, West

Miss Ida Farmer
2417 Ashland Avenue

Miss Judith Clark
Arlington Apartments
306 Highland Road

Mr. Lambert D. Brewster
5 Beechmont Drive

Miss Nellie Russell
1628 Forester Avenue

Mr. William P. Thompson
R. F. D. 3

LESSON 126

CONDITIONING PRACTICE 126
5 minutes

STROKES

The reporters quickly recognized the vexing problems of judging flaws.	70
Please notice Rule 36 on page 210 as well as Rule 85 on pages 479-482.	70
Dr. R. J. Addison is employed by the Indiana State Highway Commission.	70
Try to keep the fingers in typing position when shifting for capitals.	70

RELATED LEARNING 126—PUNCTUATION GUIDES
10 minutes

Directions. Study the explanatory statements; type each line one or more times as time permits.

Line 1: Parentheses are frequently used in legal papers to enclose figures following amounts which are expressed in words.
Line 2: The hyphen is used in compound numerals from twenty-one to ninety-nine.
Line 3: "Suspension" hyphens are used to carry the force of a modifier over to a later noun.
Line 4: Compound adjectives are written with hyphens when used to modify a noun which they precede.
Line 5: Use a hyphen in a compound adjective containing a number when it is used to modify a noun.

STROKES

The undersigned agrees to pay the sum of three hundred dollars ($300).	70
A balance of four hundred sixty-two dollars ($462) is due and payable.	70
First-, second-, and third-class mail is to be sorted before 9:30 a.m.	70
In the last five-year period, our business has increased tremendously.	70
He bought three 35-pound bags of sugar and one 50-pound sack of flour.	70

CORRECT IT AS YOU TYPE (OR DIRECT DICTATION)
5 minutes

the payee will receive the sum of two hundred forty six dollars $246
count all the five , ten , and twenty dollar bills in the cash drawer
the cost of a 50 pound bag of sugar doubled in the twenty year period

LESSON 116

STROKES

The jovial king was very puzzled when these six fine men became quiet.	70
Between 1940 and 1950, the population increased from 26,378 to 36,479.	70
EasyPac Quick Frozen Juices are processed in Santa Monica, California.	70
The manager was aware of the fact that two of the workers were absent.	70

RELATED LEARNING 116—CAPITALIZATION GUIDES   *10 minutes*

Directions. Study the explanatory statements; then type each line one or more times as time permits.

Line 1: Business or professional titles used without the name of the person are not usually capitalized.

Line 2: Capitalize first words and all other words in titles of books, articles, periodicals, headings, etc., *except* words which are articles, conjunctions, and prepositions. NOTE: The title of a book may be underscored or typed in all capital letters.

Line 3: Capitalize all proper nouns and their derivations.

Line 4: Capitalize the names of days of the week, months of the year, holidays, periods of history, and historic events.

Line 5: The seasons of the year are usually written without the capital.

STROKES

The doctor will be here at 10 a.m. The attorney is studying the case.	70
Have you read the new book by Thomas Booth, *The Value of an Education*?	95
John wrote an interesting report on European and American folk dances.	70
Capitalize these words: Tuesday, May, Christmas, and the Middle Ages.	70
There is an old saying, "When winter comes, can spring be far behind?"	70

CORRECT IT AS YOU TYPE (OR DIRECT DICTATION)   *5 minutes*

the professor and his attorney will arrive before the court convenes.

professor derek will review his book, the wake of man, today at 3 p.m.

a demonstration of south american dances will be given tuesday, may 1.

PROBLEM TYPING 116   *20 minutes*

PROBLEM 1

Directions. Type the following problem on a half sheet of paper. Use single spacing with double spacing between paragraphs. Leave a 1-inch top margin and set the marginal stops for 1-inch side margins. Indent each paragraph 5 spaces. Leave a triple space after the heading which is to be centered.

After you have typed the problem, check each of the steps listed with the typewriter you are using and do the things called for by each step.

	STROKES	WORDS
PRELIMINARY STEPS IN LEARNING TO	33	7
CHANGE THE RIBBON	51	10
Changing the ribbon on a typewriter is not difficult if you are thor-	119	24
oughly acquainted with the typewriter you are using. Listed are a few	190	38
preliminary steps which will help you learn to change the ribbon on your	263	53
typewriter quickly and easily.	295	59

demonstration. Be sure to give the time, place, and date of your meeting. Tell Mr. O'Brien of the interest of the students of your school in typewriting and ask him to demonstrate and comment on some of the things that you might do to improve your typewriting skill. Address Mr. O'Brien at 236 West 44th Street, New York 18, New York. Type his name and address below the body of the letter as shown in Illustration 43, page 174.

Until you develop skill in composing letters, etc., directly at the typewriter, you will probably make many errors. It is suggested, therefore, that you type the letter to Mr. O'Brien in rough form. Then, proofread this copy and indicate by making pencil corrections any changes that need to be made. Finally, retype the letter and make the corrections you have indicated.

PROBLEM 2

Directions. As time permits, type the letter in Problem Typing 123, page 174, to any of the addresses that you did not use in Problem 2, page 175.

LESSON 125

CONDITIONING PRACTICE 125
5 minutes

STROKES

John V. Maze is able to type six words faster by using a quick stroke. 70
The terms of discount on Order #46789 dated June 15 were: 2/10, N/30. 70
The Tri-High Commercial Club Luncheon will be held at the Regis-Plaza. 70
Keep your eyes on the copy and type with continuity to increase speed. 70

RELATED LEARNING 125—PUNCTUATION GUIDES
10 minutes

Directions. Study the explanatory statements; type each line one or more times as time permits.

Line 1: When a proper name of one syllable ends in *s,* add an apostrophe and *s* to show possession.
Line 2: When a proper name of more than one syllable ends in *s,* add an apostrophe only to show possession.
Line 3: The apostrophe may be used as a symbol for feet in billings or tabulations. The apostrophe also may be used to indicate the omission of figures; as, *The Spirit of '76.*
Line 4: Parentheses may be used to segregate from the rest of the sentence parenthetical or explanatory matter and added information.
Line 5: Parentheses may be used to enclose enumerated items in a sentence or paragraph.

STROKES

Do not pay Charles's bill for $274 today, but pay 75 cents at Jones's. 70
Anthony Roberts' automobile was parked in back of Fred Sanders' house. 70
The apostrophe may be used to express feet in billings; as, 15' x 18'. 70
The Contract (Exhibit A) and the Bill of Sale (Exhibit B) were stolen. 70
The important factors are: (1) speed, (2) accuracy, and (3) neatness. 70

CORRECT IT AS YOU TYPE (OR DIRECT DICTATION)
5 minutes

Rod Steve and Barry will ride to Charles house in Bill Francis car
permascript ink a special fast-drying ink has been recommended to us
classify the duties as follows: 1 general 2 special or 3 extra

PROBLEM TYPING 125
20 minutes

Directions. Mr. O'Brien has accepted your invitation to give a typewriting demonstration at your school. As secretary of your commercial club, you are to send cards to some former mem-

	STROKES	WORDS

1. Carefully observe how the ribbon is threaded through the ribbon-carrier mechanism. — 362 / 72, 382 / 76

2. Note the direction of travel of the ribbon on both spools. Do this by using the carriage-release lever to move the carriage from side to side while you observe how the ribbon winds and unwinds on the spools. The new ribbon must always be attached so that it will wind and unwind properly on both spools. — 454 / 91, 529 / 106, 600 / 120, 667 / 133, 693 / 139

3. Lift the right spool slightly off its hub. Notice whether the two sides of the spool are the same. If they are not, then you must be sure that the bottom side is down when you put on a new ribbon spool. Be sure to replace the right spool in its proper position on the hub. — 764 / 153, 837 / 167, 906 / 181, 972 / 194

PROBLEM 2

Directions. Use a full sheet of paper and type the following basic steps in changing the ribbon in manuscript form. Use a 5-space paragraph indention and double spacing. Leave a 2-inch top margin and center the heading. Triple-space after the heading.

	STROKES	WORDS

CHANGING THE RIBBON
20 / 4

In changing the ribbon on most standard typewriters, these are the basic steps to follow: — 87 / 17, 111 / 22

1. Wind the ribbon on one spool. Usually it is best to wind the ribbon on the right spool unless the spools are interchangeable. It may be necessary to adjust the ribbon-reverse lever so that the ribbon may be wound on the proper spool. — 184 / 37, 256 / 51, 330 / 66, 352 / 70

2. Press down the shift-lock key, and move the ribbon-indicator lever to the "red" position, the position for typing on the lower portion of the ribbon. Depress any two central keys, such as the y and u, so that the two type bars lock in front of the printing point. This will raise and lock the ribbon carrier so that the old ribbon can be removed easily and the new ribbon inserted. — 423 / 85, 498 / 100, 572 / 114, 649 / 130, 721 / 144, 743 / 149

3. Remove the ribbon from the carrier and remove both spools. On some typewriters, it will be necessary to raise the top cover of the typewriter in order to remove the spools. Be sure to note how each spool is attached to its hub and how the ribbon is attached to the empty spool. The new ribbon must be attached in the same manner. — 810 / 162, 883 / 177, 956 / 191, 1028 / 206, 1081 / 216

4. Hook the new ribbon onto the empty spool and wind several inches of the new ribbon onto it. Be sure to wind this ribbon in the proper direction. Place both spools on their holders and thread the ribbon through the ribbon carrier. Keep the ribbon straight when doing this. — 1150 / 230, 1225 / 245, 1297 / 259, 1361 / 272

5. Finally, release the shift-lock key and return the ribbon-indicator lever to the "blue" position, the position for typing on the upper portion of the ribbon. Unlock the two keys that were used to raise the ribbon carrier, and the typewriter will be ready for use. — 1443 / 289, 1508 / 302, 1582 / 316, 1629 / 326

PROBLEM 2

Directions. As time permits, type the letter given as Problem 1 to as many of the following members of the Parent-Teacher Association as possible.

Mrs. James Montgomery
1906 Robertson Blvd.
Los Angeles 34, California

Mrs. Betty Wyman
8410 Overland Street
Los Angeles 49, California

Mr. G. M. Peck
509 East Citrus Avenue
Los Angeles 32, California

Mr. John Russell
1862 Carthay Circle
Los Angeles 34, California

LESSON 124

CONDITIONING PRACTICE 124
5 minutes

STROKES

Visitors did enjoy the amazing water tricks of six quaint polar bears.   70

Express measures in figures; as, 156 quarts, 284 gallons, 7,903 pecks.   70

Marty visited Santa Catalina, Santa Barbara, and San Clemente Islands.   70

The right key stroke is made with your fingers held close to the keys.   70

RELATED LEARNING 124—PUNCTUATION GUIDES
10 minutes

Directions. Study the explanatory statements; type each line one or more times as time permits.

Lines 1 and 2: The singular possessive of a noun is formed by adding 's to the singular noun.
Line 3: When a noun is plural in form and ends in *s*, add an apostrophe after the *s* to show possession.
Line 4: When a noun is plural in form and does not end in *s*, add an apostrophe and *s* to show possession.
Line 5: Joint possession is usually indicated by using the possessive with the last noun in the series. NOTE: Words printed in italics are underscored when typed. The titles of books may be underscored or typed in all capital letters.

STROKES

In return for a fair day's pay, you must be sure to give a day's work.   70

A boy's bicycle was found early this morning in front of John's house.   70

The lawyers' offices and the accountants' offices are all in the Loop.   70

Men's hats, women's dresses, and children's toys are on sale tomorrow.   70

Mr. Warwick read *Calm Contemplation* at his son and daughter's request.   88

CORRECT IT AS YOU TYPE (OR DIRECT DICTATION)
5 minutes

dons brother will take a weeks vacation during the early part of may
girls shoes and womens hats are featured at Lanes Department Store
my brother and sisters request caused me to change my departure date

PROBLEM TYPING 124
20 minutes

PROBLEM 1

Directions. You have just learned that Mr. J. Dudley O'Brien, who is a typing expert, will be in your city during the first week of next month. As secretary of your commercial club, you are to write a letter to Mr. O'Brien inviting him to talk to your group and to give a typewriting

SECTION 18. Manuscript with Footnotes

Some of the specific details upon which there is agreement for typing manuscripts or reports with footnotes are given in the materials in this section. With respect to some details, usage sanctions more than one form. Uniformity must be maintained, however, throughout a particular manuscript.

If a title page is used with a manuscript, this display page contains (1) the title of the book or the article and (2) the name of the author. Other information is added to the title page of a book that is to be published. For example, turn to the title page of this textbook. Note that, in addition to the title of the book and the names of the authors, the name of the publisher and the places of business of the publisher are given. The copyright date may be given on the title page, or it may be given on the following page.

LESSON 117

CONDITIONING PRACTICE 117 — 5 minutes

Directions. Type each line twice, or more if time permits. This will be the uniform assignment for typing the conditioning practices in all lessons in this section.

	STROKES
The quick, ambiguous quiz on job pay vexed all who had studied for it.	70
I may buy 15 jackets, 289 blankets, 74 kits, 360 lamps, and 110 tires.	70
Mt. Rushmore National Memorial is located in the historic Black Hills.	70
Learn to space quickly between words in order to type with continuity.	70

RELATED LEARNING 117—CAPITALIZATION GUIDES — 10 minutes

Directions. Study the explanatory statements; then type each line one or more times as time permits.

Lines 1 and 2: Capitalize the names of geographic regions and localities as well as geographical names. Points of the compass are not capitalized when used to indicate direction, or when used in a descriptive sense.

Line 3: Capitalize such words as *street, avenue, company,* etc., when used with a proper noun.

Line 4: Capitalize the names of organizations, clubs, and their derivatives.

Line 5: Nouns preceding a figure are usually capitalized, although common words, such as line, page, verse, etc., are not.

	STROKES
I live in the East, but I plan to move to the Middle West next summer.	70
Drive south on Pennsylvania Avenue, and then turn west at Pitt Street.	70
Is the address of Dowe & Company 123 Fifth Street or 123 Fifth Avenue?	70
The Boy Scouts will meet at the Commercial Club at 4 p.m. on Saturday.	70
He read Judge Baxter's decision in Volume III, Section 123, page 1049.	70

CORRECT IT AS YOU TYPE (OR DIRECT DICTATION) — 5 minutes

the future business leaders of america will meet in the west this year.

although he lives on slater street, he attends washington high school.

j d morgan & company uses style 34 as shown on page 12 of catalog 5.

Directions. Study the explanatory statements; type each line one or more times as time permits.

Line 1: An exclamation mark is used after emphatic interjections and after phrases or sentences that are clearly exclamatory.

Lines 2 and 3: Use quotation marks to enclose direct quotations. NOTE: Long quotations that are set off from the body of the material by being single spaced and indented need not be enclosed within quotation marks.

Line 4: The titles of articles, poems, plays, etc., are placed within quotation marks.

Line 5: Quotation marks are sometimes used to enclose special words, phrases, and the like.

	STROKES
The teacher shouted "Stop!" but all the students kept right on typing.	72
The telegram read, "Ship Crabbe & Martin 3 cars, 2 5/8″ oak flooring."	70
In a calm voice she asked, "Why didn't you say so in the first place?"	70
Did any of you read Paul Jackson's article, "Frontier Thinking Today"?	70
What do the two expressions "buying futures" and "selling short" mean?	70

CORRECT IT AS YOU TYPE (OR DIRECT DICTATION)   *5 minutes*

fred said in his letter typewriting is my most interesting subject did he study chapter 7 entitled The History of the Westward Movement the word daughter-in-law should always be typewritten with hyphens

PROBLEM TYPING 123   *20 minutes*

PROBLEM I

Directions. As secretary of the F. B. L. A. Club of your school, you are to type the following letter in a style similar to that given for Style Letter 1, page 43; but omit the typewritten signature in the closing lines, and type the name and the address of the addressee 6 spaces below the complimentary close and at the left margin (See Illustration 43). This style is often used for official and semi-formal communications and for purely personal letters.

Use the current date and open punctuation.

Refreshments will be served by the senior cooking class. We shall look forward to seeing you.

Sincerely yours

Mrs. Betty Greenleaf
1136 Verdugo Road
Los Angeles 56, California

Illustration 43 — Name and Address of the Addressee Typed Below the Complimentary Close and at the Left Margin

	STROKES
Hamilton High School	21
Los Angeles 34, California	48
(Current Date)	64
Dear P. T. A. Member The Future	97
Business Leaders of America Club	130
cordially invites you to hear a panel	168
discussion of "School Sponsored	200
Work-Experience Activities" at our	235
monthly meeting, Friday, November	269
26, at 2 p.m. in the school audi-	301
torium. (P) Mr. Henry Addison,	329
Vice President of the Pacific Petro-	364
leum Company, Mr. John Given, Di-	396
rector of the Metropolitan Junior	430

	STROKES
College, and Miss Harriet Wilson,	464
Personnel Director of Bradley's,	497
Inc., have consented to appear on	531
the panel as our guest speakers. Fol-	568
lowing the presentations by the	600
panel members, there will be a gen-	634
eral open-forum discussion of this	669
important topic. (P) Refreshments	700
will be served by the senior cooking	737
class. We shall look forward to see-	773
ing you. Sincerely yours *(111)*	799
Mrs. Betty Greenleaf	820
1136 Verdugo Road	838
Los Angeles 56, California	865

Directions. 1. This problem introduces a short report which illustrates the use of footnotes. You are not expected to complete the report in this lesson; additional time is provided in Lesson 118.

2. The report is to be double spaced and typed in manuscript form. Quoted material of 4 lines or more is to be single spaced and indented 5 spaces from each margin. To aid you in typing the report, such quoted material is shown with shorter lines than the copy which is to be double spaced. Indent the first line of each paragraph 5 spaces. You are to assume that the report is to be bound on the left; so leave a left margin of 1½ inches. Manuscript typing is explained on page 158. If necessary, refer to this page for the general form to be used in typing manuscripts or reports.

3. All horizontal centering is to be based on the *line of writing* rather than the center of the page. A quick, easy way to get the center of a writing line of any length is to add the figure representing the point for the beginning of the line to the figure representing the point for the ending of the line and divide by 2. The result will be the exact center of the line of writing.

4. In typing copy containing footnotes, estimate 4 lines for each footnote. You must plan to save space for the footnotes in addition to leaving an inch for the bottom margin. Single-space the footnotes with double spacing between footnotes. Footnotes may be numbered consecutively throughout an article, a report, or a chapter of a book, or they may be numbered consecutively on each page, the first footnote on each page being "1." Be uniform in the numbering of footnote references. For this problem, number the footnotes consecutively on each page. This means you will have to change the superior numbers in the text and the numbers for the footnotes on the second and third pages of your manuscript. Type the superior figures a half space above the line of writing. Use a 1½-inch line to separate the last line of the text from the footnote. Illustration 42 shows the arrangement of footnotes at the bottom of the page.

If your teacher so directs, you are to erase and correct neatly all errors that you make in typing the report.

What is the chief purpose of a dictionary? This question is answered by Crabbe and Salsgiver as follows:

> The chief purpose of a dictionary is to provide reliable information on the spelling, pronunciation,

[1] Cecil B. Williams, Effective Business Writing (New York: The Ronald Press Company, 1947), p. 46.

[2] Robert Wallace, "A is for Aardvark," Reader's Digest, Vol. 58 (May, 1951), p. 10.

Illustration 42 — Footnote Arrangement at the Bottom of the Page

(Although usage sanctions more than one form, uniformity must be maintained in the form that is used in a particular report.)

THE DICTIONARY

The dictionary is one of the most popular and most useful of all reference books. It should be one of the first works of reference with which we become thoroughly acquainted, and the last one with which we should dispense. The successful student acquires the dictionary habit early in his school life. The dictionary is equally important for the typist, for the stenographer, or for the secretary in the business office. Williams emphasizes this fact by making the following statement:

> A successful businessman told me recently that he had two secretaries, a good one and a poor one. The difference was that the good one used the dictionary freely; the poor one seemed to have an aversion to it.[1]

[1] Cecil B. Williams, *Effective Business Writing* (New York: The Ronald Press Company, 1947), p. 46.

(This problem is continued on the following page.)

Directions. Type a data sheet to enclose with the application letter typed in Problem Typing 121. Use a 60-space line and center the main heading 1½ inches from the top of the sheet. Make all corrections marked in the copy.

PERSONAL DATA SHEET   *← Add 1 line space*

PERSONAL

    Name: Virginia Adams
    Address: 630 Magnolia Drive, Lexington 14, Ky.
    Telephone: MAdison 1370
    Age: 18
    Height: 5 feet 4 inches
    Weight: 120 pounds
    Physical Defects: None

EDUCATION

    High School: Lexington High School
    Major: Secretarial-Bookkeeping
    Leadership Activities: Secretary, Commerce Club
                             Vice President, Junior Class
    Technical Skills: Typewriting Speed, 60 words
                             Shorthand Dictation Speed, 100
                               words
                           Training in operation of calcu-
                             lators, adding machines, and
                             duplicating machines

WORK EXPERIENCE *← Add 1 line space*
    Worked one summer as typist-clerk in the Lexington
       National Bank

REFERENCES (by Permission)

    Mrs. Ethel Johnson, Instructor In Secretarial Science,
       Lexington High School, Lexington 4, Kentucky *← Add 1 line space*
    Mr. John A. Finch, Cashier, Lexington National Bank,
       Lexington 2, Kentucky

    Reverend James K. Edwards, 1759 Burlingame Avenue,
       Lexington 23, Kentucky

LESSON 123

CONDITIONING PRACTICE 123   *5 minutes*

                                                      STROKES

Even Jerome Quixote was puzzled by the incorrect spelling of Siskiyou. 70
Did he order the 16-, 20-, and 24-foot beams (5 7/8″ x 9 3/4″) for us? 70
Payment No. 48 for the Christmas Club will be due Tuesday, October 24. 70
Keep the stroking action in the fingers to increase your typing skill. 70

That most persons recognize the importance of the dictionary as a valuable reference source and aid is attested to by the popularity of the dictionary. Wallace [2] points out that ". . . the number of dictionaries in the United States is probably second only to the number of Bibles. And they range from pocket size at ten cents to mammoth unabridged at $175."

What is the chief purpose of a dictionary? This question is answered by Crabbe and Salsgiver as follows:

> The chief purpose of a dictionary is to provide reliable information on the spelling, pronunciation, and meaning of words. However, the fact that a dictionary contains thousands of words taken from many different fields of knowledge also makes it a great storehouse of information.[3]

Crabbe and Salsgiver indicate, in addition, that the dictionary contains a vast amount of other information. Its usefulness is not limited to answering questions concerning the spelling, the pronunciation, and the meaning of words even though this is the primary purpose of the dictionary. The scope of the modern dictionary has been extended to cover many other areas of information. For example, the dictionary contains rules for spelling, for punctuation, and for the use of capitals. It contains a guide to pronunciation. It shows the syllable divisions of words. (In writing this is an aid because if we know the syllable divisions of a word and are acquainted with the rules for word division, we can avoid errors in dividing words at the ends of lines.) The dictionary tells us whether or not words are in good usage. In addition, the dictionary usually contains a pronouncing gazetteer, common English given names and their meanings, as well as other special sections. All these furnish special information in an easy-to-use form.

Today there is a growing recognition of the fact that an extensive vocabulary is an important factor in success, not only in school work, but also in business and professional work. Here is another important reason for using the dictionary. There are many ways to increase your vocabulary to be sure, but the following suggestion warrants attention:

> One of the best ways to add to your knowledge of words is to consult your dictionary for the meaning of every unfamiliar word which comes to your attention, learn its pronunciation, and then use the word in your own writing and conversation.[4]

Once you acquire the dictionary habit, you will find that the study of words can be an interesting and fascinating pastime. Clark [5] suggests that you will "discover that dictionary reading can be fun." Such a practice is an excellent way to acquire a knowledge of words and an increased vocabulary.

---

[2] Robert Wallace, "A is for Aardvark," *Reader's Digest*, Vol. 58 (May, 1951), p. 10.

[3] Ernest H. Crabbe and Paul L. Salsgiver, *General Business*, Sixth Edition (Cincinnati: South-Western Publishing Company, 1951), p. 561.

[4] *An Outline for Dictionary Study* (Springfield: G. & C. Merriam Co., 1949), p. 8.

[5] Helen M. Clark, "Suggestions for Themes," *English Journal*, Vol. XL (June, 1951), p. 334.

(This problem is concluded on page 166.)

630 Magnolia Drive — 19   I am qualified to perform the duties — 616
Lexington 14, Kentucky — 42   of the position you wish to fill. My — 654
(Current Date) — 58   typewriting speed is approximately — 689
Box 285 The Daily Kentuckian 1647 — 92   60 words a minute, and I can take — 723
West 19th Street Lexington 13, — 123   dictation at 100 words a minute. (P) — 757
Kentucky Gentlemen Your adver- — 152   In addition to my course work in — 790
tisement for a typist in today's *Ken-* — 192   high school, I was active in several — 827
tuckian interests me very much. I — 234   school organizations. This has given — 865
should like to have you consider my — 270   me experience in working with — 895
application. (P) While in high — 298   others. (P) As requested in your ad- — 927
school, the major emphasis of my — 331   vertisement, I am attaching a per- — 960
last two years of training was on — 365   sonal data sheet which outlines my — 995
business subjects. I have completed — 402   qualifications in greater detail. (P) — 1030
courses in typewriting, shorthand, — 437   My telephone number is MAdison — 1061
bookkeeping, business English, gen- — 471   1370. May I come for a personal — 1094
eral business, and office practice. — 508   interview at a time that is conven- — 1128
This training coupled with my work — 543   ient for you. Very truly yours Vir- — 1164
experience leads me to believe that — 579   ginia Adams Enclosure *(168)* — 1185

LESSON 122

CONDITIONING PRACTICE 122   *5 minutes*

STROKES

Was Zetta Kelley able to give up any of her extraordinary quince jams? — 70
Thank you for your Order #13698 of March 25 for 470 small metal discs. — 70
F. J. Togow was elected to the United States House of Representatives. — 70
It was such a gloriously warm day that they decided to go in swimming. — 70

RELATED LEARNING 122—PUNCTUATION GUIDES   *10 minutes*

Directions. Study the explanatory statements; then type each line one or more times as time permits.

Line 1: A colon may be used to introduce an enumeration or a listing. NOTE: Space twice after the colon.

Line 2: A colon may be used to introduce a question, or a long direct quotation. NOTE: The first word after the colon is capitalized if it is part of a complete sentence.

Line 3: The colon is used between hours and minutes expressed in figures.

Lines 4 and 5: The dash (made by striking two hyphens without spacing before or after) is an abrupt and emphatic mark of punctuation. It may be used for emphasis, to indicate a change of thought, to introduce the name of an author or a reference when it follows a direct quotation, and for other special purposes.

STROKES

She bought three items at the store: a coat, a dress, and a suitcase. — 70
The question is this: Are you using good technique at the typewriter? — 70
When it is 4:30 p.m. in New York City, it is 1:30 p.m. in Los Angeles. — 70
The icy road—slippery as a silver-scaled fish—made driving a hazard. — 70
"To read good books is to enjoy life's greatest treasures."—Thompson. — 70

CORRECT IT AS YOU TYPE (OR DIRECT DICTATION)   *5 minutes*

don't forget to bring these items a pen a notebook and an eraser
i shall discuss the question what are the main duties of a secretary
the train was due at 11 30 a m but it didn't arrive until 2 25 p m

These, then, are some of the important reasons for using the dictionary. In summary, it may be said that the modern dictionary stands ready to give a vast and valuable amount of information and help if we know how to use it correctly and to interpret the information it lays before us. Upon the use that we make of the dictionary depends much of the value of our reading and much of the accuracy of our writing.

LESSON 118

CONDITIONING PRACTICE 118

5 minutes

STROKES

Judge Namy will be quite perplexed to realize the five checks are bad.	70
The books were copyrighted in 1949 and sold 278,650 copies in 3 years.	70
Magic Radios and Imperial Television Sets are sold by Land & Son, Inc.	70
We all agreed that it would be a great treat to have him as a speaker.	70

PROBLEM TYPING 118

35 minutes

PROBLEM 1

Directions. In this lesson you will complete the typing of the report given as Problem Typing 117.

If you reinsert an incomplete page, be sure to check the alignment of the last line with the alignment scale on your typewriter. Use the paper-release lever or the variable line spacer to make the necessary adjustments so that the margins and spacing will be uniform.

PROBLEM 2

Directions. A report or manuscript which contains footnotes usually requires a bibliography. The bibliography may be an alphabetic listing of the references actually used in compiling the report or it may be an alphabetic listing of references pertaining to the subject discussed even though such references were not quoted in the report itself.

Type the following bibliography which is a listing of the references used in the preceding problem. The entries as shown illustrate one form that may be used in typing a bibliography. Allow for a 1½-inch left margin. Center the heading horizontally over the line of writing approximately 2 inches from the top of the paper. Triple-space between the heading and the first entry. Start the first line of each entry flush with the left margin. The second and succeeding lines are to be indented 5 spaces. Use single spacing; double-space between the entries.

Entry 1: A pamphlet with no author listed. Alphabetized according to title.
Entry 2: A magazine reference.
Entry 3: A book reference with two authors.
Entry 4: A magazine reference.
Entry 5: A book reference.

BIBLIOGRAPHY

An Outline for Dictionary Study. Springfield: G. & C. Merriam Co., 1949.
Clark, Helen M. "Suggestions for Themes," *English Journal,* Vol. XL (June, 1951), pp. 332-336.
Crabbe, Ernest H., and Salsgiver, Paul L. *General Business,* Sixth Edition. Cincinnati: South-Western Publishing Company, 1951.
Wallace, Robert. "A is for Aardvark," *Reader's Digest,* Vol. 58 (May, 1951), pp. 9-13.
Williams, Cecil B. *Effective Business Writing.* New York: The Ronald Press Company, 1947.

LESSON 121

Max King and his pupils were very doubtful of the justice of the quiz.   70

The Smiths live at 3078 Avenue 29, just 16 blocks east of 45th Street.   70

West & Macy Co. in Olympia is having a sale on Seed's Home Appliances.   70

Have you looked carefully through both of the desks for the lost file?   70

RELATED LEARNING 121—PUNCTUATION GUIDES   *10 minutes*

Directions. Study the explanatory statements; then type each line one or more times as time permits.

Line 1: When unrelated groups of figures come together, separate them by a comma. NOTE: Whole numbers are usually divided into groups of three digits each by use of the comma (12,737), but policy, year, page, room, telephone, and most serial numbers are written without commas (KMG 3099618, Room 1134, MIchigan 54326).

Line 2: A semicolon may be used to separate the members of a compound sentence when the conjunction is not expressed.

Line 3: A semicolon is used to separate the members of a compound sentence when the clauses are joined by a conjunctive adverb (*however, consequently, nevertheless, moreover, etc.*). NOTE: A comma is used after the conjunctive adverb.

Line 4: A semicolon is used to separate a series of phrases or clauses (especially when they contain commas) that are introduced by a colon.

Line 5: The semicolon is always placed outside the quotation mark.

STROKES

During 1929, 47,280 plows were shipped C. O. D. to the African colony.   70

We cannot live on past glory; we must strive to improve and go onward.   70

He did not follow the rule; consequently, he made many serious errors.   70

Our sales were: 1950, $1,125,840; 1951, $1,531,450; 1952, $1,935,976.   70

Mr. Carr spoke on "Building Speed"; Mr. Brown, on "Building Accuracy."   70

CORRECT IT AS YOU TYPE (OR DIRECT DICTATION)   *5 minutes*

in 1952 35 new typewriters were purchased for room 168 building A470

he wrote letters on march 3 9 and 22 no reply came until august 14

the chairman is not here nevertheless we should begin the meeting

PROBLEM TYPING 121   *20 minutes*

Directions. The letter of this problem was written in answer to an advertisement for a typist. Type the letter in the modified block form with indented paragraphs. Use the current date and open punctuation. Type the box number as a separate line in the address. Type the name of the applicant on the fourth line below the complimentary close. As this is a personal-type letter, the return address should be typed with the date. Reference initials should not be used.

If time permits, retype the letter trying to make the second copy more attractive than the first.

TYPING FOR PERSONAL USE

GENERAL DIRECTIONS

If time permits when you have completed the problems for each lesson, spend the time in improving your skill in composing at the typewriter. Type personal letters to your friends, type your work for other classes, or select some topic and type a short composition, article, or report on the topic. Suggested topics are the following: Work I Enjoy Doing; My Hobby; My Favorite Television Program; Sports I Enjoy; An Interesting Trip; My Ambition; An Exciting Experience. A very worth-while activity would be to assume that you are writing an article for the local newspaper on some phase of school life. If such articles are well written, your teacher may want to submit them to the local newspaper for possible publication.

SECTION 19. Personal Typing Problems

LESSON 119

CONDITIONING PRACTICE 119   *5 minutes*

Directions. Type each line twice, or more if time permits. This will be the uniform assignment for typing the conditioning practices in all lessons in this section.

	STROKES
Murky haze enveloped a city as jarring quakes broke forty-six windows.	70
The 5 reams of 8½″ x 11″ paper (No. 24) on Order #79 will cost $16.30.	70
The Semi-Formal Dinner Dance of the Hanover Lodge was held in January.	70
I may work with them or their friends in the ancient city by the lake.	70

RELATED LEARNING 119—PUNCTUATION GUIDES   *10 minutes*

Directions. Study the explanatory statements; then type each line one or more times as time permits.

Line 1: Space once after a period within an abbreviation, except when small letters are used.
Lines 2 and 3: The question mark is used at the end of a sentence that is a direct question; however, a period is used after a question which is in the form of a request.
Lines 4 and 5: Use a comma to separate the words or the parts of a series.

	STROKES
After receiving an M. A. degree, Miss Struthers began work for a Ph.D.	70
What is the price of the khaki hunting jacket that is in the showcase?	70
When are you leaving? May we have your check for $15.45 before May 5.	70
Marvin, Jerry, George, Jack, and I are driving Bill's car to the game.	70
He ran across the athletic field, over the hill, and back to the pool.	70

CORRECT IT AS YOU TYPE (OR DIRECT DICTATION)   *5 minutes*

"C.O.D." may be written with capitals; "f.o.b.," with small letters.
when are you leaving for chicago May we have your reply immediately
if you have time today, send greeting cards to susan dick and henry

	STROKES
After he had endorsed the check, he gave it to the teller at the bank.	70
His story, which no one believed, was told in detail to many visitors.	70
I asked, "When are you leaving?" She replied, "I plan to leave soon."	70
He was born September 20, 1873, and lived in Lexington, Massachusetts.	70
That old-fashioned stove kept them warm on long, cold winter evenings.	70

CORRECT IT AS YOU TYPE (OR DIRECT DICTATION) *5 minutes*

although the schedule was visible she asked "When is No 103 due

The radio although in need of repair still had a rich tone quality

benjamin franklin was born january 17 1706 in boston massachusetts

TIMED WRITING 120 *8 minutes*

Directions. Type a 5-minute timed writing on the material given for Timed Writing 119, page 168. Work for an increased stroking rate. *Type at the skill-building level of practice.* Determine the cwpm.

PROBLEM TYPING 120 *12 minutes*

PROBLEM 1

Directions. 1. Use a ruled sheet of paper. If such paper is not available:

a. Insert a sheet of paper into the machine.
b. Type a 6-inch line across the page.
c. Operate the variable line spacer (No. 3) and move the cylinder (or platen) forward and type a 2-inch line. Move the cylinder forward several times, each time typing a 2-inch line.

2. Operate the variable line spacer and move the cylinder so that the first line is just covered by the aligning scale (No. 34).

3. Type your name and study its placement in relation to the line. The letters should be close to or on the line, but the line should not run through any of them.

4. If the copy is not properly on the line, adjust the cylinder by operating the variable line spacer. Type your name again. Continue to do this until you do type on the line satisfactorily. Then study the relation of the line and the top of the aligning scale.

5. Type your name in a similar way on each of the additional lines on the page.

PROBLEM 2

Directions. Draw a form similar to the one at the right with lines about ½-inch apart and about 6 inches long. Then type the headings shown on the form and follow each heading with information that is appropriate for yourself.

School	:
School Address	:
Your Name	:
Your Address	:
Your Age	:

Directions. Type a 5-minute timed writing. Type with ease and control but make an effort to increase your stroking rate. Keep the carriage moving steadily and smoothly in order to do this. Determine the cwpm.

Each paragraph has every letter of the alphabet and a syllable intensity of 1.30.

	STROKES	WORDS
This is an age and an era in which we are quite likely to give too	67	13
much importance to getting money and in which we are prone to give too	138	28
little thought to the real value of money. All of us are rich in time,	210	42
rich in abilities rarely used to the fullest extent, and rich in opportuni-	284	57
ties to accomplish something useful. Such riches are far greater in value	359	72
than mere money, but we do not realize their intrinsic worth. If we would	434	87
just take stock of what we have and what we are and what we desire to be,	508	102
we would find that the things that have true value are the things that all	583	117
may possess.	597	119
In taking stock of our personal assets, we must rank high in the list	667	133
of our possessions those qualities that have to do with real values. We	740	148
should not want to accumulate money just for the sake of money, but we	811	162
should want to have money for the sound social use that can be made of it.	887	177
We do not need time in order that we may squander more hours, but we	956	191
need to use time more intelligently in order that we may enrich life.	1027	205
We should not want to extend our abilities in order that we may dazzle	1098	220
our little world with a vain show of brilliance; but we need greater	1167	233
capacity to do, in order that we may add to the total wealth of the world.	1243	249
Wealth is not made up just of assets known as stocks and bonds and	1310	262
cash and real estate. We are beginning to realize that the true wealth of	1385	277
a man can be found by taking stock of his ideas and ideals, of his	1452	290
habits and attitudes, of his regard for the fine things in life, and of his	1528	306
understanding of his relationship to others. If a man excels in these	1599	320
things, we may be quite sure that he has true wealth. When he makes	1668	334
the shift in emphasis from money to ideals, he begins to achieve a sense	1741	348
of values.	1751	350

PROBLEM TYPING 119   *12 minutes*

Composing at the Typewriter. In your English classes you have learned to compose short themes and articles which you wrote in longhand. You will be able to save considerable time if you learn to compose directly at the typewriter. When you first compose at the typewriter you may make more errors than usual. These errors should be ignored or you may "X" them out and type the correct word or words.

In order to compose efficiently, it is well to think through and plan what you want to say. In the beginning, you may find that the making of a brief outline or a listing of the points to be covered will be an aid to you. *Think and type* and you will find that it is easy to gain composing skill at the typewriter. The following problem will help you develop composing skill. You can gain additional skill by using the typewriter, whenever possible, for any composing work that you do.

Directions. Use a 60-space line and double spacing. Type a short response to as many of the questions as you can. Finish the list of questions given if you can but do not hurry in order to do so. It is more important that you organize your thoughts so that you can type complete sentences. In your answers to the questions, indicate the nature of the question being answered. Number each of your responses to correspond with the questions. *Think and type!*

1. If you had your choice, what state in the United States or what country would you like to visit and why?

2. What is your favorite form of recreation? Why is this your favorite form of recreation?

3. Why are you learning to typewrite? Do you like typewriting?

4. Do you find it easy or difficult to try to compose directly at the typewriter? If you have difficulty, why does it seem difficult?

5. If you were to tell someone how to increase his typewriting speed, what would you tell him to do?

6. What one thing has caused you the most difficulty in your efforts to develop typewriting skill?

7. What is your favorite subject in school? Why is it your favorite subject?

LESSON 120

CONDITIONING PRACTICE 120   *5 minutes*

STROKES

Have you ever watched a quick jet zoom past as a bird in exact flight?   70

The new prices are as follows: 12 @ $25.50; 24 @ $48.95; 36 @ $70.50.   70

Harry Ryan flew from Los Angeles to Kansas City via American Airlines.   70

I do not know if the two pupils studied for their geometry test today.   70

RELATED LEARNING 120—PUNCTUATION GUIDES   *10 minutes*

Directions. Study the explanatory statements; then type each line one or more times as time permits.

Line 1: A comma is used to set off introductory expressions (phrases or clauses) and any phrase or clause out of its natural order.

Line 2: Commas are used to separate a parenthetical expression or a nonrestrictive clause from the rest of the sentence.

Line 3: A comma may be used before short, direct quotations. NOTE: The question mark is placed before the ending quotation mark when it punctuates the quoted matter; it is placed after the ending quotation mark when it punctuates the entire sentence. The usual practice is to type the period before the ending quotation mark in all cases.

Line 4: Commas are used to set off dates and to separate the city and state.

Line 5: A comma may be used to separate two or more parallel adjectives in a series, but compound adjectives are written with hyphens when used to modify a noun which they precede.